DEFAULT RULES IN PRIVATE LAW

Drawing on the experience of recognised experts from across a range of different fields and jurisdictions, this landmark publication tackles default rules in private law in comparative perspective. Often underestimated, but highly influential, default rules are non-mandatory rules that kick in where nothing else has been agreed or provided.

The contributions explore default rules from a variety of angles relevant to both scholarship and legal practice, including:

- behavioural aspects and the role of platform terms in the digital age;
- the remit and operation of defaults in different areas, ranging from contract and commercial law to succession, civil procedure and private international law;
- a comparison between Common law and Civilian approaches as well as the EU level;
- the perspectives of different 'players' engaged in the generation and application of default rules.

Volume 32: Studies of the Oxford Institute of European and Comparative Law

Studies of the Oxford Institute of European and Comparative Law

Recent titles in this Series

Volume 22: Passing Wealth on Death: Will-Substitutes in Comparative Perspective
Edited by Alexandra Braun and Anne Röthel

Volume 23: General Principles of Law: European and Comparative Perspectives
Edited by Stefan Vogenauer and Stephen Weatherill

Volume 24: The Future of Contract Law in Latin America: The Principles of Latin American Contract Law
Edited by Rodrigo Momberg and Stefan Vogenauer

Volume 25: The Code Napoléon Rewritten: French Contract Law after the 2016 Reforms
Edited by John Cartwright and Simon Whittaker

Volume 26: Discretion in EU Public Procurement Law
Edited by Sanja Bogojevic, Xavier Groussot and Jörgen Hettne

Volume 27: New Economic Constitutionalism in Europe
George Gerapetritis

Volume 28: French Civil Liability in Comparative Perspective
Edited by Jean-Sébastien Borghetti and Simon Whittaker

Volume 29: Better Regulation in EU Contract Law: The Fitness Check and the New Deal for Consumers
Edited by Esther van Schagen and Stephen Weatherill

Volume 30: Property and Contract: Comparative Reflections on English Law and Spanish Law
Edited by John Cartwright and Ángel M López y López

Volume 31: Demoicratic Authority: Nature and Ground of the EU's Right to Rule
Josef Weinzierl

Volume 32: Default Rules in Private Law
Edited by Birke Häcker and Johannes Ungerer

Default Rules in Private Law

Edited by
Birke Häcker
and
Johannes Ungerer

•HART•
OXFORD • LONDON • NEW YORK • NEW DELHI • SYDNEY

HART PUBLISHING

Bloomsbury Publishing Plc

Kemp House, Chawley Park, Cumnor Hill, Oxford, OX2 9PH, UK

1385 Broadway, New York, NY 10018, USA

Bloomsbury Publishing Ireland Limited, 29 Earlsfort Terrace, Dublin 2, D02 AY28, Ireland

HART PUBLISHING, the Hart/Stag logo, BLOOMSBURY and the Diana logo are trademarks of Bloomsbury Publishing Plc

First published in Great Britain 2025

A catalogue record for this book is available from the British Library.

A catalogue record for this book is available from the Library of Congress.

Library of Congress Control Number: 2024950552

ISBN: HB: 978-1-50997-352-1
ePDF: 978-1-50997-354-5
ePub: 978-1-50997-353-8

Typeset by Compuscript Ltd, Shannon

For product safety related questions contact productsafety@bloomsbury.com

To find out more about our authors and books visit www.hartpublishing.co.uk. Here you will find extracts, author information, details of forthcoming events and the option to sign up for our newsletters.

In memory of

Jürgen Basedow

(1949–2023)

PREFACE

This collection is the product of an international conference in workshop format entitled 'Default Rules in Private Law' held at Brasenose College, University of Oxford, on 24 and 25 March 2023. Co-organised by the current editors, it sought to examine in comparative perspective the phenomenon commonly referred to (in English) as 'default rules', with a view to showcasing quite how wide-ranging and diverse a phenomenon it is.

The editors are grateful to the Institute of European and Comparative Law at the University of Oxford for contributing towards the cost of the event and to Brasenose College for hosting it in its beautiful surroundings and with characteristic warmth and kindness from all of the staff involved. Thanks are also due to Hart Publishing for agreeing to publish the proceedings in this series and to the whole team seeing the manuscripts through to publication.

The two days of the conference were, in the best academic spirit, intellectually enriching and extremely stimulating, with many lively discussions lasting well into the breaks. They were also wonderfully light-hearted and marked by true scholarly comradery between participants of many different legal backgrounds. No one could have imagined that it was to be the last such excursion for one amongst us. Professor Jürgen Basedow, Emeritus Director of the Max Planck Institute for Comparative and International Private Law in Hamburg, passed away suddenly and unexpectedly on 6 April 2023. The paper he prepared for the conference, published in chapter six, reflects his wide-ranging interest in and profound mastery of European Private Law in the broadest possible sense. The editors and the other contributors remember him fondly and with great admiration. This collection is dedicated to his memory.

Birke Häcker
Johannes Ungerer

CONTENTS

LIST OF CONTRIBUTORS

Jürgen Basedow (†) was Emeritus Director at the Max Planck Institute for Comparative and International Private Law, Hamburg

Alan Bogg is Professor of Labour Law, University of Bristol; Emeritus Fellow, Hertford College, Oxford; and a Barrister at Old Square Chambers.

John Cartwright is Emeritus Professor of the Law of Contract and Emeritus Student (Fellow) of Christ Church, University of Oxford

Gregor Christandl is Professor at the Department for Civil Law, Foreign and Private International Law, University of Graz

Louise Gullifer is Rouse Ball Professor of English Law, Chair of the Faculty of Law and Fellow of Gonville and Caius College, University of Cambridge

Birke Häcker is Schlegel Professor of Civil Law, Common Law and Comparative Law, and Director of the Institute of International and Comparative Private Law, University of Bonn

Geneviève Helleringer is Professor at Essec Business School, Paris as well as Associate Professor and Fellow of Reuben College, University of Oxford

Alexander Hellgardt is Professor of Private Law, University of Augsburg, and at the time of the conference held a Chair in Private Law, Corporate Law and Jurisprudence, University of Regensburg

Florian Möslein is Professor of Civil Law, German and European Business Law, University of Marburg

Giesela Rühl is Professor of Civil Law, Civil Procedure, Private International Law, International Civil Procedure and Comparative Law, Humboldt University of Berlin

Philip Sales is a Justice of the Supreme Court of the United Kingdom

Johannes Ungerer is Erich Brost Senior Research Lecturer in German Law, European and International Private Law at the Law Faculty and St Hilda's College, University of Oxford, as well as Global Associate Professor of Law, University of Notre Dame (USA) in England

Simon Whittaker is Emeritus Professor of European Comparative Law and Emeritus Research Fellow of St John's College, University of Oxford

1

A Comparative Introduction to Default Rules

BIRKE HÄCKER

I. Background

The aim of this volume is to explore default rules in private law from a comparative perspective. Speaking simply, default rules are rules of law that apply where nothing else has been agreed or provided. They are the opposite of mandatory rules from which no derogation is possible.

Despite their tremendous practical importance for people's legal relations, default rules do not usually attract a great deal of attention. Lawyers tend to take them for granted, treating them as little more than a base or backdrop for transaction planning. Yet since the late twentieth century, academic interest in default rules has grown, particularly in the context of contract law. In the United States, the so-called 'Legal Default Project' was originally a progeny of the law and economics movement.[1] It sought to design optimal default rules that would maximise efficiency in contracting by reducing transaction costs or by providing a framework of appropriate incentives.[2] More recently, liberal choice theorists of contract law have discovered default rules as a means of enhancing individual autonomy,[3] while behavioural economists are propagating them as ideal nudging tools.[4] In Germany, over the past decade and a half, a number of monographs have been specifically dedicated to dissecting and analysing

[1] Seminal contributions include I Ayres and R Gertner, 'Filling Gaps in Incomplete Contracts: An Economic Theory of Default Rules' (1989) 99 *Yale LJ* 87; R Craswell, 'Contract Law, Default Rules and the Philosophy of Promising' (1989) 88 *Michigan L Rev* 489; JS Johnston, 'Strategic Bargaining and the Economic Theory of Contract Default Rules' (1990) 100 *Yale LJ* 615; RE Scott, 'A Relational Theory of Default Rules for Commercial Contracts' (1990) 19 *Journal of Legal Studies* 597; R Barnett, 'The Sound of Silence: Default Rules and Contractual Consent' (1992) 78 *Virginia L Rev* 821.

[2] While many authors initially adopted a 'majoritarian' approach to default rules, some began to argue in favour of so-called 'penalty defaults': see below, text to nn 80–82.

[3] See esp H Dagan and M Heller, *The Choice Theory of Contracts* (Cambridge, CUP, 2017) esp 109–13, with particular reference to so-called 'sticky defaults'. See further below, n 32 and text thereto as well as text to nn 73–74 and nn 87–88.

[4] See esp CR Sunstein, 'Deciding by Default' (2013) 162 *Univ Penn L Rev* 1. See further below, n 85 and text thereto in section VI.

'dispositive law'.[5] This literature, alongside other timely contributions,[6] has made the regulatory dimension of default rules (more) visible, and with it the phenomenon of 'governance by default'.[7]

II. (At Least) Three Layers of Comparison

Against that background, the idea behind this volume and the conference on which it is based was to bring together Common lawyers and Civil lawyers to explore in a round-table setting the nature of default rules, their aims and functions, the mechanisms by which they are generated, their impact and their remit. To what extent is one's outlook when thinking about such issues shaped by different legal traditions? How far does it depend on the specific field of law in question? And what is the view of those who are actively engaged in the creation or application of default rules? There are thus not merely one or two, but (at least) three potentially overlapping layers to the comparison.

First, there is the comparison of what different legal systems understand by default rules and how they use them. Here, commensurate with the circle of contributors, the book is dominated by Anglo-German and Anglo-French comparative perspectives, with numerous side-glances at other European jurisdictions as well as the United States. There is, it may be added, another cross-jurisdictional comparative collaboration currently under way, namely an Anglo-Australian project organised by the University of Cambridge and Melbourne Law School, whose conclusions will also be made publicly available in due course.[8] The specific 'comparative common law' angle adopted there and the numerous more traditional comparisons of Civilian systems with the English Common law in the present volume should hopefully complement one another to produce a holistic comparative overview.

Second, though usually discussed in connection with contract law, default rules as a phenomenon are in no way confined to regulating contracts. They play a role in many (quite possibly all) areas of private law, and indeed even far beyond private law. This does not, however, mean that the answer to the questions we are asking about default rules is necessarily the same in all the various fields. We must thus add to the cross-jurisdictional comparison an intra-jurisdictional survey of different private law subjects.[9] Moreover, when we look beyond national legal systems to the supra- and

[5] Most notably J Cziupka, *Dispositives Vertragsrecht* (Tübingen, Mohr Siebeck, 2010); F Möslein, *Dispositives Recht* (Tübingen, Mohr Siebeck, 2011); L Kähler, *Begriff und Rechtsfertigung abdingbaren Rechts* (Tübingen, Mohr Siebeck, 2012). On the relevant terminology, see section III below, text to nn 13–18.

[6] See eg A Hellgardt, *Regulierung und Privatrecht* (Tübingen, Mohr Siebeck, 2016) on regulation in and through private law more generally.

[7] See esp F Möslein, '"Governance by Default": Innovation und Koordination durch dispositives Recht' in S Grundmann, B Haar, H Merkt and others (eds), *Festschrift für Klaus J. Hopt zum 70. Geburtstag am 24. August 2010* (Berlin, De Gruyter, 2010) 2861; Möslein, *Dispositives Recht* (n 5) ch 3 at 120–50.

[8] The Cambridge/Melbourne project involved a series of online workshops held in April–May 2024, with the proceedings due to be published in K Barnett, W Day, J Morgan and A Robertson (eds), *Mandatory and Default Rules in Contract and Commercial Law* (Oxford, Hart Publishing, forthcoming).

[9] See section IV below, text to nn 19–45.

international plane, we find that default rules often take on an important function in coordinating people's cross-border legal relations or indeed their disputes. This angle, too, needs to be taken into account to complete the picture.[10]

Third, perspectives may also differ depending on the 'role' played by someone engaging with default rules. In particular, those generating default rules will be operating within a given framework and under certain institutional or political constraints. The most evident example is Common law systems distinguishing between default rules based on statute and judge-made default rules.[11] It has unfortunately not been possible to source a contribution outlining the approach of the Law Commission towards the design of default rules, but it is clear that it would (need to) be informed by very different considerations from those shaping the judicial approach. Indeed, a contribution from the Bench reminds us that the Common law system of precedent itself operates as a kind of default rule – in that the *ratio* of a previous decision also governs later cases, unless the former is distinguishable on the facts or until it is as a matter of law overruled by a competent body establishing a different (new default) rule.[12]

By way of an introduction, this chapter will provide a brief comparative overview of some of the salient issues that arise from – or in connection with – default rules when viewed against the backdrop of various legal systems across the so-called Civil law/Common law 'divide'. It starts by pondering the relevant terminology and the connotations that terminology invokes (section III). It then turns to examining lawyers' practical approaches and more generally social attitudes towards the use of default rules, in particular the extent to which drafters can and do place reliance on default regimes (section IV). This is followed by a consideration of three interconnected yet distinct questions, namely what kinds of default rules there are, their different forms as well as fields of application (section V), the functions they serve or could potentially serve (section V), and their conceptual basis or bases (section VI).

III. Terminology

One of the first things that meets the eye when looking at default rules in a comparative perspective is that the terminology used to describe the phenomenon varies considerably – more than is explicable by different languages alone. While 'default rules' is the term that has established itself in English law and around the Common law world,[13] German lawyers tend to speak of 'dispositive' law (*dispositives Recht*) and French typically refer to 'suppletive' rules of law (*lois* or *règles supplétives*).

All of these terms in one sense capture the essence of what is at stake, namely the peculiar mix of party autonomy and heteronomous imposition that characterises

[10] See the contributions by G Rühl and J Ungerer, chs 12 and 13 (respectively) in this volume.

[11] Consider, for instance, classical default rules in the form of 'terms implied in law', which may be imported into a contract either through statutory provision or based on the (judge-made) common law.

[12] See the contribution by Lord Sales, ch 5 in this volume.

[13] Ayers and Gertner (1989) (n 1) 91 observe that other terms occasionally used include, inter alia, 'background', 'backstop', 'fallback' 'gap-filling', 'opt-out', 'preset', 'standby' or 'suppletory' rules.

default rules.[14] On the other hand, each of them approaches the matter from a slightly different angle;[15] and it is interesting to ask what these different angles tell us about the perception and use of default rules in the various systems.

Of the three terms considered here, 'default rules' is arguably the most 'neutral'. All it tells us is that some rule applies unless the relevant parties (or party)[16] involved stipulate(s) otherwise. There is admittedly a question over whether the notion of application 'by default' has a slightly vituperative tinge, implying that something is lacking, something which really ought to have been provided for.[17] Yet if one thinks of the 'default' settings of, say, a piece of equipment or relating to a particular computer program, this connotation is by no means inevitable.

The term preferred in Germany, 'dispositive law', conveys the same idea, that of a rule applying unless superseded by specific provision, but distinctly from the side of the pre-ordained legal rule. The default rule is the starting point; one may perhaps add, the state-approved normal baseline. That starting point may be abrogated in favour of something else, but there is no sense of any expectation that the parties or party involved will or ought to make specific provision. If they do, they are actively deviating from the norm, which they are free to do, although it would also have been perfectly fine for them to stick to the baseline.

The French notion of 'suppletive' law, whilst not necessarily criticising a 'lack' of specific provision, nonetheless adopts technically the opposite approach. A suppletive rule is of a supplementary character. It is there to keep something on track by supporting and completing it. The notion therefore views the matter from the point of view of the *volonté*-based transaction (or other legal relationship) being supported. It fills in 'gaps' where and to the extent that nothing else has been provided. Metaphorically speaking, the law steps in only where the parties involved leave space for it to do so. There is, at least in the linguistic sense, no sense of any 'deviation'.

An example from contract law may serve to illustrate the difference between the approaches outlined above. Judged by reference to the local terminology for 'default rules', at least, the 'dispositive law' approach proceeds by characterising the parties' agreement as a particular *type* of legal transaction (eg, as a contract of sale) and then automatically applies to it a set of pre-determined legal rules conformable to the relevant type of transaction. The 'suppletive law' approach, on the other hand, notionally *completes* the parties' agreement by importing into it a suitable gap-filling regime where the parties have not expressly made their own provisions.[18]

[14] Nicely exposed by Möslein, *Dispositives Recht* (n 5) 45–119, who highlights the 'dipolarity' (*Dipolarität*) of dispositive law.

[15] This is also noted in the contribution by J Basedow, ch 6 in this volume, at 101.

[16] Default rules are not confined to transactions involving two or more parties, as is evident if one considers the example of succession law: see further below, esp text to nn 62–66.

[17] As suggested by Basedow (n 15) at 101.

[18] But cf B Nicholas, 'Rules and Terms – Civil Law and Common Law' (1974) 48 *Tulane L Rev* 946, 949, who characterises French law as operating the first-mentioned model as well, despite all the rhetoric about *autonomie* and *volonté* ('The parties freely make their agreement, but the law will, as far as possible, categorise that agreement as a specific typical contract, and the rights and duties of the parties will be seen as flowing from that categorisation rather than from the agreement itself'). Nicholas contrasts this with the Common law's agreement-centred approach. See also the contribution by J Cartwright, ch 7 in this volume, at 129 et seq, making a similar point. It *may* therefore be that the distinction between French and German law drawn here is no more than terminological.

IV. Practical Approaches and Social Attitudes

While the terminology of 'default rules' may not in and of itself be an indicator of how strongly or how often parties actually 'fall back' on them in everyday life and business, drafting practices in the Common law world are, as an observable fact, much more detailed than they are (traditionally)[19] in Civilian systems such as Germany or France. Common lawyers' characteristic aim for comprehensiveness and making provision for every eventuality results in much longer, perhaps more precise, yet arguably also more unwieldy, contracts and other transactional documents.[20] Rather than relying on a set of default rules and providing only for the desired derogations or additions, English lawyers typically draft 'complete' contracts, often expressly designated as such. They thereby seek to preclude any suggestion that the contract contains terms not expressly reflected on the face of the signed document. It has been held that a sufficiently clear 'entire agreement clause' can in an appropriate case exclude terms which would otherwise be implied by custom or usage.[21] And although English courts have not yet taken the next step, it is by no means impossible to envisage an extension of the same logic to non-mandatory terms implied by statute or (case) law. As things stand, such 'ousting' of contractual default rules happens frequently in practice, but usually via a designated separate exclusion clause.[22]

On the other hand, it has to be borne in mind that the phenomenon of detailed drafting is actually part of a chicken-and-egg problem.[23] By comparison with Civilian systems, there is a relative dearth of default rules within the Common law (in the widest sense of that term) on which parties could fall back, even if they wanted to. While the entire Civilian law of contract essentially emerged from the Roman law tradition of different contracts, Common law courts never developed a great number of detailed rules relating to various different 'types' of contract,[24] and statute has only rarely sought to provide even a definition, let alone a comprehensive set of provisions specifically for one such 'type'. The Sale of Goods Act 1893/1979 comes to mind as the salient

[19] But see below, text to and following n 29.

[20] Without going further into this here, at first sight the same observation could be made with respect to the drafting style of many statutes.

[21] *Exxonmobil Sales & Supply Corp v Texaco Ltd* [2003] EWHC 1964 (Comm), [2003] 2 Lloyd's Rep 686, [2004] 1 All ER (Comm) 435, at [21]–[28]. Rules implied by custom or usage sit somewhere at the blurry borderline between so-called 'terms implied in fact' (by party agreement) and 'terms implied in law' (by statute or case law).

[22] For example: 'Except as set out in this document, all warranties, representations, conditions, terms and undertakings, express or implied, whether by statute, common law, custom, trade usage, course of dealings or otherwise are hereby excluded to the fullest extent permitted by law.'

[23] See also J Cartwright, *Contract Law: An Introduction to the Common Law of Contract for the Civil Lawyer*, 3rd edn (Oxford, Hart Publishing, 2016) 63, who comes at the matter from the other angle and writes that '[the] difference of approach between the common law and the civil law to the standardisation of contract types may … sometimes have a practical consequence in the form of contract drafting. It is well known that contracts in common law jurisdictions can be significantly longer and more detailed than similar contracts in civil law jurisdictions. One reason … is the approach taken to finding the terms of the contract. … Without a fully developed theory of special contracts, there would be significant uncertainty about the scope of obligations to be implied into contracts. And so express drafting helps to make the contract "judge-proof": to anticipate and provide for possible conflicts in advance.'

[24] But cf the comment in n 25 immediately below.

example of where this *did* happen, but it is also the prime example of a statute closely resembling Civilian-style legislation.[25] For the most part, the Common law confines itself to framing the general law of contract (with rules relating mainly to contract formation, interpretation, discharge and remedies for breach)[26] as a sort of skeleton around which the parties then flesh out their specific agreement *in toto*.

In the vast majority of daily business transactions, this is of course not done through detailed negotiations over every single contract term. Rather, legal practice resorts to templates, standard terms and boilerplate clauses. One could indeed say that, as far as the Common law is concerned, the 'default rules' of many special contracts are to be found in commercial custom and usage rather than in a Civilian-type statute.[27] These customs and usages may then, in turn, seep back into other, similar contracts through the process of implication of contract terms.[28] This is in fact how it was possible for 'judge-made' default rules governing some specific contracts to emerge in the first place, like islands from what is otherwise a sea of general contract law.

Interestingly, as far as one can tell,[29] drafting practices in Civilian systems have changed significantly over the past decades. Parties' advisers no longer seem content to provide only for deviations from or additions to the default regime and otherwise to rely on statutory definitions and default rules. Maximum coverage and gap-filling appears to be the order of the day. How much of this trend is owed to the rise of international law firms, whose head offices in the UK or the US may shape the corporate sense of good drafting practice, is hard to say. It is certainly the case that some big-player business contracts one encounters in continental legal practice closely resemble the Common law model in both style and (remarkably) substance, even where a Civilian system has been chosen as the applicable law and where a potential dispute falls to be resolved before Civilian judges.

While modern Civilian drafting may thus be gradually assimilating itself to the Common law tradition, there are interestingly some debates in the Common law world which might suggest a modern movement in the opposite direction. As mentioned above, the US 'Legal Default Project' was initially conceived as a means of making the process of contracting more efficient by reducing the opt-out incidence, thus minimising overall transaction costs. At first blush, the underlying idea actually chimes with the traditional Civilian approach: providing a suitable default regime obviates the need for parties to make their own detailed arrangements. Where critics have – from a range

[25] The fact that the 1893 Sale of Goods Act by-and-large codified the pre-existing common law indicates, however, that some specific judge-made (or rather: precedent-based) default rules were developed for those special 'types' of contract which were of greatest commercial significance. These included not only the sale of goods, but also service and insurance contracts, financial guarantees (suretyship) and bailment (widely and long regarded as 'contractual' in nature, whether or not it was for a reward).

[26] Many of the rules of general contract law are of a default nature: see below, text to nn 50–54.

[27] See also S Whittaker in H Beale (gen ed), *Chitty on Contracts*, 35th edn (London, Sweet & Maxwell, 2023) [1-004]: '[I]n some types of contract, the regulation of the parties' relationship remains all but entirely in the hands of the parties themselves, who may for this purpose use standard contract terms, whether their own or ones drawn from industry practice.' *Chitty* is one of the few texts in the Common law world that has a separate part (vol 2) devoted to 'Specific Contracts' besides the 'General Principles' (in vol 1).

[28] See comment at the end of n 21.

[29] This is an important qualification. We tend to see mainly the evidence of large commercial transactions.

of different vantage points – drawn attention to the weaknesses of a one-size-fits-all regime,[30] they have either called for a radical reduction in both mandatory and default rules (thus reviving the old idea of an unfettered law merchant)[31] or concluded that what is really needed is not a general default regime, but a more fine-grained offering of selected contract 'types' (which also sounds quite Civilian).[32] Whether any of these suggestions or developments have had a meaningful impact on legal practice in the US or elsewhere in the Common law world is an open question.

Looking beyond professionally drafted contracts, different attitudes to default rules can also be perceived more widely in private law. Reliable data is not easy to come by, yet arguably the best illustration of this is to be found in the field of succession law, where the 'default' intestacy regime can be displaced by a valid will.[33] Social attitudes towards making a will (and the typical extent of testation) vary considerably between countries. In England, about half the population are thought to die testate, which is commonly regarded as an undesirably low quota.[34] On a closer analysis of the available figures, however, a leading expert concludes that 'most of those who die in England and Wales and who are the owners of property of value do not die intestate'.[35] Citizens are strongly encouraged[36] to make a will, particularly when getting married,[37] when having children, or at any rate when they purchase their first home and start climbing the property ladder.[38] It is estimated that around two thirds of those aged over 65 have made

[30] A Schwartz and RE Scott, 'Contract Theory and the Limits of Contract Law' (2003) 113 *Yale LJ* 541, esp 584–609; Dagan and Heller (n 3) chs 10–12 at 102–34.

[31] Schwartz and Scott (n 30) conclude at 619: 'Most of the mandatory rules should be repealed or reduced to defaults, and most of the defaults should vanish from the law. … A law merchant appropriate to our time would be a merchants' law; and for merchants, the less publicly supplied law the better.'

[32] Dagan and Heller (n 3) 113: 'Contract types are the locus for enhancing autonomy because each type can offer a distinctive normative balance that responds to what people seek by contracting. A variety of types in an important sphere of human activity … ensures that people have meaningful choice among the goods of contracting.' It is important to realise, however, that by 'contract types' Dagan and Heller do not mean the conventional 'nominate' Civilian categories of contract such as sale or hire, but instead refer to different 'spheres of contracting', namely the (private) 'family' and 'home' spheres and the (public) spheres of 'employment' and 'commerce': ibid ch 9, esp at 96.

[33] See further below, text to and following n 62.

[34] To get a flavour of the general attitude, see eg www.painterslaw.co.uk/news/less-than-half-of-uk-adults-have-a-will-are-you-one-of-them; www.ftadviser.com/retirement-income/2021/10/20/millions-of-brits-still-die-intestate-just-warns/; www.theguardian.com/money/2016/nov/14/writing-a-will-dying-intestate; www.thegazette.co.uk/wills-and-probate/content/103347 (all websites last accessed 22.02.2024).

[35] R Kerridge, 'Intestacy Reform in 2014 – Unfinished Business' in B Häcker and C Mitchell (eds), *Current Issues in Succession Law* (Oxford, Hart Publishing, 2016) 1 at 13–15, esp 15.

[36] For example, the website of the Law Society states (www.lawsociety.org.uk/public/for-public-visitors/common-legal-issues/making-a-will): 'If you die without a valid will, it could be difficult for your family to sort out your affairs. Your estate will be shared out according to the rules of intestacy. … It's important to make a will if you:

> own property or a business
> have children
> have savings, investments or insurance policies'.

[37] Note that under the Wills Act 1837, s 18, subject to a few exceptions, a testator's marriage automatically revokes any will previously made.

[38] This is despite the fact that joint tenancies of realty are 'will substitutes' in the sense that, upon the death of one joint tenant, the full property right automatically accrues to the other by right of 'survivorship', rather than the testator's notional share devolving in accordance with provisions in a will.

a will, rising to 82% of those aged 75 and over.[39] Even more startling rates are reported from Australia and New Zealand, being Common law countries with traditionally high rates of testation. In Queensland, for example, 79% of those aged over 35 and a remarkable 98% of the population over 70 years of age allegedly have a current will in place.[40]

By contrast, the rate of testation in many continental systems is much lower. Estimates for Germany put the number of people dying testate at around 25–30%,[41] with the average testator making his or her will in the mid-50s.[42] In France and Belgium, the relevant rate is assumed to be below 20%.[43] While it cannot be stated generally that citizens living in Civilian countries make fewer wills than those in Common law countries,[44] social expectations and conventions are something to be borne in mind when assessing the significance of opt-outs, quite independently of the quality of the default regime (here the intestacy regime), which is of course the other main factor.

Connected is the observation that rates of testation alone do not tell us much about the *content* of the will someone chooses to make. There is a big difference between simply leaving a few small bequests to friends and family members who would not otherwise receive anything in intestacy and drafting a document that makes provision for the entirety of the estate (perhaps in some respects replicating what would otherwise apply by default). In England, there is still a very real sense amongst professionals and the general populace alike that a 'proper' will, to be complete, requires the testator to nominate an executor who is then given instructions for the distribution of the estate *in toto*.[45] In the absence of such nomination, no probate can be granted, but only letters of administration 'with will annexed'. In Germany, on the other hand, the act of testation often exhausts itself in provisions that build on and complement the default regime, particularly where wills are home-drafted without expert legal advice.

The upshot is that the density, role and content of default rules, and the approach practitioners and citizens take towards them, are two factors going hand-in-hand. Some

[39] A Humphrey, G Douglas, L Mills and others, *Inheritance and the Family: Attitudes to Will-Making and Intestacy* (Report published by the National Centre for Social Research, London, August 2010) at 8, 13. The National Wills Report 2023, recently published by the National Will Register, records a figure of 66% of those aged 55 years and over as having made a will (at 5): www.nationalwillregister.co.uk/app/uploads/2023/04/The-National-Wills-Report-2023.pdf.

[40] N Peart and P Vines, 'Will-Substitutes in New Zealand and Australia' in A Braun and A Röthel (eds), *Passing Wealth on Death: Will-Substitutes in Comparative Perspective* (Oxford, Hart Publishing, 2016) 107 at 108 (fn 5).

[41] See (with further references) R Zimmermann, 'Testamentary Formalities in Germany' in KGC Reid, MJ de Waal and R Zimmermann, *Comparative Succession Law I: Testamentary Formalities* (Oxford, OUP, 2011) 175 at 204 (25–35%); D Ludwig, *Die Form des ordentlichen Privattestaments: Überlegungen zum Videotestament* (Frankfurt/Main, Wolfgang Metzner, 2019) 8–13, esp 9 (18–27%), but hinting (at 11) that the actual rate may be higher.

[42] Ludwig (n 41) 12.

[43] W Pintens, 'Testamentary Formalities in France and Belgium' in Reid, de Waal and Zimmermann (eds), *Comparative Succession Law I: Testamentary Formalities* (n 41) 51 at 57.

[44] Spain, for example, has similar or even higher rates than England and Wales: S Cámara Lapuente, 'Testamentary Formalities in Spain' in Reid, de Waal and Zimmermann (eds), *Comparative Succession Law I: Testamentary Formalities* (n 31) 71 at 72, also exploring the reasons behind the phenomenon.

[45] This is a remnant of the Roman principle that the institution of an heir (*heres*) was the 'head and foundation of the entire testament' (*caput et fundamentum totius testamenti*).

differences will be subtle and quite hard to spot, yet identifying them can teach us a great deal about people's unspoken expectations and assumptions, and it may explain otherwise puzzling observable divergences.

V. Various Forms of Rules and Fields of Application

Default rules come in various forms and (dis)guises, and they apply in many more fields than one might at first suspect. In fact, it is hard to find an area of private law where they do not play at least some small role. It is easier to see this when one thinks of default rules as 'dispositive' rather than 'suppletive' or supplementary rules,[46] for they are not always about filling gaps in people's transactions. While the default rules of contract law may only be triggered where there is a contract in the first place,[47] this is different – to give just one example – with the intestacy rules of succession law. It would be odd to say that someone who dies intestate has made an 'incomplete' will needing to be supplemented by a legal default regime!

Even within contract law, dispositive norms governing particular types of transactions (such as sales) are only a part of the picture. So far as the Common law breaks contracts down into different 'types', we often encounter them in the form of so-called implied terms, more specifically as terms implied either by statute or 'in law'.[48] Yet default rules also exist in general contract law, from the formation stage right through to the end of the life of the contract. Think, for instance, of the Common law's famous 'postal rule', whose application is displaced by a unilateral stipulation to the effect that the acceptance needs actually to reach the offeror.[49] Post-formation, in a reciprocal contract, *unless otherwise agreed* (or inevitably required by the nature of the transaction at hand),[50] neither party can enforce the other's promise without him- or herself being ready, willing and able to perform his/her side of the bargain.[51] Similarly, *unless otherwise provided*, a contract breaker will be liable for all consequential losses suffered by the other which were, at the time of contracting, reasonably foreseeable as a probable result of the breach.[52] Through legislative intervention there is now also a rule in English law stating that a person who is not him- or herself a party to a contract (ie, a third party) may nonetheless enforce a term of the contract if that term

[46] Cf section III above, text to n 13 et seq.

[47] Even that is not technically a given. Default rules governing, for instance, the manner and form in which a contractual offer can be accepted are logically *prior* to the contract whose formation they govern: see text to n 49 below.

[48] On the conventional understanding, so-called terms implied 'in fact' have nothing to do with a default regime. They derive from the parties' agreement itself, albeit that they are not made express. Terms implied 'by custom or usage' are a borderline case: see above, comment at the end of n 21 and the text following n 27.

[49] *Holwell Securities Ltd v Hughes* [1974] 1 WLR 155.

[50] In an appropriate case, the order of performance may well be determined by interpretation or derived from a term implied 'in fact'.

[51] For details of the historical evolution, see J English, 'Discharge of Contractual Obligations' (DPhil thesis, University of Oxford, 2022), esp 38 et seq concerning so-called dependent promises, soon to be published as J English, *Discharge of Contractual Obligations for Failure of Condition* (Oxford, OUP, forthcoming 2025) ch 2.

[52] This is the well-known 'remoteness' rule in *Hadley v Baxendale* (1854) 9 Ex 341, 156 ER 145.

purports to confer a benefit upon him/her, *unless* 'on a proper construction of the contract it appears that the parties did not intend the term to be enforceable by the third party'.[53] This is not to denigrate mandatory law or to deny the existence of hard-to-classify rules,[54] but to illustrate the importance and breadth of the default rule phenomenon, which reaches right into the very heart of the general law of contract.[55]

Areas connected and overlapping with contract law are of course also fertile grounds for analysis. This includes in particular commercial and company law (interesting on account of the distinct business context),[56] employment/labour law (an area where implied terms actually play a significant role)[57] and the consumer context (often involving semi-mandatory law, in the sense that derogation to the disadvantage of the consumer is not possible).[58] Unfair terms legislation is particularly instructive in that it interacts with default rules in two interrelated ways. On the one hand, it limits the extent to which parties can opt out of and deviate from the legal default regime. On the other hand, the default regime itself can become a yardstick for assessing the acceptability of a deviation. As the CJEU regularly emphasises with regard to the EU's Unfair Terms Directive:

> [I]n order to ascertain whether a term causes a 'significant imbalance' in the parties' rights and obligations arising under the contract, to the detriment of the consumer, *it must in particular be considered what rules of national law would apply in the absence of an agreement by the parties in that regard.* Such a comparative analysis will enable the national court to evaluate whether and, as the case may be, to what extent, the contract places the consumer in a legal situation less favourable than that provided for by the national law in force.[59]

The fact that unfair terms control never extends to the main subject matter of the contract or the adequacy of the price or remuneration paid for goods or services[60] is easily explicable if one considers that there has to be a contract first, defined at least by its bare essentials (*essentialia negotii*), before any national default regime can kick in.[61]

[53] Contracts (Rights of Third Parties) Act 1999, s 1(1) and (2).

[54] There are, for example, a number of contract law rules of which it is hard to say whether they are technically mandatory or dispositive. Moreover, depending on how one conceptualises doctrines such as common mistake and frustration, these may or may not qualify as 'default rules' proper.

[55] It is sometimes said that practically the whole of general contract law is dispositive in the Common law tradition, yet this overstates the case. The law of remedies in particular sets clear boundaries to what the parties are able to agree. Thus, for example, they cannot provide for penalty payments (as opposed to liquidated damages) and they cannot make specific performance available as of right (damages being the primary remedy). For further detailed analysis of default rules in contract law, see the contribution by J Cartwright, ch 7 in this volume.

[56] See the contribution by L Gullifer, ch 9 in this volume.

[57] See the contribution by A Bogg, ch 10 in this volume.

[58] See the contribution by S Whittaker, ch 8 in this volume.

[59] CJEU, C-415/11 *Aziz v Caixa d'Estalvis de Catalunya, Tarragona i Manresa (Catalunyacaixa)* EU:C:2013:164, at [68] (emphasis added). Cf Council Directive 93/13/EEC of 5 April 1993 on Unfair Terms in Consumer Contracts [1993] OJ L95/29, esp Art 3(1).

[60] Unfair Contract Terms Directive 93/13/EEC, Art 4(2).

[61] Though note that English law (of all systems!) actually contains 'default' provisions to the effect that, where a contract price is not fixed by the parties themselves, a 'reasonable' price is payable: see eg Sale of Goods Act 1893/1979, s 8. The existence of these defaults is perhaps best explained by the fact that a Common law of unjust enrichment developed at a relatively late stage and provision had to be made for goods provided by the 'seller' and already consumed by the 'buyer'.

Yet such a 'transactional base' is not always necessary before default rules apply. Succession law has already been mentioned as an instance where default rules, in the shape of the intestacy regime, are there to cater precisely for the absence of a 'last will'.[62] The example of succession law also helps draw attention to another typical shape of default rules, namely those often described as 'presumptions'[63] relating to the content and meaning of people's testamentary dispositions.[64] The Wills Act 1837 contains countless provisions setting out what applies 'unless a contrary intention shall appear by the will'.[65] In German law, so-called 'rules of interpretation' (*Auslegungsregeln*) are to the same effect.[66] Where an utterance is, by law, taken to indicate that a particular legal consequence is intended unless a different intention is made sufficiently clear, then that itself amounts to a legal default rule.

Outside the realm of substantive law, defaults also impact certain aspects of procedural law as well as conflicts questions regulating disputes with a cross-border element. There is, in particular, a (growing) degree of party autonomy when it comes to civil procedure, despite this field being traditionally dominated by mandatory rules.[67] Moreover, both international conventions and EU Regulations successfully employ what could be described as 'private international default rules' in order to determine what is, prima facie, the most appropriate legal regime to govern a dispute, ie the applicable law, and/or the most appropriate forum for a case to be heard, ie the issue of international jurisdiction.[68] We will come back to this below in the context of the functions default rules perform.

While the above-mentioned areas all have a chapter devoted to them in this book, it is of course not possible to cover all fields of or related to private law. The following further examples may suffice to give a flavour of just how widespread the use of default rules is, and how varied a phenomenon we are dealing with. Consider tort law (or, in Civilian terminology, the law of delict or extra-contractual liability): Wherever there is a question of the standard of care one person is obliged to take in order not to harm the other, even in the absence of any agreement giving rise to that obligation, it is nonetheless usually possible to agree on a modification of the expected standard, thus showing that standard to be the default. In property law, systems that in principle envisage title or ownership of goods passing as soon as a relevant contract of sale is

[62] See already above, text to and following n 33 and after n 47.

[63] The existence and terminology of such 'interpretative presumptions' can be queried on the ground that presumptions proper are a part of the law of evidence and allow inferences to be drawn about the existence of one set of facts (ultimately to be proved) from proof of another set of facts.

[64] Although this may not be obvious, this is in fact not at all dissimilar to the way most of the default rules in general contract law operate: cf the text to nn 50–53 above.

[65] See eg section 24: 'Every will shall be construed, with reference to the real estate and personal estate comprised in it, to speak and take effect as if it had been executed immediately before the death of the testator, unless a contrary intention shall appear by the will.'

[66] See eg § 2087(2) BGB, providing that a testamentary beneficiary who has been left individual objects is, *in case of doubt*, to be treated as a legatee rather than an heir, even if the term 'heir' is used in the will. (Background to this rule is that 'heirship' in law necessarily involves universal succession, though ordinary lay language will often describe someone as being 'heir' to a specific asset.)

[67] See the contribution by G Rühl, ch 12 in this volume, arguing that, conversely, party autonomy when it comes to designing arbitration proceedings seems to be in decline.

[68] See the contribution by J Ungerer, ch 13 in this volume.

concluded typically provide for the parties' option to delay the conveyancing effect at will, for instance until full payment is made. Such a reservation of title arrangement can be constructed as inserting a suspensive condition into the contract itself,[69] but under English law, it is clearly a case in which the legislative default for ascertaining the parties' intention with respect to the passing of title ('property passes … when the contract is made') is displaced.[70] In the law of real property and trusts, we find a judge-made default rule that operates in a similar fashion to this legislative model. It concerns the so-called 'common intention constructive trust'.[71] Where a family home is bought in two parties' joint names, the starting point is that they intend to 'own' the property jointly at law and in equity. This means that, unless the default 'presumption' can be displaced by showing a different common intention with regard to the equitable interest, both parties will have an equal share in the beneficial interest. One might go further and say that even the rules governing so-called 'automatic' resulting trusts are judge-made default rules of sorts: for although no settlor can escape an equitable interest 'jumping back' to him or her where it has not been properly disposed of,[72] this simply makes the default rule into one whose abrogation requires a valid disposition of the *entire* equitable interest to one or more third party beneficiaries at the point of trust creation.

Finally, the fascinating concept of 'sticky defaults' needs mentioning.[73] While this term tells us nothing specific about the exact *form* a default rule takes or its field or mode of operation, it vividly describes the *tenacity* of certain defaults. 'Sticky defaults' are hard(er) to opt out of, and one may perhaps add, deliberately so. They are designed to minimise the incidence of opt-outs without preventing them altogether, ie without becoming full-blown mandatory rules. All default rules that take a certain degree of effort to displace are, in a sense, 'sticky'. Formality requirements highlight this

[69] As (most probably) under French law: see art 2367 Code civil and B Häcker, 'Contract and Conveyance: The Further Repercussions of Different Transfer Systems' in J Cartwright and ÁM López y López (eds), *Comparative Reflections on English Law and Spanish Law* (Oxford, Hart Publishing, 2021) 89 at 94. In German law, a reservation of title (*Eigentumsvorbehalt*) is achieved by inserting an appropriate condition into the (abstract) real agreement concluded in pursuance of an underlying obligatory contract.

[70] See Sale of Goods Act 1979, ss 17, 18:

> 'Section 17: Property passes when intended to pass.
>
> (1) Where there is a contract for the sale of specific or ascertained goods the property in them is transferred to the buyer at such time as the parties to the contract intend it to be transferred.
>
> (2) For the purpose of ascertaining the intention of the parties regard shall be had to the terms of the contract, the conduct of the parties and the circumstances of the case.
>
> Section 18: Rules for ascertaining intention.
>
> Unless a different intention appears, the following are rules for ascertaining the intention of the parties as to the time at which the property in the goods is to pass to the buyer.
>
>> Rule 1.
>>
>> —Where there is an unconditional contract for the sale of specific goods in a deliverable state the property in the goods passes to the buyer when the contract is made, and it is immaterial whether the time of payment or the time of delivery, or both, be postponed.
>>
>> [… Rules 2–5 …]'

[71] The leading English cases are *Stack v Dowden* [2007] UKHL 17, [2007] 2 AC 432, and *Jones v Kernott* [2011] UKSC 53, [2012] AC 776, though it has to be said that the law is still in a state of flux.

[72] See esp *Re Vandervell Trustees Ltd* (No 2) [1974] Ch 269.

[73] See the references in n 86 below.

particularly well. The fact that one needs to execute a formal 'last will and testament' in order to 'opt out' of the intestacy regime increases the 'stickiness' of the latter. Yet no-one would suggest that formalities are always there to nudge people in a particular direction. Quite the opposite may be true, as the succession law example discussed earlier shows, bearing in mind the different social attitudes towards will-making and the fact that in some countries citizens are positively encouraged to choose their own provisions.[74] Real 'sticky defaults' have a regulatory aim and therefore fall to be considered in the next section.

VI. A Number of Different Functions and (Potential) Aims

In light of the above discussion of the many fields in which default rules operate, and the varied forms they take, it is unsurprising that they perform a range of functions and are associated with a number of different (potential) aims. Only the most salient ones can be touched upon here.

One main function of default rules, the most obvious and arguably most venerable of purposes, is to fill gaps in people's private transactions. They are then in the true sense of the word 'suppletive' and supplement what has been agreed or provided.[75] In the economic analysis of law, this supplementary function is rationalised as helping to increase the efficiency of contracting.[76] It is particularly compelling in fields such as contract, company and commercial law, where efficiency in terms of both time and money is a key driver of people's dispositions.

Sometimes, however, the aim is not – or at any rate not necessarily – to increase the efficiency of contracting or otherwise to 'complete' a transaction people have entered into, but simply to plug what would otherwise be a legal void by providing a predictable fallback position. Intestacy regimes arguably fit into this category. Rules governing failed transactions (such as the English rules on 'automatic resulting trusts') could also be placed within it,[77] though one may wonder at which point the whole of the law of restitution for unjust(ified) enrichment would then also need to be classed as a legal default.

A third function often discussed in connection with default rules is that they occasionally serve as a useful model or yardstick by which to assess private transactions. This idea is neatly captured by the (hard to translate) German description of them serving as a *Leitbild*. A good example is to be found in the previously mentioned control of contract terms, where the legal default is a type of state-approved 'best practice'

[74] See above, n 36 and text thereto.

[75] German lawyers speak of default rules having an *Ergänzungsfunktion*.

[76] See eg RA Posner, *Economic Analysis of Law*, 9th edn (New York, Wolters Kluwer, 2014) 543: 'One function of contract law … [is] to economize on transaction costs by supplying standard contract terms that the parties would otherwise have to adopt by express agreement'; AW Katz, 'Economic Foundations of Contract Law' in G Klass, G Letsas and P Saprai (eds), *Philosophical Foundations of Contract Law* (Oxford, OUP, 2016) 171 at 182.

[77] See the text around n 72 above.

and where the degree of deviation effectively becomes a measure for the 'fairness' of a proposed (standard) term.[78]

Unfair contract terms control is, of course, a field where private law's aims of allowing people to enter into binding deals overlaps with the aim of defining certain boundaries in both the private and the public interest. It has rightly been observed that lawyers typically associate mandatory rules – rather than default rules – with regulation in the public interest[79] (and the unfair contract terms regime is indeed 'mandatory' in the sense that it delimits the permissible range of deviations). Yet it is nowadays also widely recognised that default rules are not merely perfectly plausible candidates for pursuing regulatory aims, but are in fact particularly well suited as steering mechanisms, governance tools, and as powerful instruments for 'nudging'.

Well before the concept of 'nudging' entered public consciousness,[80] Ian Ayres and Robert Gertner had already coined the term 'penalty defaults' for default rules deliberately designed *not* to fit with what most parties would choose to complete their contract.[81] The avowed aim of penalty defaults is to incentivise parties to contract around them and to counter-balance existing but inefficient information asymmetries.[82]

'Default nudges' are different. From a behavioural perspective,[83] relying on the widespread tendency to accept a given or pre-determined status quo,[84] they provide a strong steer towards what the entity doing the nudging regards as a desirable choice for people to make or live by.[85] In this way, default nudges combine two related opt-out obstacles: on the one hand the economic cost of replacing the default regime with a tailor-made or even just an off-the-rack alternative, and on the other hand the observable psychological barrier composed of people's inbuilt decision inertia.

[78] See above, text before and accompanying n 59. The notion of *Leitbild* is discussed – also in the context of unfair terms control – by M Lehmann and J Ungerer, 'Save the "Mittelstand": How German Courts Protect Small and Medium-Sized Enterprises from Unfair Terms' [2017] ERPL 313, 330–31.

[79] Nicely put by M Grochowski, 'The Majoritarian Concept of Default Rules: Towards a Shift in Paradigms?' (2020) 15 *Studia Prawa Prywatnego* 63, 65: 'Under [the] classic assumption, default rules are neutral in terms of policy goals – as opposed to mandatory rules, which are, by nature, nothing but incarnations of regulatory goals.'

[80] Through the influential work by RH Thaler and CR Sunstein, *Nudge: Improving Decisions About Health, Wealth, and Happiness* (New Haven, Yale University Press, 2008).

[81] Ayres and Gertner (1989) (n 1). Critical: BE Adler, 'The Questionable Ascent of *Hadley v. Baxendale*' (1999) 41 *Stanford L Rev* 1547; EA Posner, 'There Are No Penalty Default Rules in Contract Law' (2006) 33 *Florida State Univ LR* 563.

[82] Ayres and Gertner (1989) (n 1) 91: 'Penalty defaults are designed to give at least one party to the contract an incentive to contract around the default rule and therefore to choose affirmatively the contract provision they prefer. In contrast to the received wisdom, penalty defaults are purposefully set at what the parties would not want-in order to encourage the parties to reveal information to each other or to third parties (especially the courts).' The example of a penalty default most frequently given – but also fiercely disputed – is the remoteness rule in *Hadley v Baxendale* (n 52).

[83] The behavioural aspects of default rules are explored in the contribution by G Helleringer, ch 3 in this volume.

[84] See already R Korobkin, 'The Status Quo Bias and Contract Default Rules' (1998) 83 *Cornell L Rev* 609, observing that contracting parties often fail to opt out of default rules even if the latter are inefficient.

[85] Sunstein (n 4) 5: '[D]efault rules, even or perhaps especially if they appear to be invisible, count as prime "nudges," understood as interventions that maintain freedom of choice, that do not impose mandates or bans, but that nonetheless incline people's choices in a particular direction.'

'Sticky defaults' nudge more strongly still in that they artificially increase the opt-out obstacles.[86] In the words of Ian Ayres,

> what makes a default sticky … has nothing to do with the content or desirability of the default itself. The stickiness of a default derives from the relative difficulty of contracting around – particularly if the altering rules impede fully-informed contractors from contracting for certain non-default effects because of the costs of complying with the impeding altering rules.[87]

Imposed formality or notification requirements may constitute relevant hurdles, as indeed may a serious risk of falling foul of mandatory opt-out limits.[88]

Another function default rules can potentially have is to serve as coordination or even harmonisation tools. This is the realm of international private and procedural law (think of the various Rome Regulations or the Brussels Ia Regulation aligning default conflicts rules within the EU)[89] as well as supra- and international instruments which help coordinate cross-border trade between countries.[90] The UN Convention on Contracts for the International Sale of Goods (CISG) is a well-known example of the latter, in that, where business parties based in appropriate states contract with one another, the entire CISG regime automatically governs their transaction unless they opt out either in part or *in toto*.[91] At the level of EU law, the nearest equivalent to CISG aimed at consumers and SMEs was arguably the failed 'Common European Sales Law' (CESL),[92] though that would have been an 'optional instrument' sitting alongside national law and would thus *not* have applied by default.[93] The EU's harmonisation efforts – particularly in consumer law – have instead conventionally focused on setting mandatory minimum standards to be implemented nationally.[94] Yet there is a question whether this approach should or could usefully be supplemented

[86] See eg O Ben-Shahar and JAE Pottow, 'On the Stickiness of Default Rules' (2006) 33 *Florida State Univ LR* 651; B McDonnell, Sticky Defaults and Altering Rules in Corporate Law (2007) 60 *SMU L Rev* 384, coining (at 385) the wonderful term 'Teflon rules' for non-sticky defaults.

[87] I Ayres, 'Regulating Opt-Out: An Economic Theory of Altering Rules' (2012) 121 *Yale LJ* 2032 at 2086.

[88] In the terminology of Ian Ayers, 'transaction costs' and 'error costs', respectively: see ibid 2084–109.

[89] See eg Regulation (EC) No 593/2008 of the European Parliament and of the Council of 17 June 2008 on the Law Applicable to Contractual Obligations (Rome I) [2008] OJ L177/6; Regulation (EC) No 864/2007 of the European Parliament and of the Council of 11 July 2007 on the Law Applicable to Non-Contractual Obligations (Rome II) [2007] OJ L199/40; Regulation (EU) No 1215/2012 of the European Parliament and of the Council of 12 December 2012 on Jurisdiction and the Recognition and Enforcement of Judgments in Civil and Commercial Matters (Brussels I Recast) [2012] OJ L351/1.

[90] See further ch 13 by Ungerer, esp at 246 et seq and 253 et seq. As has variously been pointed out, the parties' ability to choose the governing law in certain situations means that even mandatory provisions of national law can effectively become default rules from their perspective, subject to limits imposed by the choice of law regime (eg Rome I Regulation, Arts 3(3), 3(4), 6(2), 9(2), and 9(3)).

[91] The Principles of International Commercial Contracts (PICC) drawn up by UNIDROIT are different. Although they, too, contain a great number of substantive defaults, the PICC regime as such only applies where the parties actively choose to opt *into* it, which is typically only possible if they subject their disputes to arbitration. (Parties may under certain circumstances even empower arbitral tribunals to determine the choice of law or 'rules of law' for them, thus potentially opening a back door for PICC to be applied as a version of the general *lex mercatoria*).

[92] Proposal for a Regulation on a Common European Sales Law, COM(2011) 635 final.

[93] Once chosen, however, the CESL would have supplied a uniform default regime for all relevant contracts. Many of its provisions were dispositive, subject to certain limits in the interest of consumer protection, leading to semi-mandatory law.

[94] More recently, the trend has been towards full harmonisation by also defining maximum standards.

by a harmonisation of national default rules so as further to integrate the internal market and indeed legal cultures more generally (thinking of the '*Leitbild*'-function of default rules).[95]

In practice, different aims will at various points be pursued by means of default rules (whether or not consciously so), depending on the field of law involved and the actor(s) in charge. Most obviously, democratically elected and well-advised legislators have much greater scope and legitimacy for implementing policy than courts do. We must therefore – as has already been indicated – expect statutory default rules to be informed by a wider, or at least significantly different, range of considerations than judge-made law emerging through precedent, simply on account of the institutional and procedural framework which shapes them.[96] Less obviously, but no less interestingly, one might even ponder whether and how far the 'regulatory' aspect of default rules can or ought to vary with substantive context. For instance, it might be argued that default rules supplementing people's transactions by filling in remaining gaps (such as typically in contract law) should on the whole be less 'regulatory' than those operating in fields where the 'default' is supplied by law regardless of any underlying transaction. Although, in the latter case, it may well be possible for people to modify the given legal default governing their relationship (such as by changing the level of a tortious duty of care), there is something to be said for policy informing the default position, while in the former case the parties' hypothetical will be more relevant.[97] All of this is closely linked to the conceptual basis or bases towards which default rules are orientated, which is the final and last point we need to consider.

VII. Conceptual Basis or Bases

Having looked at the aims default rules pursue, or at any rate the aims we ascribe to them when trying to rationalise their existence, we must now dig down below the surface to their underlying root. This raises perhaps the most important set of questions shaping our perspective on default rules: What is their conceptual basis? How are they created? And what ought they to be modelled on? The influence of the procedural framework under which the rule-maker (legislator or not) operates has already been mentioned as a key factor. For present purposes, we will disregard such institutional constraints and look at the matter from point of principle alone.

There are essentially two main[98] approaches to default rule design competing with each other. Default rules can either be designed to reflect what most people would want most of the time and thus be based on the hypothetical will of the average reasonable

[95] See the contribution by Basedow, ch 6 in this volume, esp at 116: '[The proposed] set of default principles and rules need not be complete, but should aim at establishing [a] grid that could constitute a common ground for legal education all over Europe. It could also serve as a point of reference where the courts have to interpret provisions of binding and usually mandatory EU law'. The idea 'uniform default rules' as a means of market integration is one already floated in J Basedow, *EU Private Law: Anatomy of a Growing Legal Order* (Cambridge, Intersentia, 2021) 724.

[96] See above, text to and following n 11.

[97] See below, text to and following nn 100, 106.

[98] Of course there are also any number of nuances and further refinements.

person; or the rule-maker can seek to regulate private behaviour and relationships based on other considerations – by setting a particular incentive structure, by active nudging or simply by exploiting the statistic fact that individuals often fail to agree anything else.

The first approach is commonly known as the 'majoritarian' approach. It is a preference-based theory orientated towards 'what the parties would have wanted'.[99] If one regards default rules as transaction cost savers, there is a great deal to be said for this approach. Economic efficiency is maximised through minimising the need for most parties to make alternative provision. In line with the observation at the end of the previous section,[100] the strongest case for the majoritarian theory can arguably be made out in the realm of contract law and similar fields, where default rules complete parties' agreements. It is here that transaction costs really matter and where they are on people's minds. And even if one shifts from the law and economics perspective to an autonomy-centred account of contracting, the argument for majoritarian defaults remains strong. Where the whole basis for importing defaults is a will-driven transaction, there is a lot to be said for plugging gaps by reference to the parties' hypothetical wishes, thereby extending their autonomy.

This may, of course, lead to a dilemma. It cannot always be assumed that the preferences of the actual parties in a given case will coincide with those of the majority or the average reasonable person. We may perhaps even know of vastly different preferences and idiosyncrasies. That is where gap-filling by 'supplementary interpretation' or, in English terminology, the implication of terms 'in fact' can help.[101] Such party- and contract-specific gap-filling has the potential to take individual preferences and idiosyncrasies into account in a way the more generic default rules cannot. From the generic point of view, however, the majoritarian approach usually provides the best statistical approximation of parties' intentions. And – indeed – to the extent that it is impossible to establish the hypothetical intentions of the *actual* parties, systems routinely draw on the default rules regime (if and where available) to inform the process of 'supplementary interpretation' or equivalent findings of what the contracting parties would have wanted in a particular situation.

The likelihood that a majoritarian default will fit the actual parties' needs and wishes increases the more fine-grained the categories and sub-categories towards which a rule is tailored. Put differently, the broader and more general the reference point of majoritarianism, the greater the trade-off between target-specificity and widespread fit will inevitably be. Buyers and sellers have very different needs and preferences from landlords and tenants or employers and employees. The default rules of general contract law cannot therefore be nearly as specific or dense as those where the majoritarian

[99] There is a question, not pursued further here, whether majoritarian defaults should be modelled on what most people would want (the 'dominant preference' approach) or what the average person would want (the 'mean preference' approach). The two theoretical reference points may, but need not, coincide.

[100] See above, text to n 97, and below, text to and following n 106.

[101] Differently to the English common law position, where the processes of *interpretation* and *implication* of terms are seen as distinct and subject to different rules (*Marks & Spencer plc v BNP Paribas Securities Services Trust Co (Jersey) Ltd* [2015] UKSC 72, [2016] AC 742), Civilian systems such as French and German law see both as closely connected. Gaps are filled, first and foremost, through 'supplementary interpretation' (*interprétation supplétive/ergänzende Auslegung*).

approach is applied to smaller sub-sets of different contract types. This is one reason why the general default regime of English law is less detailed than the default regimes additionally governing special contracts like sale or tenancies in Civilian systems (the latter typically consisting of both dispositive general contract law and transaction-specific default rules). If, however, the transaction-specific defaults of Civilian systems are in fact informed by the majoritarian approach, then – despite the divergent techniques – we should not be surprised to find little or no substantive difference to the rules typically adopted by commercial parties under the Common law's boilerplate approach.[102]

The regulatory approach has a different starting point from majoritariansim. It does not seek to emulate what most people would (hypothetically) want, but instead pursues certain policy objectives. It deliberately 'steers' people in a particular direction, which may or may not coincide with what the protagonists themselves would have chosen. Within this phenomenon, penalty defaults are a special case, in that their objective is to provide an incentive structure that will induce parties to reveal certain efficiency-increasing information.[103] They seek do this by filling gaps in a way that is distinctly *undesirable* from the perspective of at least one of the parties, so that there is an incentive to opt out by contracting around the default. This is almost exactly the opposite of a majoritarian default.[104]

Mostly, however, regulation takes the form of the rule-setter injecting into default rules the content that the setter regards as desirable from a policy perspective, while at the same time nudging people away from opt-outs. This type of regulatory approach is, in fact, the more obvious alternative to majoritarianism. It may be paternalistically or otherwise motivated. Think for a moment not about the law, but about some appliance or piece of equipment (a widget): Here, the manufacturer always has to decide whether – and how far – to model the default settings of the widget on what most customers or users would presumably choose as their preferred mode of operation. Alternatively, the manufacturer could nudge customers and users in a particular direction by providing default settings that are supposedly advantageous for the user (even if users would not routinely choose these settings) or which are for some reason particularly desirable from the manufacturer's point of view. The problem is of course nowadays especially pertinent with respect to computer software and internet platforms, where there is an ongoing tug-of-war between program providers and state regulators over the permissible default settings, their degree of 'stickiness' and acceptable modes of nudging.[105]

Looking at default rules in private law from a distance, and coming back to a point already raised, one might argue that the regulatory approach is easier to justify

[102] See above, n 27 and the text thereto.

[103] Ayers and Gertner (1989) (n 1) 127 reason that 'when one party to a contract knows more than another, the knowledgeable party may strategically decide not to contract around even an inefficient default' and suggest that 'lawmakers may be able to undercut the incentives for this strategic rent-seeking by establishing penalty defaults that encourage the better informed parties to reveal their information', thereby making the contract to be concluded more efficient overall.

[104] I Ayers and R Gertner, 'Majoritarian vs. Minoritarian Defaults' (1999) 51 *Stanford L Rev* 1591 therefore describe penalty defaults as a form of 'minoritiarian' defaults.

[105] Specifically on the problem of default rules set by platform terms and conditions, see Möslein in ch 4, at 62 et seq, 67 et seq, 72 et seq.

conceptually where there is no 'foundational' transaction (such as a contract) with gaps needing to be filled.[106] Why, after all, should default rules seek to emulate a hypothetical transaction that the parties concerned never chose to enter? For example, why should an intestacy regime resemble a will that the testator did *not* make although he or she could have? Why should the state not instead use succession law to pursue policy-orientated regulation? Carried to its logical conclusion, however, this type of argument would mean that while there is no need for *intestacy* rules to be inspired by the hypothetical wishes of testators, the majoritarian approach would once again have to prevail when it comes to the default rules guiding testamentary *interpretation*, ie where a will does exist and needs to be construed.[107]

Ultimately, as with widget manufacturing and the default settings on computer programs and internet platforms, it is hard to envision a workable set of default rules which do not defer to majoritarianism in at least some respects. On the other hand, an element of targeted regulation seems acceptable even within an area in which the 'hypothetical will' paradigm rightly dominates. Within contract law, for instance, default limitation periods are plausible candidates for pursuing policy objectives by nudging people in a particular direction.[108]

That a mix of approaches is often unavoidable may be illustrated by reference (again) to the succession law example regarding the intestacy regime. Assume that an empirical study found most testators to prefer their eldest son over his younger or female siblings. Even if one were generally in favour of intestacy rules being informed by majoritarianism, it would in many countries nowadays be completely unthinkable (and indeed unconstitutional) for the testator's children not to be treated all alike under the law's default regime. If, on the other hand, one believed in a greater role of policy-orientated regulation, this would nonetheless still not warrant an intestacy regime leaving the bulk of the testator's estate to squeaky-clean charities or to some other worthy cause (such as perhaps paying off the national debt?[109]).

It is widely assumed that some version of 'majoritarianism' traditionally underpinned the creation and justification of default rules in private law (long before the concept even got its name)[110] and that the 'regulatory' approach is a much more recent

[106] See above, text to and following nn 97, 100.

[107] See above, text to nn 63–66.

[108] I am grateful to Jürgen Basedow for the specific example of German sales law prior to the 2002 reform of the law of obligations, where limitation periods in respect of defects were extremely short, lasting six months only in the case of movables (§ 477(1) BGB in the original version of 1900). Though this default provision was widely criticised as far too short for buyers to notice all relevant defects, it had been enacted in the late nineteenth century following pressure from the powerful business community and with distinct economic policy in mind. Prompted by the need to implement the European Consumer Sales Directive 1999/44/EC, the 2022 reform extended the default period to two years in the case of movables for all sales transactions (§ 438(1) Nr. 3 BGB in the current version).

[109] The latter was famously envisaged by the eighteenth-century Master of the Rolls Sir Joseph Jekyll, when on his death in 1738 he left £20,000 to help pay off the national debt. This is said to have prompted Lord Mansfield to the observation that it was a 'very foolish' bequest since the testator 'might as well have attempted to stop the middle arch of Blackfriars Bridge with his full-bottomed wig': E Foss, *Biographia Juridica: A Biographical Dictionary of the Judges of England from the Conquest to the Present Time, 1066–1870* (London, J Murray, 1870) 375.

[110] See, for example, FC von Savigny, *System des heutigen römischen Rechts*, vol 1 (Berlin, Veit & Co, 1840) § 16 at 57–58, referring back to Roman law and describing what Savigny himself calls 'mediating legal rules' ('vermittelnde Rechtsregeln') as 'constructions of the will [of the parties] that has remained uncomplete' ('Auslegungen des unvollständig gebliebenen Willens').

phenomenon. While that may be true in very broad terms, there are actually venerable examples where both approaches compete, or where they are in some way combined, going back right into the early modern period and probably well beyond. One such example that may be used to illustrate the point is to be found in the law of bailment.[111] It relates to the standard of care owed by a bailee to the bailor where nothing has been specifically agreed between the parties. In his landmark treatise of 1781, Sir William Jones argues for a variable standard of care, depending on whether the bailment is for the benefit of both parties or in the interest of the bailor alone or for the bailee alone.[112] He maintains that

> This distinction is conformable not only to natural reason,[113] but also, by a fair presumption, to the *intention of the parties*, which constitutes the genuine law of all contracts, when it contravenes no maxim of morals or good government; but when a different intention is *expressed*, the rule … yields to it …[114]

Compare this to what Joseph Story said half a century later in the US, arguing for a similar gradation of the negligence standard as that proposed by Jones, yet in a decidedly more worldly tone:

> The law in respect to bailments is generally founded upon the absence of any positive engagements between the parties, (for the express contract of the parties may vary or supersede those derived from the law;) and, therefore, the question arises what obligations may, *with reference to public policy and general convenience*, be implied by law in the absence of such positive engagements.[115]

The upshot is that it would be wrong to regard the 'majoritarian' and the 'regulatory' approaches as rivals in all respects. One approach may well moderate the other (as illustrated by the two scenarios of 'outrageous' intestacy rules), and default rules are often at their most persuasive where both approaches can be understood as steering the same direction (as seen in the bailment discussions by Jones and Story).

In fact, one could go as far as arguing that, outside the context where default rules are genuine 'gap-fillers' in respect of some foundational transaction, there is not very much to distinguish one conceptual approach from the other. Just think of a tortious duty of care for the purposes of a negligence claim.[116] Does it really make a difference whether we set the relevant standard of care at the level that ordinary people (who are typically strangers) would have chosen to govern their relationship, or whether we try to reflect what society as a whole regards as best in the interest of protecting

[111] I am very grateful to Franz Bauer for bringing the relevant passages to my attention.

[112] W Jones, *An Essay on the Law of Bailments* (London, J Nichols, 1781) 10: In the first case the 'ordinary' standard of care is to be applied, in the second the standard is that of gross negligence, and in the third the bailee is bound to answer even for slight negligence.

[113] William Jones was strongly influenced by the natural law thinking of his day, which in turn impacted on the justifications he put forward for proposed default rules.

[114] Jones (n 112) 11 (italics in the original).

[115] J Story, *Commentaries on the Law of Bailments* (Cambridge, MA, Hilliard and Brown, 1832) 7 (emphasis added).

[116] The duty of care owed by a bailee to a bailor with respect to the bailed goods is not meant here and is deliberately left to one side. Both Jones (n 112) and Story (n 115) saw bailment as being based on contract, even where it was a gratuitous bailment, and for that reason treated the bailee's duty of case as being of a contractual nature.

an individuals' life, limb and property, while at the same time leaving everyone maximum freedom to act as they wish? In other words, is the (wo)man on the Clapham omnibus, who concludes a hypothetical agreement in the abstract, not essentially the same person as the one who determines, as a precedent-setting judge on the bench or as parliamentary policy-maker down at Westminster, what level of care strangers *ought* to owe to one another? In both cases, a Rawlsian veil of ignorance prevents the rule-giver from fully disentangling all the various interests at stake. Nowhere perhaps is this more starkly illustrated than by the disagreement over whether the Social Action, Responsibility and Heroism Act 2015 is a policy instrument designed to privilege and reassure 'people … acting for the benefit of society or intervening to help someone in an emergency … in the event they are sued' (as the government seemed to think was necessary)[117] or a mere restatement of the common law position (and therefore potentially redundant).[118]

What those designing default rules from scratch could usefully take on board is that it pays to think expressly[119] about the right yardstick to use: when and why majoritarianism should be followed, where there is need and space for deliberate regulation and whether and how far the two approaches actually deviate. If they go hand-in-hand, then the argument for the proposed default becomes particularly strong and the resulting product should be portrayed as such. Where there is a deviation, the concomitant trade-offs need to be put openly on the table to produce a coherent and transparent justification for the rule ultimately chosen as default.

VIII. Summing Up

At first glance, the idea of 'default rules' seems relatively straightforward. They are mostly associated with contract law and related fields, where they serve to fill gaps in parties' transactions. Yet on closer inspection default rules are not merely about the terms of transactions, but play a role whenever parties are affected by legal rules they could potentially alter or 'opt out' of. Indeed, more broadly still, one could say that the default is that which applies unless and until a competent entity effects a change. And even within their 'core' fields of application, it is possible to make out various 'takes' on default rules. Their quantity and their density differs between legal traditions, as does the practice of how much – or how little – they are used. The perspective of affected parties differs from that of rule-setters, who may pursue a number of aims (from increasing efficiency to nudging) and accordingly model default rules on different ideals and templates (from the typical will of hypothetical parties to policy considerations).

[117] See the 'Fact Sheet: Social Action, Responsibility and Heroism Bill' (2014), available via https://assets.publishing.service.gov.uk/government/uploads/system/uploads/attachment_data/file/318839/sarah-bill-fact-sheet.pdf.

[118] For a discussion (with further references), see J Goudkamp, 'Restating the Common Law? The Social Action, Responsibility and Heroism Act 2015' [2017] *Legal Studies* 1.

[119] As happened, for instance, when the Law Commission of England and Wales consulted and reported in the run-up to the recent intestacy reforms: see Law Commission, 'Intestacy and Family Provision Claims on Death' (Consultation Paper No 191, 2009) paras 1.38–1.45, (Report No 331, 2011) paras 1.15 and 3.42.

The following chapters seek to elucidate these questions and aspects through a variety of lenses with different focal points. They illustrate quite how rich and interesting the supposedly simple concept of 'default rules' becomes when we allow ourselves a closer look, and particularly when we open up the vista to reveal (in the broadest possible sense) the comparative panorama. There is, one is tempted to conclude somewhat tongue in cheek, simply no typical 'default' when it comes to default rules.

2

Regulation by Means of Default Rules

ALEXANDER HELLGARDT

I. Introduction

Private law consists largely of default rules which are either laid down in a civil code or in the Common Law shaped by the courts. From a traditional continental perspective, default rules constitute the very essence of private law:[1] the state provides private parties with a legal infrastructure that enables them to organise their contracts, establish family relations and leave their property to someone else after their death.[2] Default rules preserve the principle of private autonomy as they only apply where the parties do not agree otherwise. Ideally, default rules do not merely relieve the parties of transaction costs, but also bring their conflicting interests into a fair balance which, as Savigny famously put it, corresponds to the terms the parties would have stipulated in the exercise of their private autonomy if they had entered into an explicit agreement on the relevant issue.[3] Default rules are therefore the perfect embodiment of what can be called the 'infrastructure function' and the 'balancing of interest function' of law.[4] Until recently, there was a broad consensus in German jurisprudence that these legal functions also form the boundaries of the legal domains (public law–private law).[5] According to this traditional account, regulation as a way of steering people's behaviour[6] was restricted to administrative and criminal law.

[1] H Köhler, *BGB Allgemeiner Teil*, 48th edn (München, CH Beck, 2024) § 3 para 24. See also J Drexl, *Die wirtschaftliche Selbstbestimmung des Verbrauchers* (Tübingen, Mohr Siebeck, 1998) 305.

[2] For a view of default rules as infrastructure, see F Böhm, 'Privatrechtsgesellschaft und Marktwirtschaft' (1966) 17 *Jahrbuch für die Ordnung von Wirtschaft und Gesellschaft (ORDO)* 75, 91; F Möslein, *Dispositives Recht* (Tübingen, Mohr Siebeck, 2011) 17; see also the discussion in the US on 'enabling corporate law', eg F Easterbrook and D Fischel, *The Economic Structure of Corporate Law* (Cambridge, MA, Harvard University Press, 1991) 34.

[3] FC Savigny, *System des heutigen Römischen Rechts*, vol 1 (Berlin, Veit & Co, 1840) 58. In a similar vein B Windscheid, *Lehrbuch des Pandektenrecht*, vol 1, 6th edn (Frankfurt, Rütten & Loening, 1887) 263 with fn 1.

[4] For these categories see A Hellgardt, *Regulierung und Privatrecht* (Tübingen, Mohr Siebeck, 2016) 56–62.

[5] Concisely P Kirchhof, 'Verfassungsrechtliche Grundlagen der "Privatrechtsgesellschaft"' in K Riesenhuber (ed), *Privatrechtsgesellschaft* (Tübingen, Mohr Siebeck, 2007) 83, 86: 'Deshalb ist das Privatrecht – als Recht der Freiheit – das Recht der Gesellschaft, nicht des Staates.'

[6] On the notion of regulation, see in detail section II below.

In Common Law systems, the difference between public law and private law is less pronounced, which is also reflected institutionally in the fact that there are no separate administrative courts in England and Wales. Therefore, the Civil Procedure Rules contain a part (Part 54) entitled 'Judicial Review and Statutory Review', which deals with the judicial review of sovereign acts. With reference to these rules, the claimant in a dispute between two private parties can claim that the defendant has taken 'a decision, action or fail[ed] to act in relation to the exercise of a public function' (section 54.1(2)(a)(ii) of the Civil Procedure Rules) and is therefore subject to judicial review.[7] Also, the role of statutory law in Common Law systems has always been more ambivalent. According to the 'mischief rule', which was established in 1584[8] and which is still part of the applicable rules on the interpretation of statutes, so-called 'remedial statutes' require special interpretation. In the words of William Blackstone, 'it is the business of the judges so to construe the act, as to suppress the mischief and advance the remedy'.[9] Yet the typical remedial statute, which derogates even the common law, is not at the disposal of the parties to depart from if they wish. Therefore, it is also true in the Common Law tradition that there is an essential difference between the core area of private law, which is characterised by default rules, and state regulation.

The aim of this chapter is to explore the relationship between default rules and state regulation. To this end, the notion of regulation will first be specified (section II). On this basis, the tension between private law and regulation can then be elaborated more precisely, examining particularly how default rules fit into the spectrum between state regulation and freedom of contract (section III).

Then we will explore how default rules' opt-out mechanism can be employed as regulatory instrument (section IV). Finally, we will have a closer look at the way the content of default rules can cause general steering effects (section V).

II. The Notion of Regulation

When dealing with the relationship between regulation and private law, the question inevitably arises what role the state plays in this context. Traditionally, the term 'regulation' refers to state measures taken by the legislature or the authorities in pursuit of public interests.[10] Thus, regulation first of all has a sovereign connotation, it is about measures that belong to public law. This connection becomes particularly clear

[7] See eg *R v Birmingham International Airport Limited* [2009] EWHC 1913 (Admin). The case concerned the question of whether a private airport operator was bound by public law requirements due to its monopoly-like position. In the specific case, the termination of an exclusive contract with a taxi company was at issue, and the court ruled that the airport operator had not exercised a public function in this respect (but very much in other relations!) and could therefore rely on its private autonomy and did not have to justify the termination in objective terms.

[8] *Heydon's Case* (1584) 3 Co Rep 7a, 76 ER 637.

[9] W Blackstone, *Commentaries on the Laws of England*, vol 1 (Oxford, Clarendon Press, 1765) 87. On the relationship between common law and statutory law from today's perspective, see eg A Burrows, 'The Relationship Between Common Law and Statute in the Law of Obligations' (2012) 128 *LQR* 232.

[10] On the historical development of regulation in Britain, see A Ogus, *Regulation* (Oxford, Hart Publishing, 2004) 6–12.

in the area of so-called 'command and control' regulation, as expressed primarily in criminal law. However, the classic area of regulation goes far beyond 'command and control' regulation. Since the New Deal, the US has had a large number of independent regulatory agencies, created and supervised by Congress, whose task is to regulate certain areas of economic life.[11] The industries subject to their supervision are accordingly called 'regulated industries'.[12] A classic component of this regulation is oversight of pricing in industries that serve the public interest or are otherwise closely related to public welfare concerns. In contrast to 'command and control' regulation, it is not a matter of prescribing certain rules and imposing sanctions for violations. Rather, it is a principle-based approach that aims to accompany economic processes and to steer them in the sense of a common good orientation.[13] This type of regulation, however, provokes the possibility of regulatory capture and was therefore at the centre of the deregulation discussion of the 1980s and 1990s.[14] In the EU, this kind of regulation exists as well. For example, in many areas of public services, such as telecommunications, there are Directives subjecting the access of new entrants to the market, and the pricing of network infrastructure such as telecommunications networks or rail networks, to close regulatory supervision.[15] This type of law is sometimes referred to as 'regulatory law'[16] and initially has little overlap with private law.[17] If one understands regulation as a synonym for this type of law and reduces it in essence to governmental price control, there is even a stark contrast with private law. This is because private law traditionally leaves pricing to the contractual freedom of the parties and merely checks that the conclusion of the contract was not influenced by mistake, deception or duress.[18]

For some time, however, the concept of regulation has been understood much more broadly. As early as 1998, Lawrence Lessig presented his concept of 'indirect regulation'.[19] According to this concept, the 'regulated entities' are not only subject to the influence of law, but also of markets, social norms and what he calls 'architecture'. This refers to circumstances in the real world that constrain our behaviour, such as the fact that certain places can only be reached by car. The crucial point here is that law can regulate the addressee not only directly, but also indirectly, by regulating the

[11] For an overview, see S Breyer, *Regulation and Its Reform* (Cambridge, MA, Harvard University Press, 1982) 15–35.

[12] For an introduction, see R Pierce and E Gellhorn, *Regulated Industries in a Nutshell*, 4th edn (St Paul, MN, West Publishing Co, 1999) 1–23.

[13] On principle-based regulation in general, see J Black, 'Forms and Paradoxes of Principles-Based Regulation' (2008) 3 *Capital Markets LJ* 425.

[14] See eg JJ Laffont and J Tirole, 'The Politics of Government Decision-Making: A Theory of Regulatory Capture' (1991) 106 *Quarterly Journal of Economics* 1089.

[15] On this, see J Kühling, *Sektorspezifische Regulierung in den Netzwirtschaften* (München, CH Beck, 2004).

[16] See eg the handbook by M Fehling and M Ruffert (eds), *Regulierungsrecht* (Tübingen, Mohr Siebeck, 2010).

[17] For a classification of regulatory law on the interface between public law and private law, see FJ Säcker, 'Das Regulierungsrecht im Spannungsfeld von öffentlichem und privatem Recht' (2005) 130 *Archiv des öffentlichen Rechts (AöR)* 180.

[18] For a description of this traditional 'dogma of contract law', see PS Atiya, *Essays on Contract* (Oxford, OUP, 1986) 329.

[19] L Lessig, 'The New Chicago School' (1998) 27 *Journal of Legal Studies* 661.

other factors – markets, social norms and 'architecture'. For example, we can enforce a speed limit on a highway not only by 'command and control' regulation, but also by prescribing that only cars with a technically implemented maximum speed are allowed to drive on it. In the context of indirect regulation, too, private law has a certain importance. This is obvious in the regulation of markets, which is possible not only by means of public law, but also by means of private law. One example is the right of withdrawal in online distance selling, which guarantees every consumer the possibility of comparing prices and services after receiving the goods.[20] But private law can also influence the content of social norms. For example, empirical studies show that social acceptance of homosexual partnerships increased enormously after the legalisation of gay marriage.[21] This is an example of what Cass Sunstein has termed the 'expressive function of law'.[22] Nonetheless, indirect regulation still comes from the state.

By contrast, the concept of regulation itself has for some time been extended beyond the state. Julia Black, for example, advocated a 'decentred understanding of regulation' as early as 20 years ago. According to her, regulation can be defined as 'the intentional activity of attempting to control, order or influence the behaviour of others'.[23] This means that any reference to the state is abandoned, and it implies that private individuals can also act as regulators.

When it comes to questions of definition, there is naturally no right or wrong; only considerations of expediency play a certain role. Personally, I believe that it dilutes the concept of regulation too much if one abandons any reference to the state. Regulation would then become a synonym for 'steering behaviour'. There is no doubt that control and steering of behaviour is an important element in the definition of regulation. On the other hand, not all behavioural control is regulation. Every time we walk through the city, listen to the radio or surf on the internet, advertising posters, commercials or algorithms try to steer our behaviour in a certain way. According to Julia Black's definition cited above, that would all be regulation. Now, of course, one could say that none of these are legal instruments, which is certainly true. But is all legally based control of behaviour really the same as regulation? Contractual penalties certainly also have the goal of encouraging the obligated person to fulfil the contract properly.[24] So-called smart contracts, which aim to ensure contract fulfilment beyond the state court system, for example by means of blockchain technology,

[20] On the function of the right of withdrawal, see P Mankowski, 'Right of Withdrawal' in J Basedow, K Hopt and R Zimmermann (eds), *The Max Planck Encyclopedia of Private Law*, vol 2 (Oxford, OUP, 2012) 1476.

[21] M Tankard and E Paluck, 'The Effect of a Supreme Court Decision Regarding Gay Marriage on Social Norms and Personal Attitudes' (2017) 28 *Psychological Science* 1334; J Thompson, 'Attitudes Towards LGBT Individuals After Bostock v. Clayton County: Evidence From a Quasi Experiment' (2022) 75 *Political Research Quarterly* 1374.

[22] C Sunstein, 'On the Expressive Function of Law' (1996) 144 *University of Pennsylvania Law Review* 2021.

[23] J Black, 'Critical Reflections on Regulation' (2002) 27 *Australian Journal of Legal Philosophy* 1, 25. This definition is followed by one that is even more comprehensive, according to which regulation is 'the sustained and focused attempt to alter the behaviour of others according to defined standards or purposes with the intention of producing a broadly identified outcome or outcomes, which may involve mechanisms of standard-setting, information-gathering and behaviour-modification' (ibid 26).

[24] R Zimmermann, *The Law of Obligations* (Oxford, OUP, 1996) 95–97 discusses the function of penalty clauses historically in ancient Roman law as well as in the Common Law.

also have extreme steering effects.[25] In my opinion, one should nevertheless not speak of regulation in such cases. What all the examples listed under the classical concept of regulation, but also under indirect regulation, have in common is that they are concerned with the enforcement of *public interests*. In my opinion, one should only speak of regulation if there is such a connection to the public good. Otherwise, the term seems to me to become arbitrary and interchangeable. If, however, regulation is limited to the enforcement of public interests, this results in an implicit reference to the state. For in a democratic state, it is primarily the task of parliament to define those public interests which the regulatory law is supposed to help achieve.[26]

To summarise these different aspects, regulation can best be defined as the use of law as a governmental instrument with the intention of achieving general steering effects in order to pursue public interest goals.[27]

III. The Tension between Private Law and Regulation

With this definition in mind, it is possible to describe the tension between regulation and private law more precisely: according to the traditional understanding, private law serves solely to balance conflicting interests between private parties. Ulpian's famous dictum that private law serves private interests, while public law serves public interests,[28] neatly sums up this division of labour between the different branches of the law. The question therefore arises whether private law can play *any* role in regulation, and if so, how this can be explained in terms of legal theory. In the following, it will first be shown that regulation is best understood as a function of law and that private law can also fulfil this function (sub-section A). Subsequently, we can examine in detail the question of the extent to which default rules can play a role in the regulatory function of private law (sub-section B).

A. Regulation as a Function of (Private) Law

The definition of regulation that has just been developed[29] is based on the specific way parliament, a court or a public authority (from now on: 'the rule-maker') uses the law. It is not primarily about the *content* of the law, but about a specific *purpose* the law is supposed to fulfil. This is why regulation, in my view, is best understood as a function of law. Attributing different functions to law is well-recognised in legal theory.[30]

[25] See Law Commission, *Smart Legal Contracts: Advice to Government* (Law Com No 401, 2021) para 2.14: 'A distinctive feature of smart legal contracts is automaticity: some or all of the obligations under the contract are performed automatically without the need for human intervention.'

[26] On the interplay between democracy and the regulatory state, see K Yeung, 'The Regulatory State' in R Baldwin, M Cave and M Lodge (eds), *The Oxford Handbook of Regulation* (Oxford, OUP, 2010) 64, 76–80.

[27] This definition was developed in Hellgardt (n 4) 50–55.

[28] Digest 1.1.1.2: 'publicum ius est quod ad statum rei Romanae spectat, privatum quod ad singulorum utilitatem: sunt enim quaedam publice utilia, quaedam privatim'.

[29] See the text accompanying n 27.

[30] HLA Hart, *The Concept of Law* (Oxford, Clarendon Press, 1961) 39: 'The principal functions of the law as a means of social control are … to be seen in the diverse ways in which the law is used to control, to guide,

However, these functions mainly concern what one may call the macro level, that is to say, the functions 'the law' as a whole provides for society. While one may also discern functions fulfilled by individual legal provisions on a micro level, that is to say for individual legal relationships,[31] the functions of law we are examining here are located at the meso level, that is, they relate to the way legal instruments are more generally used by the rule-maker. Thus viewed, regulation is not to be distinguished from private law, but from other *functions* of law that transcend the demarcation of legal domains. These are, for example, the function of balancing interests, the function of infrastructure or the organisational function of law.[32]

If we analyse existing legal systems in terms of these functions, it becomes obvious that regulation is by no means restricted to administrative or criminal law. In German law, the legislature has recently used private law, inter alia, to pursue sustainability goals. For example, the tenant may not reduce the rent for (the first) three months if the landlord carries out renovation works on an apartment to make it more energy efficient.[33] Also, the installation of charging stations for electric cars in apartment buildings can no longer be blocked by the landlord or individual apartment owners.[34] These rules clearly no longer serve to balance conflicting interests. It is true that 'balancing' does not mean that the rule-maker necessarily seeks a middle ground between the parties. This is shown, for example, by the rules on employee protection, which in continental Europe often protect the interests of employees at the expense of the financial interests of the employer.[35] However, the fact that the landlord receives the full rent even though the apartment can only be used to a limited extent during renovation does not aim to serve landlords, but is intended to improve the energy efficiency of residential buildings.[36] The fact that one co-owner cannot prevent another neighbour from installing a charging station in the shared garage is also not intended to strengthen the neighbour's private interests, but to help electric mobility achieve a breakthrough. In the course of the enactment and implementation of the EU Sales Directive,[37] the sustainability discussion has also found its way into sales law.

and to plan life'. An elaborate theoretical concept of the functions of law is developed by J Raz, *The Authority of Law* (Oxford, Clarendon Press, 1979) 163, 167–77. Raz distinguishes between direct and indirect functions and within the direct functions between primary and secondary ones. According to Raz, there are four direct functions (preventing undesirable behaviour and securing desirable behaviour; providing facilities for private arrangements between individuals; the provision of services and the redistribution of goods; settling unregulated disputes), while secondary functions concern the procedures for changing and enforcing the law. An indirect function, on the other hand, is the influence of law on moral values.

[31] For an example, see E Schmidt-Aßmann, 'Öffentliches Recht und Privatrecht: Ihre Funktionen als wechselseitige Auffangordnungen' in W Hoffmann-Riem and E Schmidt-Aßmann (eds), *Öffentliches Recht und Privatrecht als wechselseitige Auffangordnungen* (Baden-Baden, Nomos, 1996) 7, 26–27, identifying different functions of public law (eg enforcement) and private law (eg operating markets).

[32] For definitions of these functions, see Hellgardt (n 4) 56–63.

[33] § 536 para 1a BGB.

[34] § 20 para 1 sentence 1 no 2 *Wohnungseigentumsgesetz* [WEG = Co-Ownership Act].

[35] See F Wieacker, *Das Sozialmodell der klassischen Privatrechtsgesetzbücher und die Entwicklung der modernen Gesellschaft* (Karlsruhe, CF Müller, 1953) 21.

[36] This is expressly stated in the explanatory memorandum to the law: *Bundestags-Drucksache* 17/10485, 13.

[37] Directive (EU) 2019/771 of the European Parliament and of the Council of 20 May 2019 on certain aspects concerning contracts for the sale of goods, amending Regulation (EU) 2017/2394 and Directive 2009/22/EC, and repealing Directive 1999/44/EC [2019] OJ L136/28.

According to Recital 32 of the Directive, 'ensuring longer durability of goods is important for achieving more sustainable consumption patterns and a circular economy'. For this reason, durability was expressly elevated to an objective requirement for the conformity of the goods in Article 7(1)(d). As an objective requirement, the criterion is to be applied even if the specific purchaser intends to use the item only once and therefore has no interest in its durability. In this respect, Article 7 is also an expression of regulation by means of private law.[38]

Elsewhere, I have tried to show that the regulatory function of private law is compatible with requirements of (German) constitutional law and EU law – indeed, that the regulatory use of private law is even required by EU law.[39] At this point, therefore, just a small note on the side: if one sees regulation as a function of law per se and of private law in particular, this also offers a way out of the dilemma of defining the purpose of private law. Private law is not degraded to just another 'garden-variety mode of regulation', as Hanoch Dagan and Avihay Dorfman have argued in opposition to a regulatory view.[40] Rather, private law fulfils a variety of different functions. The balancing of conflicting interests as a core area of private law does not lose its importance by the fact that other parts of private law are used for regulatory purposes.

B. Default Rules between Contractual Freedom and Regulation

But even if one abandons the strict functional separation of legal domains and recognises that private law can also fulfil a regulatory function, it is by no means obvious that it does so in case of default rules. If the rule-maker aims to steer people's behaviour, how is that supposed to work when the parties can waive default rules at their discretion? In order to address this question, the following section will take a closer look at how regulation works in private law. In particular, the relationship between regulation and freedom of contract will be examined. Based on this, default rules can be placed along the spectrum between state control and private self-determination in a second step.

i. Regulation as a Contrast to Party Interests

Even if one recognises that the rule-maker can (legitimately) use private law to pursue public interests, that is to say, to regulate, it is undisputed that private law remains the very domain of the law in which private interests are primarily realised. The private autonomy of the parties, in particular their freedom to contract, allows them to structure their legal relationships according to their own will. Whenever the parties make use of the capacity to shape their legal relationships in order to realise their private interests, this cannot at the same time be an expression of state regulation, because the latter is directed precisely towards the pursuit of *public* interests. Even a coincidence of private

[38] On the consequences for German sales law, see B Gsell, 'Kauf- und deliktsrechtliche Haftung für das nachhaltigkeitsfehlerhafte Produkt als Schaden' (2023) 187 *Zeitschrift für das gesamte Handels- und Wirtschaftsrecht (ZHR)* 392, 405–12.

[39] Hellgardt (n 4) 175–264.

[40] H Dagan and A Dorfman, 'Just Relationships' (2016) 116 *Colum L Rev* 1395, 1430–31.

and public interests is not sufficient to term the result 'regulation', because it is then not based on state control.

However, this does not mean that we necessarily enter the realm of regulation as soon as the parties refrain from spelling out expressly all details of their legal relationship and instead rely on the (default) rules provided by state private law. In the classical understanding of private law, state private law and contracts generally coincide, because state private law only lays down what is in the supposed interest of typical contracting parties. Whether the courts develop the common law on the basis of private cases, or whether – in accordance with the traditional German understanding – the legislator merely brings the interests of the parties into a standardised balance, or whether the parties notionally replace state laws with their own inter-party 'law' as stated in the French Code civile,[41] in all cases the state and the parties principally pursue the same goals. In this setting, the task of the state is limited to facilitating the private parties' pursuit of their interests and containing excesses, especially in constellations where there is a substantial difference in bargaining power between the parties, so as to prevent one party dictating its terms unilaterally.

But if and where state private law becomes a regulatory instrument, a contrast arises between contractual autonomy and governmental heteronomy. On the one hand, what the parties have freely stipulated in their contract cannot be a means of regulation in the sense used here, because 'regulation' is restricted to governmental instruments in pursuit of public interest goals. But on the other hand, when parliament precludes the tenant's right to a rent reduction when a building is refurbished to make it more energy-efficient, this is no longer a standardisation of party interests, but an encroachment on contractual freedom. Hence, mandatory private law can be an instrument of regulation, while contracts cannot. But what about default rules?

ii. Default Rules as a Middle Ground

Default rules occupy an intermediate position between contract and statutory law. On the one hand, the parties have not included the content of the default rules in their will when concluding their transaction. Otherwise, we would not be dealing with default rules, but with a contractual clause – even if we have only identified it by way of implication or (supplementary) interpretation. On the other hand, the default rule itself empowers the parties to waive or modify the legal consequence provided by statutory or common law as they see fit. Against this background, the legal nature of default rules has long been disputed in German jurisprudence. Two basic positions can be distinguished, arising as a consequence of different perspectives: if one starts with the derogable statutory norm, it appears as if the law stipulates a particular rule and, at the same time, authorises the parties to derogate or restrict the effect of this rule and, if necessary, to replace it with a provision of their own. Oskar Bülow, for instance, is an early proponent of this position.[42] He sees default rules as the 'authorisation' of private

[41] See Art 1103 Cc (2016 version): 'Les contrats légalement formés tiennent lieu de loi à ceux qui les ont faits.'

[42] O Bülow, 'Dispositives Civilprozeßrecht und die verbindliche Kraft der Rechtsordnung' (1881) 64 *Archiv für die civilistische Praxis (AcP)* 1, 75–93.

parties to stipulate a rule, whose sole legal basis, however, is the authorising statutory provision, thereby making the will of the parties an implicit component of the statutory norm. If, on the other hand, one starts with the contract resulting from the parties' agreement and will, then default rules would appear to apply only for the reason and only to the extent that the parties themselves have not made any provision of their own. This view is reflected in Savigny's statement that default rules consist of 'rules which may be regarded as an interpretation of the incomplete will',[43] which implies that their validity is ultimately based on the (typified) will of the parties.

The prevailing view today agrees in principle with the first analysis, but makes an important modification: insofar as the parties have deviated from a given default rule, it is not the statute, but the parties' will that justifies the specific provision; however, the default rules applying in a supplementary manner are understood in accordance with Bülow as an act of state heteronomy, which has built into it an inherent limit on its own scope by permitting the parties to deviate. As a consequence of this classification, default rules are not interpreted according to the rules on the interpretation of contracts, but according to the *canones* on statutory interpretation.[44]

From a functional perspective, the debate about the legal nature of default rules is important mainly insofar as it helps us understand how default rules work in practice. Default rules can either be applied within the framework of an opt-in mechanism or be deselected by the parties by way of an opt-out.[45] Typically, default rules constitute an opt-out mechanism, not an opt-in. Because they apply unless the parties displace them, opt-out default rules are 'governmental' in nature and can in principle be an instrument of regulation.[46] Whether they actually function as a regulatory tool depends on the content of the default rules concerned and the specificities of the opt-out mechanism.

There are two different ways in which default rules can be used as regulatory instruments: on the one hand, the *act of opting out* can be made fruitful for regulatory purposes. On the other hand, the *content* of default rules can in certain situations be turned into a regulatory instrument. In the following, we will explore both modes.

IV. The Burden of Opting-Out as a Regulatory Instrument

Most default rules are based on an opt-out mechanism, that is to say, they apply unless the parties displace them. However, there are also opt-in rules, in German law for example the statutory rules on bequests.[47] This set or 'package' of provisions, some of which themselves allow for further deviations by way of opt-out,[48] apply only if the deceased has provided someone with a bequest in his or her will.

[43] Savigny (n 3) 58.
[44] See Möslein (n 2) 430–33; but cf M Schmidt-Kessel, 'Europäisches Vertragsrecht' in K Riesenhuber (ed), *Europäische Methodenlehre*, 3rd edn (Berlin, De Gruyter, 2015) 487, 501–04.
[45] For more details, see Möslein (n 2) 71–74.
[46] As to the definition of regulation, see text accompanying n 27.
[47] §§ 2147–2191 BGB.
[48] See eg § 2164 para 1 BGB, according to which, 'in case of doubt', the bequest of a thing extends to the accessories existing at the time of the testator's death. Hence, the deceased may explicitly or implicitly

A. The 'Stickiness' of Default Rules

Provided the parties behave fully rationally and there are no transaction costs, the content of default rules and whether they constitute an opt-in or apply unless opted out do not matter. In this thought experiment, if the content of the default rule does not correspond to the parties' interests, the parties will replace the rule with one that reflects their interests.

In reality, however, a certain 'stickiness' of opt-out default rules can be observed.[49] This is first due to the fact that in the real world the displacing of default rules does cause transaction costs. It is not rational for contracting parties to make explicit provisions for remote contingencies. If such an unlikely circumstance – think of a war or a pandemic – nevertheless occurs, opt-out default rules apply. The second reason is the so-called 'endowment effect'.[50] The party who receives an advantage through the default rule sees this as the natural starting point in contract negotiations and is only willing to forego this advantage in return for some consideration. This is so despite the fact that, in the absence of the default rule, the same person would not themselves be willing to provide consideration for the inclusion of the corresponding clause in the contract. And third, there are many circumstances in which it is not legally but practically impossible to deviate from default rules. This is particularly true for non-contractual obligations where the parties are not known to each other in advance. For example, it is recognised that the duty of care in tort can be modified by contract. However, if I carry a huge iron bar across the street during windy weather, I cannot foresee in advance who I might encounter in the process and with whom I would therefore have to agree on a waiver of liability. In the economic analysis of law, the problem is mainly discussed under the heading of prohibitively high transaction costs.[51] But this does not get to the heart of the problem. In reality, it is not possible to eliminate unforeseeable contingencies altogether and fully to identify all persons with whom one would have to conclude a contract, even if one were prepared to spend an extremely large amount of money.

provide otherwise, ie, opt out of this particular default rule. The default rule in § 2164 para 1 BGB might well be deemed to be regulatory in character as it ensures that assets (eg farms or factories) are regularly passed on in a way that secures their actual usability (ie including machinery etc). This supports an efficient use of resources, which reflects a genuine public interest. On default rules in the context of succession law generally, see the contribution by G Christandl, ch 11 in this volume.

[49] O Ben-Shahar and J Pottow, 'On the Stickiness of Default Rules' (2006) 33 *Florida State Univ L Rev* 651; B McDonell, 'Sticky Defaults and Altering Rules in Corporate Law' (2007) 60 *SMU L Rev* 383. See also A Schwartz and R Scott, 'The Common Law of Contract and the Default Rule Project' (2016) 102 *Virginia L Rev* 1523, 1566–68.

[50] This effect was first described by R Thaler, 'Toward a Positive Theory of Consumer Choice' (1980) 1 *Journal of Economic Behavior and Organization* 39, 43–47. The concept is based on the ideas in the seminal paper by D Kahneman and A Tversky, 'Prospect Theory: An Analysis of Decision under Risk' (1979) 47 *Econometrica* 263.

[51] R Cooter and T Ulen, *Law & Economics*, 6th edn (Boston, Addison-Wesley, 2012) 189: 'Contract law concerns relationships among people for whom the transaction costs of private agreements are relatively low, whereas tort law concerns relationships among people for whom transaction costs of private agreements are relatively high.'

B. Sticky Defaults versus Penalty Defaults

When it comes to regulation by means of default rules, the contrast between opt-in and opt-out therefore makes all the difference. The rule-maker can make use of the 'stickiness' of opt-out default rules as a regulatory instrument.[52] Yet, there are two ways of doing this. Which path the regulating rule-maker should choose depends on what assumptions it has about the parties' bargaining power and level of information.

First, provided the rule-maker assumes that the parties have roughly equivalent information and equal bargaining power, it can use the existence of transaction costs or the practical impossibility of deviating from a default rule as a regulatory instrument. In this setting, it is possible, due to the persistence of default rules on seemingly unimportant side issues, or due to the factual impossibility of deviating, to impose substantive rules that promote public interest goals. In this scenario, the rule-maker enacts default rules on the assumption that their content is desirable and should apply. In law and economics these kinds of rules are called 'majoritarian' default rules.[53]

However, the rule-maker can also employ these rules in a way that does not represent the private interests of the majoritarian parties, but to further public interest goals. One example is the already-mentioned inclusion of 'durability' as an objective requirement for the conformity of sold goods in Article 7 of the EU Sales Directive.[54] It may well be that the majoritarian parties of many consumer goods sales contracts are more interested in a low price than in the durability of a chattel, especially if they buy it for a one-off or short-period use. They could, according to Article 6(a), waive this objective requirement by defining the required durability of the purchased goods divergently. But the vast majority of parties still do not opt out of these sticky defaults, mostly because of ignorance or to avoid transaction costs. A main reason for this is that the Directive on Unfair Terms in Consumer Contracts[55] restricts the possibilities of deviating by use of standard terms,[56] so that an individual contract would be required. Yet, the offer of the seller to conclude such a contract would draw the attention of the consumer to the fact that there is a default rule guaranteeing a high durability of the good, possibly triggering the aforementioned endowment effect.

On the other hand, there are situations in which the rule-maker assumes unequal bargaining power or asymmetric information between the parties. In these circumstances, the rule-maker can shape the content of default rules in such a way that they run counter to the interests of one party, namely the one assumed to be in the superior position. Such rules are called 'penalty defaults'.[57] Penalty defaults are designed to encourage or force the stronger (better informed) party to waive the rule and thereby

[52] I Ayres, 'Regulating Opt-Out: An Economic Theory of Altering Rules' (2012) 121 *Yale LJ* 2032.
[53] I Ayres and R Gertner, 'Majoritarian vs. Minoritarian Defaults' (1999) 51 *Stanford L Rev* 1591.
[54] See above, text to nn 37–38.
[55] Council Directive 93/13/EEC of 5 April 1993 on unfair terms in consumer contracts [1993] OJ L95/29.
[56] See on this section V.B.
[57] The concept of penalty defaults was developed by I Ayres and R Gertner, 'Filling Gaps in Incomplete Contracts: An Economic Theory of Default Rules' (1989) 99 *Yale LJ* 87 and I Ayres and R Gertner, 'Strategic Contractual Inefficiency and the Optimal Choice of Legal Rules' (1992) 101 *Yale LJ* 729. It was further developed in Ayres and Gertner (n 53).

to provide important information to the weaker (worse informed) party. An example is the maximum liability limit for road transport in Article 23(3) of the CMR Convention.[58] It runs counter to the interests of senders who despatch particularly valuable goods. The default rule puts them at a disadvantage and forces them to disclose the special value of the transported goods to the carrier by asking the carrier to waive the liability limit, which is only a default rule. According to Article 24 the sender may, upon payment of an agreed surcharge, declare in the consignment note a value for the goods exceeding the limit laid down in Article 23(3), and in that case the amount of the declared value is substituted as the limit. This provision illustrates in a textbook-like manner the aim of disclosing information through the request for derogation.

V. The Content of Default Rules as a Regulatory Instrument

Let us now examine the second way in which the rule-maker can use default rules as a regulatory instrument. The content of a default rule can influence the parties, but is even more relevant for how the courts deal with the legal transaction in question.

A. The 'Expressive Function' of Default Rules

As regards the parties, default rules may have an 'expressive function'.[59] This means that they are understood by the parties as an expression of an agreement that is fair and just in substantive terms. However, in many legal questions, there is no single just solution, such as the question of whether or not the seller should, as default rule, be subject to a warranty obligation. On the one hand, there is the traditional principle of *caveat emptor*;[60] on the other hand, Article 21 of the EU Sales Directive makes the buyer's rights mandatory. Nevertheless, people regularly regard the (default) rule that applies in their legal system as resulting from a choice of moral values. Consequently, explicit contractual provisions often merely reflect what would have been the default rule anyway.

If the default rule changes, contractual practice usually follows suit. This can be seen, for example, in the wake of the German reform of the law of obligations in 2001. Prior to the reform, according to the case law of the German Federal Court of Justice (Bundesgerichtshof, abbreviated BGH), the legal default subjected the seller to a guarantee-liability for the absence of defects of title.[61] However, when reforming the law of obligations, the legislator took away the statutory basis for this line of case law by harmonising liability for defects of title and defects of quality. As a consequence, the BGH subsequently ruled that 'unlike in the past, the contractual obligation of the

[58] Convention on the Contract for the International Carriage of Goods by Road (CMR) of 19 May 1956, UNTS No 5742.

[59] On this concept, see text accompanying n 22.

[60] On this, see Zimmermann (n 24) 307–08.

[61] BGH (16.12.1952) BGHZ 8, 222, 231; BGH (28.10.1953) BGHZ 11, 16, 21.

seller alone can no longer be taken to be implying a guarantee of his ability to perform' and justified this result by stating that otherwise 'the core content of the amendments to the law by the reform, according to which the debtor should in principle only be liable for fault, would be undermined'.[62] Hence, the court stipulated a new default rule, having exactly the opposite content from the old rule, and contractual practice has followed suit.[63]

Yet while this may explain a certain steering effect of default rules, the expressive function of law is a poor basis for hard-core regulation. Regulation in the sense used here is about enforcing *public* interests. This will often involve conflicts with party interests, and possibly with the interests of *both* parties, so that only a mandatory provision can achieve the goal. Take the example of the right of withdrawal in Article 9 of the EU Consumer Rights Directive.[64] Even if the consumer is absolutely sure that she wants to buy something (for example because it is a follow-up purchase), she cannot according to Article 25 of the Directive waive the right of withdrawal, even if that would allow her to get a better price in return. The reason is that the Consumer Rights Directive, according to its Recital 3, aims to ensure a high level of consumer protection in online trade, so that consumers always have the same rights in cross-border transactions in the European internal market. Such a result cannot be achieved by mere default rules.

B. The 'Leitbildfunktion' of Default Rules

More important for regulation is the second feature of the content of default rules, namely their role model function (in German: *Leitbildfunktion*). This function is mainly discussed in the context of controlling standard term contracts, but it goes far beyond.

i. Statutory Types of Contracts Formed by Default Rules

In a codified contract law system such as the German BGB, courts always try to assign contracts coming before them to one of the 'types' of contracts provided for in the Code.[65] If the contract at issue has been classified as a sales contract, a contract for work to be done or a classic service or employment contract, because the main obligations of the parties as agreed upon correspond to the model established by the Code's default rules, the entire 'package' of default rules for this type of contract automatically applies.

[62] BGH (19.10.2007) BGHZ 174, 61, 72.

[63] At least the books containing forms and templates for legal practice do not recommend re-establishing by contract the former default rule of a guarantee-liability, even though before the reform they had not recommended waiving that liability either.

[64] Directive 2011/83/EU of the European Parliament and of the Council of 25 October 2011 on consumer rights, amending Council Directive 93/13/EEC and Directive 1999/44/EC of the European Parliament and of the Council and repealing Council Directive 85/577/EEC and Directive 97/7/EC of the European Parliament and of the Council [2011] OJ L304/64.

[65] D Medicus and S Lorenz, *Schuldrecht I: Allgemeiner Teil*, 22nd edn (München, CH Beck, 2021) § 13 para 31.

In order to avoid this consequence, it is not sufficient to choose different legal terminology when drafting a contract. For classification purposes, German courts look at the substance of the clauses, not their wording or form.[66] Therefore, the parties may choose to draft a contract that is so idiosyncratic that it cannot be assigned to any statutory type ('contract sui generis'); then only the rules stipulated in the contract apply. Yet, if the parties pursue a goal which is covered by an existing type of contract, forming a contract sui generis can only be achieved by significantly deviating from the main obligations associated with the statutory template. Such a deviation will in most cases contradict the interests of the parties, who actually want to conclude a sales contract, a contract for work or services, and so on. Another possibility is that the parties indeed choose a statutory type of contract, but waive all the default rules they dislike. As long as no restrictions apply, such as on the use of standard terms,[67] the parties can actually waive default rules.

Although the parties formally enjoy freedom of contract, considerable effort is required to avoid the application of default rules. In everyday contracts, the transaction costs are far too high to derogate from statutory types of contracts or from specific default rules. Because of this, regulatory default rules become applicable to many contracts.

ii. Default Rules as a Yardstick for Fairness Review

The role model provided by default rules may also serve as a yardstick for reviewing the substantive fairness of contracts. German judges are much more open to undertake such a fairness review of contract clauses than their English counterparts on the bench, even in the field of business contracts. When German courts conduct such reviews, they often look at the relevant default rules to assess whether the contractual provision under scrutiny disadvantages one party in a manner that makes the contract clause invalid. In this vein, the BGH has held it to be against bona fides (cf § 138 para 1 BGB, declaring contracts void if they violate the principle of good faith) to deviate too far from the 'gesetzliches Leitbild' of the default rule that determines the amount of compensation payable to the withdrawing partner of a commercial partnership.[68]

Hence, even if default rules allow the parties to stipulate divergent terms, the courts also take them as a measurement of a substantively fair agreement. If parties deviate too much from the statutory role model, without providing some kind of consideration, they risk their contract being declared void. The rule-maker can thus stipulate regulatory default rules with the potential to affect contracts even when parties waive them, because the mere stipulation of statutory defaults limits the scope of possible deviation.

iii. Default Rules and the Control of Standard Form Contracts

However, the role model function of default rules is most important in controlling standard form contracts. According to the case law of the CJEU, default rules form an

[66] BGH (8.10.2009) NJW 2010, 150, 151.
[67] See subsection 3 immediately below.
[68] BGH (09.01.1989) NJW 1989, 2685, 2686.

important yardstick for controlling standard terms in consumer contracts according to the Directive on Unfair Terms in Consumer Contracts.[69] The CJEU obliges national courts to conduct a comparative analysis between the national default rule and the standard term, in order to determine whether the term causes a 'significant imbalance' in the parties' rights and obligations in the sense of Article 3(1) of the Directive. The Directive therefore turns default rules into semi-mandatory provisions which can only be deviated from in standard terms in favour of consumers, but not to their detriment.

The national legislator has the ability to make use of this mechanism and stipulate default rules that entrust the consumer with the enforcement of public interests, for example with regard to sustainability concerns. In mass business with consumers, such unwelcome default rules can only be changed using standard terms. By giving consumers subjective rights through the default rules, the Directive effectively limits the possibility of derogation. The question remains, of course, whether and which consumer will invoke the invalidity of a clause affecting primarily public interests. However, the CJEU has ruled that invalidity must be observed ex officio.[70] In addition, Article 7(2) of the Directive guarantees consumer protection organisations the right to have the invalidity of standard terms established in judicial or administrative proceedings.

The German legislator has even extended the role model function of default rules to general terms and conditions in business transactions. § 307 paragraph 2 no 1 BGB, which transposes the role model function to German law, applies in the same way to consumer and business contracts. In this respect, too, default rules have a semi-mandatory effect, which makes them a potential regulatory instrument. The case law of the BGH provides ample evidence. After the reform of the German law of obligations standard form clauses that attempted to restore the previous statutory situation were considered to be in breach of the new statutory role model,[71] while other clauses that had previously been considered to be in breach were now declared permissible.[72] This amply demonstrates that a change of default rules has a real steering effect, which can be employed for regulatory purposes as well.

VI. Conclusion

While it still might be true that default rules constitute the very essence of private law, they are much more than this. Default rules are also an instrument of regulation, and

[69] CJEU, C-421/14 *Banco Primus SA v Jesús Gutiérrez García* ECLI:EU:C:2017:60, para 59.

[70] CJEU, C-472/11 *Banif Plus Bank Zrt v Csipai* ECLI:EU:C:2013:88; C-176/17 *Profi Credit Polska SA w Bielsku Białej v Wawrzosek* ECLI:EU:C:2018:711, para 42.

[71] BGH (05.10.2005) BGHZ 164, 196, 210–12: A home improvement business chain had included a provision in its standard terms and conditions of purchase according to which the (wholesale) seller was strictly liable for defects of title. This clause reflected the default rule before the reform of the law of obligations (see text accompanying n 61 above). The BGH nevertheless considered the clause to be a violation of § 307 para 2 no 1 BGB, and it was irrelevant that the clause corresponded to the former default rule.

[72] BGH (05.10.2005) BGHZ 164, 196, 201–03: The same home improvement business chain had included a provision in its standard terms and conditions of purchase according to which the warranty period for claims for defects was to be 36 months. Although it had previously, in a ruling on the old law of obligations, considered a corresponding clause to be violating of § 307 para 2 no 1 BGB (because the statutory period at the time was only six months), the BGH now approved the clause.

this holds true even if we restrict the concept of regulation to steering effects in pursuit of public interest goals. Regulation goes far beyond 'command and control' and is not limited to administrative law and criminal law. Private law plays an important role as an instrument of regulation as well. This applies not only to mandatory rules, but also to contract law and even default rules. Hence, there is no real tension between state regulation and default rules. From the point of view of regulation, default rules are just another part of the rule-maker's regulatory toolbox. But from the point of view of private law, it is necessary to accept the regulatory function of some of its rules. This is not merely a demand of legal theory but concerns the application and interpretation of statutory private law. A default rule with which the rule-maker pursues regulatory goals must be applied differently by the courts than a rule by means of which the interests of typical contracting parties are to be balanced.[73] In this respect, the mischief rule of English law may serve as a good starting point.

[73] For more details, see Hellgardt (n 4) 646–723.

3

Behavioural Aspects of Default Rules

GENEVIÈVE HELLERINGER*

I. Introduction

Law modifies human behaviour. It encourages some actions while discouraging others, relying for that purpose not only on mandatory rules, but also on default ones. Defaults constrain the behaviour unless the person makes an affirmative choice to modify them. They have been part of the legal toolbox since time immemorial.[1] In Roman law, tenants had a duty of care with regard to the landlord's property:[2] it was infringed if the tenant committed a 'fault' (*culpa*). The standard was an objective one, measured by reference to a reasonable person.[3] One can safely suppose that, back then as today, such default standards had meaningful impact. This is partly grounded in, for want of any meaningful biological evolution, the human brain's tendency towards 'inertia', a feature that is deeply rooted even though it has only been documented clearly in behavioural, and, later neuronal, studies from the mid-twentieth century.[4]

Although legal default rules have an impact on behaviour, they are not, of course, the only factor. Other factors, such as economic incentives, also have a significant impact, both singly and in combination. While both law and economics generally treat people as rational actors seeking to maximise their individual gains – whether in terms of monetary benefit or general welfare – the behavioural approach seeks to synthesise empirical findings and theoretical analyses to provide a richer account of reality, striving for a more reliable prediction of the outcome. And this outcome largely differs from what would be expected from a pure *homo economicus*. While economic rewards matter, human beings are also motivated by pro-social tendencies as well as specific social norms, and other psychological framing.

* I thank Johannes Ungerer for helpful suggestions.

[1] In fact rather longer if 'time immemorial' is understood in its English law sense, which dates it to run from 1189.

[2] See Ulpian, D. 19.2.11.2.

[3] See Ulpian, D. 19.2.13.7.

[4] See T Gilovich, D Griffin and D Kahneman (eds), *Heuristics and Biases: The Psychology of Intuitive Judgment* (Cambridge, CUP, 2002) (compiling research on how people make judgements); D Kahneman and A Tversky (eds), *Choices, Values, and Frames* (Cambridge, CUP, 2000). See also D Kahneman, *Thinking, Fast and Slow* (New York, Farrar, Straus and Giroux, 2011).

The behavioural analysis of law relies on the application of empirical behavioural evidence to legal analysis, but it corresponds to a broad net that encompasses multiple methods and areas of focus, and as a consequence, it remains a loosely defined enterprise. Psychology includes numerous subfields, such as cognitive studies, brain and neuronal studies, as well as laboratory or online observations of behaviours relating to judgement or decision-making. It also covers the ways in which responses reflect limitations on rationality and illustrates how the human brain predictably deal with beliefs formation and decision-making. While these observations are often described as documenting 'biases', they are indeed 'deviation' only if one agrees that welfare maximisation rationality represents the norm.[5]

In addition, psychology also encompasses social psychology and insights on interpersonal interactions in social cognition and social psychology experiments, as well as cross-cultural studies that have some elements in common with sociology and cultural anthropology. As has been noted, 'in all these, there is much – perhaps too much – for legal scholars to think about as potentially useful behavioural traits'.[6] Identifiable streams of work, with distinct methodology and ambitions, have however started to coalesce, providing useful guidance.

Default rules are a topic of interest in these various approaches. This chapter will focus on insights related to behavioural decision-making and its individuals-centred methodology ('methodological individualism'). While not explored in depth in this chapter, it is worth noting that cultural studies and their attention to the diffusion of norms and perceptions within a jurisdiction are also relevant. This may be related to the fact that default rules have an institutional dimension revealed by differences in terminology described in an earlier chapter:[7] the preferred term for default rules in different languages provides an interesting insight into the expectations of the different cultures as to the role that such rules are expected to play in the corresponding society. Thus in Germany, 'dispositive' law (*dispositives Recht*) connotes a pre-ordained legal rule: it can be superseded, but it represents 'the state-approved normal starting point'.[8] The fact that there is 'no sense of any expectation that the parties or party involved will or ought to make specific provision'[9] ties in with the cultural 'embeddedness' usually associated with Germany and modelled by Schwartz in relation to the desirable relations between the individual and the group.[10] In Schwartz's leading 'cultural value dimensions' model, 'embeddedness' characterises a cultural emphasis on the maintenance of the status quo, propriety and restraint of actions or inclinations that might disrupt the solidarity of the group or the traditional order. 'Embeddedness' is to be contrasted with the opposite pole,

[5] See, challenging this orthodoxy, G Helleringer, 'Behavioural Perspectives on Corporate Law and Corporate Governance' in Jeff Gordon and Georg Ringe (eds), *Oxford Handbook on Corporate Law and Corporate Governance* (Oxford, OUP, 2nd edn forthcoming).

[6] D Langevoort, 'Behavioral Approaches to Corporate Law' in CA Hill and BH McDonnell (eds), *Research Handbook on the Economics of Corporate Law* (Cheltenham and Northampton, MA, Edward Elgar, 2012) 442.

[7] See B Häcker, ch 1 in this volume, 3–4.

[8] ibid.

[9] ibid, 4.

[10] SH Schwartz, 'A Theory of Cultural Value Orientations: Explications and Applications' (2006) 5 *Comparative Sociology* 1937; SH Schwartz, 'Culture Matters: National Value Culture, Sources and Consequences' in RS Wyer, C-Y Chiu with Y-y Hong (eds), *Understanding Culture: Theory, Research, Application* (New York, Psychology Press, 2009) 157.

'autonomy'. 'Autonomy' describes cultures in which the person is viewed as an autonomous, bounded entity who finds meaning in his or her own uniqueness. France is often cited as an example of such culture. This makes it interesting to note that the preferred term in French for default rule is '*droit supplétif*' ('supplementary law'), conveying the idea that it is additional to the autonomously agreed upon commitment.[11] As noted by Birke Häcker, 'it fills in "gaps" where and to the extent that nothing else has been provided … the law steps in only where the parties involved leave space for it to do so'.[12]

These preliminary observations on cultural analysis bring the introductory notes to the chapter to a close. In section II, adopting individualism methodology, I will briefly consider how default rules have been analysed under the neo-classical economic cost-benefit approach, resting on the methodological assumptions of individual rationality and market efficiency.[13] I will then turn to the critics of the rational-actor paradigm, stressing how empirical and experimental observations mostly fail to recognise *homo economicus* at play,[14] which opened the way to incorporating behavioural findings in an approach now known as 'behavioural economics' (Section III). In the following Section IV, I will deal with the way in which, under the behavioural perspective, defaults retain a function, albeit a different one, often characterised by a strong social engineering intent. This aspect is somewhat controversial, raising concerns as to the democratic legitimacy of default rules as a policy tool. Then in section V, I will discuss concerns associated with default rules as well as solutions, such as personalisation, and their own limits will be discussed thereafter. In the conclusion (Section VI), I will discuss the current legacy of the behavioural analysis of default rules and its limitations.

II. The Neo-Classical Analysis of Defaults

Neo-classical economics approaches defaults as a means of enhancing efficiency (A) but its account suffers from weaknesses that have progressively been evidenced (B).

A. Defaults in the Neo-Classical Tradition

Defaults represent a meticulously studied area in the economic analysis of law.[15] From a neo-classical perspective, their double function of contractual gap-fillers,[16] as well as

[11] The autonomy of the will (*autonomy de la volonté*) is a concept heavily present in doctrinal writing about contract formation. See V Ranouil, *L'autonomie de la volonté: Naissance et évolution d'un concept* (Aix-en-Provence, Presses universitaires d'Aix Marseilles, 1980).

[12] See Häcker, ch 1 in this volume, 4.

[13] Unsurprisingly, orthodox economics often leads to conclude that existing legal constraints are at best unnecessary, and often source of inefficiencies – and therefore recommends deregulation.

[14] A critique of the deregulatory normative agenda ensues.

[15] O Bar-Gill and O Ben-Shahar, 'Optimal Defaults in Consumer Markets' (2016) 45 *Journal of Legal Studies* 137.

[16] I Ayres and R Gertner, 'Filling Gaps in Incomplete Contracts: An Economic Theory of Default Rules' (1989) 99 *Yale LJ* 87; CJ Goetz and RE Scott, 'The Limits of Expanded Choice: An Analysis of the Interactions Between Express and Implied Contract Terms' (1985) 73 *California L Rev* 261.

deviation enablers, promote efficiency, and this independently of whether or not the content of the rules reflects the actual preferences of the parties.

Default rules that are able to capture the preferences of those to whom they apply will save the cost of active adoption of similar rules. In other words, they eliminate the 'transaction costs' that would otherwise form part of the negotiation between the parties to agree on a mutually acceptable solution, including time and energy spent discussing the matter and the possible cost of a sub-optimal arrangement. Pursuant to the Coase Theorem, named after the Nobel Prize-winning economist Ronald Coase,[17] when parties figure out collaboratively how to allocate resources, or to decide on rules about how to allocate them later, they are expected to work out and reach an agreement whereby their joint wealth is maximised.[18] However, achieving this efficiency is often difficult in practice because it requires the parties to 'get together' and to find, among other things, the adequate space and time to do that. It also requires them to express offers back and forth in a way that is understandable to forge an agreement, as well as putting in place mechanisms to ensure the enforceability of the agreement. In other words, parties will then incur the 'transactions costs' of spelling out the agreed provisions relating to the contingency and putting together a privately agreed default rule.

As stated by the economist Jim Leitzel:

> [P]ublicly provided default rules are likely to call for the sorts of actions that the parties themselves would have agreed to, had they taken the time and trouble to write into the contract their preferred response to every contingency.[19]

From this perspective, while transaction costs preclude forming highly complex explicit contracts, default rules may be described as providing the complexity 'for free'. Defaults may be described as gratis or, more precisely, tax-funded transaction facilitators.

By contrast, when the default rules fail to reflect the prevailing preferences of the people to whom they apply, people will opt out of the default. The efficiency of default as regulatory tool is however maintained in such a situation under the neo-classical perspective: opting out is expected to take place whenever it is rationally a preferable solution. When a party opts out of the default solution, the other party learns potentially valuable information from this move.[20] Typically, when the default states that a supplier is liable for some defined product defects and the supplier explicitly exempts themself from such liability, this opting-out also clarifies for the buyer the scope of the supplier's liability.[21]

In addition, neo-classical analysts acknowledge that transaction costs may be artificially created. Legal formalities make it more burdensome for parties to tailor

[17] It is usually associated with an influential article Coase published in 1960, 'The Problem of Social Cost'.

[18] The underlying reasoning is that if the parties do not maximise their joint wealth, an improvement that they would unanimously prefer is available, because everyone could get a bigger portion (Pareto improvement). In other words, the bargaining goes on in a given group until the overall wealth is as much improved as it can be.

[19] J Leitzel, *Concepts in Law and Economics. A Guide for the Curious* (Oxford, OUP, 2015) 33.

[20] I Ayres and R Gertner, 'Filling Gaps in Incomplete Contracts: An Economic Theory of Defaults Rules' (1989) 99 *Yale LJ* 87.

[21] E Zamir and D Teichman, *Behavioral Law and Economics* (Oxford, OUP, 2018) 179.

their specific agreements in a way that deviates from the default: transaction costs escalate as a consequence.

B. Weaknesses of the Neo-Classical Account of Defaults

Since the 1980s, it has increasingly been recognised that neo-classical economics offers an incomplete account of observable behaviours. The discipline is based on strict hypotheses that include consistent preferences and unlimited cognitive abilities as well as a leading role for economic incentives. These scientific hypotheses are not supposed to reflect the real world in its granularity and complexity, but merely to establish limited findings. However, even under strictly controlled methodological conditions, it turns out that fundamental neo-classical assumptions are not verified: human actors do not appear to follow the behaviour expected from economic predictions.

Typically, eliminating the cost of opting out does not impact the level of opt-out in the way it would be expected if the 'stickiness' of default rules was only due to direct costs of negotiating a specific agreement or registering one's decision to opt out.

Scepticism has therefore grown toward the usefulness of the Coasian theorem and the support of real world contractualism it justifies, beyond their role as theoretical tools for producing simplified models and testing well-controlled hypotheses. One may recognise that property law and contract law typically reduce transaction costs by providing resources that make it easier for parties to craft and enforce their agreements. However, the idea that the choice for an initial assignment of entitlements does not matter and an efficient outcome will result, no matter what the starting point, could not be verified in any actual setting. Such an outcome would require the transaction costs to be so low that they would be quasi-zero, and also that parties behave rationally.[22] These two conditions do not provide a credible account of reality. Neither do they provide a sound basis to endorse contractualism.

One must acknowledge that, as soon as we consider the real world, transaction costs are ubiquitous. Beyond the possible flaw in the quality of contract and tort law, it is the increasingly well-known limits to the rationality of actor that explain this observation.

III. Behavioural Law and Economic Analysis of Defaults

Rather than providing a radical departure from the law and economics framework, the behavioural perspective retains central elements of the framework while relaxing some others (A) and offers specific insights in the impact of default rules, including their potential to architecture choices (B).

[22] J Leitzel, *Concepts in Law and Economics. A Guide for the Curious* (Oxford, OUP, 2015) 13–15; R Cooter and T Ulen, *Law and Economics*, 6th edn (Boston, Addison-Wesley, 2012).

A. The Behavioural Turn

Behavioural economics represents a branch of the discipline that takes account of 'the crooked timber of humanity',[23] and aims to provide findings that have relevance to the real world, and possibly to provide policy recommendations.

It should immediately be noted that in practice legal rules have long adjusted to behaviours expected to be less rational than average. Typically, children and vulnerable people are protected against entering legal contracts that would bind them at a time when their consent can only be sub-par. Their freedom of action and autonomy are reduced in exchange for the legal protection they enjoy. Behavioural studies have since highlighted a general lack of rationality and that the general population suffers from predictable biases in their judgement and decision-making.[24]

From an analytical perspective, behavioural economics relaxes the assumptions of neo-classical economics. Both Law and Economics and Behavioural Law and Economics rest on the assumption legal rules change the opportunity structure and that individuals' actions are a reaction to the opportunity structure. However, where the neoclassical ideal-type is a 'rational superstar' who displays consistent preferences and unlimited cognitive abilities, the 'behavioral quidam' displays a richer utility function. They display pro-social tendencies even though their ethicality is bounded, and their ability to process information is also restricted by cognitive limitations.

Although legal studies have traditionally followed the rationality assumption, they have slowly started to engage in the behavioural evolution and adopt the behavioural perspective since the programmatic book by Sunstein in 2000, *Behavioural Law & Economics*.[25] All this line of work evidences a nuanced and realistic approach to human judgement and decision-making.

B. The Behavioural Account of Defaults

In this context, defaults remain a useful legal tool and if anything have become more central both as a procedure enabling private autonomy and as regulatory instrument to promote justice at the individual and collective level.[26]

They represent well identified 'nudging' tools that behavioural scientists can use to help policy-makers harness benefits for the greater good. As part of a specifically designed architecture informed by scientific findings on choice making, defaults can increase the likelihood that certain contractual terms are more prevalent while leaving individuals un-coerced and free to diverge from the default if they feel strongly about it.

[23] 'Out of the crooked timber of humanity, no straight thing was ever made': this quote from Kant was popularised by I Berlin, *The Crooked Timber of Humanity: Chapters in the History of Ideas*, 2nd edn, H Hardy (ed) (Princeton, Princeton University Press, 2013 [original UK first edition 1990]).

[24] J Baron, 'Heuristics and Biases' in E Zamir and D Teichman (eds), *The Oxford Handbook of Behavioural Economics and the Law* (Oxford, OUP, 2014) 3–27.

[25] CR Sunstein (ed), Behavioral Law & Economics (Cambridge, Cambridge University Press, 2000). The book was preceded by seminal articles by CR Sunstein, 'Behavioral Analysis of Law' (1997) 64 Univ of Chicago L Rev 1175; C Jolls, CR Sunstein and R Thaler, 'A Behavioral Approach to Law and Economics' (1998) 50 Stanford L Rev 1471.

[26] For a detailed analysis of these functions, see F Möslein, ch 4 in this volume.

The development of default rules shows that rule-makers have to some extent recognised that there are circumstances in which rationality is more compromised than in others, and that default rules may be relied on as a protection device. This is all the more so given the behavioural effects of defaults, including their 'stickiness', which can be harnessed or reinforced for public policy purposes.

Behavioural economics relies on studies that account for possibly less than perfect heuristics (or shortcuts) in the way questions are tackled, as well as predictable biases in human answers. The mistakes attached to actual judgement and choice-making are predictable, pervasive and difficult to correct.[27]

Against this backdrop, various contributing factors to such effects have been identified that have a direct connection with the perception of default rules. The main one is 'omission bias', which is the tendency to prefer omission to commission. In general, people tend to avoid active choices in circumstances where all the options involve both advantages and disadvantages. Omission bias is reinforced by another key bias: 'status quo bias'. Status quo bias is the tendency, other things being equal, to stick to the state of affairs perceived as the status quo rather than opting for an alternative one (sometimes referred to as inertia and procrastination bias).[28]

Default rules also carry an expressive effect: the fact that a policymaker has set a default may be perceived as a governmental endorsement of that arrangement and may therefore be understood as recommended for the good of the individuals.[29] As a consequence, individuals tend to believe that they should not depart from it unless there is particular information to support the change.[30]

Finally, the default rule may be seen as establishing a kind of reference point against which the individual's decision is made. The effect can be significant, because people dislike the potential loss that may arise if they depart from that reference point.[31]

Whatever the exact cognitive reason, default rules set a reference point from which people will not easily deviate. This effect is particularly strong in connection with issues that people prefer not to think about, such as the standard for negligence or force majeure. What are the consequences of these characteristics?

IV. Harnessing the Behavioural Effects of Defaults

While defaults all share certain behavioural effects, the precise nature of these effects span various dimensions, of which I highlight four: the setting of the default as aligned with the majority's preference or rather contrary to this preference (A), the likelihood

[27] T Ulen, 'The Importance of Behavioral Law' in E Zamir and D Teichman (eds), *The Oxford Handbook of Behavioral Economics and the Law* (Oxford, OUP, 2014) 96–97.

[28] I Ritov and J Baron, 'Status-Quo and Omission Biases' (1992) 5 *Journal of Risk and Uncertainty* 49.

[29] E Zamir, 'The Inverted Hierarchy of Contract Interpretation and Supplementation' (1997) 97 *Columbia L Rev* 1710, 1758–59. See also NC Smith, DG Goldstein and E Johnson, 'Choice without Awareness: Ethical and Policy Implications of Defaults' (2013) 32 *Journal of Public Policy & Marketing* 159, 161.

[30] See CRM McKenzie, MJ Liersch and SR Finkelstein, 'Recommendations Implicit in Policy Defaults' (2006) 17 *Psychological Science* 414, 418–19.

[31] See Isaac Dinner et al, 'Partitioning Default Effects: Why People Choose Not to Choose' (2011–12) 17 *Journal of Experimental Psychology: Applied* 332, 333.

that the default will stick (B), the modalities of actively opting out of the default (C) and the limits to the freedom to construct a rule as a default rule (D).

A. Which Default Rule?

Legislators and other regulators do not set defaults at random. They are likely to choose a solution that will be beneficial for most people, even if it may not reflect the spontaneous preference of the parties in a given contract or the preference of a majority of people. On this basis, accepting the default and not opting out in favour of a different solution might be the reasonable thing to do, all the more so if examining other options would itself be costly.[32]

However, as noted,[33] while some default rules are intended to spare parties the cost of negotiating and drafting terms by providing the content that they would probably have agreed upon had they taken the time to do so, not all follow this enabling route. Many default rules have a different and more 'regulatory' purpose.[34] They are not the rules that the parties would probably have agreed upon but rules that are not aligned with their probable preferences: they are likely to induce the parties – often one of the parties – to negotiate a more suitable rule for the particular transaction, and, if not, will promote chosen policies. While defaults classically mimicked the parties' preferred terms, modern rules are more likely to be purposefully set by the regulator set as 'sticky' socially beneficial defaults.[35]

B. How Sticky?

Research shows that defaults are rarely challenged by parties even when they are chosen in a random fashion or when options that are objectively superior are available.[36] This 'stickiness' can be harnessed to promote a behaviour that policymakers want to encourage. The desired option is set as the default, with the expectation that people will assume they are automatically assigned the superior choice and will not alter this status quo.[37] One very well-established example is the default venue for dispute resolution: unless parties provide otherwise, litigation in the national courts is defined as the method for dispute resolution.[38] To increase the stickiness, the procedure to evade the default may

[32] See J Leitzel, *Concepts in Law and Economics. A Guide for the Curious* (Oxford, OUP, 2015) 136.

[33] EA Farnsworth, 'An American View of the Principles as a Guide to Drafting Contracts' in J-P Béraudo (ed), *UNIDROIT Principles For International Commercial Contracts: A New Lex Mercatoria*? (Paris, International Chamber of Commerce, 1995) 87.

[34] On this dichotomy, see Möslein, ch 4 in this volume, 54 et seq.

[35] O Bar-Gill and O Ben-Shahar, 'Rethinking Nudge' (2021) 88 *Univ of Chicago L Rev* 531.

[36] RH Thaler and CR Sunstein, Nudge: Improving Decisions About Health, Wealth, and Happiness (New Haven, Yale University Press, 2008) 159–82.

[37] See R Korobkin, 'The Status Quo Bias and Contract Default Rules' (1998) 83 *Cornell L Rev* 609, observing that contracting parties often fail to opt out of default rules even if these default rules are inefficient.

[38] See G Rühl, ch 12 in this volume.

be toughened. For example, consumer law requires some changes to the legal defaults to be expressly agreed upon by the parties.[39]

The regulatory function of defaults is particularly well illustrated by strategies combining defaults and the effect of the status quo bias to create a pathway for private parties towards more socially desirable behaviours.[40] This 'nudge' approach was popularised by the work of Cass Sunstein and Richard Thaler.[41] Such default 'nudges' are based on choice architecture: the economic cost of replacing the default with an alternative that can be standard or, even more costly, tailored, is combined with the psychological barrier of human decision inertia.[42] This approach has given rise to the introduction of 'nudge units' funded by governments,[43] with the aim of encouraging (rather than coercing) modes of behaviour that are considered to be socially beneficial.

In addition, the difficulty of opting out of a default rule may be manipulated. Policymakers may introduce or complicate obstacles to opting out, such as formalities, in order to make the default rules they want to encourage more sticky.[44]

It may however be noted that default rules may not 'stick' when they are set up in a way that it is antithetic to people's strong contrary preferences. Commercial parties often agree on an arbitration clause to solve their disputes according to a procedure that matches their preferences better, allowing for confidentiality and judges expert in the technical issues that are likely to arise in the dispute.

A related finding is that workers are not strongly affected by a default allocation of a fraction of their tax refund to US savings bonds. The reason given by the researchers is that such workers had clear pre-defined plans about how to spend their refunds.[45] The implication is that default rules will have a weaker effect, and potentially no effect, when the relevant population has a strong preference for a certain outcome.

C. Active Choice as an Alternative?

When the relevant population is diverse, a single default option may not be appropriate and an alternative strategy is to require an active choice. Under this approach, everyone is forced to make an actual choice from among different options. For example, most

[39] See S Whittaker, ch 8 in this volume, 143 et seq.

[40] P Schlag, 'Nudge, Choice Architecture, and Libertarian Paternalism' (2010) 108 *Michigan L Rev* 913, 915 (describing default rules as 'the mother of all nudges').

[41] Thaler and Sunstein (n 36). See also RH Thaler, CR Sunstein and JP Balz, 'Choice Architecture' in E Shafir (ed), *The Behavioral Foundations of Public Policy* (Princeton, Princeton University Press, 2012) 428.

[42] See Häcker, ch 1 in this volume, 14.

[43] See the account of the UK Behavioural Insight Team (that later spun out of the Cabinet Office) by its head 2012–15, D Halpern, *Inside the Nudge Unit: How Small Changes Can Make a Big Difference* (London, WH Allen, 2015). See also C Sunstein, 'Empirically Informed Regulation' (2011) 78 *Univ of Chicago L Rev* 1349, written while the author was administrator of the Office of Information and Regulatory Affairs in the Office of Management and Budget, part of the Executive Office of the US President.

[44] See, eg, O Ben-Shahar and JAE Pottow, 'On the Stickiness of Default Rules' (2006) 33 *Florida State Univ L Rev* 651; B McDonnell, 'Sticky Defaults and Altering Rules in Corporate Law' (2007) 60 *SMU L Rev* 384.

[45] See ET Bronchetti et al, *When a Nudge Isn't Enough: Defaults and Saving among Low-Income Tax Filers* (NBER Working Paper Series 16887, March 2011), online at www.nber.org/papers/w16887. Note, however, that the 'default' in this study consisted of a mere statement on a form.

legal systems require the parties to a sale contract to agree on a price, either fixed or determinable by some ascertainable process, in order for the contract to become legally enforceable. Some systems accept that, in the absence of an agreed price, the contract may nevertheless be valid and the judge may determine the price at an objectively reasonable level based on comparable transactions. In England and Wales, for example, section 8 of the Sale of Goods Act 1979 provides that, in a contract of sale, where the contract itself does not determine the price or include a manner to fix it, and the course of dealing between the parties does not offer a basis to determine the price, 'the buyer must pay a reasonable price'. What corresponds to a 'reasonable price' is a question of fact and depends on the circumstances of each case. Other legal systems, like French law, will insist that if parties do not agree on a price or a manner to calculate it, there is no contract,[46] but for limited exceptions for framework and supply of service contracts. This compels the parties to make an active choice.

In some contexts, inertia and procrastination play a non-trivial role, typically because they relate to issues associated with displeasure, such as old age and retirement or healthcare. In such situations, it may be expected that the majority of people will fail to opt in to their preferred outcome, and that the necessity of making an active choice will decrease the likelihood that they will end up with their preferred option.[47]

Of course, active choosing also comes with downsides. This is particularly true where people do not have, or do not have access to, all the relevant information, or where they lack the skills or experience necessary to interpret it. The more complex the decision, the greater the demands are on the decision-maker. Even where expertise is not an issue, the time and effort required to analyse the information, and to reach a reasoned decision, may be such that the choices made are sub-optimal.[48] Where setting the default in an optimal manner is difficult, significant benefits might be obtained merely by simplifying and easing the available choices and making active choice easier.

D. When is a Rule a Default?

It is sometimes controversial whether a rule is a default,[49] and as such can be contracted out of, or whether it is in fact a mandatory legal requirement. Here again, behavioural studies can provide some insight. As an example, corporate lawyers may dispute whether it is permissible for fiduciary duties to be contractually waived: are such duties imposed by law, or are they simply presumed to have been agreed upon? Findings from empirical studies suggest that if fiduciary duties are treated as default rules that can be freely contracted out of, confidence in the commitment of the directors to put the interests of the company ahead of their own is weakened. This in turn has the

[46] See French Civil Code art 1163: an obligation has as its subject-matter a present or future act of performance. The latter must be possible and determined or capable of being determined.

[47] See Sunstein (n 43) 1400–01.

[48] ibid 1401.

[49] See J Cartwright, ch 7 in this volume, 135.

consequence of diluting the value of the information available to investors, which then creates costs for all firms in the market.[50] In other words, there are sound commercial reasons for preferring to treat fiduciary duties as legal imperatives rather than as contractual default rules.

V. Behavioural Risks and Concerns Raised by Default Rules

It is important to recognise that regulatory intervention, however well-intentioned, should not place unwarranted limits on freedom and autonomy: the possibility of opting out creates an asymmetric paternalism (or libertarian paternalism).[51]

Default rules work by exploiting known biases in the way people tend to make their decisions. To be effective, they operate subliminally. However, from one perspective this kind of paternalistic manipulation can be seen as somewhat sinister: in some ways, it is more oppressive than overt coercion.[52] On the other hand, it may be thought that since mundane choices are often made with little or no deliberation, what is the harm in 'encouraging' a benign outcome by designing the architecture in such a way as to make it more likely? There are good arguments on both sides. Explicit mandatory rules are easier to identify and, where appropriate, challenge.

Another area of possible concern arises from the fact that sophisticated and educated individuals are generally better placed to make their own informed decisions, and consequently may be more likely to opt out of a default scheme. This should be taken into account in designing the default options, so as to ensure, if possible, that the cost of opting out is borne by those who are most likely to be able to afford those costs.

Those designing default rules also need to bear in mind the fact that certain arrangements may be beneficial to one class of people but disadvantageous to another class. For example, employees who would, if left to their own devices, have made saving plans at a high level will be disadvantaged if the automatic enrolment plan chosen by their employer as a default has the effect of encouraging them to save less than they would otherwise have done; meanwhile the same scheme would benefit those employees who might otherwise not have saved at all. When planning for a heterogeneous group, therefore, it is necessary to have regard to the fact all of the members' interests may not be exactly aligned.[53]

[50] See MA Blair and LA Stout, 'Trust, Trustworthiness, and the Behavioral Foundations of Corporate Law' (2001) 149 *Univ of Pennsylvania L Rev* 1735, 1780–89.

[51] C Camerer et al, 'Regulation for Conservatives: Behavioral Economics and the Case for "Asymmetric Paternalism"' (2003) 151 *Univ of Pennsylvania L Rev* 1211; CR Sunstein and R Thaler, 'Libertarian Paternalism Is Not an Oxymoron' (2003) *Univ of Chicago L Rev* 1159.

[52] L Bovens, 'The Ethics of Nudge' in T Grüne-Yanoff and S Ove Hansson (eds), *Preference Change: Approaches from Philosophy, Economics and Psychology* (Heidelberg, Springer, 2009) 207.

[53] Thaler and Sunstein (n 36). See also R Bubb and R Pildes, 'How Behavioral Economics Trims Its Sails and Why' (2014) 127 *Harvard L Rev* 1593, 1616–25.

Finally, there is the important issue of public scrutiny: open mandatory rules are more likely to be properly investigated and challenged than default rules designed to create a 'nudge' effect.[54]

Various proposals may be considered as a means of addressing these concerns, such as supplementing the default rules with mechanisms to encourage or make it easier to opt out. Perhaps the most interesting, though controversial, approach involves the 'personalisation' of default rules, based on information about particular needs and preferences of specific groups, or even each individual.[55] Such personalisation may identify particular groups of people by reference to their income, or their age or their geographic region, or indeed any relevant demographic marker. Alternatively, information about an individual's past choices, for instance regarding financial investment choices, may be used to select the most suitable default for future investment offers.[56] Advances in technology and data gathering may improve the reliability and robustness of such systems. On the other hand, appropriate safeguards are also necessary, both to protect privacy and to ensure that the process is not corrupted by inaccurate data or erroneous statistical assumptions.

VI. Conclusion

In this chapter, it is discussed how economic analysis of default rules has evolved alongside the development of behavioural economics out of neo-classical economics. While neo-classical economics focused on the cost-benefit analysis of such rules, behavioural economics takes into account the observation that behaviours are not necessarily purely rational and value maximising. The chapter then stresses how defaults continue to represent a cornerstone of legal structures designed to support individual autonomy, and how the regulatory aims associated with the definition of defaults have grown under the influence of the nudge paradigm. Meanwhile professional private actors enjoy the freedom allowed by the elective nature of default, and resort to the same nudging tools in dealing with their customers. The chapter underlines how behavioural findings have been harnessed to reinforce the social and commercial engineering of default, and the democratic concerns that this may raise.

As a final note, it is useful to remind ourselves that in legal scholarship, 'behavioural analysis'[57] mainly refers to the application of empirical behavioural evidence

[54] ibid.

[55] PM Bender, 'Limits of Personalization of Default Rules: Towards a Normative Theory' (2020) 16 *European Review of Contract Law* 366. See also O Ben-Shahar and A Porat, *Personalised Law: Different Rules for Different People* (Oxford, OUP, 2021).

[56] See G Helleringer, 'Consumer Finance 3.0. Behavioural insights, Big Data and Digital Technologies' in N Aggarwal et al (ed), *Autonomous Systems and the Law* (Munich, CH Beck, 2019) 51.

[57] Sometimes also referred to as 'behavioural law and economic approach', especially in the Anglo-American sphere, which implies that law and economics is a baseline and the behavioural dimension a twist to it. On the European continent, the expression 'behavioural law' is not uncommon. See on the vocabulary and the connotations, A Alemanno, G Helleringer and AL Sibony, 'L'analyse comportementale du droit manifeste pour un nouveau champ de recherche en Europe' (2016) 3 *Revue Internationale de Droit Economique* 315, 316–18.

to legal analysis. In practice, it denotes relying on established insights from psychology and predictions of human behaviour – usually gained via extensive experimental efforts or collection of data – to gain specific insights into the ways in which legal requirements impact behaviours. Although this approach makes good sense in principle, recent alarms as to the value of experimental studies[58] remind us that, as in any empirical science, the quality of the insights directly depends upon the choice of data that is collected, the integrity of the data itself, the methodology applied to the analysis and the restraint in the conclusions drawn. As with every empirical discipline, flaws in the sampling methodology will distort or invalidate the conclusions sought to be drawn.

It is widely acknowledged that the behavioural approach has since its inception suffered from some intrinsic limitations. An important limitation relates to the fact that the statistical inferences disregard individual differences: for example, cognitive biases may be shown to be statistically significant, but will differ from individual to individual. Typically, bounded rationality should hardly be described as a uniformly universal characteristic: some individuals remain more rational, even under time pressure or while suffering intellectual fatigue and cognitive depletion, than others.[59] Beyond these differences, there are reasons to describe rationality as a social norm specifically associated with the market and other social environments where agents' best strategic response is to maximise gain, however that may be defined.[60]

Another important limitation, common to law and economics, and to law and social sciences more generally, relates to how behavioural law and economics models may be treated as a guide for policy-making:[61] it would be a methodological error to rely uncritically on them for that purpose, since the models they provide are merely tools for generating hypotheses to be subjected to empirical testing. Models are expected to be driven by new data and theory. These findings lead to the revision of the assumptions (such as the rational actor model) underlying the model. However, even models that are more realistic remain tentative claims, not authoritative conclusions.

To conclude this chapter and final observations on the aims of research in behavioural law, a distinction may be drawn between work on existing norms and work on theoretically possible norms. So far as existing norms are concerned, the approach may be descriptive or geared towards assessment of the impact and quality of the norm. Such research may also have a role in assessing past behaviour in bulk in order to devise

[58] See A Jack and A Hill, 'Harvard fraud claims fuel doubts over science of behaviour' (*Financial Times*, 30 June 2023) stressing that the field has gained traction with businesses and governments, with the 'nudge' theory in particular, but some findings are contested. See also S Keynes, 'Behavioural scientists suffer from bias – but so do their critics' (*Financial Times*, 10 August 2023).

[59] See S Sah, 'The Professionalism Paradox: A Sense of Professionalism Increases Vulnerability to Conflicts of Interest' (2022) 36 *Academy of Management Perspectives* 896–918.

[60] See H Mercier and D Sperber, *The Enigma of Reason* (London, Allen Lane, 2017).

[61] See S Deakin, 'Rational Choice and Its Limits for the Solution of Social and Legal Problems: Three Questions for Behavioural Law and Economics' in S Grundman and P Hacker (eds), *Theories of Choice: The Social Science and the Law of Decision Making* (New York, OUP, 2021).

tools to adjudicate future disputes: an accurate description of possible motivations is instrumental in devising a framework to allocate liability and decide remedies. So far as potential norms are concerned, the endeavour is directed towards promoting more effective regulatory and legislative efforts by providing fact-based guidance on designing better public policy.[62]

[62] See A Tor, 'The Methodology of the Behavioral Analysis of Law' (2008) 4 *Haifa L Rev* 237. See also E Zamir and D Teichman, *Behavioral Law and Economics* (Oxford, OUP, 2018); Y Feldman, *The Law of Good People – Challenging State's Ability to Regulate Human Behavior* (Cambridge, CUP, 2018); E Shafir (ed), *The Behavioral Foundations of Public Policy* (Princeton, Princeton University Press, 2013).

4

Digitising Defaults: Methods and Mechanisms of Generating Default Rules in the Digital Age

FLORIAN MÖSLEIN

I. Introduction

Default rules are a fundamental cornerstone of private law. The design of default rules for contracts, for example, ranks as 'one of the most thoroughly studied areas in the economic analysis of contract law'.[1] By providing terms to fill gaps in contracts, but also by allowing for deviations, default rules provide the necessary legal infrastructure for the functioning of private autonomy. They spare private actors the need to negotiate and draft contractual terms for every conceivable eventuality.[2] On the other hand, however, the generation of default rules poses considerable challenges for rule-makers, both in terms of their content and the formulation of the conditions for deviation. From the perspective of regulatory theory, default rules are a fruitful area of research because they raise sophisticated questions about what kind of rule-makers are best suited to generate default rules, whether these rules should better be formulated by the legislature or be developed by judicial interpretation, and what degree of precision or complexity seems appropriate.[3] It is not surprising that legal scholars regard default rules as one of the most ingenious features of our private law system.[4] How to fill gaps in incomplete contracts is considered 'perhaps the most important question in contract law',[5] and it has sparked 'the most provocative debate in contemporary contract law scholarship'.[6]

[1] O Bar-Gill and O Ben-Shahar, 'Optimal Defaults in Consumer Markets' (2016) 45 *Journal of Legal Studies* 137.

[2] For broader discussions see, for instance, I Ayres and R Gertner, 'Filling Gaps in Incomplete Contracts: An Economic Theory of Default Rules' (1989) 99 *Yale LJ* 87; CJ Goetz and RE Scott, 'The Limits of Expanded Choice: An Analysis of the Interactions Between Express and Implied Contract Terms' (1985) 73 *California L Rev* 261.

[3] For a detailed discussion of these questions, see F Möslein, *Dispositives Recht: Zwecke, Strukturen und Methoden* (Tübingen, Mohr Siebeck, 2011).

[4] W Zöllner, 'Vertragskontrolle und Gerechtigkeit' [2006] *Neue Zeitschrift für Arbeitsrecht: Beilage* 99, 99 ('geniale[n] Eigenschaft[en] unserer Privatrechtsordnung').

[5] O Ben-Shahar, 'A Bargaining Power Theory of Default Rules' (2009) 109 *Columbia L Rev* 396, 396.

[6] LA Cunningham, 'Hermeneutics and Contract Default Rules: An Essay on Lieber and Corbin' (1995) 16 *Cardozo L Rev* 2225, 2225.

Their inherent alterability makes default rules particularly sensitive to changes in non-legal, factual circumstances: If their content no longer meets the needs of those to whom they are addressed, these rules run the risk of being replaced en masse by deviating contractual arrangements. Economic, social and technological changes, therefore, affect the relevance of default rules.[7] More specifically, the current digital transformation fundamentally challenges default rules because digital technologies have the capacity to create alternative regulatory structures. By their technological design, digital devices such as online platforms, artificial intelligence and distributed ledger technologies embody their own rules of conduct by enabling certain behaviours and discouraging others.[8] Long after Lawrence Lessig formulated the famous, if controversial equation that 'Code is Law',[9] digital regulatory architectures increasingly compete with the law, and in particular with default rules.[10]

Against this background, we will discuss the impact of digitalisation on default rules in more detail, in particular by examining whether default rules are at risk of losing their relevance and, if so, which regulatory strategies promise to counter this risk. After a brief overview of the classical mechanics of default rules (Section II), some of the most important digital technologies will be examined in more detail in order to assess their impact on default rules (Section III). These observations raise the question of the potential risks of such developments (Section IV) – and how the legislator can possibly counteract these dangers (Section V). Simple answers, however, are not to be expected. Nevertheless, the aim is to develop appropriate regulatory strategies for the digital age, although the motto coined by Michael Trebilcock 30 years ago, when discussing default rules in general, still applies: 'For the moment, "muddling through" may define our aspirational limits'.[11]

II. Classical Mechanics of Default Rules

Default rules create a unique tension between private autonomy and regulatory impact.[12] The generation of the rules that ultimately apply in individual circumstances is shared between the state and private actors: default rules provide certain regulatory content, but they also allow the private actors to whom they are addressed to deviate from them. In terms of content, therefore, default rules only apply ex post if no other

[7] See Möslein (n 3) 444 et seq. For a specific application in a commercial law case, cf BGH (31.11.1978) NJW 1979, 1705, 1706 ('Das dispositive Gesetzesrecht wird … den geänderten wirtschaftlichen Verhältnissen nicht mehr gerecht').

[8] Similar: JR Reidenberg, 'Lex Informatica: The Formulation of Information Policy Rules through Technology' (1998) 76 *Texas L Rev* 553.

[9] L Lessig, *Code and Other Laws of Cyberspace* (New York, Basic Books, 1999) 89; see also L Lessig, 'Code is Law: On Liberty in Cyberspace' (2000) 1 *Harvard Magazine*, https://harvardmagazine.com/2000/01/code-is-law-html.

[10] More extensively, F Möslein, 'Conflicts of Laws and Codes: Defining the Boundaries of Digital Jurisdictions' in P Hacker, J Lianos, G Dimitropoulos and S Eich (eds), *Regulating Blockchain. Techno-Social and Legal Challenges* (Oxford, OUP, 2019) 275.

[11] MJ Trebilcock, *The Limits of Freedom of Contract* (Cambridge, MA and London, Harvard University Press, 1993) 126.

[12] Möslein (n 3) 43 et seq.

rule has been agreed ex ante by the private parties concerned. However, the effect of default rules is not limited to filling contractual gaps.[13] Instead, default rules also have a procedural effect by shaping the bargaining situation between private parties.[14] They place the burden of negotiation on the actor who wishes to deviate from the substantive content of the default rule that would otherwise apply.[15] From a regulatory perspective, therefore, default rules are by no means limited to their enabling function as gap-fillers, but also exercise regulatory functions,[16] even if their regulatory intensity is lower than that of mandatory law. In fact, default rules can be seen as a tool to create a choice architecture to nudge private parties towards personally and socially desirable behaviour.[17] Rather than imposing a specific regulatory content, they trigger a dynamic governance process that oscillates between state and private rule-making.[18] Their regulatory intensity and the relative importance of their enabling and regulatory functions therefore depend on the rule-specific features of the regulatory design as well as on the behaviour of the private actors to whom the default rules in question are addressed.[19] Given the pervasiveness and diversity of default rules in private and commercial law, the dynamics of their operation can only be understood by taking a closer look at these parameters.

A. Legal Infrastructure for Private Autonomy

When private actors negotiate legal transactions, they cannot take into account every conceivable future development that may need to be provided for. Contracts are therefore inevitably incomplete and must be supplemented by the legal order. Default rules are a necessary element of the legal infrastructure without which exchange and cooperation between private actors would be impossible.[20] Even if private law allows

[13] Still, the term 'gap-filling rules' is used as a synonym: see eg Ayres and Gertner (n 2); O Ben-Shahar, 'Agreeing to Disagree: Filling Gaps in Deliberately Incomplete Contracts' [2004] *Wisconsin L Rev* 389. Note that supplementary interpretation of contracts by judges in courts is another, alternative mechanism of filling gaps: see, from a comparative perspective, N Kornet, *Contract Interpretation and Gap Filling: Comparative and Theoretical Perspectives* (Antwerp, Intersentia, 2006).

[14] In a similar vein, some argue that default rules cast a shadow on contract negotiations: see references in n 66 below.

[15] Möslein (n 3) 41 et seq. In the law and economics debate, the term 'penalty default rules' is being used: cf Ayres and Gertner (n 2) 91; more extensively: I Ayres and R Gertner, 'Strategic Contractual Inefficiency and the Optimal Choice of Legal Rules' (1992) 101 *Yale LJ* 729; I Ayres and E Talley, 'Solomonic Bargaining: Dividing a Legal Entitlement to Facilitate Cosean Trade' (1995) 104 *Yale LJ* 1027.

[16] On this aspect, see section II.B. below as well as the contribution A Hellgardt, ch 2 in this volume.

[17] Similar: P Schlag, 'Nudge, Choice Architecture, and Libertarian Paternalism' (2010) 108 *Michigan L Rev* 913, 915 (describing default rules as 'the mother of all nudges'); more generally on the concept itself: RH Thaler, CR Sunstein and JP Balz, 'Choice Architecture' in E Shafir (ed), *The Behavioral Foundations of Public Policy* (Princeton, Princeton University Press, 2012) 428. See also the contribution by G Helleringer, ch 3 in this volume.

[18] For more detail, see F Möslein, 'Governance by Default: Innovation und Koordination durch dispositives Recht' in S Grundmann, B Haar and H Merkt (eds), *Festschrift für Klaus J. Hopt* (Berlin, de Gruyter, 2010) 2861.

[19] See Möslein (n 3) 43 et seq.

[20] On the concept of private law as an infrastructure for private autonomy, cf F Möslein, 'Genuine Self-Regulation in Germany: Drawing the Line' in H Baum, M Bälz and M Dernauer (eds), *Self-Regulation in Private Law in Japan and Germany*, Special Issue of the *Zeitschrift für Japanisches Recht* (Köln, Carl Heymanns, 2018) 83, 91, with further references.

these actors contractually to design their relation with each other autonomously, it must provide them with a substitute order in order to avoid legal gaps. In this sense, default rules do not restrict private autonomy, but rather support it. They are enabling rules.[21]

Whether private parties actually deviate from default rules is primarily a question of individual human behaviour, however.[22] Predicting the likelihood of deviation therefore requires behavioural assumptions, such as those provided by the economic and social sciences with the model concepts of *homo oeconomicus* and *homo sociologicus*.[23] Despite their significant differences, these concepts include some common key factors that are likely to determine the incentives to deviate from default rules.[24]

The first factor depends on the degree of preference autonomy: deviations from default rules are less likely when private individuals are guided by these rules and develop conforming preferences. Indeed, human preferences are not immutable.[25] Preferences for certain rules can develop through learning processes, in a way that these rules become internalised over time. In addition, such preferences may be based on psychological causes such as 'ownership' effects or the so-called 'status quo bias', but they may also be rooted in the social and cultural identities of individuals.[26] Obviously, the regulatory impact of default rules is significantly enhanced if the legislator's choice of terms alters the parties' preferences for contract terms by increasing the strength of their preferences for the stipulated default term and decreasing the strength of their preferences for alternative terms.[27]

[21] See eg F Cafaggi, 'Self-Regulation in European Contract Law' in H Collins (ed), *Standard Contract Terms in Europe* (Aalphen aan den Rijn, Kluwer, 2008) 93, 100.

[22] Similar: R Korobkin and TS Ulen, 'Law and Behavioral Science – Removing the Rationality Assumption from Law and Economics' (2000) 88 *California L Rev* 1051, 1072: 'To be useful for legal policy, behavioral theories need to predict (with reasonable success) the likely responses to legal rules of the particular classes of actors to whom the rules are geared, whether or not the responses of other classes of actors would likely be identical'.

[23] The former serves as the starting point for behavioural economic analysis, whereas the latter may well be regarded as the role model for socio-legal research. For a similar contrast see T Raiser, 'Homo Oeconomicus, Homo Sociologicus, Homo Juridicus – Leitbilder wissenschaftlicher Forschung?' in M Mahlmann (ed), *Festschrift für Hubert Rottleuthner* (Baden-Baden, Nomos, 2011) 347, 347–53. On further models of human behaviour (or rather: variations), see J Cohen, *Homo Psychologicus* (Crows Nest, Allen & Unwin, 1970); C Elworthy, *Homo Biologicus: An Evolutionary Model for the Human Sciences* (Berlin, Duncker & Humblot, 1993); M Faber, R Manstetten and T Petersen, 'Homo Politicus and Homo Oeconomicus: Political Economy, Constitutional Interest and Ecological Interest' (1997) 50 *Kyklos* 457; H Simon, *Reason in Human Affairs* (Stanford, Stanford University Press, 1983) (*homo rationalis*).

[24] For greater detail, see F Möslein, 'Behavioural Analysis and Socio-Legal Research: Is Everything Architecture?' in H Micklitz, A Sibony and F Esposito (eds), *Research Methods in Consumer Law: A Handbook* (Cheltenham, Edward Elgar, 2018) 441, 472–75.

[25] Similar: Trebilcock (n 11) 21; Möslein (n 3) 314; cf, however, GJ Stigler and GS Becker, 'De Gustibus Non Est Disputandum' in KS Cook and M Levi (eds), *The Limits of Rationality* (Chicago, University of Chicago Press, 1990) 191.

[26] See, for instance, GA Akerlof and RE Kranton, 'Economics and Identity' (2000) 115 *Quarterly Journal of Economics* 715, 717 ('Identity … changes the "payoffs" from different actions').

[27] Similar R Korobkin, 'Behavioral Economics, Contract Formation, and Contract Law' in CR Sunstein (ed), *Behavioral Law & Economics* (Cambridge, CUP, 2000) 116, 137: 'If lawmakers' choice of default terms alters parties' preferences for contract terms – causing an increase in the strength of their preferences for the default term and a decrease in the strength of their preference for alternative terms – the choice of default terms has the potential to affect *any* private contract'.

A second determinant of human behaviour relates to the costs of contracting around: the higher the transaction costs involved, the lower the likelihood of deviation.[28] As is well known, transaction costs are incurred in searching for and obtaining information, in negotiating and making decisions, and in monitoring.[29] Private individuals, for example, inevitably incur higher costs if they focus not only on their contract partner and the price, but also on the terms of the contract by comparing different contract options both with each other and with the otherwise applicable default rules. Negotiating deviations from default rules costs additional time and money. Finally, monitoring and enforcing individual agreements can also be costly, because, unlike default rules, these arrangements have not yet been applied frequently and over a long period of time.[30] Overall, therefore, the costs of deviation depend on many factors, some of which offset each other. The legislator can influence these costs to some extent at least, for example by imposing formal requirements for deviations.[31]

The third and probably most important factor concerns the knowledge limitations of those to whom the default rules are addressed.[32] Compared to other market decisions, these limitations are particularly obvious when it comes to contracting around default rules. Such rules point to the future, and future events are inherently unpredictable.[33] For example, the decision to accept a shorter warranty period in exchange for a price reduction can only be made in a fully rational way if there is sufficient information available about the quality and lifetime of the product in question.[34] The degree of ignorance may decrease as individuals learn and gain experience.[35] New information is likely to trigger adaptation processes that strengthen the incentives to contract around default rules. Conversely, the knowledge of rule-makers is also limited. In particular, they are confronted with the unpredictability of the future on a much larger scale, both in terms of the large number and variety of cases and the typically much longer timeline that needs to be envisaged.

B. Default Rules as a Regulatory Instrument[36]

From the perspective of the rule-makers, however, the paramount question concerns the fundamental substantive guideline on which the default rules should be based: in formulating default rules, should rule-makers simulate the autonomous intentions of

[28] See eg Ayres and Gertner (n 2); extensively on the different categories of transaction cost involved in contracting around: Möslein (n 3) 302–08.

[29] For an overview over transaction cost economics, see OE Williamson, 'Transaction Cost Economics: The Natural Progression' (2010) 100 *American Econ Rev* 673, 675 et seq.

[30] Goetz and Scott (n 2) 265–73.

[31] I Ayres, 'Regulating Opt Out: An Economic Theory of Altering Rules' (2021) 121 *Yale LJ* 2032; with regard to corporate law, see also BH McDonnell, 'Sticky Defaults and Altering Rules in Corporate Law' (2007) 60 *Southern Methodist Univ L Rev* 383.

[32] Information deficits already play a role, albeit a limited one, in the context of transaction cost analysis: see J Fairfield, 'The Cost of Consent: Optimal Standardization in the Law of Contract' (2009) 58 *Emory LJ* 1401.

[33] For a more extensive discussion, see Möslein (n 3) 309 et seq.

[34] W Emons, 'On the Limitation of Warranty Duration' (1989) 37 *Journal of Industrial Economics* 287, with further references.

[35] Möslein (n 3) 312–14.

[36] On the regulatory aspect, see A Hellgardt, ch 2 in this volume.

the parties as precisely as possible? Or should they instead lay down heteronomous regulatory content in default rules? The methodological discussion on the generation of default rules has always oscillated between these two seemingly incompatible alternatives.[37]

On the one hand, democratically legitimated legislators are for constitutional reasons bound to the common good and the public interest.[38] Rule-making should therefore be orientated towards an ideal of justice that is not necessarily limited to 'exchange justice' in the Aristotelian sense (*iustitia commutativa*), but can also include aspects of 'distributive justice' (*iustitia distributiva*).[39] For all the vagueness of these different concepts, there is in any case a fundamental difference to the paradigm of autonomous, even though hypothetical, intentions of private parties. The guidance of public and of private interests does not point in the same direction, simply because the group of actors whose interests are taken into account differs from the outset.[40] Even the idea of 'exchange justice', which focuses exclusively on the two-person relationship, differs from the paradigm of hypothetical party agreements because it largely abstracts from the actual negotiation scenario and assumes idealised negotiating partners. When enacting default rules, rule-makers must therefore make a fundamental choice between these normative guidelines and that of hypothetical party agreements.

On the other hand, it has been argued that rule-makers need to orientate themselves towards the hypothetical intentions of private parties, simply because the latter will otherwise deviate from the default rules in question.[41] The great German jurist Savigny once argued that statutory default rules had the task of providing norms that the parties would have agreed on if they had included the problem in their contract negotiations.[42] Similarly, Justice Holmes stated in a US Supreme Court decision of 1903 that default rules must complement 'what the parties probably would have said if they had spoken about the matter'.[43] Today it is still commonly taught that default rules 'must mimic efficient arrangements'.[44] In the detail, this view can be justified in very different ways, namely with arguments of indifference, efficiency and correctness. Most frequently, it is argued that default rules otherwise 'impose needless transaction costs upon parties

[37] Recently, for instance, O Bar-Gill and O Ben-Shahar, 'Rethinking Nudge' (2021) 88 *Univ Chicago L Rev* 531 ('from the classic works on "mimicking" defaults for contracts to the modern rush to set "sticky" default rules to promote policies'). For an extensive discussion, see Möslein (n 3) 89–119.

[38] See eg A Vermeule, *Common Good Constitutionalism* (Hoboken, Wiley, 2022), showing that US law was, from the outset, subsumed within the broad framework of the classical legal tradition, which conceives law as 'a reasoned ordering to the common good'.

[39] For a discussion from the perspective of (German) contract law, see CW Canaris, *Die Bedeutung der iustitia distributiva im deutschen Vertragsrecht* (Berlin, de Gruyter, 1997).

[40] In addition, different procedural frameworks need to be taken into account: see Möslein (n 3) 104 et seq as well as 110 et seq.

[41] In this vein, for instance, RE Scott, 'Rethinking the Default Rule Project' (2003) 6 *Virginia Journal* 84, 94: 'Choosing a default rule on the basis of some normative conception of fairness would be wrong, in the sense that it would not increase the amount of fair contracts in the world, but it would increase the amount of contracting costs in the world, as parties contracted out of the codes'.

[42] FC von Savigny, *System des heutigen römischen Rechts*, vol 1 (Berlin, Veit & Co, 1840) 58.

[43] *Globe Refining Co v Landa Cotton Oil Co* 190 US 540 (1903).

[44] O Ben-Shahar and JAE Pottow, 'On the Stickiness of Default Rules' (2006) 33 *Florida State Univ L Rev* 651, 651.

who seek to opt out of them to reach more efficient positions'.[45] Conversely, however, the question remains as to how to carry out such a simulation of the hypothetical will of the parties. If, with Friedrich August von Hayek, one understands competition as a discovery process and markets as a spontaneous order,[46] then any simulation of contractual terms amounts to a pretence of knowledge.[47] Even the smartest rule-maker cannot depict with sufficient precision the 'invisible hand' of the market that has been proverbial since Adam Smith.[48] Instead of precise predictions, however, generic patterns might be sufficient for the formulation of default rules.[49] In any event, the rule-maker also faces a knowledge problem when trying to simulate private agreements.[50]

However, rule-makers not only decide on the content of default rules, but also on the necessary and sufficient requirements for deviating from them. By setting the conditions for opting out, rule-makers can determine the 'stickiness' of default rules,[51] at least in part. That depends not only on the (non-legal) deviation behaviour of those to whom the rules are addressed,[52] but also on the (legal) conditions for deviation. On closer inspection, these 'altering rules'[53] can vary considerably.[54] On the one hand, they differ with regard to the substantive scope of such deviations. In sales law, for example, parties have traditionally been allowed to deviate from the rules on liability for substantive defects, for example if the buyer accepted a more lenient warranty rule.[55] However, the scope for such derogations has now been severely restricted: Article 21 of the EU Sales Directive[56] excludes contractual arrangements that derogate to the detriment of the consumer, while derogations in the opposite direction, in favour of the consumer, remain possible. In the case of consumer contracts, therefore, warranty

[45] Ben-Shahar and Pottow (n 44). See also RA Posner, *Economic Analysis of Law*, 6th edn (Boston, MA, Aspen Publishers, 2003) 98: '[C]ontract law cannot readily be used to achieve goals other than efficiency. A ruling that fails to interpolate the efficient term … will only impose additional – and avoidable – transaction costs'.

[46] FA von Hayek, 'Der Wettbewerb als Entdeckungsverfahren' in FA von Hayek (ed), *Freiburger Studien: Gesammelte Aufsätze* (Tübingen, Mohr Siebeck, 1969) 249; English translation in FA von Hayek, 'Competition as a Discovery Procedure' (2002) 5 *Quarterly Journal of Austrian Economics* 9. In the same vein already A Ferguson, *An Essay on the History of Civil Society* (Dublin, Boulter Grierson, 1767) 187: 'the result of human action but not of human design'.

[47] This was the title of Hayek's Nobel Prize speech and also the *leitmotif* of his late work: FA von Hayek, *Die Anmaßung von Wissen* (Tübingen, Mohr Siebeck, 1996).

[48] A Smith, *The Theory of Moral Sentiments* (Carmel, Liberty Fund, 1759) 264 (part IV, ch 1). On today's reception across disciplines see NE Aydinonat, *The Invisible Hand in Economics* (London, Routledge, 2008); D Lal, *Reviving the Invisible Hand* (Princeton, Princeton University Press, 2006); H Micklitz, 'The Visible Hand of European Private Law: The Transformation of European Private Law from Autonomy to Functionalism in Competition and Regulation' (2009) 28 *Yearbook of European Law* 3.

[49] In more detail Möslein (n 3) 96–102.

[50] Similar, though with regard to transaction costs: I Ayres, 'Preliminary Thoughts on Optimal Tailoring of Contractual Rules' (1993) 3 *Southern California Interdisciplinary LJ* 1, 14.

[51] See Ben-Shahar and Pottow (n 44); McDonnell (n 31). See also I Ayres, 'Menus Matter' (2006) 73 *Univ Chicago L Rev* 3.

[52] See eg R Korobkin, 'The Status Quo Bias and Contract Default Rules' (1998) 83 *Cornell L Rev* 608.

[53] Ayres (n 51) 6.

[54] For a comprehensive account with particular regard to German law, see Möslein (n 3) 186–264.

[55] See eg Y Listokin, 'The Meaning of Contractual Silence' [2010] *Journal of Legal Analysis* 397, referring to the Uniform Commercial Code, sec 2-314, which lays down the warranty of merchantability as a default rule.

[56] Directive (EU) 2019/771 of the European Parliament and of the Council of 20 May 2019 on certain aspects concerning contracts for the sale of goods, amending Regulation (EU) 2017/2394 and Directive 2009/22/EC, and repealing Directive 1999/44/EC [2019] OJ L136/28.

rules are no longer of a default nature, but have a semi-mandatory and semi-default character.[57] Further variations on the scale between 'mandatory' and 'default' can result from provisions that allow deviations only on the condition that adequate compensation is provided.[58] Instead of allowing arbitrary deviations from specific default rules, private actors can also be given a predefined choice between different regulatory options (or 'menus'), for example between different legal forms or between different types of contracts.[59] On the other hand, in addition to these substantive restrictions on permissible alterations, deviations can be made subject to different procedural requirements prescribing what parties must do in order legally to opt out of a given default. Some altering rules require specificity or unambiguity of deviations, while others require full disclosure to the other party (or even justification for alterations), and still others require compliance with certain formal requirements.[60] A prime example of such requirements is the Unfair Contract Terms Directive,[61] which allows certain deviations only if they are made by individual agreements and not by standard terms.[62] Finally, it should not be overlooked that the basic procedures for derogations may also differ. While deviations in contract law usually require the consent of both parties, other standard rules can be waived by a unilateral decision and still others require a majority decision.[63] All these substantive and procedural differences determine the likelihood of deviations from the legal default. Different default rules go hand in hand with different altering rules and thus allow very different degrees of private autonomy. This is why Ian Ayres, in his paper on the regulation of opt-outs, aptly concludes that 'altering rules matter'.[64]

C. Dynamics of Operation

Default rules turn out to be a very subtle regulatory instrument, based less on sovereign intervention than on mutual coordination. By casting a kind of 'shadow' over private negotiations, default rules channel private behaviour.[65] Conversely, private autonomy interacts with this legal infrastructure as a second steering mechanism – negotiation and hierarchy are intertwined. Like other reflexive instruments of governance, default rules help to reconcile individual and common interests as smoothly as possible in a

[57] In more detail: K Riesenhuber, 'Party Autonomy and Information in the Sales Directive' in S Grundmann, W Kerber and S Weatherill (eds), *Party Autonomy and the Role of Information in the Internal Market* (Berlin, de Gruyter, 2001) 348, 359 et seq.

[58] See Möslein (n 3) 208–16.

[59] Cf Ayres (n 51).

[60] For an extensive account and many examples, in particular with regard to German law, see Möslein (n 3) 217–59.

[61] Council Directive 93/13/EEC of 5 April 1993 on unfair terms in consumer contracts [1993] OJ L95/29.

[62] See eg F Möslein, 'Optional Regulation of Standard Contract Terms' in K Purnhagen and P Rott (eds), *Varieties of European Economic Law and Regulation: Liber Amicorum for Hans Micklitz* (Dordrecht, Springer, 2014) 71, 73 et seq.

[63] Möslein (n 3) 227–49. Similar, albeit with different categories: Ayres (n 31) 2068 et seq.

[64] Ayres (n 31) 2114.

[65] This terminology is used by H Fleischer, 'Der Einfluß der Societas Europaea auf die Dogmatik des deutschen Gesellschaftsrechts' (2004) 204 *Archiv für die civilistische Praxis (AcP)* 502, 535 ('im Schatten der default rule'); RH Mnookin and LA Kornhauser, 'Bargaining in the Shadow of the Law: The Case of Divorce' (1979) 88 *Yale LJ* 950.

pre-formed bargaining process.[66] The state provides the infrastructure for private bargaining, but also defines its limits.[67]

The dynamics of default rules cannot be understood by looking separately either at the rule-maker or at those to whom the stipulated rules are addressed. From an evolutionary perspective, it is instead the interaction between these two (sets of) actors that proves to be the decisive advantage of default rules: they create feedback dynamics that can help overcome specific knowledge and regulatory deficits.[68] Both the state and the private sector play a dual role in this process as they each provide models for the rule-making undertaken by the other actor, while at the same time benefiting from the regulatory competencies of the other actor in order to supplement or update their own sets of rules. Default rules thus provide a sophisticated governance mechanism of knowledge production that operates by means of the interaction between public and private rule-making.[69] The interplay between regulatory structures and private rationalities allows default rules to involve as many minds as possible in the rule-making process, all with different incentives and limited knowledge.[70] The dynamic feedback between rule-makers and rule-addressees can help compensate for the knowledge gaps of both private and state actors.[71] Default rules thus operate as an evolutionary mechanism of permanent error correction in the tradition of critical rationalism. They trigger a 'quasi-Darwinian evolutionary process'.[72]

III. Digital Transformation of Default Rules

In the course of digital transformation, these dynamics are about to change fundamentally. Digital platforms provide alternative regulatory infrastructures that could eventually outdo default rules. If combined with artificial intelligence and machine

[66] See the reference in n 18 above. For broader discussions of governance perspectives on contract law, see F Möslein and K Riesenhuber, 'Contract Governance – A Draft Research Agenda' (2009) 5 *ERCL* 248, 269; S Grundmann, F Möslein and K Riesenhuber (eds), *Contract Governance: Dimensions in Law and Interdisciplinary Research* (Oxford, OUP, 2015).

[67] In more detail on contract law was a regulatory infrastructure, see S Grundmann, 'Regulating Breach of Contract: The Right to Reject Performance by the Party in Breach' (2007) 3 *ERCL* 121, 143; Möslein and Riesenhuber (n 66) 269; C Windbichler, 'Neue Vertriebsformen und ihr Einfluss auf das Kaufrecht' (1998) 198 *Archiv für die civilistische Praxis (AcP)* 261, 271.

[68] For an empirical study of an evolutionary process in law, see A Niblett, RA Posner and A Shleifer, 'The Evolution of a Legal Rule' (2010) 39 *Journal of Legal Studies* 325. For more general considerations on the evolution (and innovations) of legal rules, see S Grundmann and M Grochowski, 'The Creation of Norms: An Evolutionary View on European Contract Law' in S Grundmann and M Grochowski (eds), *European Contract Law and the Creation of Norms* (Cambridge, Intersentia, 2021) 3; JF Duffy, 'Inventing Innovation: A Case Study of Legal Innovation' (2007) 86 *Texas L Rev* 1; R Romano, 'The States as a Laboratory: Legal Innovation and State Competition for Corporate Charters' (2006) 23 *Yale Journal on Regulation* 209; TS Ulen and N Garoupa, 'The Market for Legal Innovation: Law and Economics in Europe and the United States' (2008) 60 *Alabama L Rev* 1555.

[69] For more detail, see Möslein (n 18) 2877–79.

[70] On the general benefits of pooling information, see C Sunstein, *Infotopia: How Many Minds Produce Knowledge* (Oxford, OUP, 2006).

[71] More extensively on the advantages of this process: Möslein (n 3) 128 ('Königsweg, um eine Evolution und Innovation sachgerechter Regeln zu fördern oder gar erst zu ermöglichen').

[72] Goetz and Scott (n 2) 278.

learning technologies, data collection and analysis enable learning processes that work much faster and much more effectively than on the basis of default rules. Smart technologies provide tools that can not only anticipate, mitigate and resolve contractual risks of all kinds, but that also provide for mechanisms of automatic enforcement that functionally resemble and partially replace judicial enforcement.

A. Digital Platforms as Alternative Regulatory Infrastructures

To begin with, online platforms are key drivers and indispensable prerequisites for both the so-called 'platform economy' and the 'sharing economy'.[73] By creating digital structures that allow two groups of users (suppliers and customers) to meet and transact with each other, they form a central pillar of digital markets. They enable consumers to find information online and allow businesses to exploit the advantages of e-commerce.[74] On the other hand, they raise widely discussed competition and private law questions, for instance about their responsibility in respect of illegal or harmful content or products hosted as part of their operation.[75] As a centrepiece of Europe's digital strategy, the Digital Markets Act was recently adopted.[76] It aims to ensure fair behaviour by large online platforms that act as gatekeepers in digital markets.[77]

From a regulatory theory perspective, the characteristic feature of online platforms is that transactions are governed by the respective platforms' terms and conditions, in addition to – or even in place of – state-made contract law. Platforms provide the framework 'that shapes the way in which supply and demand are matched, in which products are perceived, and hence in which a vast number of individual contracts are formed'.[78] Platforms typically operate as marketplaces with a triangular structure, where users must first conclude a 'user contract' with the platform to be subsequently able to conclude contracts amongst themselves.[79] As part of this user contract, users agree to

[73] See eg B Devolder, *The Platform Economy* (Antwerp, Intersentia, 2018); NM Davidson, M Finck and JJ Infranca, *The Cambridge Handbook of the Law of the Sharing Economy* (Cambridge, CUP, 2018).

[74] European Commission, Commission Staff Working Document: Online Platforms – Accompanying the document: Communication on Online Platforms and the Digital Single Market, SWD(2016) 172 final, 1. In greater detail: OECD, *An Introduction to Online Platforms and Their Role in the Digital Transformation* (Paris, 2019).

[75] Cf, on the one hand, JCL Valente, *From Online Platforms to Digital Monopolies Technology, Information and Power* (Leiden, Brill, 2021); and, on the other hand, European Parliamentary Research Service (ed), *Liability of Online Platforms* (Brussels, 2021); G Frosio, *The Oxford Handbook of Online Intermediary Liability* (Oxford, OUP, 2020); F Maultzsch, 'Contractual Liability of Online Platform Operators: European Proposals and Established Principles' (2018) 14 *ECLR* 209.

[76] Regulation (EU) 2022/1925 of the European Parliament and of the Council of 14 September 2022 on contestable and fair markets in the digital sector and amending Directives (EU) 2019/1937 and (EU) 2020/1828 (Digital Markets Act) [2002] OJ L265/1.

[77] In more detail: H Schweitzer, 'The Art to Make Gatekeeper Positions Contestable and the Challenge to Know What Is Fair: A Discussion of the Digital Markets Act Proposal' [2021] *Zeitschrift für Europäisches Privatrecht (ZEuP)* 503; R Podszun, P Bongartz and S Langenstein, 'The Digital Markets Act: Moving from Competition Law to Regulation for Large Gatekeepers' (2021) 2 *Journal of European Consumer and Market Law* 60.

[78] S Grundmann and P Hacker, 'Digital Technology as a Challenge to European Contract Law' (2017) 13 *ERCL* 255, 273 et seq.

[79] C Twigg-Flesner, 'Online Intermediary Platforms and English Contract Law' in PS Davies and T Cheng-Han (eds), *Intermediaries in Commercial Law* (Oxford, Hart Publishing, 2022) ch 9.

the platform's terms and conditions.[80] The regulatory content of user contracts often extends far beyond the bilateral relationship between the user and the platform as it has a profound impact on the individual transactions between users.[81] In this way, online platforms largely substitute the default rules of contract law for their own, private rules. In fact, they act 'as de facto "lawmakers" for the platform environment'.[82]

In contrast to the traditional mode of application of standard terms, these indirect effects of online platform terms do not fit well with the rules of the Unfair Terms Directive as they do not form part of 'contracts concluded between a seller or supplier and a consumer' (as envisaged by Article 1 paragraph 1 of the Directive). To market partners, the platform is a third party.[83] Platforms also call the applicability of other consumer law rules into question. Differently to bank lending, for instance, peer-to-peer lending is not subject to regulatory safeguards such as bank deposit guarantee schemes, and it is unclear whether respective lenders are protected by the rules on consumer credit contracts.[84] Generally speaking, the emergence of online platforms modifies both the nature of transactions and the regulatory framework within which they occur. Platforms have a fundamental impact both on contract formation and on the mode of operation of default rules.[85] Their emergence is therefore a challenge both for our regulatory understanding of default rules and for their dynamic mode of operation. By redefining the operation of markets, be it in goods or in services, online platforms substitute their own platform terms for the otherwise applicable default rules, thereby affecting the sophisticated governance mechanism of knowledge production characterised by the interaction between public and private rule-making. Platforms substitute the conventional legal framework of private autonomy by their own, private rules, at least in part.[86]

B. Information Advantages Through Data Analysis

In addition, digital technologies provide tools for handling large amounts of data. They enable data analytics aimed at discovering useful information, drawing conclusions and

[80] See eg C Riefa, *Consumer Protection and Online Auction Platforms* (London, Routledge, 2016) 50.

[81] V Mak, 'Private Law Perspectives on Platform Services' (2016) 5 *Journal of European Consumer and Market Law* 19, 20–23.

[82] Grundmann and Hacker (n 78) 274; similar H Schweitzer, 'Digitale Plattformen als private Gesetzgeber: Ein Perspektivwechsel für die europäische "Plattform-Regulierung"' [2019] *Zeitschrift für Europäisches Privatrecht (ZEuP)* 1 (digital platforms as private law-makers); LK Kumkar, 'Plattform-Recht revisited: Umgang mit den Marktordnungen digitaler Plattformen de lege lata et ferenda' [2022] *Zeitschrift für Europäisches Privatrecht* 530, 530 ('Platform law'); MK Land, 'The Problem of Platform Law: Pluralistic Legal Ordering on Social Media' in P S Berman (ed), *The Oxford Handbook of Global Legal Pluralism* (Oxford, OUP, 2020) 974.

[83] V Hatzopoulos, *The Collaborative Economy and EU Law* (Oxford, Hart Publishing, 2018) 44 et seq; cf also Grundmann and Hacker (n 78) 275; Kumkar (n 82) 545 et seq.

[84] In detail: F Möslein and C Rennig, 'Anleger- und Verbraucherschutz bei Crowdfunding-Finanzierungen' in F Möslein and S Omlor (eds), *FinTech-Handbuch*, 2nd edn (Munich, CH Beck, 2021) 505; M Ebers and BM Quarch, 'EU Consumer Law and the Boundaries of the Crowdfunding Regulation' in P Ortolani and M Louisse (eds), *The EU Crowdfunding Regulation* (Oxford, OUP, 2021) 83.

[85] Twigg-Flesner (n 79).

[86] Similar: Grundmann and Hacker (n 78) 274.

supporting decision-making, by transforming and modelling data on a large scale.[87] The underlying data often originates from online platforms and includes market participants' preferences, for instance for particular contract terms. Artificial intelligence and machine learning can dynamically adjust prices based on data about supply and demand, competitor activity and delivery schedules.[88] While such practices of so-called algorithmic pricing, which automatically set prices for items in order to maximise the seller's profit, are among the best-known and most widely discussed manifestations of this technological development,[89] the same technological means also allow algorithmic adjustments to other contractual terms, in particular dynamic deviations from default rules.[90] Online platforms are therefore in a position to use data analytics so as dynamically to adjust or even to personalise their platform terms and conditions.

However, when algorithms and artificial intelligence devices influence contractual decisions, private autonomy may be challenged. Technological advances in data analytics and artificial intelligence enable algorithmic agents to replace human choice in contractual transactions and decisions.[91] Algorithmic capabilities for personalising interactions with consumers so as to exploit information asymmetries and consumer biases also raise private autonomy concerns.[92] The fundamental challenge for any regulatory assessment is understanding the differences between human and machine decision-making in order to assess the impact on private autonomy.[93] Legislators are currently considering regulatory strategies to avoid discriminatory or self-interested algorithmic decisions, notably in the context of the European AI Act.[94] At a more fundamental level,

[87] See eg A Zobaa and T Bihl, *Big Data Analytics in Future Power Systems* (London, Routledge, 2018) 57 et seq.

[88] Briefly: P Rott, 'A Consumer Perspective on Algorithms' in L de Almeida, M Cantero Gamito, M Durovic and KP Purnhagen (eds), *The Transformation of Economic Law: Essays in Honour of Hans Micklitz* (Oxford, Hart Publishing, 2021) 43.

[89] See eg M Grochowski, A Jabłonowska, F Lagioia and G Sartor, 'Algorithmic Price Discrimination and Consumer Protection: A Digital Arms Race?' (2022) 36 *Technology and Regulation* 36; G Alper, 'Contract Law Revisited: Algorithmic Pricing and the Notion of Contractual Fairness' (2022) 47 *Computer Law & Security Rev* 105741; P Chapdelaine, 'Algorithmic Personalized Pricing' (2020) 17 *New York University Journal of Law & Business* 1; cf also the reference in n 92 below.

[90] Even though platforms have significantly better access to the necessary data than legislators, at least in the field of contract law, the focus of the legal debate has so far been exclusively on personalised default rules (rather than on personalised platform terms): C Sunstein, 'Impersonal Default Rules vs. Active Choices vs. Personalized Default Rules: A Triptych' (2012), available at https://papers.ssrn.com/sol3/papers.cfm?abstract_id=2171343; A Porat and L Strahilevitz, 'Personalizing Default Rules and Disclosure with Big Data' (2014) 112 *Michigan L Rev* 1417; cf also C Busch and A de Franceschi (eds), *Algorithmic Regulation and Personalized Law* (Munich, CH Beck, 2021).

[91] M Gal, 'Algorithmic Challenges to Autonomous Choice' (2018) 25 *Michigan Telecommunications & Technology L Rev* 59; L Scholz, 'Algorithms and Contract Law' in W Barfield (ed), *Cambridge Handbook of the Law of Algorithms* (Cambridge, CUP, 2019) 141; M Schmidt-Kessen, H Eenmaa and M Mitre, 'Machines That Make and Keep Promises – Lessons for Contract Automation from Algorithmic Trading on Financial Markets' (2022) 46 *Computer Law & Security Rev* 105717; cf also, with regard to financial markets: G Scopino, *Algo Bots and the Law* (Cambridge, CUP, 2020).

[92] G Wagner and H Eidenmüller, 'Down by Algorithms? Siphoning Rents, Exploiting Biases, and Shaping Preferences: Regulating the Dark Side of Personalized Transactions' (2019) 86 *Univ Chicago L Rev* 519.

[93] For an introductory overview, see J Turner, *Robot Rules: Regulating Artificial Intelligence* (Basingstoke, Palgrave, 2019) 39–80.

[94] Regulation of the European Parliament and of the Council laying down harmonised rules on artificial intelligence and amending Regulations (EC) No 300/2008, (EU) No 167/2013, (EU) No 168/2013, (EU) 2018/858, (EU) 2018/1139 and (EU) 2019/2144 and Directives 2014/90/EU, (EU) 2016/797 and (EU) 2020/1828.

algorithmic data analysis is redefining the way markets operate, similar to, but also in interaction with online platforms, thereby additionally affecting the traditional governance mechanism of knowledge production by default rules.

C. Enforcement by Self-Executing Technologies

Finally, digitalisation increasingly enables private parties to restrict certain actions or forcibly bring about certain events by technological means. Digital technologies make it possible to prevent or restrict the use of data and networked devices, for example by preventing smart locks from opening if rent is not paid. In such a case, the architecture of digital goods replaces legal mechanisms, and a kind of 'lex cryptographica' emerges.[95] In particular, blockchain and distributed ledger technologies enable the design of so-called smart contracts. Smart contracts are self-executing agreements written in code on the blockchain.[96] Because such 'agreements' can be automated by computers and are enforceable through the tamper-proof execution of software code, they take on tasks traditionally assigned to legal institutions.[97] Blockchain technologies provide alternative, digital mechanisms for contract enforcement, but their relationship with the legal sphere is still unclear.[98] At the very least, such devices shift the burden of litigation onto the other party.[99] By fundamentally strengthening the enforceability of alternative contractual arrangements, these self-executing technologies are likely to contribute to the impact of the other digital technologies on the operation and relevance of default rules.

IV. Default Risks of Default Rules

In short, default rules are at risk of losing their relevance as a result of digital transformation. Taken together, online platforms, supported by algorithmic data analysis and self-executing technologies, have the potential fundamentally to change the methods and mechanisms for generating the rules that fill gaps in contracts. State-created default

[95] P De Filippi and A Wright, *Blockchain and the Law* (Cambridge/Mass, Harvard University Press, 2018), 49 et seq; and already P De Filippi and A Wright, 'Decentralized Blockchain Technology and the Rise of Lex Cryptographia' (2015) *Social Science Research Network Electronic Journal*, available at www.ssrn.com/abstract=2580664; cf also K Becker, 'Blockchain Matters – Lex Cryptographia and the Displacement of Legal Symbolics and Imaginaries' (2022) 33 *Law Critique* 113; F Möslein and S Grundmann, 'Vertragsrecht und Innovation – Gedanken zur Gesamtarchitektur' in F Möslein and S Grundmann (eds), *Vertragsrecht und Innovation* (Tübingen, Mohr Siebeck, 2020) 5, 46.

[96] For a detailed discussion, see F Möslein, 'Smart Contracts im Zivil- und Handelsrecht' (2019) 183 *Zeitschrift für das gesamte Wirtschafts- und Handelsrecht (ZHR)* 254; see also F Möslein, 'Legal Boundaries of Blockchain Technologies: Smart Contracts as Self-Help?' in A de Franceschi and R Schulze (eds), *Digital Revolution – New Challenges for Law* (Munich, CH Beck, 2019) 313.

[97] Similar: eg K Werbach and N Cornell, 'Contracts Ex Machina' (2017) 67 *Duke LJ* 313.

[98] From a Civil Law perspective, see F Möslein, 'Smart Contracts and Civil Law Challenges: Does Legal Origins Theory Apply?' in I Chiu and G Deipenbrock (eds), *Routledge Handbook on Financial Technology and Law* (London, Routledge, 2021) 27.

[99] Möslein (n 96) 254.

rules are increasingly being replaced by platform terms.[100] These terms follow a very different pattern from default rules. They are generated by private institutions, adapt more dynamically and possibly even individually, and can be enforced by technological means. These kinds of differences are likely dramatically to change the institutional framework within which private autonomy can be exercised.[101]

The impending loss of importance of default rules as a governance mechanism may well be further accelerated by other contemporary developments, some of which are related to digital transformation. Increasing globalisation adds to the possibility of altering default rules within the applicable legal system with the further possibility of choosing between different national legal systems and their respective sets of default rules.[102] Since party autonomy under conflict-of-law rules constitutes an extra level of private freedom, the heteronomous efficacy of default rules is even more limited in those transnational private law transactions which are at least facilitated by digital technologies, in particular by globally operating online platforms.[103] In addition, innovations may lead to the regulatory models provided by the legislator no longer reflecting the changed reality, or are no longer being fit for purpose, because they do not address certain issues raised by these innovations.[104] Such innovations are often, but not necessarily, driven by digitalisation. Until recently, for example, the law of sales did not offer any suitable default rules for payment with data on online platforms.[105] Hand-in-hand with the digital transformation, globalisation and innovation can thus also contribute to default rules' loss of significance as a governance mechanism.

However, the resulting shift does not necessarily have to be judged negatively. The replacement of default rules, by platform conditions in particular, may even prove to be beneficial if it helps achieve more appropriate contractual solutions and outcomes.[106] In any case, the risks associated with the imminent demise of default rules require a normative assessment based on the functional mechanisms of this instrument of governance as described above.[107] In order to assess these risks, the dual function of default rules, as legal infrastructure for the exercise of private autonomy on the one hand, and as a regulatory instrument on the other, must be taken into account.[108]

[100] Similar M Grochowski, 'Default Rules Beyond a State: Special-Purpose Lawmakers in the Platform Economy' in S Grundmann and M Grochowski (eds), *European Contract Law and the Creation of Norms* (Cambridge, Intersentia, 2021) 227.

[101] On the creation of contractual default rules by private actors, see M Cohen and A Sundararajan, 'Self-Regulation and Innovation in the Peer-to-Peer Sharing Economy' (2015) 82 *Univ Chicago L Rev* 116; Grundmann and Hacker (n 78) 274. Cf also, from a consumer law perspective, N Helberger, M Sax, J Strycharz and H Micklitz, 'Choice Architectures in the Digital Economy: Towards a New Understanding of Digital Vulnerability' (2022) 45 *Journal of Consumer Policy* 45, 175.

[102] Möslein (n 3) 450–57.

[103] F Möslein, 'Dispositive Regeln im transnationalen Privatrechtsverkehr: Same Same, but Different?' in GP Calliess (ed), *Transnationales Recht: Stand und Perspektiven* (Tübingen, Mohr Siebeck, 2014) 155.

[104] Möslein (n 3) 441–49.

[105] In greater detail: H Grigoleit and T Winkelmann, 'Technische Innovation und Vertragsrecht' in Möslein und Grundmann (n 95) 101; see also C Langhanke and M Schmidt-Kessel, 'Consumer Data as Consideration' (2015) 4 *Journal of European Consumer and Market Law* 218; S Lohsse, R Schulze and D Staudenmeyer (eds), *Data as Counter-Performance: Contract Law 2.0?* (Baden-Baden, Nomos, 2020).

[106] Similar: Grundmann and Hacker (n 78) 274, observing that 'this does not necessarily invite regulatory intervention'.

[107] For a similar approach, see Grochowski (n 100 above) 227, highlighting risks of fragmentation and heterogeneity.

[108] See above, sections II.A and II.B.

A. Threats to Private Autonomy

When platforms 'shape the contractual relationships and economic incentives for their users' by setting their terms and conditions in individual user contracts, they provide a functional alternative to traditional default rules.[109] This so-called 'platform law'[110] is, of course, by no means the only instance of private regulation. On the contrary: as a result of globalisation and privatisation, this form of rule-making has become almost ubiquitous. In fact, our times have already been described as the 'era of self-regulation'.[111] The origins of private regulation reach back far, however. Almost exactly 90 years ago, the ordo-liberal Hans Grossmann-Doerth gave his inaugural lecture in Freiburg on the self-made law of the economy.[112] His discussion of standard contract terms as a form of private regulation led the legislator to limit the scope for such deviations from default rules. Today, the corresponding procedural and substantive requirements are laid down in the European Unfair Contract Terms Directive.[113] Yet there is a fundamental difference between unfair contract terms control and the regulatory infrastructures of digital platforms: whereas the rules on standard contract terms are tailored to bilateral situations, platform law arises from a tripartite situation, where the terms are set by the platform, but affect both parties to the contract in question as users of the platform.[114] How this fundamental difference affects private autonomy is fiendishly difficult to assess. On the one hand, platform law risks creating unbalanced conditions; on the other, it makes these conditions appear coercive.[115]

i. Imbalances in Platform Conditions

Because platform terms are not set by either of the two parties to the exchange contract, but by the platform as a third party, these terms could be regarded as 'impartial', at least under certain circumstances. They are not directly affected by the same imbalance of information and motivation that characterises bilateral terms. Quite the opposite, in fact. The traditional core argument for limiting deviations from default rules through standard terms relates to the bilateral asymmetry in respect of transaction costs. In a bilateral contractual relationship, it is not worthwhile for the customer to invest the time and money that would be required, either to negotiate a change in terms, or to find other

[109] Cf Grundmann and Hacker (n 78) 274.

[110] See references in n 82 above.

[111] C Estlund, 'Rebuilding the Law of the Workplace in an Era of Self-Regulation' (2005) 16 *Columbia L Rev* 319; see also F Möslein, 'Ambiguities of Self-Regulation' in Grundmann and Grochowski (n 100) 175 (with further references ibid in fn 3); Möslein (n 20).

[112] H Großmann-Doerth, *Selbstgeschaffenes Recht der Wirtschaft und staatliches Recht* (Freiburg, Wagner, 1933), reprinted and discussed in U Blaurock, N Goldschmidt and A Hollerbach (eds), *Das selbstgeschaffene Recht der Wirtschaft: Zum Gedenken an Hans Großmann-Doerth* (Tübingen, Mohr-Siebeck, 2005); in a similar vein: H Großmann-Doerth, 'Das autonome Recht des Welthandels' [1929] *Juristische Wochenschrift* 3447.

[113] On the much longer tradition and history of the regulation of standard contract terms in Germany, see eg Möslein (n 111) 175.

[114] Similar: Kumkar (n 82) 557, stressing the hybrid character between bipolar exchange agreement and organisational contract ('polymorpher Charakter'); cf also Schweitzer (n 82) 7–10.

[115] See also Kumkar (n 82) 557–59 (somewhat vaguely pleading for a flexibilisation of control instruments).

suppliers whose terms are more favourable from the customer perspective.[116] Reading and comparing multiple sets of terms and conditions, formulating counter-proposals, and conducting negotiations involves effort and costs that are not justifiable for most day-to-day transactions. For the entrepreneur who signs countless similar contracts, the calculation is different. His efforts are worthwhile because the relative cost per contract is significantly lower for 'multiple players' than for 'one-shotters'.[117] The resulting asymmetry in the transaction costs incurred by the two parties negotiating the contract is thus likely to create a partial market failure, and competition alone may therefore not lead to appropriate standard terms.[118]

A comparable asymmetry does not necessarily exist in the three-party constellation on platforms. Instead, there the terms are formulated by the platform as a third party, so that platform law is more akin to the traditional *lex mercatoria* (law merchant), whose rules are nowadays laid down by so-called 'formulating agencies'.[119] The absence of this asymmetry is no guarantee of impartiality, however. Platform terms can still create significant imbalances in the allocation of risk between the parties contracting on their basis.[120] For example, while Airbnb's terms provide for a 'host guarantee' in order to cover loss or damage sustained by hosts and caused by their guests, the platform did not initially provide a comparable guarantee for loss or damage sustained by guests and caused by the host (until the introduction of just such a 'guest guarantee' in 2019).[121] Such unbalanced terms may be motivated by platforms wanting to be particularly attractive to certain users. Airbnb, for instance, needs to attract as many hosts as possible in order to ensure a sufficient supply of accommodation.[122] In addition, users vary in their sensitivity to the design of platform terms. Again, due to different transaction costs, repeat users are more sensitive to different (platform) terms than one-off users. Furthermore, users' sensitivity also crucially depends on whether they have a choice of alternative platforms. Such choice does not exist for monopolistic platforms likely to emerge through network effects.[123] Compared with bilateral terms and conditions, the risk of imbalances in platform terms therefore depends much more on the specific market structure.

[116] For a concise overview of the different lines of argument, see M Fornasier in FJ Säcker, R Rixecker and others (eds), *Münchener Kommentar zum BGB*, vol 2, 9th edn (München, CH Beck, 2022) Vor § 305 paras 4–8.

[117] This terminology goes back to the influential and controversial article by M Galanter, 'Why the "Haves" Come Out Ahead: Speculations on the Limits of Legal Change' (1974) 9 *Law & Soc Rev* 95.

[118] See eg R Korobkin, 'Bounded Rationality, Standard Form Contracts, and Unconscionability' (2003) 70 *Univ Chicago L Rev* 1203; M Meyerson, 'The Efficient Consumer Form Contract: Law and Economics Meets the Real World' (1990) 24 *Georgia L Rev* 583; D Gilo and A Porat, 'The Hidden Roles of Boilerplate and Standard-Form Contracts: Strategic Imposition of Transaction Costs, Segmentation of Consumers, and Anticompetitive Effects' (2006) 104 *Michigan L Rev* 983.

[119] R Michaels, 'The True Lex Mercatoria: Law Beyond the State' (2007) 14 *Indiana Journal of Global Legal Studies* 447, 457.

[120] Grundmann and Hacker (n 78) 274.

[121] In more detail: Hatzopoulos (n 83) 193; cf also N Sheffi, 'The Fast to the Furious' in D McKee, F Makela and T Scassa (eds), *Law and the 'Sharing Economy': Regulating Online Market Platforms* (Ottawa, University of Ottawa Press, 2018) 73.

[122] Grundmann and Hacker (n 78) 274; in a similar vein: Schweitzer (n 82) 9.

[123] Schweitzer (n 82) 8 et seq. More generally on the importance of network effects for the emergence of private norm-setting power, see A Engert, 'Private Normsetzungsmacht' (2014) 5 *Rechtswissenschaft* 301, 310 et seq.

ii. The 'Coercive' Nature of Platform Conditions

The loss of relevance of default rules also impinges on private autonomy for reasons other than the risk of imbalances. In particular, restrictions on private autonomy flow from the particularly coercive, almost 'mandatory' nature of platform conditions.[124] From the perspective of regulatory theory, these conditions are of course not to be qualified as 'mandatory law' in a technical sense,[125] but as standard terms established by the platform operator as a private party. While standard terms form part of a contractual arrangement (in the case of platform terms: the user contract), they are only based on a very formal sort of consent, given that the other party is often not even consciously aware of their substance. As Ludwig Raiser once aptly observed, standard terms are established in a 'zone of diluted autonomy' ('Zone verdünnter Freiheit'), and their rules, therefore, have a partly heteronomous character.[126] With regard to platform terms, autonomy would appear to be even more diluted. For various reasons, the possibilities and incentives for bargaining these terms away are significantly more limited than in the case of bilateral terms. First, due to network effects, there is a tendency for platforms to become natural monopolies, leaving users with no choice of alterative.[127] Users cannot switch to another platform whose conditions better suit their preferences.[128] Second, even if deviations are possible, they are in practice much less likely to occur. This is because the conditions are established in the (earlier) user contract, not in the (later) agreement with the other party to the exchange contract. Because of this separation, deviations from the terms cannot be negotiated directly with that other party. The separation, which removes platform terms from the transaction cost logic of bilateral contracts, also gives such terms an even more ancillary character than traditional standard terms. For behavioural reasons, users will pay less attention to terms accepted *in toto* up-front than if they were confronted with them at the time of concluding the exchange contract.[129] At the time of accessing the platform, users tend to focus on other criteria (such as the platform's reach). Since humans are cognitively unable to consider and weigh all relevant information by means of multiple regression, they tend to base their decisions on single criteria and one-dimensional heuristics.[130] Third, platform

[124] Similar: Schweitzer (n 82) 9 ('heteronome[s] Recht', at least under certain conditions).

[125] See generally HC Grigoleit, 'Mandatory Law: Fundamental Principles' in J Basedow, KJ Hopt and R Zimmermann (eds), *Max Planck Encyclopaedia of European Private Law* (Oxford, OUP, 2012) 1126.

[126] L Raiser, 'Vertragsfunktion und Vertragsfreiheit' in E von Caemmerer, E Friesenhahn and R Lange (eds), *Festschrift Hundert Jahre Deutsches Rechtsleben* (Karlsruhe, CF Müller, 1960) 101, 126; cf also Möslein (n 111) 175.

[127] See F Ducci, *Natural Monopolies in Digital Platform Markets* (Cambridge, CUP, 2020) 88, as well as references n 123 above; cf, on the other hand, on the profit-oriented peculiarities of that monopoly, L Khan, 'Amazon's Antitrust Paradox' (2017) 126 *Yale LJ* 710.

[128] Generalising: Kumkar (n 82) 551; see on the other hand, however, A Hellgardt, 'Privatautonome Modifikation der Regeln zu Abschluss, Zustandekommen und Wirksamkeit des Vertrags' (2013) 213 *Archiv für die civilistische Praxis (AcP)* 760, 808.

[129] Similar: Grundmann and Hacker (n 78) 273 et seq.

[130] Heuristical behaviour of 'one-reason decision-making' has been empirically proven: R Shepard, 'On Subjectively Optimum Selections Among Multi-Attribute Alternatives' in W Edwards and A Tversky (eds), *Decision Making* (London, Penguin Books, 1967) 257; J Shanteau, 'How Much Information Does an Expert Use? Is it Relevant?' (1992) 81 *Acta Psychologica* 75; J Rieskamp and U Hoffrage, 'When do People use Simple Heuristics and How Can we Tell?' in G Gigerenzer and PM Todd (eds), *Simple Heuristics that Make us Smart* (Oxford, OUP, 1999) 141.

conditions restrict private autonomy additionally when combined with self-enforcing mechanisms. For example, if the lock on the rental apartment is blocked because certain Airbnb terms have not been met, these conditions do not first have to be enforced by courts. While courts would check the terms' content for compliance with legal rules, their self-enforcement reinforces their coercive character.[131] In a similar vein, platforms' own dispute resolution mechanisms partially remove their terms from judicial control, much as arbitration does with respect to the *lex mercatoria*.[132]

B. Risks of Regulatory Failure

In the long run, the digital transformation may deprive default rules of their function as a subtle coordination mechanism. From the perspective of legislators, the emergence of platform terms carries the risk that default rules will fail as a regulatory instrument. In addition, default rules are likely to lose their function as a standard of substantive fairness control, particularly with regard to the provisions on standard contract terms.

i. Alteration of Altering Rules

Default rules fulfil regulatory functions, even though their content is not mandatory. In spite of their default character, they are still based on one mandatory legal rule, namely the altering rule that they apply unless and until the parties deviate from them. Deviations, in other words, are subject to the mandatory requirement of an alternative arrangement.[133] It is only the modification, not the application, of default rules that requires positive action on the part of those to whom they are addressed. In case of uncertainty or doubt, default rules therefore apply heteronomously.[134] By contrast, platform terms reverse this starting point. If parties use a digital platform, its terms apply instead of the otherwise applicable default rule. Differently to legal default rules, these terms do not apply entirely automatically, of course, but their application requires nothing more than a previous access by the parties to the specific platform.[135] When the exchange contract itself is concluded, the platform terms then apply automatically,

[131] Similar: M Rudanko, 'Smart Contracts and Traditional Contracts: Views from Contract Law' in M Corrales Compagnucci, M Fenwick and S Wrbka (eds), *Smart Contracts: Technological, Business and Legal Perspectives* (Oxford, Hart Publishing, 2021) 59, 75.

[132] Michaels (n 119) 459.

[133] Möslein (n 3) 71; similar: F Kirchhof, *Private Rechtsetzung* (Berlin, Duncker & Humblot, 1987) 87.

[134] See Möslein (n 3) 71; in a similar vein already W Buckhardt, *Methode und System des Rechts* (Zürich, Polygraphischer Verlag AG Zürich, 1936), 173, arguing that default rules demand obedience; different, however, C Sunstein, 'Autonomy by Default' (2016) 11 *American Journal of Bioethics* 1, arguing that 'taken as such, default rules do not intrude on autonomy, even if they influence people without persuading them'. Cf also C Mills, 'The Heteronomy of Choice Architecture' (2015) 6 *Review of Philosophy and Psychology* 495. In general, heteronomy is regarded as a key indicator for rule-setting: A Engert, 'Private Normsetzungsmacht: Die Standardisierung von Regelungen im Markt als Form der Fremdbestimmung' (2014) 5 *Rechtswissenschaft* 301, 303 and 308, with further references in fn 35 of Engert's contribution.

[135] The choice of the specific platform will typically depend on criteria other than the platform terms: Grochowski (n 100) 227, arguing that it 'may be driven by other types of inclinations than sheer preference for one contract type over the other', in particular by the price of the specific good or service, or by the accessibility of the platform established through internet research.

without any (additional) intervention of the parties to that contract. In that respect, it is no longer the deviation from the default rules, but the deviation from the platform conditions that would require action on their part.[136]

As a consequence of digital transformation, the conventional altering rule of default rules therefore changes fundamentally. The more widely platform terms are accepted as an alternative infrastructure for contractual transactions, the more significant is the loss of relevance of the legal infrastructure of default rules. These rules are no longer the fall-back option, but are replaced by platform terms. They cease to serve as a coordinating mechanism because they can no longer overshadow private transactions and thus channel private behaviour. Default rules are thus in danger of failing as regulatory instruments.

ii. Failure as Fairness Standards

In addition, default rules conventionally provide a fairness standard. They serve as a benchmark against which private contractual agreements can be assessed.[137] Contractual agreements that deviate too much from this benchmark are either discarded or replaced, typically by the default rule itself. A prime example of a legal provision that makes default rules into the standard of control is provided by Directive 93/13/EEC on unfair terms in consumer contracts in its Article 3 paragraph 1. Even though this European provision, unlike its implementation in German law (cf § 307 paragraph 2 no 1 BGB), does not explicitly refer to default rules, they unambiguously serve as a reference point in the interpretation of the CJEU:

> When assessing whether a contract term 'causes a significant imbalance in the parties' rights and obligations, to the detriment of the consumer', national courts have to carry out, in the first place, a comparison of the relevant contract term with any rules of national law which would apply in the absence of the contract term.[138]

Even more clearly, the Commission stresses that as far as there exist default rules from which the contract terms deviate, 'those will be the primary yardstick for assessing a significant imbalance in the rights and obligations of the parties'.[139] In addition to the judicial control of standard terms, national laws also rely on the yardstick of default rules in other contexts, for example in relation to the concept of good faith or to abuse provisions in antitrust and tax law.[140]

[136] Similar: Grochowski (n 100) 227 ('turns from a classic unitarian system based upon default rules into a set of parallel universes, composed of mandatory rules that are offered by the market as alternatives to be opted-into').

[137] Möslein (n 3) 35 et seq, with further references ibid fn 135 ('Kontrollfunktion').

[138] CJEU, C-415/11 *Aziz* ECLI:EU:C:2013:164, para 68; see also C-226/12 *Constructora Principado* ECLI:EU:C:2014:10, para 21; C-421/14 *Banco Primus* ECLI:EU:C:2017:60, para 59; C-186/16 *Andriciuc* ECLI:EU:C:2017:703, para 59; C-229/19 and C-289/19 *Dexia* ECLI:EU:C:2021:68, para 48.

[139] European Commission, Guidance on the interpretation and application of Council Directive 93/13/EEC on unfair terms in consumer contracts [2019] OJ C323/4, at 31.

[140] From a comparative perspective: F Möslein, 'Inhaltskontrolle und Inhaltsregeln im Schuldvertragsrecht' in K Riesenhuber and Y Nishitani (eds), *Wandlung oder Erosion der Privatautonomie* (Berlin, de Gruyter, 2007) 233.

The legislative idea behind these uses of default rules as a fairness standard is the basic assumption that default rules embody the 'ideal' of a fair balance of interests.[141] Default rules are therefore only a suitable yardstick for contractual agreements if they can claim to reflect the ideas of justice of those to whom they are addressed.[142] At the very least, they must represent the usual, widely accepted market standard. If default rules lose their relevance because platform terms are more and more widely accepted and therefore develop into the typically applicable rule, this requirement is no longer met. On the other hand, platform conditions can increasingly themselves claim to represent the market standard. This claim gains credibility not merely on account of increasing use and dissemination of platform terms. It can also be based on the information advantages that are associated to their dissemination. By analysing the extensive contract data available to platform operators, user preferences may well be reflected better and more quickly in platform terms and conditions than in old-style default rules. With the help of modern data technology, platforms are in a position to overcome the knowledge gaps that legislators have traditionally faced when enacting default rules. Regardless of whether platform operators *actually* aim to map user preferences congruently, data technologies used on platforms at least have the *potential* to replace the sophisticated governance mechanism of knowledge production provided by the instrument of default rules, which operates through the interaction of public and private rule-making. Data technology could ultimately replace the invisible hand of the market with comprehensive knowledge of the preferences of market participants.[143] Indeed, it has the potential to usher in what has been called the 'age of surveillance capitalism'.[144] As a consequence of this fundamental change, there is a significant risk that default rules will cease to serve as fairness standards because they can no longer credibly claim to represent the market standard.

V. Regulatory Strategies to (Re-)Create an Architecture of Choice

If digital transformation threatens the tried and tested architecture of choice based on default rules, legislators will have to develop regulatory strategies to preserve this architecture. This task, however, seems no less daunting than the great challenge of the twentieth century: to ensure the functioning of private autonomy in the face of the advance of standard contract terms. Compared to the self-made law once analysed by Hans Großmann-Doerth,[145] digital regulatory architectures pose additional,

[141] Path-breaking: L Raiser, *Das Recht der allgemeinen Geschäftsbedingungen* (Bad Homburg, Gentner, 1961) 295; see also C Canaris, 'Wandlungen des Schuldvertragsrechts – Tendenzen zu seiner "Materialisierung"' (2000) 200 *Archiv für die civilistische Praxis* (*AcP*) 273, 285.

[142] Möslein (n 3) 71.

[143] Similar: A Moazed and N Johnson, *Modern Monopolies: What It Takes to Dominate the 21st Century Economy* (New York, Saint Martin's Griffin, 2016) 125 ('The Visible Hand').

[144] S Zuboff, *The Age of Surveillance Capitalism* (New York, PublicAffairs, 2019).

[145] See Großmann-Doerth (112).

fundamentally different challenges. The regulatory instruments once developed for standard terms in bilateral agreements are unlikely to be sufficient for digital regulatory architectures.[146] Instead, new regulatory tools need to be developed.[147] Beyond the traditional focus on rules, they must address the structures of rule-making itself.

A. Regulating Standard Terms

i. Transparency Requirements

One of the key regulatory tools of the Unfair Terms Directive is the requirement of transparency of standard terms. Accordingly, Article 5 of the Directive provides that standard terms shall 'always be drafted in plain, intelligible language'. The guiding principle that 'sunlight is the best disinfectant' has long been shaped by market-based regulation,[148] and the so-called information model based on disclosure is considered paradigmatic for all of European private law.[149] The potential – but also the limitations – of this information model has long been a central issue in the debate on the rules on standard terms.

In the context of digitalisation, the European legislator relies on that same regulatory approach. The Regulation on promoting fairness and transparency for business users of online intermediation services ('P2B Regulation') not only bears the term in its title, but also declares transparency to be one of its central regulatory objectives (cf Article 1 paragraph 1).[150] In particular, the core provision of Article 3 requires providers of online intermediation services to ensure transparency in a number of different respects. In general, however, it seems doubtful whether the regulatory instrument of transparency will be sufficient to allow the functional mechanisms of default rules to take effect and private autonomy to prevail in the face of the digital challenges outlined above.[151] While disclosure rules can help overcome information asymmetries and promote informed decisions, the information model proves ineffective insofar as restrictions on private autonomy have other causes. In particular, transparency rules cannot counteract the increasingly coercive nature of platform conditions which results from network effects and which is reinforced both by behavioural effects and self-enforcing mechanisms.[152]

[146] Kumkar (n 82) 557.

[147] Similar: Schweitzer (n 82) 12 ('Für die Zukunft gilt es, ein flexibles und differenziertes zivilrechtliches Kontrollregime zu entwickeln, das der legitimen Funktion der Regelsetzung durch Plattformen ebenso Rechnung trägt wie den im Einzelnen noch zu klärenden regelsetzungsspezifischen Grenzen der Richtigkeitsgewähr').

[148] L Brandeis, 'What Publicity Can Do' in L Brandeis, *Other People's Money And How The Bankers Use It* (New York, Frederick A Stokes, 1914) 92.

[149] See eg S Grundmann, W Kerber and S Weatherill, 'Party Autonomy and the Role of Information in the Internal Market: An Overview' in S Grundmann, W Kerber and S Weatherill (eds), *Party Autonomy and the Role of Information in the Internal Market* (Berlin, de Gruyter, 2021) 3, 18; S Grundmann, 'The Future of Contract Law' (2011) 7 *ERCL* 490, 521.

[150] Regulation (EU) 2019/1150 of the European Parliament and of the Council of 20 June 2019 on promoting fairness and transparency for business users of online intermediation services [2019] OJ L186/57.

[151] Similar: Schweitzer (n 82) 12.

[152] See section IV.A.ii above.

After all, the possibility of an informed decision presupposes that freedom of choice exists in the first place. Transparency rules can therefore only prove to be an effective regulatory instrument if the addressees of these rules can either choose between different platform terms or if there is a chance that they will negotiate different terms. As these conditions are typically not met for the reasons explained above, transparency rules alone are at any rate not sufficient to achieve the desired regulatory objective.[153] At best, they can complement a broader regulatory strategy as an additional regulatory instrument.

ii. Fairness Control

Another key regulatory tool dealing with the challenges of standard terms is the judicial control of their fairness. Article 6 paragraph 1 of the Unfair Terms Directive provides that unfair terms 'shall not be binding on the consumer', and Article 3 paragraph 1 specifies that 'a contractual term which has not been individually negotiated shall be regarded as unfair if, contrary to the requirement of good faith, it causes a significant imbalance in the parties' rights and obligations arising under the contract'. As has already been stated, the default rules from which the standard terms deviate typically serve as the primary yardstick for assessing such imbalances.[154]

Similarly to transparency requirements, fairness control of standard terms, too, serves the European lawmaker as a regulatory instrument in the context of digitalisation. The P2B Regulation also includes the term 'fairness' in its title and lists fairness among its regulatory objectives (cf Article 1 paragraph 1). As a regulatory instrument, however, fairness control is not strongly articulated in this Regulation. On the one hand, Article 8 expressly refers to the standards of good faith and fair dealing, but only with respect to very specific contractual terms and situations (such as retroactive changes to terms and conditions). The much broader provision on standard terms and conditions in Article 3, on the other hand, does not explicitly refer to fairness in its paragraph 1 lit a), but focuses on issues of transparency instead. While in most jurisdictions, judicial review of standard terms is considered to be justified only in B2C relations, there may nevertheless be 'a case for a special control of P2B terms and conditions based on the established rationale for controlling general terms and conditions in contract law' where a platform has become a gatekeeper.[155] Accordingly, some (especially German) authors argue in favour of judicial fairness review in the context of the P2B Regulation, even in the absence of an explicit provision.[156] Beyond the P2B Regulation, a much

[153] G Spindler and A Seidel, 'Die Regulierung von Online-Plattformen' [2022] *Neue Juristische Wochenschrift* (*NJW*) 2730, 2733.

[154] See section IV.A.ii above.

[155] H Schweitzer and F Gutmann, 'Unilateral Practices in the Digital Market: An Overview of EU and National Case Law, e-Competitions Unilateral Practices in the Digital Market' 15 July 2021, Art No 101045, available at www.concurrences.com/en/bulletin/special-issues/unilateral-practices-in-the-digital-market/new-article-no101045; see also C Twigg-Flesner, 'The EU's Proposals for Regulating B2B Relationships on Online Platforms: Transparency, Fairness and Beyond' (2018) 7 *Journal of European Consumer and Market Law* 222, 223.

[156] See, in particular, F Graf von Westphalen in C Busch (ed), *P2B-VO* (Munich, CH Beck, 2022) Art 3 paras 60 et seq.

more explicit provision is provided for in Article 13 of the Data Act.[157] The provision aims at contractual terms that concern 'the access to and use of data or the liability and remedies for the breach or the termination of data related obligations', and it reaches beyond consumer protection by covering standard terms that are imposed on micro, small or medium-sized enterprises. Similarly to the regulatory approach of the Unfair Terms Directive, unfair contractual terms 'shall not be binding on the [affected] enterprise' (cf Article 13 paragraph 1). Moreover, the concept of fairness is not only related to the general principles of good faith and fair dealing, but is specified by means of a more specific black and grey list in paragraphs 3 and 4.[158] In contrast to the Unfair Terms Directive, however, 'good commercial practice in data access and use' serve as a yardstick according to paragraph 2 – instead of legal default rules.[159] The subject matter of data access and use is simply not yet sufficiently covered by legal default rules.[160] Article 13 paragraph 2 of the proposed Data Act thus illustrates the general observation that technological innovation potentially leads to a lack of default rules. However, the regulatory way forward cannot generally rely on referring to 'good commercial practice[s]' instead of default rules either. In the long run, such practices can only develop in an environment characterised by the structural risks of digital transformation outlined above. Due to the corresponding lack of private autonomy, commercial practices will therefore not be able to provide a neutral, balanced benchmark against which terms can be effectively tested and assessed. Moreover, self-enforcing technologies increasingly reduce judicial control over standard terms. By providing alternative mechanisms for enforcing platform terms, these technologies reduce the need to go to court.[161] Both because of the impending lack of a fairness benchmark and because of these enforcement deficits, fairness control does not promise to be an appropriate regulatory tool for strengthening default rules in times of digital transformation.

iii. Restrictive Altering Rules

A more intensive regulatory approach could consist in restricting deviations from default rules more generally, regardless of the substantive content (and, in particular, the fairness) of the respective standard terms. Ultimately, this approach of 'regulating opt-out'[162] amounts to a restrictive alteration of the applicable altering rules, in particular by providing that deviations require an explicit agreement between the two parties to the

[157] Regulation (EU) 2023/2854 of the European Parliament and of the Council of 13 December 2023 on harmonised rules on fair access to and use of data and amending Regulation (EU) 2017/2394 and Directive (EU) 2020/1828 (Data Act).

[158] See L Specht-Riemenschneider, 'Der Entwurf des Data Act' [2022] *Beilage Multimedia und Recht* 809, 822; T Gerpott, 'Vorschlag für ein europäisches Datengesetz' [2022] *Computer-Recht* 271, 278.

[159] M Hennemann and B Steinrötter, 'Data Act – Fundament des neuen EU-Datenwirtschaftsrechts' [2022] *Neue Juristische Wochenschrift* (*NJW*) 1481, 1485.

[160] A Metzger and H Schweizer, 'Shaping Markets: A Critical Evaluation of the Draft Data Act' [2023] *Zeitschrift für Europäisches Privatrecht* (*ZEuP*) 42, 65: 'Once the market has developed business practices, those practices may be further developed into (majoritarian) default rules to be applied by courts in case of incomplete contracts. Up to now, neither model terms nor default rules suitable for the implementation of mandatory access rights are sufficiently developed'.

[161] See the reference in n 132 above.

[162] Ayres (n 31).

exchange contract in question. Such a statutory provision would exclude any possibility of platform terms and conditions agreed in the contracts between the platform operator and individual platform users indirectly spilling over into the contractual relationships amongst the platform users themselves. In a (roughly) comparable way, Article 5 of the Unfair Contract Terms Directive excludes deviations by standard terms unless they are drafted in plain, intelligible language. Incomprehensible, ambiguous terms are therefore not able to alter default rules, regardless of their substantive content. This provision aims to ensure that default rules can only be waived in a transparent manner; it thus counts among the 'clarity-requiring altering rules'.[163] The same transparency requirement could be transferred to three-party situations on digital platforms by arguing that alterations are generally not intelligible enough if only provided for in the platform terms. The alterations, one could reason, are not sufficiently accessible and therefore insufficiently known to the two parties when they agree bilaterally on the exchange contract in question.

However, such a restriction would go far beyond a mere transparency requirement. It would effectively prevent platform terms and conditions from serving as an alternative legal infrastructure which complements the exchange contracts concluded on the respective platform. However, completely to exclude the contractual freedom of platform operators through such a restriction seems problematic with regard to their constitutionally guaranteed private autonomy.[164] Such a restriction would not only affect significantly unbalanced platform conditions, but would also restrict 'impartial' platform operators.[165] In addition, such a restriction would significantly impede the platform economy, especially with regard to transactions for which the legal default regime fails to offer suitable provisions for supplementing incomplete contractual agreements, such as agreements on data access and use. Filling these kinds of contractual gaps with 'good commercial practices' could even have a counterproductive regulatory effect. If such practices were, in turn, predetermined by platform terms and conditions, any reference to commercial practices would once again give effect to the platform terms and conditions, albeit in a more indirect, supplementary way. In fact, European law as it stands does not seem to be considering such a far-reaching restriction of altering rules. Instead, legislation limits itself in Article 3 paragraph 1 lit b) of the P2B Regulation to improving the transparency of platform conditions. Providers of online intermediation services are required to ensure that their terms and conditions are 'easily available to business users at all stages of their commercial relationship with the provider of online intermediation services, including in the pre-contractual stage'.[166] Although this provision requires terms and conditions to be made available at all times, it does not restrict the ability of platform operators to provide terms and conditions that result in deviations from default rules in bilateral contractual relationships between platform users. The provision does not therefore restrict altering rules in substance.

[163] ibid 2072 et seq.
[164] Schweitzer (n 82) 7.
[165] Similar Schweitzer (n 82) 9, arguing for a differentiated regulatory approach.
[166] Extensively on this provision: Graf von Westphalen in *P2B-VO* (n 156) Art 3 paras 177–81; cf also Twigg-Flesner (n 155) 226.

B. Regulating Private Rule-Makers

The regulatory challenge is therefore to strike the right balance between protecting the private autonomy of (inter alia) platform operators on the one hand and avoiding significant imbalances in platform terms on the other hand, while also recognising that default rules are increasingly failing as a fairness standard. This weighty condition suggests that the focus of regulation should not be primarily on the fairness of terms, as is the case in the Unfair Terms Directive and – more broadly – in conventional rules on judicial control of bilateral standard terms. In order to do justice to the role of the platforms as rule-makers, the focus of regulation should instead be on the platforms themselves. After all, standard terms which are not set by either party to the exchange contract, but by the platform as a third party, are not necessarily less balanced than ordinary (typically statutory) default rules.[167] In some circumstances, platform terms may even work better than default rules in supplementing incomplete contracts, because platform operators have greater access than the lawmaker does to the data needed in order to reflect the parties' preferences in fall-back provisions.[168] A necessary condition, however, is that the platform in question can actually be regarded as impartial. To ensure this impartiality, two different regulatory strategies are conceivable: either imposing certain restrictions on private rule-makers who are potentially subject to conflicts of interest, or, conversely, privileging private rule-makers who appear to be particularly trustworthy. Both regulatory strategies are already being applied in digital-related legislation, but the question is whether and how these approaches can be transferred to secure the architecture of choice based on default rules.

i. Restrictions on Conflicted Rule-Makers

The requisite impartiality of platforms as rule-makers is particularly doubtful when platform operators themselves – or persons associated with them – also act as participants on this platform (so-called dual-role platforms).[169] On Amazon Marketplace, for example, products are sold both by independent parties as well as by Amazon itself. While all sellers are equally subject to Amazon's platform terms, it is obvious that Amazon has an interest in formulating terms that are favourable towards sellers rather than for buyers.[170] In general, dual-role platforms have their own particular interests in shaping the content of the platform terms and conditions.[171] As a rule-maker, such platform operators cannot be considered to be impartial, even if they happen also to act as a third party in relation to some platform transactions, namely those where only independent parties interact with one another. Due to the potential conflict of interest between the functions of rule-maker and market participant, neutral and balanced

[167] Similar Schweitzer (n 82) 9, arguing that platform terms retain a certain guarantee of correctness ('Richtigkeitsgewähr'), albeit only under certain conditions.

[168] See above, at nn 143 et seq.

[169] C Busch, 'Towards a "New Approach" for the Platform Ecosystem: A European Standard for Fairness in Platform-to-Business Relations' (2017) 6 *Journal of European Consumer and Market Law* 227, 227.

[170] L Khan, 'Amazon's Antitrust Paradox' (2017) 126 *Yale LJ* 710, 780.

[171] Schweitzer (n 82) 9 et seq.

platform conditions are unlikely, and the law cannot expect other market participants to trust these conditions.

There are, of course, many different legal rules on conflicts of interest that could potentially serve as a model for regulation. A provision that also covers digital platforms seems particularly relevant and appropriate, albeit in a specific context and not primarily with a view to platform conditions: Article 8 of the European Crowdfunding Service Providers for Business Regulation (ECSPR)[172] sets out provisions on conflict of interests of crowdfunding service providers who operate or manage digital platforms in order to provide crowdfunding services by matching business funding interests of investors and project owners (cf Article 2 paragraph 1 lit. a, d and e ECSPR). The various requirements that Article 8 ECSPR imposes on crowdfunding service providers include a ban on participating in crowdfunding offers on their platform (paragraph 1), restrictions on project ownership by related parties (paragraph 2), the obligation to maintain and operate effective internal rules to prevent conflicts of interest (paragraphs 3 and 4) and various disclosure obligations (paragraphs 4 to 6).[173] While this provision is primarily concerned with the operation of a platform rather than with its rule-making capacity, it nevertheless illustrates the general principle that platform operators with actual or potential conflicts of interest are subject to legal constraints. Similar restrictions should therefore also apply to their rule-making powers,[174] for example by rendering the terms and conditions of conflicted platform operators completely non-binding. Alternatively, in these circumstances, the law should at least exclude the spillover effects of platform terms and conditions on contracts concluded on the platform. In the specific case of conflicts of interest, a corresponding restriction on altering rules seems entirely appropriate (as opposed to more general restrictions as discussed in section V.A.iii above). Moreover, Article 8 ECSPR can serve as a model for specific questions of regulatory design, for instance with regard to the persons who are considered to be 'related parties' or with regard to accompanying disclosure requirements.

ii. Promotion of Trustworthy Rule-Makers

Restrictions on conflicted platform operators can only help prevent particularly problematic, potentially unbalanced platform terms. They do not, however, make a positive contribution to the dissemination and further development of rules that are particularly well suited to filling gaps in incomplete contracts. On the contrary, such restrictions once again raise the question of what rules should replace the platform terms which they declare to be non-binding.

In order to promote rules that are suitable as gap-fillers, a regulatory instrument is needed that encourages the emergence of balanced terms and conditions rather than having a purely restrictive effect. Rather than sanctioning the most problematic,

[172] Regulation (EU) 2020/1503 of the European Parliament and of the Council of 7 October 2020 on European crowdfunding service providers for business, and amending Regulation (EU) 2017/1129 and Directive (EU) 2019/1937 [2020] OJ L347/1.

[173] More extensively on this provision: D Pereira Duarte, 'Intermediation Risk and Conflicts of Interest' in E Macchiavello (ed), *Regulation on European Crowdfunding Service Providers for Business: A Commentary* (Cheltenham, Edward Elgar, 2022) 136.

[174] In a similar vein Schweitzer (n 82) 11.

conflicted rule-makers, a regulatory instrument should privilege rule-makers who appear to be particularly trustworthy. Such an approach would take advantage of the fact that platforms are, in principle, particularly well placed to design rules that mimic the market, since they have access to data on the preferences of market actors that is usually unavailable to the legislator.[175] If default rules have traditionally provided a sophisticated governance mechanism of knowledge production, and if this mechanism is becoming less functional as a result of the current digital transformation, then a regulatory instrument that promotes private regulatory knowledge could prove helpful in restoring the interaction between public and private rule-making, in order to recreate the necessary legal infrastructure for a well-functioning framework of private autonomy.

The specific regulatory design of provisions privileging trustworthy rule-makers is challenging, however, both in terms of the scope of application and the nature of the privilege. One digital-related regulatory model that could provide some guidance is to be found in the Data Governance Act,[176] as its provisions on data altruism also aim to promote specific, particularly trustworthy intermediaries.[177] The provisions of the Data Governance Act in Chapter IV (Articles 15 et seq) concern data intermediaries, not platforms as rule-makers. Nevertheless, knowledge production is a common denominator. Both sets of rules deal with the use of data, and the common regulatory challenge is the need to define criteria for distinguishing and privileging intermediaries considered to be particularly trustworthy.

With regard to the scope of application, in order to qualify as a trustworthy organisation, Article 16 of the Data Governance Act requires legal entities to be established to achieve objectives of general interest and to operate on a non-profit basis. Similar criteria, though with some adaptations, could be applied to trusted private rule-makers, given that we have identified economic incentives to be the main driving force for significant imbalances in platform terms. Platforms which, for economic reasons, want to be particularly attractive to one of the two sides of the market tend to have a correspondingly unbalanced set of terms and conditions. If, on the other hand, profit orientation is excluded, this danger does not exist. To ensure that the actual operation of the platform remains commercially attractive, the rules could, for example, allow the task of rule-making to be outsourced to independent, not-for-profit bodies. Instead of – or in addition to – the requirement of meeting general interest objectives, dominant platforms as well as their associated rule-makers could be excluded from the regulatory privileges, since such market dominance severely limits the regulatory choices of market players.

In terms of regulatory privileges, the Data Governance Act grants these only in relation to data access and collection, whereas the privileges of trusted private rule-makers should aim to strengthen their rules. In the long term, this approach could encourage balanced terms and conditions becoming a market standard of 'good commercial practice'. In particular, the terms of trusted rule-makers could benefit from an exemption from fairness review under the Unfair Terms Directive. After all, the asymmetric

[175] See above, at nn 143 et seq.

[176] Regulation (EU) 2022/868 of the European Parliament and of the Council of 30 May 2022 on European data governance and amending Regulation (EU) 2018/1724 [2022] OJ L152/1.

[177] See, for instance, B Steinrötter, 'Datenaltruismus' [2021] *Zeitschrift für Datenschutz* 61; more generally on the rules on data intermediaries: M Hennemann and L v Ditfurth, 'Datenintermediäre und Data Governance Act' [2022] *Neue Juristische Wochenschrift (NJW)* 1905.

relationship between the two contracting parties to which the Directive was originally tailored (cf Recital 2 of the Unfair Terms Directive, referring to 'many disparities'), does not exist in the three-party constellation on platforms. Significant imbalances can still occur, but their likelihood is limited if the scope of trusted rule-makers is tailored to reduce their incentives and potential interests to treat certain addressees better than others. On platforms where the risk of such influence is comparatively low, the prospects for fair platform conditions are good enough to exempt them from the Unfair Contract Terms Directive. Such an exemption would, in turn, promote platform terms that are better suited than default rules to fill gaps in incomplete contracts. As a result of digital transformation, after all, platform operators tend to have better access than legislators to the data needed to reflect the preferences of the parties and to 'mimic efficient arrangements'.[178] A regulatory architecture of choice must take advantage of this superior knowledge to be fit for the digital age.

VI. Conclusion

Almost 30 years after Nicholas Negroponte's prediction that 'everything that can be digitized will be digitized',[179] we are witnessing the digitisation of default rules. The emergence of online platforms, supported by algorithmic data analysis and self-enforcing technologies, is increasingly replacing state-created default rules with platform terms. However, platform terms follow a very different regulatory pattern from default rules, fundamentally changing the methods and mechanisms for generating the rules that fill gaps in contracts. The resulting shift is ambiguous. Because of their access to data, platforms are now in a better position than the legislator to design contractual solutions that match the preferences of the parties, but because of their economic incentives and their potential market power, their terms risk being unbalanced and coercive. The more widespread the use of platform terms, the less relevant default rules will become, thus ceasing to serve as a meaningful coordination mechanism and also failing as a persuasive standard for judicial fairness review. In order to preserve (or rather: to recreate) the architecture of choice for private contracting, this chapter has argued for a new regulatory strategy. The regulatory tools once developed for standard terms in bilateral agreements – transparency requirements, fairness review, and restrictions on contracting around – are simply no longer adequate to meet the challenges of digitalisation. To strike the right balance between protecting private autonomy and avoiding significant imbalances, the regulatory objective should nowadays rather be to ensure the impartiality of platforms by focusing on the structural conditions of their rule-making capacity. In addition to discussing restrictions on conflicted rule-makers, the chapter builds on the model of the Data Governance Act and its data altruism provisions to propose regulatory instruments that privilege trustworthy rule-makers. These tools promise to provide a regulatory framework which increases confidence in unbiased rule-making while taking advantage of digital platforms' access to the data needed to generate rules that mimic market preferences.

[178] See Ben-Shahar and Pottow (n 44) 651.
[179] N Negroponte, *Being Digital* (New York, Alfred A Knopf, 1995).

5

Default Rules in the Common Law: Substantive Rules and Precedent

PHILIP SALES*

I. Introduction

In this chapter, I consider a particularly pervasive form of default rule in the common law which constitutes its structure: precedent. I also review, at a high level, the operation of a series of default rules to be found in case law as stipulated by judges in the exercise of the powers given to them by the common law to set rules by formulating them in authoritative decisions.

Precedent is the foundation of the common law and operates as a default rule throughout all of it. Precedent as default rule has an internal aspect, when the substantive rules of the common law are established by judges. The ratio decidendi of a case becomes a rule, which will be followed by future decision-makers unless deviation is warranted in the subsequent case in such a way that the precedent can be distinguished. Those substantive rules are also themselves often formulated as kinds of default rule, reflecting the inherent capacity of the common law to bring a variety of different considerations to bear on a given situation, with different weightings accorded to them by the governing law. Thus, at the level of doctrine, defeasibility is built into the common law through a wide range of techniques, including the practice of distinguishing precedents (that is, looking for reasons to justify not applying them in a later case) and by judges building defeasibility into the rules which they articulate in the precedents they create.

Precedent as default rule also has an external aspect in the common law. This is a feature of the authority structure within the court system, according to which superior courts lay down precedents which bind lower courts and are to be followed unless they are, in accordance with the stare decisis rules, overturned. At the apex level, the Supreme Court is bound by its own previous decisions (or those of its predecessor in that role, the House of Lords), but can overturn them in certain limited circumstances. So, in principle, no rule of the common law is ever definitively fixed and unchangeable

* I am grateful to my Judicial Assistant, Robert Steele, for his invaluable assistance in preparing this chapter.

for ever. Even Supreme Court precedents operate as default rules, applicable only so long as no sufficient justification is found to exist to override them.

I begin by addressing the challenges posed by pluralism and incommensurability within the law and the way in which rules can accommodate and ameliorate these challenges. Second, I examine the nature of default rules and the way in which such rules seek to strike a balance between the competing social needs of certainty and flexibility. I also consider more specific aspects of the role of default rules, including cost savings, the injection of certain values into the law, the promotion of rule of law principles and as a means of addressing information asymmetries. Third, I explore four areas of the internal aspect of precedent as a system of default rules, relating to substantive or adjudicative rules in the form of contract, tort, structured discretions and burdens and standards of proof. Finally, I turn to precedent itself (from the external aspect), where I consider how precedent is applied and the circumstances in which a rule of precedent can be revised, with particular reference to the circumstances in which the Supreme Court will overturn its own precedents.

II. Pluralism and Rules

Since it will be helpful for understanding the place and role of default rules in a system of precedent, I should state at the beginning that value pluralism and its conceptual companion, incommensurability, permeate law generally, including the common law.[1] Their significance for the common law reflects the authority which a common law system gives to judges to fashion rules of law when articulating their application to particular cases. This tends to lead judges to examine the reason of the law and to seek to conform the content of legal rules to a material degree with the underlying rationale or rationalia for the rules. As Sir Edward Coke said in the seventeenth century, '[r]eason is the life of the law, nay the common law is nothing else but reason', albeit this is a technically trained and, in that sense, artificial form of reason.[2]

A judge, in adjudicating upon a dispute involving competing incommensurable values, strikes a balance. In a common law system with the doctrine of precedent, that determination becomes a rule. When tasked with rule design, judges bring into account the values internal to the particular rule, together with those values promoted by *having* a rule.

There is, therefore, an internal and an external aspect to rule design in the common law, based as it is on a system of precedent. The internal aspect relates to the creation and formulation of a rule (expressed in the ratio decidendi of a judgment) in the individual case. The external aspect relates to the values promoted by the common law, as a system, comprising rules. These values are the stability that comes from a system of precedent: the knowledge that certain legal questions are settled.

[1] P Sales and F Wilmot-Smith, 'Justice for Foxes' (2022) 138 *LQR* 583.

[2] P Sales, 'The Common Law: Context and Method' (2019) 135 *LQR* 47, 51–52. In this chapter I leave to one side how common law reasoning of this kind informs statutory interpretation.

A rule can be under- or over-inclusive by reference to the rule's underlying justification.[3] To take an example given by Frederick Schauer,[4] if the justification of the rule 'no dogs allowed' in a restaurant is to prevent disruption to customers, then the rule might be under-inclusive in relation to animals other than dogs (including humans) who are disruptive. On the other hand, it might be over-inclusive in relation to quiet, well-behaved, or even stuffed toy dogs. The success of a rule might be defined by its relationship with its justification, as to how probable it is to get it right in the general run of situations, in the context of the costs of getting it wrong (whether through its under- or over-inclusivity), the benefits of getting it right and the benefits of having a rule at all, as opposed to leaving it to the discretion of a waiter on the night.

It is inherent in a rule, as a norm which aims to stipulate the determination of legal outcomes prior to the crystallisation of specific factual circumstances, that it is liable to be sub-optimal in terms of the risk of its under- or over- inclusiveness. Since following a rule may produce a sub-optimal decision in some particular case, judged in terms of the rationale for the rule, the question of the comparative value of relying on rules is the question of the extent to which a decision-making environment is willing to tolerate sub-optimal results in order that those affected by the decisions in that environment will be able to plan certain aspects of their lives.[5] We may tolerate rules, including bright-line rules, which incorporate the risk of a certain level of mistakes in exchange for the rule of law values they promote.

These factors influence the decision as to *whether* to have a rule in particular circumstances, and also the *design* of a rule. The knowledge that the determination of the norm to be applied in the case at hand may create a rule for other cases can affect the balance to be struck in stating that norm. There is a rule design spectrum. At one end of the spectrum, bright-line rules may be required, giving a clear but inflexible rule to determine disputes; at the other, there may be broad and open-textured standards, requiring something closer to *de novo* decision-making in each particular case.[6] Bright-line rules may take a form which makes them mandatory, or which makes them more or less defeasible, either according to the choice of a court applying them in the light of the circumstances of a particular case or according to the choice of parties negotiating a contractual relationship in their shadow, so there is a middle ground.

The latter end of the spectrum allows for the application of the rule to be tailored more precisely to its underlying rationale but leads to potential conflict with rule of law values. These include the idea that individual cases should be determined by abstract and general laws, without excessive recourse to the individual discretion of the decision-maker; the idea that laws should be declared as precisely as possible in advance so that citizens can plan their affairs in the knowledge of how they will be applied; and the

[3] F Schauer, *Playing by the Rules: A Philosophical Examination of Rule-Based Decision-Making in Law and Life* (Oxford, OUP, 1991) ch 2.

[4] ibid, esp ch 2.

[5] ibid, 140.

[6] See, for example, L Alexander and E Sherwin, *The Rule of Rules: Morality, Rules and the Dilemmas of Law* (Durham, NC, Duke University Press, 2001); C Sunstein, *Legal Reasoning and Political Conflict* (Oxford, OUP, 1996) ch 1.

idea that cases should be determined directly by rules promulgated by the body with authority to lay down the law for all (ie the legislature or, in the context of the common law, earlier judges with sufficient authority in the judicial hierarchy).[7] If judges have the power to do what they like in applying the law, the law does not govern; the judge does. The rule of law therefore demands that legal rules exert sufficient control over a judge's decision.[8] The former end of the spectrum best alleviates those rule of law concerns. However, as Aristotle said, 'there are some things about which it is not possible to pronounce rightly in general terms'.[9] A bright-line rule may therefore purchase clarity at the expense of flexibility and a lack of responsiveness to what may be significant shifts in the balance between the competing values which the rule in question seeks to accommodate.[10]

III. Default Rules and their Role

From consideration of rules in general, I now turn to default rules and their role within the common law. The tension discussed above between flexibility and certainty is endemic throughout the law. HLA Hart saw all legal systems as the product of a compromise between these two social needs.[11] The force of one value as opposed to the other will vary by context.

The tension between these two values in a particular context can be accommodated or ameliorated through the design of a rule. For these reasons, many rules of law, which give priority to one particular value (or set of values), are defeasible:[12] they are default rules. In articulating these rules, judges can assign legal weight to incommensurable values, providing a reasonable degree of certainty without unduly abandoning flexibility. In so doing, the judicial scales are calibrated prior to the adjudication of a particular case. Rather than a simple 'no dogs allowed' rule, the rule may instead be formulated as 'no dogs allowed, *other than with the express agreement of the restaurant manager*'. Whilst that initial guidance or presumptive resolution regarding the weighting of competing values is open to change and can be overcome at the point of application of the rule, this will require a greater countervailing weight than would be the case if the scales were evenly balanced from the outset. The level of defeasibility will vary by context.

Default rules are a compromise between the certainty provided by bright-line rules and the flexibility provided by fact-specific adjudication. They seek to provide the best of both worlds by promoting the rule of law benefits of having a rule whilst alleviating

[7] P Sales, 'The General and the Particular: Parliament and the Courts under the Scheme of the European Convention on Human Rights' in M Andenas and D Fairgrieve (eds), *Tom Bingham and the Transformation of the Law: A Liber Amicorum* (Oxford, OUP, 2009) 170; Schauer (n 3) esp chs 5–8; Sunstein (n 6) esp chs 4–7; K Sullivan, 'Foreword: The Justices of Rules and Standards' (1992) 106 *Harvard L Rev* 24; R Posner, *How Judges Think* (Cambridge, Harvard University Press, 2010) 176 et seq.

[8] Sales and Wilmot-Smith (n 1) 590.

[9] Aristotle, *Nicomachean Ethics* (tr JAK Thomson, London, Penguin, 1976) 199.

[10] Sales and Wilmot-Smith (n 1) 593.

[11] HLA Hart, *The Concept of Law* (Oxford, OUP, 1961) 127. See also Lord Reid, 'The Judge as Law-Maker' (1972) 12 *Journal of the Society of Public Teachers of Law*. 22.

[12] JH Wilkinson III, 'Toward a Jurisprudence of Presumptions' (1992) 67 *NYU L Rev* 907.

the more severe errors brought about by pre-formulated rules of general application. However, it might be objected that, if a rule operates merely as a default or presumption, the rule itself is undermined. If the default rule can be overcome in certain circumstances, it might be said, the decision-maker needs to go through the same adjudicative process to decide if the defeasibility threshold has been met as would be the case if considering the matter afresh, without a rule. If dogs can, at all times, be permitted into the restaurant by the agreement of the restaurant manager, notwithstanding the preceding prohibition, why have the rule at all?

This objection misunderstands the role which a default rule plays. As Schauer has explained:

> It is one thing to inspect the world on the assumption that everything in it is part of the decision, and it is another thing to inspect the same world on the quite different assumption that something in it might but probably will not be relevant to the decision to be made. The latter process is more of a *glimpse* than any kind of careful scrutiny, and rules may exert their focusing function by determining what shall be examined with care and what shall only be glimpsed. And although the glimpse may in some cases indicate some reason to examine more closely that which was just glimpsed, the rules have their force in the way in which, in every case, they justify a much more casual examination than would otherwise have been the case.[13]

To return to the example, the proper operation of the 'no dogs allowed, other than …' rule does not allow the restaurant manager to displace the rule at will, in an open exercise of discretion. The default rule has a certain weight, depending on contextual factors such as (for example) the nature of the restaurant. Its weight may also depend on how it is phrased or structured, since it may be formulated in a way which indicates that its displacement is possible to a greater or lesser degree: a rule that 'dogs are allowed other than those expelled by the manager' would tend to make it harder for a dog to be excluded.[14] In a high-end restaurant, for example, the importance of preventing disturbances to customers will be high, allowing a high tolerance for over-inclusiveness, leading to a higher threshold for displacing the presumptive rule. The restaurant manager will not need to undergo full scrutiny on every occasion a dog appears at a restaurant; he or she can merely 'glimpse' the situation, given the presumptive weight of the rule, and swiftly be guided by the rule to the conclusion that the dog should not be permitted. In the exceptional case, however, such as a guide dog, the rule may be displaced. In doing so, the benefits of the rule of law values can be realised, whilst the sharpest corners of errors can be mitigated.

There are four main purposes served by default rules within the common law which I will explore in this chapter. These purposes are promoted both at the level of the structure of the common law as a legal system governed by the doctrine of precedent and at the level of the detail of specific rules laid down by judges operating within that system:

1) *Saving transaction (and other) costs*: default rules save the parties the time and expense of expressly agreeing and recording all the terms of their agreement.

[13] Schauer (n 3) 230 (emphasis in the original).

[14] Sunstein (n 6), ch 1 has a good discussion of the different drafting techniques and the different effects they have in terms of making a default rule presumptively stronger or weaker.

Such default rules maximise the aggregate welfare of the contracting parties (or society as a whole), notwithstanding that one of the parties may end up worse off as a result.[15] Whilst these default rules may provide for terms that the parties would themselves have chosen anyway,[16] that is not necessarily the case. They may seek to improve the parties' bargain, rather than merely helping them to reach the (possibly sub-optimal) terms that they would have otherwise chosen. Default rules may therefore aspire to mimic the terms that would be chosen by idealised contracting parties who enjoy perfect information, face zero transaction costs, and seek to maximise their joint gains.[17]

Precedent as the basis for a legal system can also save on transaction costs, in two ways. First, from the perspective of the parties, the legal certainty and predictability afforded by a system of precedent reduces transaction costs by allowing them reasonably to predict and anticipate the legal consequences of their actions. The common law is itself, in a sense, a collection of default rules formed (at least predominantly) through precedent which create the legal framework by which parties live and the background against which they can bargain with each other for different outcomes, should they choose them. Second, from the perspective of the court and on a wider view of cost saving, the resource burden is drastically reduced by the availability of a compendium of precedent, providing ready-made answers to the same or similar legal questions. A need to decide each legal dispute afresh would, inevitably, create a significant burden.

2) *Injection (or prioritisation) of values*: as mentioned above, the creation of default rules crystallises competing values into a pre-formed compromise or resolution. The deployment of those rules as precedent – and particularly from apex courts downwards through the judicial hierarchy, along the transmission lines constituted by the relevant conception of authority in the judicial system – allows certain values to be prioritised in the common law. It ensures judges do not ignore, at the point of application of legal rules, certain special values which the system as a whole has picked out as having special weight. Whilst such values might be defeated in any particular case by a value or set of values which happen to have overwhelming force in that specific situation (which is a condition of a rule being defeasible), a judge must grapple directly with why that is and justify the non-application of the presumptive rule by reference to compelling competing values which are themselves worthy of respect. By way of example, default rules in contract may seek to prioritise autonomy and consent over fairness, but in certain marginal contexts fairness may inform, qualify or even result in the disapplication of the presumptive autonomy-focused rules. Similarly, default rules in tort may seek to prioritise certain core interests of persons (such as bodily integrity) over consent, unless perhaps the consent is especially precisely targeted and well-informed.
3) *Rule of law principles*: I have set out the rule of law concerns associated with the balancing of incommensurables and the way in which bright-line rules can alleviate

[15] CA Riley, 'Designing Default Rules in Contract: Consent, Conventionalism and Efficiency' (2000) 20 *OJLS* 367, 384. See also G Helleringer, ch 3 in this volume.

[16] D Charny, 'Hypothetical Bargains: The Normative Structure of Contract Interpretation' (1991) 89 *Michigan L Rev* 1815, 1840–48. See also B Häcker, ch 1 in this volume.

[17] Riley (n 15) 385. See also L Gullifer, ch 9 in this volume.

those concerns by ruling out reference back to the underlying value compromise which justifies them in the first place and the way in which default rules can alleviate those concerns by limiting the extent to which such reference back may be made and the extent to which that value compromise (and hence the rule itself) may be displaced. Such principles are a subset of the broader 'injection of values' purpose discussed above. The choice between a mandatory, non-defeasible bright-line rule or a default, presumptive rule, and how strong the presumptive rule is, will reflect the extent to which importance is assigned to controlling what a judge does at the point of application of the rule (thereby limiting decision-maker error). It will also reflect the importance attached in a given context to promoting predictability of outcome, which may be relevant to allowing parties to know where they will stand if a matter comes to court and hence may assist them to bargain 'in the shadow of the law' without the need to have recourse to it. The choice may also reflect the need within certain legal regimes to avoid capricious or arbitrary differences in outcomes between the same or similar cases. The formulation of a rule, and constraints on the application of that rule in future cases, promote legal certainty, predictability, and consistency across the law. The mere existence of a rule is of particular importance given the context of value pluralism. Whilst we cannot unequivocally say, a priori, that one answer is better than another, we cannot let the best be the enemy of the good in failing to articulate any answer (in a rule) at all. The consistent application of a position through a rule is, itself, valuable. Indeed, it may be the highest the law can aspire to. However, use of a default rule allows scope for recognition of particularly compelling combinations of countervailing values to be recognised as justifying different legal outcomes towards the margins of the underlying rationale for the rule itself.

4) *Addressing information asymmetries*: a more adjudicative function of default rules is to create structures for the alleviation of information asymmetries and incentivisation of parties to fully cooperate in a bargaining process or in the adjudicative process.

At a more general level, the common law system of precedent operates as a system of default rules. Every common law rule (even those formulated as non-defeasible bright-line rules) is in theory capable of being overridden if later judges, having sufficient authority in the system, decide it should not be followed – although some rules are more embedded and immoveable than others. This has led Schauer to describe the common law as a system of 'presumptive positivism', which directly draws upon the value of default rules (which he terms presumptive rules):

> Commonly [common law rules, including those established by precedent,] will be presumptive rather than absolute, thereby providing some constraint while allowing for the possibility of override in particularly exigent circumstances. When rules or their equivalents function in this presumptive manner, the values served by rules are promoted but tempered by the way in which presumptions … allow a decision-maker to retain the ability to glimpse at the full array of available factors to determine if this case is a case in which those factors might provide a reason of such exceptional strength as to provide a stronger reason for overcoming the exclusion of those factors than the rule provides for the exclusion itself.[18]

[18] Schauer (n 3) 196–97.

A final point here is to consider to whom the default rule is addressed. Whilst some default rules are nominally directed towards the court, their primary target is the parties. This is most obvious in substantive rules, such as in contract and tort, but also within precedent itself as a system of default rules. An important institutional and functional limitation of the court in a common law system is that it only adjudicates upon the particular dispute brought before the courts by the parties, who argue for a view of the facts and the law which offers them victory. Therefore:

> The parties set the ambit of their dispute and present the materials which they say are relevant to its determination. The court does not conduct a roving inquiry into all factors which might potentially influence a legislature seeking to frame a law appropriate for a particular topic. The law is born out of the argument of party versus party, almost as a side product of the resolution of specific disputes. Accordingly, a court's law-making [or, in this context, we could say rule-making] function, though it can be real, is set within modest parameters.[19]

The system of precedent is therefore facilitative to the parties, informing them of the rules of the game and the route to victory, and thereby helping them to define the case and assemble the evidence which they bring to court. It is the parties' role to argue as to whether a particular ratio decidendi does (or does not) apply, why that is the case and the relevant consequences. Similarly, if a party is seeking to overturn precedent in the Supreme Court, that is a matter for them to raise and to engage with the relevant test, which I discuss below. Further, where the law creates other forms of default rules for a court (eg governing the exercise of a discretion which the court enjoys) the presumptive burden falls on the party who seeks to persuade the court to override the rule's presumptive effect, since it is that party who has to marshal arguments and evidence to persuade the court to do so.

I now turn to consider default rules in practice, first by reference to their internal aspect (in the substantive law and as adjudicative mechanisms) and second by reference to their external aspect (as precedent).

IV. Substantive Rules: The Internal Aspect of Precedent as a Default Rule

A. Contract

The parties to a contract are free to determine the primary obligations that they will accept. These obligations will typically be set out in express terms, in which case they will (ordinarily) be determinative. But express terms are not the sole source of contractual obligations.[20] Whether through inertia, lack of opportunity or foresight, or deliberate choice, parties will not have negotiated express terms to cover certain significant contingencies.[21]

[19] Sales (n 2) 55.
[20] See, for example, *Photo Production Ltd v Securicor Transport Ltd* [1980] AC 827, 848 (Lord Diplock).
[21] *Barton v Gwyn-Jones* [2023] UKSC 3, [2023] AC 684 at [128] per Lord Leggatt.

Many default rules in contract apply to contracts of all types. For example, it is unusual for a contract explicitly to state that a breach of an obligation within it will render the other party liable to pay damages for losses caused by the breach. However, such a consequence is the basis of contractual remedies. Indeed, most damages issues arise from the default rules which the law devises to give effect to principles of compensation.[22] This is seen in the rules of remoteness, causation, mitigation, and so on. These may be overridden by agreement, if the parties choose to do so.

Other default rules apply only to certain types of contracts, such as for the sale of goods.[23] Lord Radcliffe suggested that 'the corpus of commercial law has been built up largely by [the] process of supplying from the common usage of the trade what is the unexpressed intention of the parties'.[24] Lord Steyn employed 'default rules' terminology, used more widely in the United States, in relation to implied terms. He described how terms implied by law operate as 'general default rules' and how terms implied by fact (according to the business efficacy or officious bystander test) operate as 'ad hoc gap fillers'.[25]

By reason of the default nature of these rules, the parties are able to reject or modify obligations which would otherwise be incorporated, by use of express terms.[26] The default rules thus fulfil a facilitative function. They provide a basic platform or menu of standard terms fashioned by reference to what are likely to be the reasonable expectations of the parties, which helps make the parties' bargain for them (thus promoting economic efficiency and doing justice between them) whilst also giving them a background against which they can bargain in a more focused way for what they want to achieve by their agreement.

Saving transaction costs is an obvious reason for having such contractual default rules, and is itself a value which the common law recognises and to which it gives weight in the formulation of doctrine in the precedents created by judges. Their calibration crystallises the balance of certain incommensurable values, protected by contract, subject to the overriding values of party autonomy and consent. At the same time, the use of default rules, through a system of precedent, saves contracts from being unenforceable through incompleteness (contrary to the intention of the parties) and promotes legal certainty and predictability, thereby alleviating rule of law concerns.

B. Tort

Many of the same issues will apply in the context of tort, though the primary obligations will not necessarily (and often will not) be imposed by agreement. In a given context a person may owe a duty of care to another, and be subject to remedies for its breach as set

[22] *Globalia Business Travel SAU (formerly TravelPlan SAU) of Spain v Fulton Shipping Inc of Panama* [2017] UKSC 43, [2017] 1 WLR 2581 at [29].

[23] Codified in the Sale of Goods Acts 1893 and, now, 1979. See also J Cartwright, ch 7 in this volume.

[24] *Tsakiroglou & Co Ltd v Noblee Thorl GmbH* [1962] AC 93, 122. See also the chapter by Gullifer, ch 9 in this volume.

[25] *Equitable Life Assurance Society v Hyman* [2002] 1 AC 408, 458–59.

[26] *Photo Production Ltd* (n 20).

out in the general law of tort. The duty of care is, typically, itself a default rule which is capable of being disapplied or modified by express agreement between the parties. The rules on remedies are default rules in the same way. Parties may contract out, or modify, the operation of those rules by sufficiently clear agreement. The ability to do so may be moderated by statute,[27] reflecting the limits of consent and party autonomy as values injected into the law, against which competing identified human values may have to be weighed, which will vary in the tort context.

The tacit consent of the parties is not in itself the rationale for default rules in a contract or tort setting. Whilst default rules may reflect the parties' tacit intentions – and the court may, in general terms, seek (objectively) to deduce what the parties thought, but which they failed to articulate, and may not even have been consciously addressing, at the moment of their agreement – a theory of tacit consent cannot provide a convincing or full rationale for such rules.[28] Primarily, this is because default rules will often come into play only when the legitimising power of the agreement is exhausted.[29] As a result, a theory based on consent, which purports to justify the binding force of actual promises, has limited implications for the content of the law's default rules.[30] Rather, it is the judges themselves, engaging in the activity of creating law by the formulation of doctrine in precedents laid down over time, who identify what they take to be the likely preferred rule which reasonable persons (as constructed by the judges) located in the parties' positions would have chosen. A focus on a theory of tacit consent can also misstate the problem which default rules seek to address. The real problem may not be unplanned contingencies, but rather the fact that parties may avoid gaps only by adopting otherwise suboptimal contractual arrangements.[31] In other words, the substantial resources required to effect any and all of the parties' intentions may itself undermine the coherence and efficiency of the agreement. Again, the judges bring their own practical experience to bear in laying down precedents articulating default rules which they believe reasonable persons so located would be likely to prefer, so sparing the parties the burden of negotiation to reach such a position for themselves.

C. Structured Discretions

Structured discretions present perhaps the clearest articulation of the rule design spectrum alluded to previously. These principles have been articulated by the Supreme Court in *AIC Ltd v Federal Airports Authority of Nigeria*.[32] This case was concerned with the weight to be given to the principle of finality in litigation in the context of the exercise of discretion by a judge in what, from one perspective, was a matter of the exercise of discretion in a case management decision (where, usually, the discretion for a judge is taken to be very wide and unconstrained). In considering when a judge should

[27] See, generally, the Unfair Contract Terms Act 1977 and the Consumer Rights Act 2015.
[28] Riley (n 15) 370–74.
[29] SJ Burton, 'Default Principles, Legitimacy, and the Authority of a Contract' (1993) 3 *Southern California Interdisciplinary LJ* 115, 117.
[30] R Craswell, 'Contract Law, Default Rules, and the Philosophy of Promising' (1989) 88 *Michigan L Rev* 489.
[31] Riley (n 15) 374.
[32] *AIC Ltd v Federal Airports Authority of Nigeria* [2022] UKSC 16; [2002] 1 WLR 3223.

reconsider a final judgment or order before that order has been sealed, the court held that 'a judge should not start from anything like neutrality or evenly-balanced scales'.[33] This was because of the particular weight to be given to the principle of finality in the judge's initial exercise of their discretion.

However, nor was it possible to pre-determine the balancing exercise entirely through the application of a bright-line rule. To do so would 'be to impose a straitjacket upon the judicial exercise of a discretionary jurisdiction', which would be 'alien to the essentially flexible nature of the judge's task when weighing competing considerations of potentially limitless variety against each other'.[34] Instead, '[a]n evaluative judgment has to be made, but it has to reflect and respect the importance in this context of the principle of finality'. That starting point creates a default rule, by structuring the exercise of discretion in a particular way.[35] In exercising that discretion, a judge 'will err in law if he or she does not act in accordance with the principles which govern that exercise'. Having considered bright-line rules at one end of the rule design spectrum, with structured discretions in the middle, the court went on to consider the other extreme: '[i]n other contexts, by contrast, a discretion may be more open-ended, such as in relation to ordinary case management decisions, and leave greater choice to the judge to decide the weight to be given to each factor'.[36]

D. Burdens and Standards of Proof and Information Asymmetry

A further form of default rule, serving an adjudicative function, is those which lay down burdens and standards of proof. Any such rule is a default rule: if the party tasked with overcoming an evidential threshold fails to do so, they will have failed on that particular cause of action or defence,[37] such failure being the default rule. Where these are matters specified in precedents created by judges, the question of on whom the relevant burden falls (and the standard of proof to be satisfied to discharge that burden) will, itself, reflect certain underlying values in the law as identified and articulated by the judges. Ordinarily, the claimant will be tasked with discharging the burden, given it is they who have made the allegation. It will therefore, in general terms, be harder to prove a claim than not to. By comparison, in the context of the criminal procedure, this architecture gives effect to the common law's value system to avoid the punishment of the innocent, even if doing so is at the expense of a failure in some cases to punish the guilty.[38]

[33] ibid, at [32].

[34] ibid, at [33].

[35] Which, the court noted at [37], arise quite often in the law: eg the principles governing the grant of injunctive relief (*American Cyanamid Co v Ethicon Ltd* [1975] AC 396; *Fourie v Le Roux* [2007] UKHL 1, [2007] 1 WLR 320 at [16], [25] and [30]) and the exercise of discretion regarding service out of the jurisdiction (*Spiliada Maritime Corpn v Cansulex Ltd* [1987] AC 460; *VTB Capital Plc v Nutritek International Corpn* [2013] UKSC 5, [2013] 2 AC 337).

[36] *AIC Ltd v Federal Airports Authority of Nigeria* (n 32) at [37].

[37] See *FII (SC) 2* [2020] UKSC 47, [2022] AC 1 at [210].

[38] This is reflected in Blackstone's old adage that '[i]t is better that ten guilty persons escape than that one innocent suffer'.

This in itself demonstrates the lack of tolerance for over-inclusiveness in rule design, given the stakes involved in a criminal context. The differing standards between the criminal and civil procedures reflects the greater coercive power of the state consequent on an adverse finding in the former than the latter, and the underlying values of freedom and justice implicitly (but powerfully) endorsed by the common law. By contrast, a balance of probabilities standard of proof in civil procedure reflects the fact that for one side to win means that the other loses, while the background value context for favouring one outcome rather than the other is more or less evenly balanced.

However, the burden of proof will not always and for all purposes fall upon the party asserting the claim. The circumstances in which there is a departure from this reveal a further purpose of default rules. The historic example is *Armory v Delamirie*.[39] In that case, the defendant goldsmith had retained a jewel given to him by the claimant (a chimney-sweeper's boy who had found the jewel and had taken it to the defendant to find out what it was worth) and would not produce it for it to be valued for the purposes of the damages claim brought against him. The Chief Justice's direction to the jury was that 'unless the defendant produce the jewel and show it not to be of the finest water, they should presume the strongest against him, and make the value of the best jewels the measure of their damages'. It was not acceptable for the defendant to fail to participate fully in the adjudicative process, seeking to rely on information asymmetry to render the claimant unable to discharge the usual evidential burden upon him. Instead, where a party has sole or privileged access to evidence relevant to the determination of a claim but elects not to bring forward that evidence, the court may draw inferences of fact against that party, and thereby deviate from the default rule.[40]

Another example, in the context of security for costs, is the stifling principle. The burden is on the party resisting security for costs, in claiming that its claim would be stifled by virtue of an order to provide security, to that its claim would indeed be stifled; it has the best information about this, and the law puts the onus on it to explain the position with full candour.[41] The use of default rules in this context injects values of equality of arms, whilst also furthering principles of justice in facilitating the court's ability fairly and properly to adjudicate in a dispute. The mechanism also incentivises both parties to cooperate fully with the judicial process, which can save costs.

A classic example of another common law rule which addresses information asymmetry is the rule in *Hadley v Baxendale*,[42] which governs remoteness of damage in claims for breach of contract. A party will only be able to claim for 'abnormal damages', that is, beyond what might have been expected in the ordinary course of events as contemplated by both parties at the time of contracting, if the other party is actually aware (when the contract is made) of the likelihood of such loss being incurred. As a result, a claimant who is (privately) aware that it will suffer abnormally high losses if the contract

[39] (1721) 93 ER 664.

[40] See *The Law Debenture Trust Co Plc v Elektrim* [2009] EWHC 1801 (Ch), [2009] 7 WLUK 535 at [176]; *AstraZeneca AB v KRKA dd Novo Mesto* [2014] EWHC 84 (Pat), [2014] 1 WLUK 565 at [41]–[42].

[41] See, for example, *Responsible Development for Abaco (RDA) Ltd v Christie* [2023] UKPC 2, [2023] 4 WLR 47 at [67].

[42] (1854) 9 Exch 341.

is breached will not be able to recover those losses unless they bring this information to the attention of the defendant at the time of contracting, thereby giving the defendant an opportunity to bargain regarding whether and to what extent to accept responsibility for such potential losses in the case of breach. The default rule remains in place to allow recovery of a 'normal' level of damages, unless and until that party displaces the rule through disclosure. However, this also incentivises the provision of information to enhance the bargaining process.

V. Precedent: The External Structural Aspect

So far, I have dealt with the internal aspect of precedent as a default rule, in a substantive or adjudicative context. I now turn to the external aspect, which is to address, at a higher (or meta) level, the nature of the common law itself as a default system. This has two dimensions. First, when a rule has already been created by an existing precedent, there is the way in which it is applied (or not) or distinguished (or not) as a potential constraint in the adjudicative process. Second, and of equal or perhaps even greater interest for present purposes, is when superior judges, and particularly judges in the Supreme Court, decide that the particular balance of values crystallised by an existing rule (precedent) is imperfect and the rule should be remade (thereby returning to the internal aspect of rule creation).

A. The First Dimension: Whether the Rule Applies

The first dimension is a distinguishing feature of reasoning from precedent as opposed to reasoning from a rule.[43] It introduces an antecedent question: what is the rule? The factual predicate of a rule, a generalisation necessarily encompassing a multiplicity of events, is part of the rule's canonical formation. Where the 'rule' is a previous decision without express rule-formulation, the source of the factual predicate is obscure, and consequently the manner in which the previous decision constrains subsequent decision-making becomes problematic.[44] In order to proceed, the ratio decidendi must first be established to provide the rule. This may be more or less difficult, depending on the case, and the parties will often disagree. Even where the core of the rule is identified, its lack of canonical formation will often leave the edges, in terms of the rule's scope and applicability, unclear and undefined. However, identifying and applying the ratio decidendi – the rule – is routine for the common lawyer, through the orthodox application of reasoning by analogy and principle.[45] The core of the rule will ordinarily be clear, even if the boundaries are not.

[43] Schauer (n 3) 183.
[44] ibid.
[45] S Green and P Sales, 'Law, Technology and the Common Law Method in the United Kingdom' (2023) 34(5) *Europäische Zeitschrift für Wirtschaftsrecht* 212.

Once the rule has been identified, the second question will be whether it applies to the present case and what the consequences of applicability are. The nature of the rule (and the applicable freedom or constraint of a judge when deciding whether to apply it) will vary depending on the court applying the rule and the court from where the rule derives. However, according to the orthodox application of a superior court precedent in a lower court, the judge is to apply the rule or, if he or she determines that the ratio decidendi does not apply, they can consider whether to distinguish it (thereby justifying non-applicability) and articulate another rule to be applied instead (of course, they might decide that although not strictly bound by the previous authority, the reason for the rule it laid down does extend to cover the case at hand).[46] Some rules will be obviously applicable; some will be obviously inapplicable. However, where there is some uncertainty, though the rule appears to (at least) nominally apply, and a judge distinguishes it, they add or subtract factors thought to be of sufficient importance to take the case outside the rule.

Once the antecedent hurdles of rule identification and delimitation are passed, ordinary rule-based reasoning applies. The precedent rule, by which a norm formulated by a superior court is imposed on a lower court, is therefore a bright-line rule. If it applies, it is an indefeasible, pre-formulated crystallisation of the resultant of the vectors of competing values which must be applied to the present case. The operation of precedent is an important means of ensuring that the law is clear and predictable.[47] However, such values may come at the price of flexibility. From the late nineteenth century until the 1966 Practice Statement was issued,[48] the House of Lords[49] could not depart from its previous decisions at all.[50] This inflexibility led to what has been described as 'judicial gymnastics' as the Law Lords sought to distinguish precedent that they did not wish to follow.[51] That was itself damaging to certainty and consistency, the very values the rule sought to promote.[52] By 1966, there was an acceptance that greater flexibility was needed to enable the highest court to correct wrong turns and to enable the common law to develop in response to changes in society.[53] The previous bright-line rule was an imperfect balance of competing values requiring reformulation.

[46] See generally, J Raz, 'Law and Value in Adjudication' in *The Authority of Law: Essays on Law and Morality* (Oxford, OUP, 1979).

[47] See, for example, *Knauer v Ministry of Justice* [2016] UKSC 9, [2016] AC 908 at [21] per Lord Neuberger and Lady Hale.

[48] Practice Statement (Judicial Precedent) [1966] 1 WLR 1234.

[49] For readers outside the United Kingdom, the Appellate Committee of the House of Lords was the predecessor to the United Kingdom Supreme Court, which was created by the Constitutional Reform Act 2005. Judges there were 'Lords of Appeal in Ordinary', also referred to as 'Law Lords'; judges of the Supreme Court are referred to as 'Justices'. The 1966 Practice Statement provided the test for when the Law Lords could overturn their own decisions and continues to apply to the Supreme Court.

[50] The doctrine of self-binding precedent is usually attributed to *London Tramways v London County Council* [1898] AC 375. However, the rule that the Appellate Committee of the House of Lords was bound by its own previous decisions can be traced to earlier decisions. See D Pugsley, 'London Tramways (1898)' (1996) 17 *Journal of Legal History* 172 and L Blom-Cooper, '1966 and All That: The Story of the Practice Statement' in L Blom-Cooper, B Bickson and G Drewry (eds), *The Judicial House of Lords 1876–2009* (Oxford, OUP, 2009) 129.

[51] N Duxbury, 'Final Court Jurisprudence in the Crystallisation Era' (2023) 139 *LQR* 153, 159.

[52] *R v National Insurance Commissioner, ex parte Hudson* [1972] AC 944, 966 (Lord Reid).

[53] See Blom-Cooper (n 50); A Paterson, *Final Judgment: The Last Law Lords and the Supreme Court* (Oxford, Hart, 2013) 263–68.

B. The Second Dimension: Whether the Rule should be Remade

So, the question arises at the highest level: when can a judge overturn precedent? The nature of the rule depends both on the court applying the rule and the court which originally formulated it. In broad terms, focusing on the superior courts in England and Wales: (i) High Court judges are bound by decisions of the Court of Appeal and the Supreme Court; and (ii) the Court of Appeal is bound by decisions of the Supreme Court.[54] Further rules are introduced when it comes to courts of co-ordinate jurisdiction. So, in broad terms (a) High Court judges are not technically bound by decisions of their peers, but they should generally follow a decision of a court of co-ordinate jurisdiction unless there is a powerful reason for not doing so;[55] (b) subject to limited exceptions, the Court of Appeal will bind itself;[56] and (c) the Supreme Court, under the 1966 Practice Statement, regards its decisions (or those of the House of Lords) as 'normally binding', but it will depart from them 'when it appears right to do so'.[57]

At each level, therefore, the same (or similar) values are attributed different weight, resulting in differently structured rules, from bright-line rules to structured discretions. I will explore this balance principally by reference to the test applied by the Supreme Court under the 1966 Practice Statement.

There are various meta-values – values about how the law's rules should be modified or maintained – which affect whether the power under the Practice Statement should be invoked.[58] The rule within the Practice Statement is structurally different from the equivalent rules in lower courts. Whilst still restrictive, it explicitly provides for defeasibility in certain circumstances. In exploring the circumstances where this defeasibility is available, it is clear that the benefits flowing from predictability and certainty in the law continue to weigh heavily in the scales.

Before considering the operation of the Practice Statement, it is instructive to consider the impact of *who* is applying a particular rule on the design of the rule itself. This helps explain why the rule applicable to the Supreme Court might differ to the rules applicable to lower courts.

Rules serve primarily as vehicles for the allocation of power and the extent to which a system adopts rule-based decision-making modes is likely to embody social judgements about the distribution of jurisdiction.[59] It is not just that we want a clear rule, such as 'no dogs allowed', it is also that we want outcomes to be determined by the rule, rather than at the discretion of a particular waiter on a particular night. As set out by Schauer:

> Rules, including legal rules, apportion decision-making authority among various individuals and institutions, reflecting a society's decisions about who will decide what, who is to

[54] *Willers v Gubay* [2016] UKSC 44, [2018] AC 843 at [5].
[55] ibid, at [9]; *Roberts (A Child) v Soldiers, Sailors, Airmen and Families Association-Forces Help* [2019] EWHC 1104 (QB), [2019] 5 WLUK 34.
[56] *Young v Bristol Aeroplane Co* [1944] KB 718, [1944] 2 All ER 293.
[57] Practice Statement (n 48).
[58] Sales and Wilmot-Smith (n 1) 595–96.
[59] Schauer (n 3) 173.

> be trusted and who not, who is to be empowered and who not, whose decisions are to be reviewed and whose are to be final, and who is to give orders and who is to take them.[60]

We can see these considerations at each stage of the judicial hierarchy when considering the rules on whether and when a court may depart from precedent. Given the importance of the rule-based values set out above, our legal system has explicitly distributed jurisdiction only to the Supreme Court, as the apex court, to overturn its own decisions and those of the courts below.

This reflects an allocative function, but also a related functional one. As noted above, rules are sub-optimal, because of their inherent under- or -over-inclusiveness. We accept this type of error partly in exchange for a reduction in decision-making errors, that is, errors at the point of application of a norm by the decision-maker. A very clear rule offers more limited scope for it to be applied wrongly through error by the decision-maker, even if that clarity comes at the cost of insensitivity to the particular facts and therefore under- or over- inclusiveness errors, where the source of potential errors lies in the formulation of the rule itself. By contrast, a highly open-textured rule allows greater sensitivity to the particular facts in its application, so that its application can be tailored to eliminate or reduce under- or over-inclusiveness, but such discretion will inevitably invite and increase decision-making errors at that stage, on the part of the decision-maker. The two types of errors are inversely related: an increase in one will generally lead to a decrease in the other, and vice versa.

Against the backdrop of the rule of law values promoted by having a rule, we trade one type of error for the other in designing a particular rule. The risk and frequency of these errors depends, at least in part, on who will be making the decisions.[61] The Justices of the Supreme Court are the most senior and experienced in our judiciary. Where the court has been asked to overrule a previous decision of its own, or of the House of Lords, it sits in an enlarged panel to consider the question.[62] The risk of decision-maker error might therefore be thought to be (at least potentially) lower in such circumstances. If we accept that such a risk might be lower, we may feel more confident about introducing more open-textured rules, thereby (it is hoped) reducing errors arising from the form of the rule itself. If the potential for decision-maker error is lower, it reduces the pressure to seek a reduction in that type of error by creating more hard-edged rules which carry their own distinct risk of error. This creates space to reduce rule-based error, where we think the potential for decision-maker error might be lower, thereby (potentially) lowering the aggregate risks of errors arising from both sources. This partly explains why the Practice Statement, applicable only to the Supreme Court, as the apex court, to precedent, has a relatively significant level of defeasibility in its default rule.

However, the threshold to overrule a precedent remains high. This can be seen in the operation of the 1966 Practice Statement and, in particular, by considering the values which will *not* be sufficient to override the default rule. The most obvious is that judges cannot, and should not, update the rule simply because they take a different view about

[60] ibid.
[61] Schauer (n 3) 152.
[62] See the 'Panel numbers criteria' on the Supreme Court website: www.supremecourt.uk/procedures/panel-numbers-criteria.html.

where the balance of competing values should lie.[63] That is reflective of the pluralistic backdrop I have explained. Where it is difficult to say that an updated rule is unequivocally better than an earlier one, then rule-conservatism in the interests of predictability favours the status quo. This reveals a significant compromise which the law is willing to make. Such weight is attributed to the values of predictability and certainty that, even where the Supreme Court considers a previous decision to be wrong, that will not be sufficient to overcome the default rule. Thus, the default rule set out in the Practice Statement is willing to tolerate the sub-optimality inherent in a rule formed by precedent,[64] in exchange for the benefits of *having* a rule. Even though the Practice Statement formulates the relevant rule as a defeasible default rule to allow the Supreme Court to overturn its own decisions in a way which is not available elsewhere in the judicial hierarchy, the toleration for rule-based errors remains significantly greater than tolerance for decision-maker errors, given the rule of law values in play. Such a sentiment was reflected by Justice Louis Brandeis of the Supreme Court of the United States in suggesting that 'in most matters it is more important that the applicable rule of law be settled than that it be settled right';[65] in the English Court of Chancery, it was similarly suggested, 'better that the law should be certain than that every judge should speculate on improvements'.[66]

In what circumstances, then, will the defeasibility inherent in the rule become operative? To maintain its legitimacy, the law must be kept in line with social expectations. As the community's commitments on the best balance of incommensurable values shift, so, eventually, must the law's.[67] This balance is reflected in the wording of the Practice Statement. It begins by emphasising the importance of precedent in providing 'at least some degree of certainty upon which individuals can rely in the conduct of their affairs, as well as a basis for orderly development of legal rules'. It goes on to recognise, however, that 'too rigid adherence to precedent may lead to injustice in a particular case and also unduly restrict the proper development of the law'. The default rule favours the status quo; its presumptive weight is heavy and difficult to displace. The court will be 'very circumspect'[68] before accepting an invitation to invoke the Practice Statement, because it considers it to be 'important not to undermine the role of precedent and the certainty which it promotes'.[69] The discretion is therefore constrained, albeit formulated as allowing departure from precedent when it appears 'right to do so'.

[63] *Peninsula Securities Ltd v Dunnes Stores (Bangor) Ltd* [2020] UKSC 36, [2021] AC 1014 at [49] (Lord Wilson), citing *Horton v Sadler* [2007] 1 AC 307 at [29] (Lord Bingham). See also H Dagan, *Reconstructing American Legal Realism & Rethinking Private Law Theory* (Oxford, OUP, 2013), 194: '[b]ecause private law institutions are supposed to consolidate expectations and express ideals of interpersonal relationships, private law pluralism supports, even requires, relatively stable and internally coherent – albeit properly narrow – doctrinal categories'.

[64] Schauer (n 3) chs 2–4.

[65] *Burnet v Coronado Oil & Gas Co* (1932) 285 US 393, 406 (Brandeis J, dissenting).

[66] *Sheldon v Goodrich* (1803) 8 Ves 481, 497, 32 Eng Rep 441, 447.

[67] See, for example, the account in Dagan (n 63); cf B Cardozo, *The Paradoxes of Legal Science* (New York, Columbia University Press, 1928) 51: 'The common will must have made itself known for so long a time as well as in so distinct a manner as to have gained stability and authority'; for discussion see Sales (n 2).

[68] *Knauer v Ministry of Justice* (n 47) at [23] (Lord Neuberger and Lady Hale).

[69] *Henderson v Dorset Healthcare University NHS Foundation Trust* [2020] UKSC 43, [2021] AC 563 at [87] (Lord Hamblen).

Whilst this is rather amorphous in the abstract, the context of the exercise – in which competing meta-values of legal certainty and flexibility in the interests of maintaining the legitimacy of the law fall to be balanced through the structure of a default rule – is well known to the court. The question is always whether the disruptive movement of social and other values have reached sufficient force to displace the incumbent weight of legal certainty and predictability. That tipping point will vary according to the particular context.

There is, for example, a particular need for certainty in relation to property transactions, as the 1966 Practice Statement makes clear. In general terms, it will be easier to reconsider a recent precedent than one which has stood for a long time, since people are more likely to have relied on a decision in the latter category.[70] The court may be quicker to reconsider a decision which is thought to be impeding the proper development of the law,[71] or is clearly causing uncertainty,[72] administrative difficulties or individual injustice.[73] However, the court will be slower to overrule a previous decision where it risks retrospectively disturbing the basis on which contracts and other commercial transactions have been entered into. The court will be slower to reverse decisions on detailed questions of construction of legislation or other documents, which are often a matter of impression, than broader questions raising issues of legal principle.[74] The court will also consider whether any proposed change in the law is so complex, or carries with it potential injustices or wider implications, so that the matter is more appropriately left to the legislature.[75]

VI. Conclusion

Precedent operates as a system of default rules both in its internal and external aspect. The reach of default rules through these combined aspects is extensive, permeating the entire body of the common law. The prevalence of default rules as a form of rule design within the common law should therefore be better understood. The use of default rules in this context can achieve, or contribute towards, the maximised realisation of a range of goals, including by tempering rule of law concerns brought about by the incommensurability inherent in pluralism. Default rules can serve a compromise function, promoting rule of law values in the clear articulation of a presumptive rule so far as it is possible or appropriate to do so, whilst permitting sufficient flexibility in rule application to avoid the worst excesses of rule-based error. This approach therefore balances rule-based and decision-maker errors in a way which is capable of adjustment in particular contexts in an attempt to limit the scope for errors occurring in each one. Nonetheless, in view of the importance of the rule of law values at the heart of the

[70] *Ex parte Hudson* (n 52) 993 (Viscount Dilhorne).
[71] ibid, 966 (Lord Reid).
[72] *Oldendorff v Tradax Export* [1974] AC 479, 533 and 535 (Lord Reid).
[73] *Ex parte Hudson* (n 52) 1024 (Lord Simon of Glaisdale).
[74] *Ex parte Hudson* (n 52) 966 (Lord Reid) and 1024 (Lord Simon of Glaisdale). See also *R v G* [2004] 1 AC 1034 at [30]–[35] (Lord Bingham).
[75] *Ex parte Hudson* (n 52) 1025 (Lord Simon of Glaisdale); *Knauer* (n 47) at [26].

legal system and of which that system as a whole is an expression, there is a marked preference to seek protection against the risk of decision-maker error, which requires the adoption of binding rules. This set of priorities is reflected in the authority system inherent in the judicial hierarchy, extending down from the Supreme Court. Where the Supreme Court considers that the particular balance of values crystallised by an existing rule (precedent) is imperfect, it is open to this Court in narrow circumstances to recast the particular rule, returning from the external to the internal aspect of precedent. In each case, the exercise is the displacement of a default rule, namely the (defeasible) rule that precedents should be followed.

6

Default Rules as a Means of European Integration

JÜRGEN BASEDOW[†]

I. Concepts: Default Rules, European Integration and European Private Law

The topic of this chapter requires some preliminary observations on concepts. The English term 'default rules' results from the perspective of a contract that does not contain rules on certain issues; it is 'defaulting' in this respect. The same perspective also underlies the French term '*règles supplétives*'. This perspective focuses on supplementing an agreement and does not appear to address contractual modifications of legal rules. By contrast, the German concept of '*dispositives Recht*'[1] and the Italian equivalent of '*norme derogabili*'[2] refer to legal rules as being subject to private modification; that is the starting point of the classification. The difference is noteworthy since the supplementation of an incomplete text differs from the modification of legal rules and provisions. However, the difference does not seem to have significant consequences: all four legal systems recognise freedom of contract as a basic principle governing, in particular, the law of contract. Thus, it does not matter whether default rules are conceived as supplementing an agreement that exhibits some gaps, or the contract as replacing and modifying rules of law that would otherwise apply. The precedence of the contract and freedom of contract are acknowledged in any event.

When legal scholars talk about 'European integration' they usually think of an increase of commonalities in the field of law: a growth of the *acquis* of EU law, closer academic links between legal scholars in various European countries, the gradual emergence of common principles and concepts, the publication of European textbooks and

[†] The publication of this chapter is posthumous (see the note in the Preface of this book); the author has thus not approved the final version of the text, which was finalised by Jannis Gries without any changes or additions to the substantive content as it stood at the time of the conference in March 2023.

[1] See F Möslein, *Dispositives Recht* (Tübingen, Mohr Siebeck, 2011) 9.

[2] See CU Majello, 'Situazioni soggetive et rapporti giuridici' in M Bessone (ed), *Istituzioni di diritto privato* 4th edn (Torino, Giappichelli, 1997) 64, 72 et seq, as well as G Alpa, 'Disciplina generale dei contratti', in Bessone (ibid) 523, 538 et seq.

law journals, the foundation of European professional associations or the establishment of European institutions. While European integration can certainly be promoted by these activities, it reaches far beyond the sphere of law and legal scholarship. Integration is a concept of the social sciences and relates to a process. In the course of this process the participants who were initially separate are increasingly perceived as belonging to a common group, even if they keep their independence within that group. This wide concept is applied to very small groups such as the family and extends to very large groups such as the European Union.[3] Integration can be assessed from the perspective of the participants, that is to say, from inside, but also from outside, in the case of European integration for example from a Chinese or American perspective. Integration is dynamic, as reflected in the founding treaties of the European Union, which refer to 'an ever closer union among the peoples of Europe'.[4] It is moreover not an objective fact, but a matter of subjective perception, which is not confined to governments, but includes the peoples, that is, private persons as relevant participants.

Numerous forces in all parts of society may promote integration in this sense. When we talk about the specifically legal aspect of European integration, we should keep in mind that economic exchange, touristic contacts, sporting events and competitions, cultural meetings and many other encounters strengthen the feeling of commonality of Europeans. The same is true of the growing commitment to common values and symbols. All in all, and by contrast to many other integration projects around the world, European integration can be conceived as bottom-up integration to be promoted by private parties. The shift from top-down to bottom-up integration was the basic decision taken in the 1950s after the failure of the top-down integration model envisaged by the European Defence Community in 1952.[5]

'European private law' lies at the crossroads of private law and European integration. The concept is, however, far from unambiguous. It includes the multiple enactments of the European Union dealing with private relations, that is, EU private law. It also embraces a body of non-binding principles and proposals submitted by groups of scholars from various European countries and covering areas such as contract law, security interests, insurance contracts, private international law and even family law. A third component are uniform law conventions on various matters, especially in commercial law and transport law; although many of these instruments have a universal scope, they constitute compromises that have essentially been achieved through cross-fertilising processes of legal comparison between European legal systems. Further contributions to European private law have been made by the common legal history going back to Roman law. All this constitutes an amorphous body of precise provisions, non-binding rules, general principles and values and cross-fertilising ideas. Much like the private law taught in the major law schools of the United States, this body of European private

[3] See R Münch, 'Integration: Social' in N Smelser and P Baltes (eds), *International Encyclopaedia of the Social & Behavioural Sciences*, vol 11 (Amsterdam, Elsevier, 2011) 7591, 7594.

[4] See the first paragraph of the Preamble of the Treaty on the Functioning of the European Union (TFEU), consolidated version in [2016] OJ C202/1; in a similar vein, several paragraphs of the Preamble of the Treaty on European Union (TEU) refer to the 'peoples'.

[5] For further references, see J Basedow, *EU Private Law – Anatomy of a Growing Legal Order* (Cambridge, Intersentia, 2021) para I-15 et seq (in the following, all citations of this book are by reference to chapter and para number).

law cannot be said to be 'in force' anywhere, but it is constantly evolving into a realm of common legal thought. The binding portions tying everything together are some international conventions and the enactments of the European Union.

The following considerations on default rules will focus on EU private law. It will however turn out that default rules of European private law in a broader sense are indispensable both for the functioning of the Internal Market and for a more comprehensive integration of the national legal systems. To this end, we shall first take a closer look at the Internal Market (Section II) and thereafter inventorise existing default rules in EU private law (Section III); the final Section IV will address the functions of default private law rules as a tool of further integration.

II. The Internal Market and Default Rules

A. The Common Market and National Private Law

As pointed out above, default rules of private law and freedom of contract are two sides of the same coin. Default rules are needed where contracts fail to deal with relevant issues, that is, where they exhibit gaps. Such gaps are unavoidable. Even the most detailed and comprehensive contract is incomplete when unforeseen events occur and uncalculated risks materialise that have to be assigned to one of the parties. Such gaps need to be filled by legal default rules. Where the law is silent, those rules must ultimately be developed by the courts. However, the gaps usually relate to details of an agreement that is otherwise workable; where freedom of contract is basically recognised, it is primarily a matter for the parties to anticipate the gaps, that is, future risks, and to deal with them by appropriate contract clauses if they do not want to rely on the law.

In the eyes of contemporaries of the 1950s, the Treaty on the European Economic Community (EEC)[6] may have appeared as an enhanced version of former trade agreements, although one concluded in a multilateral setting; the public law aspects clearly prevail. However, the unconditional and largely unrestricted instruction to establish a Common Market, which is nowadays the Internal Market, was of a new quality. Even though traditional trade agreements try to liberalise international trade between countries, they still provide for certain quotas; moreover, they still restrict cross-border trade by imposing customs duties, and they do not remove non-tariff barriers; they are always inspired by the intention of the participating governments to maintain control over trade and over the national currency balance. In this sense, they can be designated as 'anti-trade' agreements. By contrast, the EEC Treaty was conceived as a 'pro-trade' agreement. The Common Market envisaged was intended to foster the cross-border flow of goods, capital, persons and services to a point where all quota, customs duties and non-tariff trade restrictions would ultimately be abolished.

In a regime of limited trade concessions, as provided by traditional trade agreements, such permits are a scarce resource, and the demand for those permits will usually exceed

[6] Treaty establishing the European Economic Community, signed on 25 March 1957, 298 UNTS 14.

the available supply. This is different in the Common Market. The objective pursued by national governments under the Common Market regime was the unlimited expansion of cross-border trade in goods and services as well as the cross-border movement of persons. The repeal of all state-driven restrictions put into effect by the implementation of the basic freedoms means that the welfare-enhancing success now depended essentially on the willingness of private individuals actually to engage in cross-border commerce and movements. The founding Member States could only establish a framework of rules. Private market participants and their transactions governed by private law would have to supplement them; this highlights the significance of private law for the Common Market.

Could the demand for private law be satisfied by the national contract laws of the Member States? Initially, that was the general assumption and not a real problem. The economic actors who made use of the Common Market were large businesses as well as traders and professionals experienced and specialising in import and export transactions. Contractual freedom secured by the national laws of all Member States allowed the drafting of contracts with sufficient precision so as to cope with the legal risks of cross-border trade. Where an unexpected risk materialised, the contracting parties might of course have been confronted with an unknown foreign law designated by private international law. But the default character of contract law recognised in all Member States allowed them to adjust the contract terms and conditions for *subsequent* transactions. Commercial operations within the Common Market proceeded on a trial-and-error basis. Moreover, legal unification promoted outside the European Community, in particular the 1964 Uniform Sales Laws which were of a default nature as well,[7] reduced those risks. The EEC Treaty built on freedom of contract, as can be inferred from its Article 85 (2), which is now Article 101 (2) Treaty on the Functioning of the European Union (TFEU). The sanction of nullity for anticompetitive agreements only makes sense if the parties are basically free to conclude binding contracts at will.

B. Freedom of Contract as a Principle of EU Law

Things changed from the 1970s onwards. When the Common Market turned out to be a success, medium-sized and smaller businesses as well as consumers gradually entered the market, that is, people who were not experienced repeat players and often lacked financial resources to accommodate risks inherent in foreign trade. It was also in those years that individual Member States increasingly adopted mandatory regulations affecting private relations. This occurred in fields such as labour law or commercial agency; it also happened with regard to the protection of the environment, of investors and of consumers. The growing national divergences in these areas were mirrored by the scope of contractual freedom which differed from country to country. More and more calls for the harmonisation of mandatory national provisions were voiced. The 1985

[7] Convention relating to a uniform law on the international sale of goods (ULIS), done at The Hague on 1 July 1964, 834 UNTS 107; Convention relating to a uniform law on the formation of contracts for the international sale (ULFIS), done at The Hague on 1 July 1964, 834 UNTS 169; both instruments were ratified by five of the six founding Member States of the EEC (not by France).

Internal Market Program[8] suggested a series of harmonising EU measures, and the Single European Act allowed for their adoption by qualified majority.[9] Ever since, the body of mandatory EU legislation designed to overcome national divergences has been growing constantly. As a result, the Court of Justice has increasingly often been asked to clarify concepts, rules and principles of those acts and to decide on their extension to borderline issues. It is in this context that the Court has referred, from the 1990s onwards, to the freedom of contract governing matters not covered by a binding EU act.

In subsequent years, the Court of Justice repeatedly asserted the existence of a general principle ensuring freedom of contract. While the Court for some time acknowledged 'the contractual freedom of the parties as exercised under the applicable national law',[10] it has also endorsed contractual freedom as a principle of EU law which 'cannot … be limited in the absence of Community rules imposing specific restrictions in that regard'.[11] As a principle of EU law, contractual freedom has been acknowledged by the Court in respect of various aspects, such as the content of the contract, the choice of contract partner and the modification of a prior agreement.[12] One has to keep in mind, however, that there are only few provisions of EU law which may be derogated from by parties who make use of their freedom to contract. Thus, the Court's assertion of contractual freedom generally amounts to a derogation of national rules of Member States. Since the Court has no jurisdiction over the interpretation of national law, it can rarely be certain when it comes to assessing the dispositive or mandatory nature of a national rule of contract law. Therefore, the Court's assertion of freedom of contract, which is never unbounded, must be approached with great caution. Ever since the Charter of Fundamental Rights[13] became binding law in 2008, the freedom to conduct a business secured by Article 16 provides a more solid basis for contractual freedom.[14]

However, the resulting legal situation is still uncertain. This explains Advocate General Szpunar's impression that

> [F]reedom of contract is the elephant in the room. In my opinion it has not yet found its rightful place in the system of EU law. However, it underpins its framework, above all in the context of the operation of fundamental freedoms. The internal market and a highly competitive social market economy, as referred to in Article 3(3) TEU, as well as the adoption of an economic policy which is conducted in accordance with the principle of an open market economy with free competition, as referred in Article 119 TFEU would be inconceivable without it. Yet, it remains hidden behind the entire system of other EU principles and laws.[15]

The frictions between an *EU principle* of contractual freedom and *national* contract law, including its default rules, will certainly become more visible over the years. While the

[8] Completing the internal market – White Paper from the Commission to the European Council (Milan, 28–29 June 1985), COM(1985) 310 final.

[9] Single European Act, signed at Luxembourg on 7 February 1986 and at The Hague on 28 February 1986 [1987] OJ L169/1; the Act introduced Article 100A EEC, which later became Article 114 TFEU.

[10] CJEU, C-421/05 *City Motors Groep v Citroën Belux* ECLI:EU:C:2007:38, para 24; C-125/05 *Vulcan Silkeborg v Scandinavisk Motor* ECLI:EU:C:2006:531, para 47.

[11] CJEU, C-240/97 *Kingdom of Spain v Commission* ECLI:EU:C:1999:479, para 99.

[12] For further details of the case law, see Basedow (n 5) paras V-45 et seq, V-66 et seq.

[13] Charter of Fundamental Rights of the European Union [2002] OJ C83/391.

[14] See CJEU, C-426/11 *Alemo Herron v Parkwood Leisure* ECLI:EU:C:2013:521, paras 34 and 35.

[15] CJEU, Opinion of Advocate General Szpunar, C-261/20 *Thelen Technopark Berlin v MN* ECLI:EU:C:2021:620, para 76.

Union persistently adopts mandatory rules of its own in order to harmonise or forestall national mandatory rules, the efforts for the creation of default rules in the field of contract law have currently come to a standstill. But they will have to be renewed. Before pursuing this line of thought, it is useful to shed some light onto existing provisions of EU law that allow parties to derogate by agreement.

III. Default Rules in EU Private Law

In the present context, the term 'default rules' relates to the ability of *private parties* to replace legal rules by their agreement. Provisions which allow the *Member States* to opt out are not included. The starting point of our survey is the general characterisation of secondary EU law, which can be described as positive, written law that is in a constant state of flux, policy-driven, fragmentary and for the most part mandatory.[16] Secondary law lends itself to the adoption of default rules to various degrees, depending on whether it is adopted as a Directive, a Regulation or a Decision approving an international convention.

A. Directives

Many Directives are still of a semi-mandatory nature; this is true in particular of Directives in the field of labour law or consumer law. For example, the Working Time Directive explicitly lays down 'minimum … requirements for the organisation of working time'.[17] It thereby implicitly allows agreements between employers and workers that establish working time standards above those minimum requirements. And the Sale of Goods Directive only invalidates a 'contractual agreement which, to the detriment of the consumer, excludes the application of national measures transposing this Directive [or] derogates from them'. A second paragraph goes a step further by stating that the Directive 'shall not prevent the seller from offering to the consumer contractual arrangements that go beyond the protection provided for in this Directive'.[18] The minimum harmonisation achieved by these Directives primarily respects the competence of the Member States for legislation ensuring a protection above the EU minimum level. An explicit provision such as Article 21(2) of the Sale of Goods Directive even confirms the contractual freedom of the contracting parties as a matter of EU law. In the absence of such express confirmation, for example in the Working Time Directive, it is up to the Member States to decide whether the parties to the employment contract enjoy contractual freedom for arrangements above the EU minimum level. And Member States are also entitled to enact default rules providing for a better protection of workers and consumers.

[16] See Basedow (n 5) para III-95.

[17] See Art 1(1) of Directive 2002/88/EC of the European Parliament and of the Council of 4 November 2003 concerning certain aspects of the organisation of working time [2003] OJ L299/9.

[18] See Art 21 of Directive (EU) 2019/771 of the European Parliament and of the Council of 20 May 2019 on certain aspects concerning contracts for the sale of goods, amending Regulation (EU) 2017/2394 and Directive 2009/22/EC, and repealing Directive 1999/44/EC [2019] OJ L136/28.

The admission of an unrestricted derogation by contract is a rare occurrence in EU Directives. Only very few isolated provisions allow parties to agree on deviating terms in either direction, usually in commercial contracts. Thus, the Commercial Agency Directive, which mainly lays down mandatory provisions, also refers to some issues which are left to the agreement of the parties, for example the conclusion of the contract for a definite or an indefinite period.[19] And the provision in Article 18 of the Sale of Goods Directive on the seller's redress against an upstream supplier is equally of a default nature. Since Article 21(1) declares that agreements made to the buyer's detriment 'shall not be binding *on the consumer*' (emphasis added), it can be concluded that Article 18 of the Directive can be abrogated or modified by agreement concluded between several businesses involved. In general, however, Directives confine their own scope of application, so as to exclude issues which may be settled by an agreement of private parties.

B. Regulations

More common is the endorsement of contractual freedom in EU Regulations which are directly binding under Article 288(2) TFEU. However, these Regulations have a specific form and content. A substantive provision that pertains to a traditional issue of contract law concerning matters of currency can be found in the Regulation dealing with the introduction of the Euro. Article 3 provides that

> [T]he introduction of the Euro shall not have the effect of altering any term of a legal instrument or of discharging or excusing performance under any legal instrument nor give a party the right unilaterally to alter or terminate such an instrument. This provision is subject to anything which parties may have agreed.[20]

In a similar vein, the one-to-one conversion rate from the European Currency Unit (ECU) to the Euro in legal instruments, which is laid down in Article 2 of the Regulation, is drafted as a rebuttable presumption, 'taking into account the intentions of the parties'. The explicit assurance of respect for private agreements was apparently meant to build up confidence in the new currency.

Since the turn of the millennium, the Union has the legislative competence for private international law. EU legislation based on that competence now covers substantial parts of the discipline. Most of the Regulations determining the applicable law allow parties to choose that law, or at least, as far as personal status is concerned, to select from a number of options. The conflict rules determining the applicable law in the absence of choice thereby adopt the nature of default rules.[21] This is above all true for the detailed conflict rules that establish connecting factors for contracts having a cross-border dimension.[22]

[19] See Art 15(1), (4) and (5) of Council Directive 86/653/EEC of 18 December 1986 on the coordination of the laws of the Member States relating to self-employed commercial agents [1986] OJ L382/17.

[20] Council Regulation (EC) No 1103/97 of 17 June 1979 on certain provisions relating to the introduction of the Euro [1997] OJ L162/1.

[21] See further the contribution by J Ungerer, ch 13 in this volume.

[22] See Arts 4 et seq of Regulation (EC) No 593/2008 of the European Parliament and of the Council of 17 June 2008 on the law applicable to contractual obligations (Rome I) [2008] OJ L177/6.

As compared with the freedom of contract in substantive law, party autonomy in private international law only allows for what may be called package deals: parties may select the law of country A for the whole agreement or for one 'part' of the contract, for example for its formation, and the law of country B for another 'part', for example its performance, so-called *depeçage*. But it is not possible to select a mix constituted by provisions derived from several laws for a specific single part of the contract. Thus, a clause referring to the law of country A for the consequences of a default in payment, while designating the law of country B for the interest rate, does not appear to be covered.[23] Reasonable parties would not do such a thing anyway. In this respect, however, the choice of the applicable law differs from the drafting of a contract subject to a given legal system, which may put together terms and clauses from various origins. With this qualification, the rules that apply in the absence of an agreement on the applicable law may be addressed as default rules.

A further group of provisions that could be referred to as default rules are to be found in Regulations which provide for optional instruments. Such Regulations have been enacted in the field of company law and intellectual property; the Societas Europaea (SE)[24] and the Union Trade Mark[25] are the most relevant examples in legal practice. They only come into being where the private parties involved opt for these legal institutions. Another example is the European Certificate of Succession, which is only issued upon application by one of the parties concerned.[26]

All instruments of this type enlarge individual liberty by creating institutions of EU law which are available for private individuals as alternatives to the institutions and rules that would otherwise apply. These other institutions and rules might be classified as default rules in this sense. However, those other institutions and rules are of national origin and not part of EU law. Shareholders can choose between the Societas Europaea and a public corporation under national law. Moreover, we are again confronted with the package deal. A party can choose only the complete set of rules governing the Societas Europaea or, in the alternative, a set of rules governing a corporation established under national law; specific derogations are only possible if permitted by the governing legal framework. It is difficult to compare this with default rules that may be abrogated individually.

C. Decisions Approving International Conventions

A further category of sources of EU private law are Decisions which the Council adopts under Article 218 TFEU for the conclusion of international agreements with third

[23] See Art 3(1) sentence 3 of the Rome I Regulation.

[24] Council Regulation (EC) No. 2157/2001 of 8 October 2001 on the Statute for a European company (SE) [2001] OJ L294/1.

[25] Regulation (EU) 2017/1001 of the European Parliament and of the Council of 14 June 2017 on the European Union Trade Mark (codification) [2017] OJ L154/1.

[26] See Arts 62 et seq of Regulation (EU) No 650/212 the European Parliament and of the Council of 4 July 2012 on jurisdiction, applicable law, recognition and enforcement of decisions and acceptance and enforcement of authentic instruments in matters of succession and on the creation of a European Certificate of Succession [2012] OJ L201/107.

States, in particular uniform law conventions. The Union is a party to several such conventions, for example the Montreal Convention on the carriage by air[27] and the Railway Convention COTIF as amended by the Vilnius Protocol.[28] According to settled case law, the international conventions become an integral part of the legal order of the Union through the implementing Decision of the Council.[29] Consequently, the Court of Justice has jurisdiction to interpret such international conventions under Article 267 TFEU. Where an instrument allows private parties to set aside, by their agreement, one of its provisions, the default character of that provision is thus transposed into EU law.

This has recently been confirmed by the Court of Justice in a case concerning the relationship between the manager of the Austrian rail infrastructure and the German owner of locomotives operating, inter alia, on the Austrian rail network. That relationship was governed by the Uniform Rules concerning the Contract of Use of Infrastructure in International Rail Traffic (CUI) that is attached to COTIF as an Appendix E and is an integral part of COTIF under its Article 6 § 2.[30] While the rules of the CUI are mandatory, the parties to the infrastructure use contract may 'assume a liability greater and obligations more burdensome than those provided for in these Uniform Rules or fix a maximum amount of compensation for loss of or damage to property'.[31] Under Article 8 § 1(b) CUI, the manager of the infrastructure is liable 'for loss of or damage to property (destruction of, or damage to, movable or immovable property)'; this non-fault liability is thus confined to compensation for physical harm.

In the case submitted to the Court of Justice, two locomotives had derailed in Austria and suffered damage. During the time of repair, the German owner replaced them by leased locomotives. He brought an action against the Austrian manager of the infrastructure for compensation, alleging a culpable breach of the latter's duties. The owner claimed not only compensation of the damage to its own locomotives, but also of the costs incurred for the leased locomotives. It relied on a clause of the infrastructure use contract that referred to the CUI and in a very general manner to the Austrian Civil Code (ABGB) supplementing the CUI. The fault-based liability under the ABGB also allows for the compensation of economic loss such as the costs of the leased locomotives. The Court of Justice considered the permission of certain agreements of the parties laid down in Article 4 CUI as an expression of the 'parties' contractual freedom'. It did not interpret that contractual freedom strictly, but concluded that even a general

[27] Council Decision (2001/539/EC) of 5 April 2001 on the conclusion by the European Community of the Convention for the Unification of certain rules for international carriage by air (Montreal Convention) [2001] OJ L194/38.

[28] The Union has not acceded to COTIF, but has approved it by an agreement concluded with the Intergovernmental Organisation for International Carriage by Rail, see the Council Decision (2013/103/EU) of 16 June 2011 on the signing and conclusion of the agreement between the European Union and the Intergovernmental Organisation for International Carriage by Rail on the accession of the European Union to the Convention Concerning International Carriage by Rail (COTIF) of 9 May 1980, as amended by the Vilnius Protocol of 3 June 1999 [2013] OJ L51/1 (with the agreement at 8); the consolidated version of the convention and various appendices is reproduced on the website www.otif.org/en → about OTIF → convention.

[29] See eg CJEU, C-344/04 *The Queen ex parte IATA v Department of Transportation* ECLI:EU:C:2006:10, para 36 with regards to the Montreal Convention; C-300/98 *Parfums Christian Dior v Tuk Consultancy* ECLI:EU:C:2000:688, para 33 concerning TRIPS which is annex 1C to the Agreement establishing the World Trade Organisation, done at Marrakesh on 15 April 1994, 1869 UNTS 299, [1994] OJ L336/213.

[30] The text of the CUI is available on the website referred to at the end of n 28 above.

[31] See Art 4 sentence 3 of the CUI.

reference to national law is covered by that provision and has the effect of extending the manager's liability.[32]

The Court interpreted an international convention as a part of the private law of the Union. It did not directly refer to any provision of EU law that can be classified as a default rule. But the judgment implies that a hypothetical agreement of the parties limiting the compensation for loss of or damage to property to a maximum amount, a contractual limitation that is also permitted by Article 4 sentence 3 of the CUI, would be treated in the same way. Thus, the rule on compensation for physical harm contained in Article 8 § 1(b) CUI is a default rule with regards to the amount of damages.

All in all, default rules are still a rare phenomenon in the private law of the European Union. Moreover, the specific provisions which allow for contractual derogations and thereby confer the character of the default rule to the dispositive provisions, are not based on any overarching principle. While the Court of Justice has recognised the existence of such a general principle, the single emanations in secondary EU law are based on diverse reasons: the desire to promote confidence in a new currency, the wish to provide a background to other mandatory provisions contained in the same instrument, or importing ideas laid down in international conventions into the law of the EU. While the principle of the freedom of contract appears to have inspired some Regulations in the field of private international law, the permissibility of party autonomy in others relating to family law and succession is instead due to the fact that a compromise had to be struck between the nationality and the habitual residence as connecting factors being endorsed by different Member States. The piecemeal approach of EU legislation on the one hand, and the growing consensus on an overarching general principle of contractual freedom in the Court of Justice on the other, are an unwelcome contradiction which ought to be resolved in due course.

IV. Functions of Default Rules in EU Private Law

The preceding analysis has pointed to deficits of EU law with regard to default rules: the frictions arising from the co-existence of an EU principle of contractual freedom and the absence of default rules at the level of the Union, as well as the inconsistent rationales underlying scattered provisions of EU law that may be described as default rules. One might conclude that the absence of a consistent body of default rules in the law of the Union signals that there are no positive functions for such rules in EU law. This conclusion is underpinned by the deliberate rejection of corresponding proposals. In fact, the Commission proposal for a Common European Sales Law would have introduced a regime which the parties could in principle have excluded, modified or derogated from, that is, a regime of default rules on sales and contracts in general.[33]

[32] CJEU, C-500/20 *ÖBB-Infrastruktur v Lokomotion Gesellschaft für Schienentraktion* ECLI:EU:C:2022:563, para 72 et seq, *Transportrecht* 2022, 388, with a note concerning the particular rail law aspects by R Freise at 395 et seq.

[33] See Art 1 and Recital 21 of the proposal for a regulation of the European Parliament and of the Council on a common European Sales Law, COM(2011) 635 final.

It is well known that several Member States which could have blocked its adoption in the Council prompted the Commission to withdraw this initiative.[34]

These events indicate that the opposing Member States do not consider that European integration will substantially be promoted by a body of default rules. While this was an accurate assessment at the time when the Community was founded, it is doubtful at present. As shown above, the fragmentary and mandatory laws of the Union have in the meantime penetrated large areas of private law; their application in practice invariably leads to the need to demarcate them from other component parts of the respective legal framework, parts which often are of a dispositive nature and of national origin. Since the national laws diverge, there may be detrimental repercussions on the uniform application and enforcement of the law of the Union itself (see sub-section A below). Moreover, default rules have a system-building effect in a growing legal order such as that of EU private law (see sub-section B).

A. Specific Functions of Default Rules for EU Law[35]

i. Standard Contract Terms

The Court's case law on unfair contract terms provides a telling example of the disturbing effect of national default rules and the absence of EU default rules. In one of the early cases decided under the relevant Directive, *Freiburger Kommunalbauten*, a municipal construction company was about to build a multistorey carpark and sold a parking space located therein to Mr and Mrs Hofstetter. In accordance with the contract, the whole of the purchase price was due once the contractor provided a security. When Freiburger Kommunalbauten delivered a bank guarantee, the Hofstetter couple nevertheless refused to make a payment, alleging that the contract clause at issue violated the German statute on standard conditions of contract which, inter alia, implemented the Unfair Contract Terms Directive.[36] They argued that under § 641 BGB, the relevant provision of the German Civil Code, payment is due only after completion of a building and its acceptance by the customers. They maintained that a contractual derogation from this rule was possible, but not by means of a standard clause in a consumer contract.

The German Federal Court of Justice (BGH) was nevertheless inclined to approve the clause because of the security furnished by the contractor. Upon a request for a preliminary ruling, the Court of Justice held that the balancing of the pros and cons of a clause which is needed for the assessment of its unfairness 'requires that consideration be given to the national law', which the Court of Justice has no jurisdiction to interpret.[37]

[34] See the letter to the Commission dated 28 November 2014 and signed by the governments of Austria, Finland, France, Germany, The Netherlands and the United Kingdom. The German version is published in J Basedow, 'Gemeinsames europäisches Kaufrecht – Das Ende eines Kommissionsvorschlags' [2015] *Zeitschrift für Europäisches Privatrecht (ZEuP)* 432–35.

[35] Parts of the following section are reproduced, also posthumously, in J Basedow, 'Codification of Private Law: The European Perspective' in E Veress (ed), *Codification of Civil Law: Assessment, Reforms, Options* (Budapest, FMI & CEA Publishing, 2024).

[36] Council Directive 93/13/EEC of 5 April 1993 on Unfair Terms in Consumer Contracts [1993] OJ L95/29.

[37] CJEU, C-237/02 *Freiburger Kommunalbauten v Hofstetter* ECLI:EU:C:2004:209, para 21.

The Court concluded that it may only 'interpret general criteria used by the Community legislature in order to define the concept of unfair terms, … [but] should not rule on the application of these general criteria to a particular term'.[38] The latter formula has been constantly repeated in judgments dealing with the Unfair Contract Terms Directive.[39] It has turned into a true barrier to the effective enforcement of the Directive, although the Court of Justice has tried to find other ways of implementation more recently.[40]

What matters in the present context is that the absence of default rules in EU law has been an impediment to the effective transposition of EU law and that the default rules of the Member States cannot fill this lacuna in the law of the Union. Default rules established by EU legislation could provide guidelines for the policing of standard contract terms. In *Freiburger Kommunalbauten* it would obviously have been an advantage for the effective implementation of the Directive, had EU law contained a simple rule stating that in a contract for work, and in the absence of an agreement of the parties, remuneration falls due after or before or simultaneously with the acceptance of the work by the customer. Such a rule would have established a basic principle regarding the sequence of the parties' performances and would have allowed the Court of Justice to proceed to further details, for example, on the validity, form and fairness of a derogating agreement. Similar default rules would also be useful in other contexts, such as causation, the concept of sale or agency.

ii. Agency

The Court often accepts agency as being regulated by national law; and without any hesitation, it sometimes considers agency as a factual question.[41] It acknowledges that agents bind their principals and not themselves. Consequently, intermediaries concluding agreements on behalf of their principals do not themselves infringe the prohibition of cartels under Article 101 TFEU.[42] In a consumer case, a garage owner (the dealer) obtained a used car from a consumer with a view to selling the car, in its capacity as an agent, to another consumer. When defects of the car became manifest and the final buyer brought an action against the dealer, the Court considered the latter not as an agent, but as a seller for the purposes of the Consumer Sales Directive.[43]

The judgment gives rise to some questions. What would have happened if the final buyer had sued the original owner jointly with the dealer? Would the Court have asserted, under the Directive, the existence of two sellers (the original owner and the dealer) in respect of a single sales contract? Or would the liability of the first seller be governed by national law? Would the ultimate buyer thus be entitled to contractual

[38] ibid, para 22.

[39] See the survey by M Fornasier in FJ Säcker, R Rixecker and others (eds) *Münchener Kommentar zum BGB*, vol 2, 9th edn (München, CH Beck, 2022) Vor § 305 para 45 et seq.

[40] Fornasier in *Münchener Kommentar* (n 39) vor § 305 paras 36 et seq, 51 et seq.

[41] See eg CJEU, C-8/98 *Dansommer v Götz* ECLI:EU:C:2000:45, para 8.

[42] CJEU, C-279/06 *CEPSA v Tobar* ECLI:EU:C:2008:485, para 41, distinguishing between the principal-agent relationship subject to what is now Art 101 TFEU, and the relationship between the intermediary, acting on behalf of the principal, and the third party, a relationship that is outside the scope of Art 101.

[43] CJEU, C-149/15 *Wathelet v Garage Bietheres* ECLI:EU:C:2016:840 with regard to Directive 1999/44/EC of 25 May 1999 on certain aspects of consumer goods and associated guarantees [1999] OJ L171/12.

claims against the dealer and, in addition, against the original owner? And what about the dealer's recourse against the original owner? The Court's assessment was strongly motivated by considerations of consumer protection and the principle of effectiveness. But would the same motivation, applied to other sectors, not turn a travel agent selling flight tickets into a contracting air carrier (as opposed to the actual carrier) and an insurance intermediary into an insurer, both being liable under EU legislation when the much larger principals they represent become insolvent?

The Court dwells (only) upon the concept of seller and the policy of consumer protection pursued by the Directive. It does not take account of possible complications and ramifications in other areas of the law. The judgment would have been more convincing had the Court focused on the transparency of the dealer's position. Transparency plays an important role in the law of agency, as can be inferred, for example, from § 164(2) of the German BGB: 'If the intent to act on behalf of another is not evident, the lack of intent on the part of the agent to act on his own behalf is not taken into account.'[44] The same result is achieved elsewhere by reference to reasonableness or good faith,[45] or on the basis of what the third party 'ought to have known'.[46] These provisions apply to the whole area of contract law and do not suggest that there is anything special about consumer sales.

Transparency is also acknowledged as a general principle of EU law. It has been invoked by the Court, for example, in matters of public procurement;[47] likewise, Article 4(2) of the Unfair Contract Terms Directive, which requires contract terms to be drafted in 'plain intelligible language', has been interpreted as demanding transparency.[48] By implication, the Court also referred to it in the present agency case, when it pointed out that the seller had 'not duly informed the consumer of the fact that the owner of the goods sold [was] a private individual'.[49] The Court should have extended the principle of transparency to contract law instead of spending great amounts of time and much deliberation on consumer protection. Again, some default rules of EU law on the basic principles of agency would have been helpful; they would likely have induced the Court to consider the consequences of the expansion of the seller concept, to substantiate its line of thought and to provide a fertile ground for application of the principle in other contexts.

[44] Translation as published on the website of the Federal Ministry of Justice: www.gesetze-im-internet.de. In Italian law, a similar rule requires, under the heading of *contemplation domini*, that it must be obvious for the third party that the effects of the agent's contract-related action concern the principal, see G Cian and A Trabucchi, *Commentario breve al Codice civile* 5th edn (Padova, CEDAM, 1997) Art 1388 para VI/1.

[45] For the Netherlands, see Article 3:35 of the Civil Code (*Burgerlijk Wetboek*): 'The absence in a declaration cannot be invoked against a person who has interpreted another's declaration or conduct, in conformity with the sense which he could reasonably (*redelijkerwijze*) attribute to it in the circumstances, as a declaration of a particular tenor made to him by that other person.' English translation by PPC Haanappel and E MacKaay, *New Netherlands Civil Code: Patrimonial Law* (Netherlands and Boston/MA, Kluwer and Deventer, 1990) 21.

[46] See Art 2.2.4 (1) of the UNIDROIT Principles of International Commercial Contracts 2016, on the website www.unidroit.org → instruments → commercial contracts.

[47] CJEU, C-769/21 *BTA Baltic Insurance Co v Iepirkumu uzraudzības birojs, Tieslietu ministrija* ECLI:EU:C:2022:973, para 32.

[48] CJEU, C-776/19 *VB v BNP Parisbas Personal Finance* ECLI:EU:C:2021:470, para 62 with further references.

[49] CJEU, *Wathelet* (n 43) para 45.

iii. Prescription

A further area of private law that would benefit from default rules regulating some key issues is the prescription of claims and actions. Time limits are intended to restore legal certainty and, as it is put in German, to establish '*Rechtsfrieden*', that is, 'legal peace'; they are an indispensable corollary of every claim. Multiple rules of this kind exist in the law of the Union as well.[50] Every claim must be subject to a time bar *in extremis*. It is disconcerting if the Court holds, as it recently did, 'that an application brought by a consumer for a declaration that a term in an agreement concluded between a seller or supplier and a consumer is unfair cannot be subject to any limitation period'.[51] Not even when distant heirs start litigation after a century? That was not the problem in the case decided by the Court, but its statement is misleading and would be more understandable if made against the backdrop of a default rule of EU law ordering a general prescription after a period of some decades. That period would be absolute and start with the event giving rise to the claim.

More reasonable and even suitable for codification is another rule established by the Court: it provides that the limitation period does not start to run before the creditor becomes aware of the facts giving rise to his or her claims.[52] This is a sound principle for shorter prescription periods and applies in the years before the absolute prescription period mentioned above expires. It is mirrored by more recent national legislation both within and outwith the European Union which often adds an additional and absolute prescription period starting from an objective fact.[53] These examples show that a set of default rules which need not be complete can be of further assistance in the development of the private law of the Union and is helpful when it comes to the implementation of mandatory EU laws.

B. The Systematic Function of Default Rules

A second function of default rules is of a general significance and less visible. Default rules are components of the overall framework of rules, principles, concepts and values

[50] See eg for damages claims arising from the non-contractual liability of the Union (Art 340(2) TFEU) Art 46 of the Protocol (No 3) on the Statute of the Court of Justice of the European Union [2016] OJ C202/210; Art 10 of Directive 2014/104/EU of the European Parliament and of the Council of 26 November 2014 on certain rules governing actions for damages under national law for infringements of the competition law provisions of the Member States and of the European Union [2014] OJ L349/1; Art 10 of Council Directive 85/374/EEC of 25 July 1985 on the approximation of the laws, regulations and administrative provisions of the Member States concerning liability for defective products [1985] OJ L210/29.

[51] *VB v BNP* (n 48) para 38.

[52] ibid para 46; see G Straetmans and J Werbrouck, 'Cases VB and Others v. BNP Paribas Personal Finance SA and AV and Others v. BNP Paribas Personal Finance SA and Procureur de la République (C-776/19 to C-782/19): New Jurisprudential Levers to Combat Unfair Terms in B2C Contracts' [2022] *European Journal of Consumer Law* 183, 188 et seq; in the same vein with regard to a damages claim arising from an anticompetitive agreement: CJEU, C-637/17 *Cogeco Communications v Sport TV Portugal* ECLI:EU:C:2019:263, paras 49, 51 and 53. See now Art 10(2) of Directive 2014/104 (n 50).

[53] On the trends towards a double-tracked regime of prescription periods, see R Zimmermann, 'Prescription' in J Basedow, K Hopt and R Zimmermann (eds), *The Max Planck Encyclopedia of European Private Law*, vol 2 (Oxford, OUP, 2012) 1306, 1307 et seq.

which shapes the legal mind and builds up what we usually refer to as the legal system. This framework helps allocate cases and issues to places within that system; it presages the legal analysis in the minds of lawyers. It is like the layout of a building; although we may need and seek only specific rooms for specific purposes, such as a bedroom for sleeping, a kitchen for cooking and a bathroom for washing, the layout is the device that helps us understand how the various rooms relate to one another and where to find what. EU legislation focuses on the single rooms. It builds more and more of them and will end up in a labyrinth where nobody finds the destination they are heading for.

A comprehensive network of default rules may be 'irrelevant' in the sense that no private actor is really bound by them. But it is essential for the intellectual grid that facilitates access to the specific legal information required to cope with a particular situation and conflict. It is not the only aid that helps build up such a grid; other expedients include the basic principles of EU law which drive the legal developments, the procedural embeddedness of its implementation, and the basic freedoms of the Internal Market; but a comprehensive network of non-binding rules of private law is an element that is indispensable in the long run. Given the multi-ethnic and multi-cultural composition of European institutions, that grid of orientation is unlikely to emerge from the sole interaction between the EU judiciary, national courts and legal scholarship. Legislation could play an important role in a task that relates to the long-term legal unification of Europe, as opposed to the short-run measures that are adopted every year and respond to the political programmes established by the European Commission in five-year-intervals.

The outlined function of default rules in the evolution of EU law in long-term perspective takes us to a final consideration concerning legal education. We teach law students not for the problems of the present, but in order to enable them to solve problems of the future: to settle disputes that arise in 10 or 20 or 30 years, or even further beyond. What they need for that distant future is precision in the handling of language, the capacity of legal analysis, of establishing links between the general and the specific, of forging legal arguments that appear plausible or even convincing to others, of drawing conclusions from multiple and often contradictory values for specific conflict situations. With regard to the law of the European Union, these abilities can hardly be acquired on the basis of the fragmentary legislation of the Union that is often intended to accommodate specific conflicts of the moment in response to current political goals. Participating in such discussions on legislative policy is certainly an important ability as well, but it cannot substitute for the capacity described above, which is geared towards the orientation of the lawyer in a complex and changing environment of statutes and case law. A comprehensive body of default rules covering the major parts of the law of obligations would certainly help to make students all over Europe acquainted with the same intellectual grid that helps locate and organise on a mental map the multiple specific enactments and thereby provides a common ground in cross-border debates.

V. Conclusion

This chapter has elaborated on the fragmentary and mandatory nature of EU private law – a body of law which is, moreover, undergoing rapid and repeated change. While default rules are rare in EU legislation, the Court of Justice has increasingly acknowledged the reverse of default rules, that is, contractual freedom of private parties. This has given rise to some significant frictions, since the recognition of contractual freedom brings about difficulties where the scope of that freedom is unclear due to divergences between the abrogated national laws. The metaphor of the elephant in the room used by Advocate General Szpunar actually grasped this problem. The absence of default rules in EU law has a weakening impact on the implementation of some enactments of the Union, and it renders the application of others insecure. What appears equally serious in the long run is the risk of causing disorientation to lawyers and law students in the complex legal environment resulting from the uncoordinated co-existence of a large and ever-growing number of fragmented measures. All this is not beneficial for European integration understood as a process of social and intellectual convergence.

Legal scholars who have made important contributions with a view to an ultimate codification of EU private law over recent decades should resume their work. However, they should not aim at a code incorporating existing mandatory acts. Instead, a non-binding comprehensive set of principles and rules should provide a grid of orientation that clarifies and harmonises concepts and allows us to allocate and compartmentalise specific binding measures at a later stage. Of course, such default rules would be superseded by the manifold specific provisions of EU law as *leges speciales*, most of them of a mandatory nature. That set of default principles and rules need not be complete, but should aim at establishing the said grid that could constitute a common ground for legal education all over Europe. It could also serve as a point of reference where the courts have to interpret provisions of binding and usually mandatory EU law, such as the Unfair Contract Terms Directive.

7

Default Rules in Contract Law

JOHN CARTWRIGHT

I. The Scope of the Discussion

The topic of this chapter is *default rules in contract law*. There are a few points to note at the outset. First – as in all chapters in this volume – we are concerned with *default rules*: rules[1] which apply in the absence of contrary provision made by the parties, but which the parties are free to supplement, vary or exclude by contrary provision. There are two dividing lines to bear in mind: between mandatory rules and default rules; and between default rules and no rules provided by the law. The latter line asks why the law should provide rules at all, rather than leaving it to the parties themselves to identify all such rules as they wish to apply. The former line assumes that the law does provide rules, but asks which of those rules the parties should be free to supplement, vary or exclude. The line between default rules and mandatory rules may sometimes not be easy to draw, but for our purposes the line has to be drawn. We shall see that we can learn much about the nature and function of default rules by considering how they relate to mandatory rules.

Second, we are concerned with default rules *in contract law*. This is wider than simply default rules *in contracts*, which would focus more narrowly on the terms of the contract – the content of the parties' obligations, and how the law fills out the unexpressed intentions of the parties, providing content for their transaction which will apply except and insofar as the parties otherwise provide. The rules of *contract law* govern not merely the terms of the contract, but the whole framework within which contracts exist and operate, including the rules for formation of the contract and the rules governing the consequences of failures in performance. We must inevitably be selective in the discussion, given the range of relevant areas. We shall also exclude detailed discussion of areas which fall within other chapters such as consumer law, which is relevant insofar as it provides a specific context for consumer contracts,[2] and employment law with its context for contracts of employment.[3]

[1] We do not here make a distinction between default *rules* (eg that a party take a particular action) and default *standards* (eg that a party act in accordance with a particular standard on which the court will retrospectively adjudicate, such as reasonableness): cf A Schwartz and RE Scott, 'The Common Law of Contract and the Default Rule Project' (2016) 102 *Virginia L Rev* 1523.

[2] See the contribution by S Whittaker, ch 8 in this volume.

[3] See the contribution by A Bogg, ch 10 in this volume.

Third, there are various perspectives from which this topic could be approached and, indeed, from which the topic has already been explored in the literature,[4] including philosophical (legal theory) and economic analysis. Given the international framework of this volume, the aim here is to discuss the substantive law of contract, but comparatively, looking at how systems of different traditions address the issues, and at what we can learn from similarities and differences in their approaches. To make the discussion manageable, we shall focus on examples drawn from English law and French law.

Fourth, the discussion is based on the way in which default rules operate in English law and in other legal systems, *not* the way in which they *ought to* operate. There is of course a place for debate in any system about whether the current use of default rules is too limited or too extensive,[5] but a full discussion of such matters of policy in the operation of contract laws of different legal systems is beyond the scope of this chapter.

II. The Use of Rules Supplied by Law, and Drawing the Line between Mandatory Rules and Default Rules: The Particular Context of Contract Law

The nature and function of default rules – and the relative places for default rules and mandatory rules – will depend on the context. In contract law, the distinction between mandatory and default rules is well known and much discussed.[6] If we see a contract as a set of obligations freely entered into by the parties in a whole multitude of different kinds of transaction which the parties themselves choose to fashion, there is a place for the law to complete the contract by supplementing the parties' own express provision where it is incomplete or otherwise inadequate, but the law cannot provide all rules for every contract. Nor should those rules which the law does provide all be mandatory. Such an absolute control of contracts by the law would deny the parties' freedom of contract. On the other hand, the idea that some of the rules should be mandatory is natural. In part, at least, the role allowed to default rules depends on the nature and purpose of mandatory rules.

The most obvious role of mandatory rules is to give effect to the limits that must be placed on the parties' freedom of contract. There are matters of public policy about the kinds of agreement that are acceptable as contracts, recognised and enforced by law – acceptable either in their content or in the way in which the parties have behaved in

[4] See eg R Craswell, 'Contract Law, Default Rules, and the Philosophy of Promising' (1989) 88 *Michigan L Rev* 489; TD Rakoff, 'The Implied Terms of Contracts: of "Default Rules" and "Situation Sense"' in J Beatson and D Friedmann (eds), *Good Faith and Fault in Contract Law* (Oxford, Clarendon Press, 1995) 191; CA Riley, 'Designing Default Rules in Contract Law: Consent, Conventionalism, and Efficiency' (2000) *OJLS* 367; E Peden, 'Policy Concerns Behind Implication of Terms in Law' (2001) 117 *LQR* 459.

[5] For a critical discussion of the use of default rules in English commercial law, arguing that default rules should be strictly limited, see J Morgan, *Contract Law Minimalism: A Formalist Restatement of Commercial Contract Law* (Cambridge, CUP, 2013).

[6] For examples in the common law, see Morgan (n 5) and the articles cited in nn 1 and 4 above. In French law, see C Pérès, 'Mandatory and Non-mandatory Rules in the New Law of Contract' in J Cartwright and S Whittaker (eds), *The Code Napoléon Rewritten: French Contract Law after the 2016 Reforms* (Oxford, Hart Publishing, 2017) 167, and the much more detailed study in C Pérès, *La Règle Supplétive* (Paris, LGDJ, 2003).

their formation or performance. Such policies may vary from time to time, and from one legal system to another, but in all legal systems there will be limits to contractual freedom which find their articulation through mandatory rules of contract law.

In addition to giving effect to particular issues of policy, however, there is another general role for mandatory rules of contract law: to provide the mandatory legal framework of contracts. Even in a system of contract law which adheres to the most liberal version of the parties' freedom of contract, there must be a framework, including an essential legal definition of the minimum contents and incidents of the contractual relationship into which the details are to be added by the parties. This is where the default rules come in. The parties are free to add their own details, but the law may also provide for them a picture of the kind of contract that normally results, a template which assists them in various ways. It saves them having to fill in all the details themselves if they are content to accept the law's normalised picture, or if they do not have the time or inclination to shape it for themselves or, indeed, if they do not even think about it – to avoid leaving gaps by error or inadvertence. And, taken together with the mandatory rules, the default rules provided by the law assist the parties by providing an overall, coherent picture of a complete contractual relationship – a default contract, some parts of which (the default rules) are negotiable between the parties. The contractual framework, provided by the law, contains both mandatory rules and default rules.

Modern legal systems accept that there are essential elements of a contract: every transaction recognised as a contract must fit some framework of essential rules and incidents. It is too simple, however, to assume that there is only one contractual framework defined by the law: in practice there is a master framework, applicable to all contracts, supplemented by other, different frameworks for different types of contract. We must first consider the (master) framework of contract law in general: the mandatory rules (and the scope left for default rules) in determining the essential nature of every contract. Then we consider the place of (subsidiary) frameworks: the role of default rules (by contrast with mandatory rules) in relation to particular types of contract.

III. The Framework of Contract Law

A transaction is not a contract just because the parties say that it is, but because it fits the definition given by the legal system. The law provides not only a definition of contract, but also a whole framework of rules governing the incidents of the contractual relationship. Some of these rules are mandatory, others take effect in default of the parties' provision to the contrary; and what is mandatory in one system may be a default rule in another system. Such differences can be evidence of significant differences between the very notion of 'contract' within the different systems.

In English law, we tend to think that very little is mandatory, most is negotiable. Jonathan Morgan has written that 'virtually all of contract law consists of merely default rules',[7] although this is in the context of his discussion of the nature and function of commercial contract law, where he presents a foundational claim that 'commercial

[7] Morgan (n 5) 87.

contract law's function is to provide workable rules for business-to-business transactions' – rules which, he argues, should be minimal, not only as regards mandatory rules but even as regards default rules, in order to maximise freedom of contract and to dispose of commercial disputes with maximum efficiency.[8] In the last substantive part of this chapter (Section IV), we shall consider the extent to which the law sets mandatory frameworks for particular types of contract, but the general framework of rules which applies to all contracts in English law certainly appears at first sight to be predominantly negotiable, rather than mandatory.

The terms of the contract – its content – are generally for the parties to determine, with very limited control, and such control as exists is mainly found in legislation and is mainly aimed not at contracts generally but at particular types of contract.[9] Even the legislative rules that appear to apply to contracts generally are often nuanced in their operation to apply only to a sub-set of transactions.[10] There are some mandatory rules set by case law which apply to the content of all contracts, such as the prohibition of terms that are illegal or contravene public policy,[11] the prohibition on excluding by a term of the contract a party's liability for personal fraud in inducing the formation of the contract,[12] and the rule against penalty clauses.[13] These are, however, marginal issues in most contracts, where freedom of contract prevails as to the contract terms.

As regards the rules governing the incidents of the contractual relationship, the parties also have significant freedom of contract within the framework of default rules set by the law. The common law provides rules to the effect that every breach of contract gives rise to a right to damages, and how to calculate those damages (including the limit by way of remoteness of damage),[14] as well as when the innocent party has a right to terminate the contract.[15] But such rules are not mandatory: indeed, they are classic default rules, setting the normal consequences for a breach which will apply unless the parties have otherwise agreed in the contract – and in negotiated commercial contracts it is very common for the contract to make provision for remedies which may override the (default) common law rules.[16] A more recent example of a default rule in English contract law – this time set by statute, overriding an earlier mandatory rule of the

[8] ibid 89. Morgan distinguishes consumer transactions, where mandatory rules may be required to regulate fairness, thus limiting his 'minimalist hypothesis' to commercial contracts: ibid 108.

[9] See section IV.B below (at 128).

[10] See eg the Unfair Contract Terms Act 1977 (now amended by the Consumer Rights Act 2015 so as to limit its regulatory scope to non-consumer contracts) which applies only to either particular types of contract (ss 6 and 7) or (more generally) to contracts entered into on one party's written standard terms of business (s 3); and in any event it excludes certain types of contract from its scope (sched 1). However, the Misrepresentation Act 1967, s 3 (also now applicable only to non-consumer contracts), requires *all* exclusions or restrictions of liability for precontractual misrepresentation to be reasonable.

[11] J Beatson, A Burrows and J Cartwright, *Anson's Law of Contract* 31st edn (Oxford, OUP, 2020) ch 11.

[12] *HIH Casualty & General Insurance Ltd v Chase Manhattan Bank* [2003] UKHL 6, [2003] 1 All ER (Comm) 349.

[13] *Anson's Law of Contract* (n 11) 567–73. However, this may in practice have less application to negotiated contracts between parties of roughly equal bargaining power.

[14] *Anson's Law of Contract* (n 11) 542–54.

[15] *Photo Production Ltd v Securicor Transport Ltd* [1980] AC 827 (HL) 848–49.

[16] For instance, clauses providing for the remedy of suspension (which is not generally covered by the common law remedies), or for extended or restricted (or simply more precisely defined) rights of termination, or (subject to the rule on penalties, n 13 above) defining the scope of recoverable damages. See eg R Christou, *Boilerplate: Practical Clauses* 8th edn (London, Sweet & Maxwell, 2019) chs 3, 7.

common law to the contrary – is that a contract will in certain defined circumstances create rights enforceable directly by third party.[17]

Some rules, however, cannot be varied by the parties. The most obvious is that the core definition of a contract is not negotiable. Every legal system must define what a contract is (and therefore what transactions do not constitute contracts if they fail to comply with the definition), and in English law the rule is that there must be an agreement between the parties as to the existence of the contract and (at least) a minimum sufficiency of certain terms, and the content of the agreement must fit the bilateral model of the English contract in accordance with the doctrine of consideration.[18] The parties cannot agree that a promise of a gift is a contract, because that does not fit the mandatory rule, although they may use another mechanism provided by the law to give effect to such an agreement, by entering into a deed – but only if they then comply with the mandatory legal rules for the creation of a deed.[19] The core rules governing the interpretation of contracts are also mandatory – indeed, they are part of the definitional rules of contract, since the law must provide a mechanism, beyond the parties, to determine whether (and what) the parties have agreed and whether it is in law to be accepted as a contract. This does not prevent the parties giving special meanings to particular words in their contracts, such as through the classic 'definitions' clauses of commercial contracts drafted by English lawyers. But the underlying principle of objective interpretation, both of the parties' communications to one another[20] and of written contracts,[21] is a legal rule outside the parties' control. And although the parties have considerable freedom in defining the consequences of breach of contract,[22] the remedy of specific performance is within the court's discretion which cannot be fettered by the terms of the contract.[23]

Other legal systems have mandatory rules relating at least to the constitution of the contract, and for the same reason as English law: if 'contract' is a general category of legally regulated transaction or relationship – recognised, protected and enforced by the law – there must be a clear definition of the notion of contract which is outside the parties' control. The definitions will differ, of course, from one system to another, and in codified systems the rules setting out the elements required by the law for the formation of a contract will often be set out conveniently in the text of the code. For example, the definition of a contract in French law is now[24] 'a concordance of wills of two or more persons intended to create, modify, transfer or extinguish obligations',

[17] Contracts (Rights of Third Parties) Act 1999, which can be excluded (either in whole or as regards some of its particular rules) by the parties' contrary intention. This overrides the general mandatory common law doctrine of privity of contract.

[18] See generally *Anson's Law of Contract* (n 11) chs 2, 4; H Beale (ed), *Chitty on Contracts* 35th edn (London, Sweet & Maxwell, 2023) chs 4, 6. There being no formal legislative definition of a 'contract' in English law, any definition is necessarily a summary drawn from the case law.

[19] Law of Property (Miscellaneous Provisions) Act 1989, s 1. Certain different rules apply to the execution of deeds by corporations.

[20] *Smith v Hughes* (1871) LR 6 QB 597, 607.

[21] *Investors Compensation Scheme Ltd v West Bromwich Building Society* [1998] 1 WLR 896, 912–13.

[22] See n 16 above.

[23] *Quadrant Visual Communications Ltd v Hutchison Telephone (UK) Ltd* [1993] BCLC 442, 451–52.

[24] The current provisions of the French Code civil ('Cc') dealing with the general law of contract were created by Ordonnance n° 2016-131 of 10 February 2016 (with some revisions made to the text by Loi no 2018-287 of 20 April 2018). In this chapter, English translations of the new French provisions are taken from the translation by J Cartwright, B Fauvarque-Cosson and S Whittaker, commissioned by the Direction des

supplemented by provisions to the effect that 'a contract is formed by the meeting of an offer and an acceptance by which the parties demonstrate their will to be bound' and that the validity of a contract requires the consent of the parties, their capacity to contract and content which is lawful and certain.[25] French law, however, goes further than English law in its legal regulation of the contractual relationship. Of particular note is the provision that not only the performance of the contract itself but also the period at and before the formation of the contract – the negotiations – are governed by good faith, a provision that is expressly made mandatory as a matter of public policy (*ordre public*).[26] The French Code civil expressly addresses the principle that some of its provisions are mandatory and thereby override the parties' freedom of contract:

> Everyone is free to contract or not to contract, to choose the person with whom to contract, and to determine the content and form of the contract, within the limits imposed by legislation.
>
> Contractual freedom does not allow derogation from rules which are an expression of public policy.[27]

The reference to the limits being 'imposed by legislation' is natural in a system, such as France, where the ultimate source of the legal rules governing contract is legislation, by contrast with English law, where some rules will be set out in legislation, but others rest on the authority of the common law (case law). In other respects, however, this is a general statement which would not be out of place in England nor, indeed, in other systems in either the Common law or Civil law traditions. What is particular to each system, however, is the scope given to 'rules which are an expression of public policy'. We have already noted that English law, too, prohibits terms that are illegal or contravene public policy.[28] But the notion of 'public policy' here is more restrained than the operation of *ordre public* in French contract law.

The example of the duty of good faith illustrates that a primary purpose of the use of mandatory rules of contract law in a legal system is to give a definite shape to the contract – to the very notion of contract. Finding this framework is critical to understanding and comparing the law of contract across legal systems. The absence of any mandatory duty of good faith in English law – not only in the performance of the contract (although the parties may supplement their contract by making performance in good faith an obligation),[29] but especially in the formation of the contract

affaires civiles et du sceau, Ministère de la Justice, République française. The French text and translation of the 2016 Ordonnance is printed in full as the appendix to J Cartwright and S Whittaker, *The Code Napoléon Rewritten: French Contract Law after the 2016 Reforms* (Oxford, Hart Publishing, 2017) at 409 et seq.

[25] Art 1101 Cc ('Le contrat est un accord de volontés entre deux ou plusieurs personnes destiné à créer, modifier, transmettre ou éteindre des obligations'), Art 1113 Cc ('Le contrat est formé par la rencontre d'une offre et d'une acceptation par lesquelles les parties manifestent leur volonté de s'engager') and Art 1128 Cc ('Sont nécessaires à la validité d'un contrat: 1° Le consentement des parties; 2° Leur capacité de contracter; 3° Un contenu licite et certain').

[26] Art 1104 Cc ('Les contrats doivent être négociés, formés et exécutés de bonne foi. Cette disposition est d'ordre public').

[27] Art 1102 Cc ('Chacun est libre de contracter ou de ne pas contracter, de choisir son cocontractant et de déterminer le contenu et la forme du contrat dans les limites fixées par la loi. La liberté contractuelle ne permet pas de déroger aux règles qui intéressent l'ordre public').

[28] See n 11 above and the text thereto.

[29] See eg *Compass Group UK and Ireland Ltd v Mid Essex Hospital Services NHS Trust* [2013] EWCA Civ 200, [2013] BLR 265.

(where it is said that the parties cannot even contract expressly to negotiate in good faith)[30] – tells us much about the different conceptions of the contractual relationship in England and France. Indeed, the absence of even default rules requiring good faith in English contract law reinforces this difference. If the parties do not expressly contract to perform in good faith, the terms of a contract governed by English law will not generally be supplemented by such a duty, and the parties' other duties will be interpreted simply in their own terms. There may be an exception for certain types of contract, where duties of good faith will be implied by a default rule, and which will therefore shape that type of contract, distinct from contracts generally.[31] Some other Common law systems take a different view, and see contracts as generally containing implied obligations of good faith in performance.[32] But the contrast between English law and French law on this point is particularly stark, and it is the line drawn between mandatory rules and default rules (or not even positive default rules) that helps us to make the comparison and to understand differences between the systems.

It should not be assumed, however, that it is always easy to draw the line between mandatory rules and default rules. A Common law system such as England is unlikely to offer easy answers to which rules of contract law are mandatory, at least for those (very many) rules which are contained in the case law rather than in legislation which may address the issue. In a codified system we might expect the definition to be clearer. It would be possible for the code to contain a general provision to the effect that the parties may exclude or vary the operation of any of its rules except as otherwise expressly provided by the code – that all rules of contract law are default rules unless expressly made mandatory.[33] But where there is no such provision, we have to fall back on general rules of interpretation of legislation within the legal system to work out the answer for any particular rule on which the code is silent as to its mandatory or default character. The French law of contract provides a good illustration of this problem: as Cécile Pérès has shown, although the latest reform of the general law of contract in France gives us a text which is sufficiently clear about whether certain provisions are mandatory or negotiable,[34] for some it fails to give a clear answer, leaving uncertainty for the contracting parties and the courts.[35]

Where, however, we can distinguish between the mandatory and default rules of general contract law, we can see that even the default rules have a significant part to play in shaping the contract by giving us a picture of normalised, typical contractual

[30] *Walford v Miles* [1992] 2 AC 128, 138; cf, however, *Petromec Inc v Petroleo Brasileiro SA* [2005] EWCA Civ 891, [2006] 1 Lloyd's Rep 121 at [121].

[31] See section IV.B below.

[32] In the United States, see § 205 of the Restatement (Second) of Contracts (American Law Institute, 1981) as well as § 1-304 of the Uniform Commercial Code.

[33] Such provisions are contained in the Draft Common Frame of Reference (Art II.-1:102(2)) and the UNIDROIT Principles of International Commercial Contracts (Art 1.5).

[34] Pérès, 'Mandatory and Non-mandatory Rules' (n 6) 172–73, noting that the starting point is that rules in the Ordonnance by which the Code civil was reformed (see n 24 above) are in principle non-mandatory, and listing examples where the drafters have expressly attributed a mandatory character to a certain number of provisions, but also certain provisions which the Ordonnance formally classes as non-mandatory.

[35] Pérès, 'Mandatory and Non-mandatory Rules' (n 6) 168 ('one might have expected the drafters of the *Ordonnance* to resolve this difficulty by establishing the mandatory or non-mandatory nature of the new rules once and for all. Not a bit of it'), 175–81 (listing and discussing a number of particular uncertainties).

incidents. The more extensive the default rules, the more extensive the picture becomes. Much of the contract, and in particular the detail and balance of the contractual terms, depends on the particular transaction and requires the parties to make provision accordingly, either expressly or being drawn from what they have expressly agreed relating to the transaction (what English lawyers would refer to as implication in fact,[36] and lawyers from other systems, such as French law, might call supplementation of the terms by interpreting the intention of the parties[37]). There is a limit to the scope of default rules in completing the substantive terms of the particular transaction, although some such rules may exist – even to the point of filling in the gap in a main term of the transaction, such as the price in a contract where the parties have clearly intended there to be a price but have failed to say what it is.[38] As we shall see in section IV of this chapter, it is more likely that default rules can fill gaps in the substantive terms of particular types of contract than in contracts generally. But the use of default legal rules – even though (by definition) they are only part of the contractual framework to the extent that the parties do not make provision in the contract to the contrary – assists by providing a (more or less) complete framework of a legally workable contract as defined by the legal system. Given that such rules are not mandatory, however, they are only an illustration of the kind of acceptable contractual framework that the parties might use, and therefore we might assume that it would be sensible for the legal system to adopt default rules which the parties would tend to adopt if they made express provision.[39] Otherwise, there may become a regular practice of parties excluding or overriding the rule,[40] which may undermine the validity of the choice of the rule as a default rule. The picture of the contract, as drawn by the combination of mandatory and default rules, then fails to match the expectation of parties and the reality of contracts as they are used in practice.[41] There may be a further consequence if a wide range of default rules is adopted in general contract law: by providing a very complete picture of the contract and its framework through rules which go much beyond those that are (as a matter of policy) mandatory, the inertia of parties in accepting the default rules rather than considering them and exercising their freedom to vary them may result in the (default) framework becoming more concrete than it could (and perhaps even should) be – the defaults become 'sticky' or quasi-mandatory.[42]

Much of the practical operation of default rules, at least in relation to the terms of the contract itself, depends not on the general framework of all contracts, but on the

[36] E Peel, *Treitel on the Law of Contract* 15th edn (London, Sweet & Maxwell, 2020) [6-050].

[37] '*Interprétation créatrice*', although this extends beyond simply finding the (implied) intention of the parties: S Rowan, *The New French Law of Contract* (Oxford, OUP, 2022) 130.

[38] In England, see s 8 of the Sale of Goods Act 1979 (reasonable price). This is, of course an example of a particular type of contract (sale, discussed further in section IV below) but it illustrates the general point.

[39] This is the 'majoritarian' basis of default terms: see the contribution by B Häcker, ch 1 in this volume, at 17–18. See also *Barton v Morris* [2023] UKSC 3, [2023] AC 684 at [128] (Lord Leggatt JSC).

[40] Cf the not uncommon practice in commercial contracts of excluding the operation of the Contracts (Rights of Third Parties) Act 1999 (on which see n 17).

[41] See Pérès, 'Mandatory and Non-mandatory Rules' (n 6) 168, citing also the point made by Carbonnier that when ineffectiveness of the law reaches a certain threshold, it is a sign that there is something badly wrong with it: J Carbonnier, 'Effectivité et ineffectivité de la règle de droit' in *Flexible droit, Pour une sociologie du droit sans rigueur* 10th edn (Paris, LGDJ, 2001) 136.

[42] Morgan (n 5) 92. See also Häcker (n 39) at 15.

particular context of the type of transaction – and therefore the type of contract. We therefore need to consider the use of types of contract ('special' contracts) within the structure of the law of contract.

IV. One Framework or More? The Structure of the Law of Contract(s)

In the same way that a transaction is not a contract just because the parties say that it is, but because it fits the definition given by the legal system,[43] a transaction is not a particular *type* of contract just because the parties say that it is. As Lord Templeman observed in a case which turned on whether the parties had entered into a tenancy (a lease) or merely a contractual licence to occupy land,

> If the agreement satisfied all the requirements of a tenancy, then the agreement produced a tenancy and the parties cannot alter the effect of the agreement by insisting that they only created a licence. The manufacture of a five-pronged implement for manual digging results in a fork even if the manufacturer, unfamiliar with the English language, insists that he intended to make and has made a spade.[44]

This example is from English law, although the systematic categorisation of types of contract – 'special contracts' – is more widely recognised in the Civil law. The approach in Civilian systems to special contracts follows largely from their historical roots in Roman law; the different approach taken by the Common law may follow from the very different historical development of contract law in England, as well as from the general techniques of legal reasoning in the Common law. However, we shall see that the categorisation of special contracts (and, therefore, the use of both mandatory and default rules in drawing the distinction between different types or categories of contract) is used in English law. But first we should consider the established use of 'special contracts' in the Civil law tradition.

A. 'Special' Contracts in the Civil Law Tradition: Roman Law and French Law

In Roman law, although the notion was developed that obligations may arise by contracting, and the separate types of contract had certain general features,[45] they were not united into a general principle, at least not in the modern sense of a general law of contract. A list of discrete forms of contracting, or of contractual transaction, was

[43] See section III above.
[44] *Street v Mountford* [1985] AC 809, 819. The clauses of the document referred to it as a 'licence', and a statement at the end of the document, signed by Mrs Mountford, that 'I understand and accept that a licence in the above form does not and is not intended to give me a tenancy protected under the Rent Acts' did not have the effect of making it into a licence where the legal incidents of the relationship that the parties had agreed constituted a tenancy.
[45] JAC Thomas, *Textbook of Roman Law* (Amsterdam, Oxford, North-Holland, 1976) ch 17.

recognised over time: some were defined by their form,[46] others by their content.[47] The requirements of each of the contracts were developed and refined, and new contracts were added to the list, responding both to the need for new legally-protected transactions and to the perception that, as the existing contracts were refined and redesigned in their rules and in the scope of their operation, gaps appeared which needed to be plugged.[48]

The Romans did not, however, take the final step of producing a general law of contract to which the list of contracts could form a supplement. Turning the specific contracts into a general principle did not fit the Roman approach – particularly given the law of procedure of the classical period of Roman Law, in which every claim before the courts had to fit a recognised formula, within a recognised cause of action. The development of law within this 'formulary system' of procedure[49] – not unlike the development of the English common law within the writ system before it was reformed in the nineteenth century[50] – meant that there was a tendency to add new actions to solve new problems, rather than to replace the existing actions. The consequence of such a system, however, is that the lawyer advising on the validity or effect of a transaction asks the question in a particular way. Rather than 'is this a contract?', the legally significant question becomes 'is this one of the contracts in our list?'

The Roman system of private law was not adopted directly by the modern Civilian legal systems, but was inherited indirectly through the reception of Roman law and its further development within the *ius commune* of continental Europe,[51] and then individual nations re-thought the system and enacted their own models of private law, typically within their codifications of private law. But the modern approach has interjected a prior question, not asked by the Romans. The modern Civil lawyer, faced with a transaction to analyse, asks first whether the transaction is valid, and what are its effects, *as a contract*. But that is not the end of the inquiry. If the transaction is a contract, a second question still remains: *which contract* is it? The second question is more akin to the question that the Romans would have asked, because it is only by placing the transaction within a particular, recognised category of contract that the analysis of the effects of the transaction can be complete.

The Roman legacy can be seen in its echoes within the lists of 'special' contracts in the modern codes. In the French Code civil,[52] for example, there are sections on (inter

[46] Notably, the *stipulatio* with its formality of words: B Nicholas, *An Introduction to Roman Law* (Oxford, Clarendon Press, 1962) 159–60, 193–96.

[47] Contracts of sale or hire, for example: Nicholas (n 46) 161–62, 171–85.

[48] One notable later development was the so-called 'innominate contacts', which covered the case of a bilateral agreement where performance by one party of his obligation gave rise to an enforceable claim for the other party's obligation. However, this was only used to fill gaps between the specific ('nominate') contracts and did not become a general principle underlying all contracts. Indeed, the class of innominate contracts was developed to include named transactions of particular content (such as exchange/barter): see Nicholas (n 46) 189–91; Thomas (n 45) ch 22.

[49] Nicholas (n 46) 20–21, 166.

[50] See text to n 75 below.

[51] Nicholas (n 46) 45–54; P Stein, *Roman Law in European History* (Cambridge, CUP, 1999).

[52] For French law, see generally P Malaurie, L Aynès and P-Y Gautier, *Droit des Contrats Spéciaux* 13th edn (Paris, LGDJ, 2024); F Collard Dutilleul, P Delebecque and C-E Bucher, *Contrats Civils et Commerciaux* 12th edn (Paris, Dalloz, 2024).

alia) sale, hire (of things and of services), partnership, loan (including loan for use and loan for consumption), deposit and mandate,[53] all of which were in the list of contracts devised by the Romans. It also extends to certain transactions which were known to the Romans but not fully developed as categories of contract within the Roman law scheme, or not placed by them in the list of contracts,[54] as well as to new forms of contractual transaction that have been developed in the modern context.[55] And although a transaction can be a contract within the general law of contract without being in any special category or type (and therefore subject only to the general law of contract and the particular terms of the contract which the parties may choose to agree), there are also types of contract which are not specially regulated by legislation, but which have been developed by legal practice and recognised as special contracts by the case law which often draws on the rules of other, legislatively defined special contracts by analogy to determine their incidents.[56] The modern codes of other jurisdictions follow a similar pattern, although in most jurisdictions – including in France – some of the modern developments of new forms of contracts have been placed not in the Code civil but (depending on their subject matter) in other codes or in special legislation.

The legislative treatment of the special contracts in Civil law systems is very extensive. This is not surprising: each of the numerous special contracts has its own regime precisely because it is different from the others and from the general law. And within the regime of each of the special contracts some rules will be mandatory, others will be default rules, variable by the parties.

Taking again the French model of special contracts, it is commonly said that most of the rules set out in the 1804 Code civil were (and remain) default rules,[57] although many recent legislative provisions addressing particular categories of contract include much more extensive mandatory rules.[58] This shows that in relation to particular types of contract, as much as in relation to contracts in general,[59] mandatory rules of law play a regulatory role as an instrument of public policy, reducing the place for default rules and therefore limiting the power of the parties to exclude or vary rules which are seen as fundamental to the nature of the contract in question. And just as in the definition of a contract itself,[60] the definition of each separately regulated 'special' contract is itself governed by a mandatory rule. Many of the incidents of the contract of sale may be a

[53] Book III of the Cc, titles VI (sale: *la vente*), VIII (hire: *le contrat de louage*), IX (partnership: *la société*), X (loan: *le prêt*), XI (deposit: *le dépôt*), XIII (mandate: *le mandat*).

[54] Such as the contracts of exchange (*l'échange*: book III, title VII of the Cc) and settlement of a dispute (*les transactions*: book III, title XV of the Cc), common transactions which the classical Romans had difficulty classifying, although they were eventually listed as *permutatio* and *transactio*, two of the (nominate) forms of innominate contract: see n 48 above.

[55] For instance, the contract of development of immovable property (*le contrat de promotion immobilère*: book III, title VIII bis of the Cc) and *la fiducie* (book III, title XIV of the Cc, designed to replicate to some extent the common law trust).

[56] Malaurie, Aynès and Gautier (n 52) 21.

[57] Pérès, 'Mandatory and Non-mandatory Rules' (n 6) 168, who gives a list of various turns of phrase which indicate the non-mandatory nature of a rule; Malaurie, Aynès and Gautier (n 52) 34; Collard Dutilleul, Delebecque and Bucher (n 52) 17.

[58] Malaurie, Aynès and Gautier (n 52) 34 (giving as examples leases and consumer protection legislation); Collard Dutilleul, Delebecque and Bucher (n 52) 17 (giving as examples labour law, construction law and consumer law).

[59] See section III above.

[60] See text to n 25 above.

matter for the parties if they choose to exclude or vary the default rules provided by the Code civil, but they are not free to decide that a transaction is a contract of sale if it does not meet the legal definition of that type of contract. The point of the structure of a system of contract law based on special, as well as general, rules of contract law, is that the categorisation not just of contract, but of each type of contract, is fundamental, based on legal rules, and therefore mandatory. There may be a sense in which the parties 'contract into' the law on sale when they enter into a contract of sale: their act of will in choosing that transaction places it within the 'Title' of the Code regulating contracts of sale – and this has the benefit that the default rules set out in that Title apply, without the parties having to make special provision, although they will be free to vary default rules. But they only contract into that Title if their transaction really is a contract of sale, which is a matter for the court to determine. Once a transaction has been characterised by the law, and therefore the type of contract is settled, the relevant legislative text, with its extensive, systematic and detailed provisions, give us a fuller picture of the incidents of that contract, which must also be read with the general law of contract insofar as the special regime for the type of contract does not override the rules provided by the general regime.

Many of the incidents attributable to the contract by virtue of its type may be excludable or variable by the parties, as in the case of any default rules. But providing the detailed picture of the type of contract, even in a default (not mandatory) form, brings the attendant general advantages of default rules – including certainty for the parties that they have a definite, sufficient set of standard terms and other incidents of the contractual relationship, without having to draw up a complete list of their own detailed terms beyond those that are specific to their own transaction. It is commonly observed that there is a difference in style – and, notably, in length and detail – of contract drafting in relation to commercial contracts, between the Common law (prolix) and Civil law (laconic). If the main incidents of a contract are provided by the Code, the French lawyer will be able to rely on them without extensive detailed negotiation and drafting of the contract.[61] The English lawyer has a very different approach to the drafting of commercial contracts – and, as we shall see, this may be a result of a very different view of the structure of contract law, of the place of 'special' contracts, and of the place of default rules of contract law. This must also be seen in the context of the very different history of the law of contract within the common law – and, indeed, the very structure of the Common law system, with its relationship between judge-made law (the 'common law') and legislation.

B. 'Special' Contracts in English Law

The general law of contract in England[62] was created not by legislation but through judicial decisions. Legislation has intervened from time to time to add to, vary or override

[61] H Kötz (trans G Mertens and T Weir), *European Contract Law* 2nd edn (Oxford, OUP, 2017) 102 ('The aim of these suppletive or default rules laid down by the legislature and developed by the courts is not only to accommodate the typical interests of the parties in a just manner, but also to save the parties the expense of prolonged negotiation by offering them appropriate "default rules"').

[62] See generally *Anson's Law of Contract* (n 11) ch 1.

the rules of contract law as they were laid down by the courts, and the legislative intervention has grown in extent and in significance in recent years. But the general pattern is for legislation to intervene on particular issues within the law of contract: the common law of contract, created and still developed by the judges, remains the general law to which legislation constitutes the exception. And the general law of contract, being in the modern law still a development of cases, many of which date from the middle of the nineteenth century when freedom of contract was the underlying philosophy,[63] has at its centre a conception of contract that assumes that the parties are free and independent actors, who should be allowed to take their own decisions. The role of the court is to give effect to their intentions, not to override them. This model of contract based on free, equal and independent parties may appear unsatisfactory in the modern age, but the courts see it as generally a matter for the legislator, rather than the courts themselves, to intervene to regulate inequalities between the parties.[64]

The general approach of the English courts to their role in giving effect to the intentions of the parties can be seen in establishing the terms of the contract. In the Civil law, a significant purpose of the classification of contracts by type is to provide legal rules (whether mandatory or default) to determine the parties' obligations by reference to the nature of the contract. However, according to the traditional thinking, the common law is different: it is for the parties themselves to define the content of the contract. This comparison between the Civil law and the Common law was explained by Barry Nicholas:

> In the field of contract, a fundamental difference between French law and the traditional Common law is that the Common law habitually attempts to derive all the consequences of a contract from the will of those who made it[65] (or at least ostensibly to do so, for the French lawyer would say that the will from which those consequences are derived is a very artificial or objective one), whereas the French law (and the Civil law generally) will often have recourse to rules. This may seem paradoxical, for the Common lawyer who comes to French law may well be struck by the unity and coherence which traditional *doctrine* derives from its emphasis on intention and the *autonomie de la volonté*. But there is another aspect. The unifying concept of *volonté* has been superimposed on, but has not eliminated, the Roman foundations. … The parties freely make their agreement, but the law will, as far as possible, categorise that agreement as a specific typical contract, and the rights and duties of the parties will be seen as flowing from that categorisation rather than from the agreement itself.[66]

Nicholas here refers to the general approach in the Common law to define the content of the contract by reference to the will of the parties, although such a reference is not to the actual, *subjective* will or intention of the parties, but to their *objective* will or intention. The general approach in English contract law is to determine parties' intentions by reference to the interpretation that a reasonable person would give to

[63] *Anson's Law of Contract* (n 11) 4, 17.

[64] *National Westminster Bank Plc v Morgan* [1985] AC 686, 708; *Times Travel (UK) Ltd v Pakistan International Airlines Corp* [2021] UKSC 40, [2023] AC 101 at [26].

[65] Cf the dictum of Lord Radcliffe in *Davis Contractors Ltd v Fareham Urban District Council* [1956] AC 696, 728 ['the tendency of English courts to refer all the consequences of a contract to the will of those who made it'].

[66] B Nicholas, 'Rules and Terms – Civil Law and Common Law' (1974) 48 *Tulane L Rev* 946, 948–49.

their intentions.[67] In recent decisions the Supreme Court continues to insist that the interpretation of the contract is objective, but also that is not for the law generally to override the clearly expressed intentions of the parties. If there is some ambiguity in a (commercial) contract, the courts may favour the (commercially) sensible conclusion, but this is only because such a construction is more likely to give effect to the intention of the parties.[68] 'The purpose of interpretation is to identify what the parties have agreed, not what the court thinks that they should have agreed.'[69]

Similarly, when the English courts engage in the (different) exercise of completing the contents of the contract by adding terms which the parties have not expressed – finding the 'implied terms' – it is often said that the aim is to add terms by reference to the parties' intentions. This is again an exercise in objectivity rather than looking simply for the unspoken subjective intentions of the parties, and the courts admit that they sometimes go beyond what they believe the parties really intended, so that it may be better to say that the courts presume, or impute, an intention to the parties as to the terms that are implied.[70] But this insistence on the contract and its terms being based on the (objective) intention of the parties runs deep in English law.[71]

This picture of a law of contract where the terms are based on the parties' intentions in the context of their particular contract – however attenuated that notion of 'intention' may be (implied, presumed, imputed) – is not the whole story. There are plenty of situations where the law will say that, because the contract that the parties entered into is of a particular type, they are bound (at least if they do not provide expressly to the contrary) by certain standard terms which normally belong in that type of contract – rather like the Civil lawyer's categorisation of 'special' contracts. We shall consider further below the significance of such standard types of contract within the modern English law of contract. But here we should note that, even in these cases, the traditional approach of the courts has been to say that terms implied into standard types of contract follow broadly the same idea as other implied terms: parties who enter into such a contract can be taken (objectively) to have intended the terms because they are the normal incidents of that type of contract:

> The task of ascertaining what the parties to a contract of any kind have agreed shall be their legal rights and liabilities to one another as a result of the contract is a familiar one in all systems of law. It is accomplished not by determining what each party actually thought those rights and liabilities would be, but by what each party by his words and conduct reasonably led the other party to believe were the acts which he was undertaking a legal obligation to perform. There are some rights and liabilities which arise by implication of law from the nature of the contract itself such as a contract of sale of goods or land, a contract of carriage or bailment, a contract of service or a contract of insurance. In offering to enter into a contract of a particular kind a party leads the other party reasonably to believe that he undertakes a legal obligation to perform all those acts which a person entering into a contract of that kind usually performs, unless his words or conduct are such as would make it reasonably clear to

[67] See n 20 and n 21 above.

[68] *Mannai Investment Co Ltd v Eagle Star Life Assurance Co Ltd* [1997] AC 749, 771.

[69] *Arnold v Britton* [2015] UKSC 36, [2015] AC 1619 at [20] (Lord Neuberger).

[70] *The Moorcock* (1889) 14 PD 64, 68.

[71] *Anson's Law of Contract* (n 11) 4, 7; *Chitty on Contracts* (n 18) [2-003], [2-004].

> the other party that this is not so and also makes it clear which of those acts he does not intend to undertake to perform and which of them he intends to undertake to perform only in some other and specified manner.[72]

Another reason why the English courts, when they were developing the general rules of modern contract law,[73] did not see the same significance in the categorisation of contracts as the lawyers in Civil law systems, can be found in the history of the law of contract within the broader historical development of English private law – both the substantive law and the law of procedure. This is not the place to discuss the history of English contract law in detail,[74] but we should note that from the medieval period until the nineteenth century the availability of a claim in court depended on there being a relevant procedure for making the claim: a 'form of action', which in the King's courts required the claimant to obtain one of a list of writs.[75] From an early stage, a claim for a fixed sum of money due under a contract (such as the unpaid price in a sale contract) fell within the writ of 'debt'; the action to enforce other promises was the writ of 'covenant'. Debt remained the action for payment of a debt of money but, building on the fact that the claim for misfeasance in the performance of a contract which caused loss to the claimant was more in the nature of a tort, by the beginning of the seventeenth century the courts had accepted that not only misfeasance (defective performance) but also nonfeasance (non-performance) of an agreement could be brought under a single, general action – an action based historically within the law of tort but now seen as an action in contract, on the basis that the defendant had failed in an obligation which he had undertaken ('*assumpsit*'). This generalisation of a contractual form of action, rather than (as in Rome) a list of special contracts with their own separate actions,[76] lay behind the development of the modern English law of contract. As Nicholas wrote:

> There remains … the difference that historically the Civil law starts from typical contracts and eventually reaches a single principle, whereas we reverse the process. We first of all evolved, through assumpsit, a general principle of contract, and then, by the device of the implied term, we isolated certain typical contracts, in which the same terms are held to recur.[77]

Insofar as English law has developed – and continues to develop – special contracts, it is therefore not a matter of inheritance from the earlier law, but a response to the need to categorise different, typical forms of contractual transaction, to *break away from* the nineteenth century vision of the contract as a general principle based on the intentions of the parties.

There is nothing novel about seeing a balance within English law between the general law of contract and a list of special contracts. *Chitty on Contracts* has been structured in two volumes (vol I: General Principles; vol II: Specific Contracts) since the twenty-first

[72] *Hardwick Game Farm v Suffolk Agricultural Poultry Producers Association* [1966] 1 WLR 287, 339 (Diplock LJ).
[73] See text to n 63 above.
[74] For a short account, see *Anson's Law of Contract* (n 11) 10–18; and for fuller discussion, see J Baker, *An Introduction to English Legal History*, 5th edn (Oxford, OUP, 2019) 338–85.
[75] Baker (n 74) ch 4.
[76] See nn 46–48 above.
[77] Nicholas (n 66) 950.

edition in 1955, and from its earliest editions in the nineteenth century the (one-volume) book contained separate chapters dedicated to contracts governing particular relationships, as well as the main chapters on the general rules of contract law.[78] This is an exception to the general structure of the books on contract law, although there are many books, often aimed at practitioners, on specific types of contract. Indeed, the list of 'specific contracts' in *Chitty* is rather eclectic, by no means a complete coverage of all the types of contract that one might expect to encounter in practice, nor containing all those contracts that would generally be included in the Civil lawyer's list of special contracts.[79]

The reality is that in English law the classification of contracts by type is important and has become increasingly so in recent decades. There are benefits for the Common law as much as for the Civil law in recognising distinctions between contracts. In finding the terms of the contract, if they have not been fully set out by the parties, it is of assistance to the parties and to the court to have a sense of the normal incidents of that type of transaction, at least to provide a default position against which to set the particular arrangements agreed between the parties. But there can also be a place for more active regulation of contracts: rules relating to particular types of contract can be designed to reflect the appropriate balance of the parties' interests, including protections for the party who typically needs them in the context of such a contract.

We have seen that the general approach of the Common law within the general law of contract is non-interventionist: it is not the role of the courts themselves to override the intentions of the parties, nor to create a regulatory framework to depart from the general principle of freedom of contract.[80] However, the courts have been able to identify types of contract which, by virtue of their inherent characteristics, or the inherent relationship between their parties, can be given special treatment, typically by implying terms into such a contract as default rules. Even before the legislature intervened in 1893 to put the implied terms in contracts of sale of goods on a statutory footing, the courts had already decided that in the contract of sale of goods by description there are implied terms that the goods are of merchantable quality and in conformity with their description, and reasonably fit for their purpose.[81] And the case law made clear that in

[78] In the first edition (1826) the author included a chapter entitled 'Of the Subject Matter of Contracts', containing sections dealing with contracts relating to land (in particular, leases of premises for occupation by the tenant); contracts relating to personal property (eg sale of goods, and bailment – covering the loan of things by deposit, mandate, *commodatum*, pledge and hire); marriage; contracts of services and works by a range of different kinds of professionals and tradesmen; and contracts relating to money, including loans. There were also sections on contracts requiring particular formalities, including contracts of guarantee and contracts relating to land.

[79] The current (35th) edition of *Chitty on Contracts* (n 18) has chapters on Arbitration, Bailment, Bills of Exchange and Banking, Carriage by Air, Carriage by Land, Construction Contracts, Consumer Contracts, Credit and Security, Employment, Gambling Contracts, Insurance, Restrictive Agreements and Competition, Sale of Goods and Suretyship. For another example, similarly selective in its list of contracts, see A Burrows (ed), *English Private Law* 3rd edn (Oxford, OUP, 2013) ch 8 ('Contract: In General') followed by separate chapters on Agency, Sale of Goods, Carriage of Goods by Sea, Carriage of Goods by Air and Land, Insurance, Banking, Employment and Bailment.

[80] See section III above.

[81] These terms were implied by statute by Sale of Goods Act 1893, ss 13, 14; see now Sale of Goods Act 1979, ss 13, 14 (where 'merchantable quality' is replaced by 'satisfactory quality'). On the earlier law, and its development, see M Bridge (ed), *Benjamin's Sale of Goods* 12th edn (London, Sweet & Maxwell, 2023) paras 11-002 to 11-003, 11-025.

a contract for the supply of services, the supplier's normal obligation is to supply the service with reasonable care and skill, before this was provided by statute in 1982.[82] Typical terms have also been implied by the courts into other kinds of contract: the implied obligation of mutual trust and confidence between the parties to an employment contract;[83] the obligation of the landlord in a lease of a flat within a block of flats in multiple occupation to maintain the common parts over which he retains control;[84] and the obligation of the housebuilder to provide a house fit for habitation.[85]

However, in the modern law, there has been an increasing tendency for the legislature to regulate particular types of contract, not only taking over by legislation the regulation of some contracts that were already identified by the courts at common law as having particular defining characteristics,[86] but also giving effect to new forms of contract.[87] There are advantages in defining types of contract by legislation, which can provide in much more precise detail than the common law for standard implied terms to regulate the performance of the contract itself[88] – even if these are default rules, rather than mandatory. And the legislator can lay down authoritatively and in greater detail the consequences of the categorisation of a particular form of transaction, and can apply a range of policy decisions to shape the content of each type of contract, based on the inherent nature of the relationship between the parties to such a transaction – such as imposing duties of disclosure on one of the parties,[89] or setting requirements of formality,[90] with a view to protecting the party who is generally perceived as being weaker in that type of relationship. In their definition of particular types of contract the courts may themselves sometimes apply policy decisions,[91] but this is necessarily much more limited

[82] Supply of Goods and Services Act 1982, s 13.

[83] *Malik v Bank of Credit and Commerce International SA* [1998] AC 20, 45 (Lord Steyn: 'a standardised term implied by law, that is, on a term which is said to be an incident of all contracts of employment … Such implied terms operate as default rules. The parties are free to exclude or modify them'). For a discussion of this implied term in the employment context, see the contribution by A Bogg, ch 10 in this volume.

[84] *Liverpool City Council v Irwin* [1977] AC 239, 254 (Lord Wilberforce: 'such obligation should be read into the contract as the nature of the contract itself implicitly requires, no more, no less: a test, in other words, of necessity').

[85] *Miller v Cannon Hill Estates Ltd* [1931] 2 KB 113.

[86] Such as contracts for the sale of goods (n 81) and for the supply of services (n 82).

[87] Such as contracts for digital content, regulated by the Consumer Rights Act 2015, Part I, Chapter 3, and various forms of consumer and non-consumer finance contract.

[88] See eg the detailed definition of the implied terms under the contract of sale, under the Sale of Goods Act 1979, as well as the precise definition of the contracts to which they apply – such as s 14(1), (2), which makes clear that it is not all sellers, but only those who sell in the course of a business, that guarantee the quality of their goods and their fitness for purpose.

[89] The common law developed the rule that the parties to a contract of 'utmost good faith' had duties of disclosure in the formation of the contract; however, this was applied only to a limited group of contracts, in particular contracts of insurance and of partnership. There are many more new duties of disclosure in modern statutes, particularly in favour of the consumer but also in non-consumer contexts. See *Anson's Law of Contract* (n 11) 365–67, and for detailed discussion J Cartwright, *Misrepresentation, Mistake and Non-Disclosure* 6th edn (London, Sweet & Maxwell, 2022) ch 17.

[90] See *Anson's Law of Contract* (n 11) 80–91; and for detailed discussion J Cartwright, *Formation and Variation of Contracts* 4th edn (London, Sweet & Maxwell, 2024) chs 5 and 6.

[91] See *Crossley v Faithful & Gould Holdings Ltd* [2004] EWCA Civ 293, [2004] ICR 1615 at [36] (Dyson LJ: 'rather than focus on the elusive concept of necessity, it is better to recognise that, to some extent at least, the existence and scope of standardised implied terms raise questions of reasonableness, fairness and the balancing of competing policy considerations: see Elisabeth Peden, "Policy Concerns behind Implication of Terms in Law" (2001) 117 LQR 459, 467–475. Such considerations are, I believe, reflected in the recent significant developments in the field of the employer/employee relationship').

than in the case of the legislator. Moreover, the courts' view that contracts are designed to give effect to the intentions of the parties means that there is a well-established general rule that any term that would otherwise be implied into a contract by the common law (judge-made law) must give way to the express terms of the contract: 'any terms which the courts imply into a contract must be consistent with the express terms. Implied terms may supplement the express terms of the contract but cannot contradict them. Only Parliament may actually override what the parties have agreed.'[92] Where there is a desire to protect one party in a typical contractual relationship by a mandatory rule of law, it will have to be done by statute – as, indeed, is commonly done in the field of consumer protection.[93] The very concept of the 'consumer' as a legally protected category of contracting party, and the recognition of the various forms of consumer contract which have built-in protections for the consumer against the trader, are creations of the legislature, not of the courts.

From the perspective of English law, however, there are disadvantages in leaving the classification of contracts to the legislator: the fact that the type of contract to which the legislation applies has to be defined in the text means that lines around the forms of contract can become sharp, leaving gaps. The Civil lawyer may not see a significant difficulty in this: if a contract under analysis is not specially regulated, but is analogous to a type of contract for which special provision is made by the legislator, the court may be able to reason by analogy from the special regulation to determine how the legislative intent behind that provision should be translated to cover the analogous contract. The traditional approach of the English courts, however, is not generally to draw analogies from statute. There have been some suggestions that this view is too narrow, and that the courts could, and sometimes do, rely on statute in the development of the common law,[94] but this has not been developed by the courts as a general approach.

By contrast, the courts have greater freedom when they are engaged in the categorisation of contracts by type for the purposes of the common law, and within the limits of what they can achieve at common law – typically, for the purpose of implying terms into the contract as default rules, having no power to make such terms mandatory. The fact that they are not constrained by immutable definitions in the case of contracts that have already been recognised, and that they can develop new rules by analogy with existing common law rules, allows them to work out the appropriate categorisation of a new transaction. An example is the contract which has the overlapping features of two other, different contracts, such as goods and services, in identifying the inherent (implied) obligation on the party who both designs and supplies a product.[95] Another advantage of the classification of contracts by the courts within the case law is that, not bound by a textual definition of categories, the courts can build up sub-groups of forms of contract, and particularise the terms to be implied by reference to each individual form of contract.

[92] *Johnson v Unisys Ltd* [2001] UKHL 13, [2003] 1 AC 518 at [37] (Lord Hoffmann). But cf the critical discussion by Bogg (n 83) at 196 et seq in this volume, in the employment context.

[93] *Chitty on Contracts* (n 18) ch 41; and see the contribution by S Whittaker, ch 8 in this volume.

[94] See esp J Beatson, 'The Role of Statute in the Development of Common Law' (2001) 117 *LQR* 247; A Burrows, *Thinking About Statutes* (Cambridge, CUP, 2018) 45 ('Lecture 2: The Interaction Between Common Law and Statute').

[95] *Samuels v Davis* [1943] KB 526.

The courts may also take bolder steps, and expand the rules of contracts already established at common law to cover new situations. A notable recent example is the way in which some judges have sought to identify 'relational contracts' as a broader category than contracts of partnership, or joint venture, but which (like partnership, but contrary to contracts generally in English law) may contain an implied term requiring both parties to perform the contract in good faith.[96] The recognition of new types of contract – new 'special contracts' – within which the courts then identify particular terms or other incidents as default rules of each type of contract, is still possible within the common law, alongside any further legislative regulation of particular contracts.

V. Conclusion

In this chapter we have focused on the different approaches of the Common law (represented by English law) and the Civil law (represented by French law) in their use of default rules of contract law: the way in which the law in each system provides rules of contract law – both terms in contracts, and a broader framework within which contracts exist and operate – independently of the parties' agreement. This requires us to take into account the distinction between mandatory and default legal rules. At first sight, these are fundamentally different in function: mandatory rules are designed to fulfil some general or particular policy which the law decides should override the freedom that the parties would otherwise have in constructing their own contractual framework and terms; default rules are to facilitate the parties' contracting, furthering (by their purely default nature) the parties' freedom but assisting them by filling out the transaction, saving the parties having to address everything in detail (or even at all) apart from the elements of their transaction that cannot be generalised as part of a default template for their contract. However, the distinction between the roles of mandatory and default rules of contract law, whilst clear in theory, is porous in practice. Not only can there be doubt about the mandatory or non-mandatory status of some individual rules, but even those that are clearly default rules also further aims similar to the mandatory rules: they are devised to sit alongside any mandatory rules, and to form part of a coherent template for the framework of the contract – an image of the whole contract which (particularly where parties generally do not contract out of them, whether by choice or by inertia or by simple ignorance or inadvertence) can become normalised as the standard form.

Integral to an understanding – and especially a comparative understanding – of the nature and function of default rules in different systems of contract law is not only the extent of the use in fact made of default rules in each system, but the *reasons* for any differences. This may include not only the systems' theories of default rules (are they designed to give effect to the intention of the parties, or at least to the (likely) intentions of parties who enter into such contracts, or are they designed to complete the model for the contract set out as a matter of policy by the legal system for the contract, a model whose framework may be defined in the mandatory rules which they supplement?), but

[96] See, in particular, *Yam Seng Pte Ltd v International Trade Corporation Ltd* [2013] EWHC 111 (QB), [2013] 1 CLC 662; *Al Nehayan v Kent* [2018] EWHC 333 (Comm), [2018] 1 CLC 216.

also the different structures of the systems' law of contract, including the different sources of law through which contracts are defined and regulated. History also has a part to play in understanding this topic – as, indeed, it generally does in comparative law.

We have seen that there is a traditional contrast between the Common law and the Civil law in their approach to default rules in contract law. Civilian systems, drawing on their Roman heritage, see a necessary role for the categorisation of contracts by type, not simply as a means of defining different mandatory rules for each type, but (and perhaps especially) to provide individualised contractual frameworks for different, standard types of transaction. This is then reflected also in contractual practice in the analysis of transactions, and in the drafting of contracts – which can be relatively brief, relying on the relevant default rules to complete the details. This traditional role for default rules in the modern Civil law systems is furthered by the fact that the source of the default rules is predominantly legislation – the 'special contracts' set out in the code, supplemented by courts' interpretation of the legislation in light of commercial practice.

By contrast, the traditional Common law model is fundamentally different. From its very different history, English law is said to have a general law of contract, based on the (objectively determined) common intention of the parties. Contracts are more individualised, not categorised by law, and the courts generally do not see it as their role to impose terms – even normal, standard terms – on the parties: the content of default rules appears not to fulfil a regulatory function in the same way as in a Civil law system, where default rules have the authority of the legislator.[97] However, the picture is more nuanced than the traditional model might suggest. Even in the nineteenth century, when the general theory of English contract law, rooted in the intention of the parties, was in its heyday, the courts were also identifying contracts by type – the contract of sale is a classic example – and typical incidents to be implied (by default) in each contract. But in the modern law not only have the courts themselves identified a broader range of typical contracts for which, through their case law, they have set out the kind of terms that it can normally be assumed the parties would intend, but also there has been significant legislative intervention to regulate particular types of contract, which includes the provision of not only mandatory but also default rules.

In the modern English law, there is therefore greater fragmentation of contract law, with a greater reliance on not only mandatory rules but also default rules for different types of contract. This appears to be a movement away from the old model of a general contract law.[98] However, it would be misleading to assume that it involves convergence with the Civil law. The building blocks of the English law of contract remain in place: legislation is still seen as an exception to the general rules of the common law and the courts' approach to the further development of common law rules is different from (and potentially broader than) their development of rules whose authority is based on legislation. And it is commercial practice not to rely on default rules – even those that are clearly provided by a legislative text – but to provide certainty by writing them into contracts.

[97] cf the contribution by A Hellgardt, ch 2 in this volume.

[98] Cf text to n 77, where Nicholas contrasts the development of the Common law with the historical development of the Civil law.

8

The Nature and Function of Default Rules in English Consumer Contract Law

SIMON WHITTAKER

I. Introduction

Consumer contract law provides a striking exception to the general pattern of English contract law as many of the special rules governing consumer contracts apply irrespective of any contrary or derogating agreement: they are mandatory rather than default rules.[1] This reflects a general acceptance that, in consumer law, the principles of freedom of contract and the binding force of contract should give way to the need to protect consumers as the 'weaker parties' compared to traders both as regards their bargaining power and their level of knowledge.[2] This may suggest a very limited role for default rules in the consumer context, but in fact they remain significant in some situations and also play a number of roles in the general controls on the fairness of the terms of consumer contracts. By way of preliminary, though, I need to clarify my understanding both of 'default rules' and 'consumer contract law' for present purposes.

II. The Nature of 'Default Rules'

The recent judgment of Lord Leggatt JSC in *Barton v Morris* provides a convenient explanation of what most, if not all, English lawyers understand by 'default rules'.[3] He noted first the general role of contract law in a way which gives them a central role.

[1] See more generally on the differences between the general law of contract and the law governing consumer contracts S Whittaker, 'Distinctive Features of the New Consumer Contract Law' (2017) 133 *LQR* 47.

[2] This description of consumers is taken from the case law of the CJEU: see C-453/10 *Pereničová v SOS finance spol sro* EU:C:2012:144 para 27 (unfair contract terms) and C-59/12 *BKK Mobil Oil Körperschaft des öffentlichen Rechts v Zentrale zur Bekämpfung unlauteren Wettbewerbs eV* EU:C:2013:634 para 35 (unfair commercial practices).

[3] *Barton v Morris* [2023] UKSC 3, [2023] 2 WLR 26. According to the majority (Lady Rose, Lord Briggs and Lord Stephens JJSC) the members of the Court did not disagree fundamentally about the underlying

> The idea of freedom of contract is that contractual obligations should be freely chosen. But that does not mean that the choice to be bound by an obligation must be expressly stated. If it did, there would be very little to the law of contract. A principal function of contract law is to provide a framework of rules which apply to contractual relationships unless the parties expressly opt out of them. … Establishing default rules serves to reduce the costs and inconvenience of negotiating terms and also to avoid unfair outcomes in cases where parties, whether through inertia, lack of opportunity or foresight, or deliberate choice, have not negotiated express terms to cover certain significant contingencies.[4]

Default rules may apply in principle to all types of contract (such as the rules governing remoteness of damage) or to particular types or categories of contract (for example, sale of goods or contracts for services).[5] Lord Leggatt then explained the prominent role in English law of implied terms in setting these default rules, whether they are implied in fact or in law (and as regards the latter, whether by the common law or legislation).[6] While Lord Leggatt made these observations in the context of a commercial contract, I think that his views reflect the general understanding of the nature of 'default rules' in English contract law, that is, that they are legal rules which apply to a contract unless parties make contrary or different express provision. Also reflecting the general position in the positive law, Lord Leggatt's discussion of 'default rules' reflects the much lesser prominence given to legal rules governing contracts (whether generally or particular types of contracts) which are *incapable* of exclusion or modification by express term.[7]

Here, there are both similarities and contrasts with the traditional framework adopted by many Civil law systems. In French law, for example, lawyers have long distinguished between *lois supplétives* (*de volonté*) (legislative rules which supplement

principles themselves: at [107]. The majority held, first, that, on its construction, the contract before them provided for payment of a sum as remuneration of the service provided 'if, and only if' certain conditions were satisfied; they saw this as inconsistent with the implication of a term implied in fact as to a reasonable remuneration where the conditions were not satisfied and held that the type of contract did not attract any term implied in law: as a result, no reasonable sum was payable, at [25]–[26], [43], [50], [68] and [76]. By contrast, in the view of Lord Leggatt JSC, the contract contained a term implied in law that the party providing the service would be paid a reasonable remuneration for it; this recognition then placed the burden of proof as to whether this term had been excluded by the agreement of the parties on the party so claiming; given the trial judge's unchallenged findings as to the silence of that oral agreement as to remuneration in the circumstances, the implied term was not excluded and so should be applied and a reasonable remuneration paid: esp at [135]–[136], [160]–[161], and [185]–[188]. Lord Burrows JSC also dissented on the ground that the contract included a term implied in law which had not been excluded by the contract: at [205], [214]–[220] and [225].

[4] *Barton v Morris* (n 3) at [126] and [128].

[5] *Barton v Morris* (n 3) at [129]–[130].

[6] *Barton v Morris* (n 3) at [131]–[135].

[7] A key example of such a rule at common law is liability in tort for personal fraud which at common law cannot be excluded or restricted by agreement: *S. Pearson & Son Ltd v Dublin Corp* [1907] AC 351, 353, 362; *HIH Casualty and General Insurance Ltd v Chase Manhattan Bank* [2003] UKHL 6, [2003] 2 Lloyd's Rep 61 at [16], [76], and [98]. There are, of course, other examples where the common law does not give effect to an express contract term, notably, where the term provides for a 'penalty' or where it is in unreasonable restraint of trade. In all these cases, though, it is not usual to describe these controls in terms of the mandatory character of the law which is purportedly modified by the express terms in question. For example, a contract term is ineffective which seeks to impose the payment of a sum of money on breach of contract and which is qualified as a penalty clause, but this is not said to render the rules governing the measure of damages for breach mandatory, not least as (subject to any applicable legislative control) that liability may be limited or even excluded entirely. And in the case of the law on unreasonable restraint of trade, it would be not be usual to refer to the general position of a party's freedom to trade as providing a default rule which may be excluded or restricted (but only reasonably).

the will of the parties) and *lois impératives* (legislative rules which apply by authority), a distinction which reflects the medieval distinction between *ius dispositivum* and *ius cogens*.[8] This distinction can be referred to conveniently in English as one between 'non-mandatory legal rules/law' and 'mandatory legal rules/law',[9] but the difference in the usual terminology of English lawyers (which refers to default rules and rules incapable of exclusion by agreement/contract) and in the Civil law tradition reflects a significant difference in starting-point. As Barry Nicholas explained, while the Common law 'evolved, through assumpsit, a general principle of contract and then by the device of the implied term, … isolated certain typical contracts, in which the same terms are held to incur', the Civil law developed a unitary theory of contract from the 'scattered materials' in the *Corpus Iuris*, but

> this leaves unaffected the explicit contribution which the *Corpus Iuris* makes in the shape of the elaborate structure of the rules which lay down the essential elements of those typical contracts and the rights and duties of the parties to them. The parties freely make their agreement, but the law will, as far as possible, categorise that agreement as a specific typical contract, and the rights and duties of the parties will be seen as flowing from that categorisation rather than from the agreement itself.[10]

For French civil lawyers, therefore, while the parties may in principle add what terms they wish and may make a contract which does not fall within a listed category, the starting-point is that legislation (and in particular the Civil Code) sets the incidents of a series of typical contracts and then supplements this with a law common in principle to all contracts.[11] Given this starting-point, the question whether the *legislative* rules applicable to a contract made between particular parties are capable or incapable of modification by express intention (that is, whether they are *lois supplétives* or *lois impératives*) arises naturally and is to be resolved by reference to general principle and by interpretation of the particular legislative provision in question. In this respect, Article 6 of the Civil Code (as enacted in 1804 and still in force) frames the proper question generally by providing that '[o]ne cannot derogate by individual agreements from legislation which concerns public policy [*ordre public*] or good morals',[12] and since its reform in 2016 and specifically in the context of contract law, Article 1102 provides that:

> Everyone is free to contract or not to contract, to choose the person with whom to contract, and to determine the content and form of the contract, within the limits imposed by legislation.

[8] See B Rudden 'Ius Cogens, Ius Dispositivum' (1980) 11 *Cambrian L Rev* 87 who traces the Roman origins of the Latin distinction; see also C Pérèz, 'Mandatory and Non-mandatory Rules in the New Law of Contract' in J Cartwright and S Whittaker (eds), *The Code Napoléan Rewritten, French Contract Law after the 2016 Reforms* (Oxford, Hart, 2017) ch 9 at 167.

[9] The terminology can, however, be confusing as we need to distinguish the question whether rules are mandatory or non-mandatory as a matter of domestic law (which is discussed in the text) and whether they are internationally mandatory in the sense that they apply whatever the choice of law to govern the contract by the contracting parties. Sometimes the two coincide as noted below, s IV.

[10] B Nicholas, 'Rules and Terms – Civil Law and Common Law' (1973–74) 48 *Tulane L Rev* 946, 949.

[11] This body of law is known as *le droit commun contractuel* and is typically distinguished from *le droit des contrats spéciaux*, that is, the law applicable to special (or nominate) contracts.

[12] Author's translation (*'On ne peut déroger, par des conventions particulières, aux lois qui intéressent l'ordre public et les bonnes moeurs'*). Rudden (n 8) 89 explains that Art 6 is a conflation of two ancient texts: D.50.17.45.1 *'Privatorum conventio iuri publico non derogat'* and C.2.3.6 *'Pacta, quae contra leges constitutionesque vel contra bonos mores iunt, nullam vim habere indubitati iuris est.'*

> Contractual freedom does not allow derogation from rules which are an expression of public policy [*ordre public*].[13]

For the French Ministry of Justice, Articles 6 and 1102 affirm the generally non-mandatory character of the new provisions on the general law of obligations and that the mandatory character of a particular rule is therefore exceptional.[14] This does not of itself settle the status of individual provisions, although sometimes the provision itself makes this clear by providing that it is 'a matter of public policy'.[15] Where this is not the case, there remains a degree of uncertainty which has to be resolved by interpretation of the particular text.[16]

There is therefore a contrast of approach between the English law and Civil law traditions. In English law the idea of default rules (unlike 'non-mandatory' or 'dispositive' rules) *itself* refers to the idea that they apply only in the absence ('in default') of express agreement. Moreover, the widespread Common law technique of implying terms in law to set these default rules necessarily requires that they are susceptible to exclusion by express terms, except where legislation provides specially and explicitly that this is not the case. As a result, and putting aside the law governing illegality of contract, situations where the rules of contract law apply regardless of the agreement of the parties are indeed seen as exceptional, both in the sense that they are relatively rare and in the sense that their source is typically legislative rather than found in the common law generally applicable.

III. 'Consumer Contract Law'

What do I mean by 'consumer contract law' for the purpose of this discussion of default rules? Consumer contract law could include *all* the law which governs the conclusion, contents, performance and non-performance of contracts made between a trader and a consumer.[17] This would also include the law applicable to contracts more generally (typically under the common law, such as the law governing the conclusion of contracts, or rescission or damages for misrepresentation, and termination or the measure of damages for breach of contract) and whether or not any duty or liability arising were classified as contractual or (notably) tortious. However, I think that for most English lawyers 'consumer contract law' refers instead to that body of law which is *dedicated* to the regulation of the legal relations of parties (or would-be parties) to a consumer contract, a special body of law put in place by the legislature (and it *is* the legislature rather than the common law) for the protection of consumers. Such a dedicated body

[13] English translation by J Carwright, B Fauvarque-Cosson and S Whittaker.

[14] Péréz (n 8) 172 referring to *Rapport au Président de la République relative à l'ordonnance n°2016-131 du 10 février 2016 portant réforme du droit des contrats, du régime général et de la prevue des obligations* (2016) available at www.legifrance.gouv.fr/jorf/id/JORFTEXT000032004539/.

[15] Eg Art 1104 Civil Code. For other examples, see Pérèz (n 8) 173.

[16] See Péréz (n 8) 175–81 as to the range of arguments which can be relevant for this purpose. She notes (at 176), in particular, that the Ministry revised its preliminary draft so that in the enacted text a number of provisions *omit* the phrase 'subject to any term to the contrary' so as to avoid the argument *a contrario* that provisions which do not contain this form of words are mandatory.

[17] For present purposes, I will adopt the now standard legislative definitions of 'trader' and 'consumer' in the UK legislation: see, in particular, the Consumer Rights Act 2015 s 2.

of law may govern the contract itself, providing the consumer with contractual rights against the trader or controlling the fairness of the express terms of the contract between them, but it may sometimes be non-contractual, notably when it imposes liability in tort in traders in respect of their conduct towards consumers.[18] In this respect, the actual *content* of the law dedicated to governing the legal relationship between the consumer and trader may reflect (more or less closely) the law which would apply outside the consumer context (as in the case of some, though not all, of the statutory terms in Part 1 of the Consumer Rights Act 2015 (CRA 2015),[19] but sometimes the dedicated consumer law may differ significantly or even radically from the position under the general law (for example, in the duties of information in traders and rights of cancellation for consumers applicable to off-premises and distance contracts[20]). In the remainder of this chapter, I will focus on consumer contract law in the narrower, dedicated sense, but we will see that the wider sense of consumer contract law as the law which happens to apply to the legal relationship of consumers and traders is also significant for our discussion.[21]

IV. Most Consumer Contract Law is Mandatory

What, therefore, is the role of default rules in consumer contract law? Or perhaps I should say, *is* there a role for default rules in consumer contract law? For, as I earlier indicated, what is immediately clear is that many of the dedicated rules of consumer contract law (whether they are expressed as rights in the consumer, duties in the trader or terms 'treated as included' in the contract) are incapable of exclusion or restriction by express term. Or, to put it another way, much of consumer contract law is mandatory. This is true of all the statutory terms inserted by the CRA into 'goods contracts'[22] and all but one of those inserted into 'digital content contracts'[23] and it is true of the *exclusion* of liability for breach of the statutory terms inserted into 'services contracts' though the treatment of *restrictions* on liability is more nuanced.[24] Moreover, many of the other legislative rules governing consumer contracts are incapable of exclusion or modification by agreement: this is true of the trader's duties of information, the consumer's rights to cancellation and the controls on additional charges in the Consumer Contracts

[18] Eg the liability in damages of a trader under the consumer's rights to redress in respect of misleading actions or aggressive commercial practices under the Consumer Protection from Unfair Trading Regulations 2008 (SI 2008/1277) reg 27J.

[19] See, notably, the statutory terms as to quality and fitness for particular purpose in CRA 2015 ss 9–10, which were modelled on s 14 of the Sale of Goods Act 1979, though with differences (in s 9(5)–(7)) required for consumer sales by the Consumer Sales Directive 1999 Art 2. Cf CRA 2015 s 11: s 11(1) reflects closely s 13 of the 1979 Act (sale by description) but s 11(4)–(6) and s 12 include a distinctive treatment of information which is provided by the trader to the consumer. In the case of services contracts (CRA 2015 Pt 1 Ch 4), several of the statutory terms reflect the law applicable outside the consumer context (ss 49, 51 and 52) but again there is special treatment of information provided by the trader to the consumer (s 50).

[20] Consumer Contracts (Information, Cancellation and Additional Charges) Regulations 2013 (SI 2013/3134) Pts 2 and 3.

[21] See below, s V.B in relation to unfair contract terms.

[22] CRA 2015 s 31 referring to ss 9–17 (though with qualifications as regards s 17 in relation to contracts for the hire of goods).

[23] CRA 2015 s 47 referring to ss 34–37.

[24] CRA 2015 s 57 and see below, s V.B.

(Information, Cancellation and Additional Charges) Regulations 2013,[25] and the legislative rights for consumers in respect of timeshare contracts,[26] package holiday contracts,[27] distance contracts for the provision of financial services[28] and consumer credit.[29] Moreover, in looking more closely at the consumer law provisions, we can see that there are a number of significances to their mandatory nature, or perhaps a number of *levels* of mandatoriness. This may be seen particularly clearly in the case of the rules on goods contracts in Part 1 and the general controls on unfair contract terms in Part 2 of the CRA 2015. In both these situations, the rules are mandatory in three senses: they cannot be excluded or amended by the contract directly;[30] where the contract has a close connection with the UK they cannot be excluded as a result of a choice of law other than the UK;[31] and their application is not left to the parties to any litigation (and in particular to the consumer to raise) as, in principle, the court has a duty to raise the issue of the fairness of a contract term of its own initiative.[32] On the other hand, they are *not* mandatory in the sense that they apply to the consumer contract whatever the views of the consumer. This is particularly clear in the case of the law on unfair terms where the Court of Justice of the EU has declared that the duty of a national court to raise the issue of the fairness of a term of its own initiative does not apply where 'the consumer, after having been informed of it, does not intend to assert its unfair or non-binding status',[33] a position adopted explicitly by section 62(2) of the CRA 2015. The control may be mandatory, but it is not compulsory for the consumer! Finally, we should also note that in the case of most rules for the protection of consumers, their application is not merely left to the consumer to enforce, or courts to raise, as they are buttressed by a series of enforcement measures available on the application of designated public bodies, these measures including the possibility of court orders forbidding the trader's

[25] This is not stated by the 2013 Regulations themselves, but is clear from Art 25 of the Consumer Rights Directive 2011: H Beale (gen ed), *Chitty on Contracts*, vol II, 35th edn (London, Sweet & Maxwell, 2023) para 41-074. Chapter 41 'Consumer Contracts' is written by the present author.

[26] Timeshare, Holiday Products, Resale and Exchange Contracts Regulations 2010 (SI 2010/2960) reg 19. There is also provision against loss of the consumer's rights by contractual choice of law: reg 5.

[27] Package Travel and Linked Travel Arrangements Regulations 2018 (SI 2018/634) reg 30(2) and (3).

[28] Financial Services (Distance Marketing) Regulations 2004 (SI 2004/2095) reg.16(1) (any contract term inconsistent with the application of the Regulations is void); reg.16(2) provides that the Regulations will apply notwithstanding any contract term which applies or purposes to apply the law of a country other than the UK. The Financial Services and Markets Act 2023 provides, inter alia, for the repeal of the 2004 Regulations as part of a wider revocation of retained/assimilated EU law governing financial services: s.1 and, specifically, Sch 1 Pt 2.

[29] The Consumer Credit Act 1974 s 173(1) ('Contracting-out forbidden').

[30] CRA 2015 s 31 (goods contracts). In the case of the controls on unfair contract terms, this is not stated explicitly either by the CRA 2015 or by the 1993 Directive, but follows from their providing that an unfair contract term is not binding on the consumer and is clear from the case law of the CJEU which has declared that the consumer 'may not legitimately waive, for the future, the legal protection and the rights that he or she derives from [the 1993 Directive]', though the Court distinguished this situation from an agreement between a trader and a consumer to settle their disputed rights under an earlier consumer contract: C-452/18 *XZ v Ibercaja Banco SA* EU:C:2020:536 esp at para 77.

[31] CRA 2015 s 32 (sales contracts, which originally implemented the Consumer Sales Directive 1999 art 7(2)); s 74 (unfair contract terms, which originally implemented art 6(2) of the 1993 Directive). In both cases, the provisions were amended on IP completion day so as to change references to the EEA to ones to the UK.

[32] CJEU, C-497/13 *Faber v Autobedrijf Hazet Ochten BV* EU:C:2015:357, esp at paras 36–48 (sale of goods); in the case of unfair terms the CRA 2015 s 71 put into legislative form the duty required by a series of decisions of the CJEU, notably, C-168/05 *Mostaza Claro v Centro Móvil Milenium SL* EU:C:2006:675; C-243/08 *Pannon GSM Zrt v Erzsébet Sustikné Győrfi* EU:C:2009:350. On the details of this case law and its continuing significance for English law, see *Chitty on Contracts* (n 25) paras 41-021–41-023.

[33] *Pannon GSM Zrt v Erzsébet Sustikné Győrfi* (n 32) para 33.

infringement of consumer rights, various types of 'redress' (including compensation), and sometimes criminal sanctions.[34] Where this is the case, the rules are as mandatory as the law can make them. Overall, therefore, the contrast between mandatory and non-mandatory rules can indeed be said to exist along a spectrum rather than being a simple dichotomy.[35]

V. Consumer Default Rules

Nevertheless, in some situations the dedicated legislative rights or protections for consumers are not mandatory even in the most obvious sense of being always impervious to exclusion or derogation by contract. Here, there are, I think, two different phenomena: on the one hand, rules which apply only in the absence of contrary or differing agreement and, on the other hand, rules which I will call conditionally non-mandatory rules.

A. Rules which Apply Only in the Absence of Contrary or Differing Agreement

First, sometimes a particular legal provision will itself provide that a particular rule or duty will apply only in the absence of agreement on the issue in question: here, the absence of an express provision on the issue is a condition for the application of the rule. For example, section 51 of the CRA 2015 (which reflects closely earlier provision in the general law[36]) provides that:

> (1) This section applies to a contract to supply a service if—
>
> (a) the consumer has not paid a price or other consideration for the service,

[34] For a summary see Whittaker (n 1) 66–77. The most general public enforcement powers are contained in Enterprise Act 2002 Pt 8 (due to be repealed and replaced by the Digital Markets, Competition and Consumers Act 2024 Pt 3), but some legislative schemes provide for dedicated enforcement regimes, as in the case of unfair contract terms: CRA 2015 s 70 and Sch 3. An example of the availability of criminal sanctions may be found in the 2008 Regulations Pt 3.

[35] Cf Rudden (n 8) 88 who remarks of the distinction between *ius cogens* and *ius dispositivum* that '[a]s one might expect, of course, the picture is of a spectrum rather than a split', referencing G Del Vecchio, *Philosophy of Law* (tr TO Martin, 1953) 291 et seq. Del Vecchio (in the original Italian, *Lezioni di filosophia del diritto* 11th edn (Milano, A Giuffrè, 1962) 242 accepted the distinction between *norme tassative e dispositive* (or *jus cogens* and *jus dispositivum*), and defined the former as 'those which command independently of the will of the parties so that it is not permissible to derogate from them either absolutely, or even in relation to a certain purpose which the parties intended to achieve, and which is precisely governed by the same rules'. However, Del Vecchio's concern was to argue that recognition of this distinction should not lead to a mistaken view of the nature of law in general as for him the law is always imperative even as regards *jus dispositivum*. This is the case because 'the command, which is implicit in every legal norm, is always subordinated to the presence of certain elements or *factual conditions*, which are indicated in the norm itself, and the latter precisely and solely comes into force only when the conditions which it has itself established are verified'. And these conditions (or premises) 'can consist in the fact that the parties have manifested a particular intention [*volontà*]. This is the case as regards norms which are called dispositive'. As a result, in his view, even dispositive norms are, strictly speaking, a *jus cogens* as 'in a word, all law is coercive in that it establishes the limits of its coerciveness and imperative nature': ibid at 243 (present author's translations, original emphasis).

[36] Supply of Goods and Services Act 1982 s 15, which provides for payment of a reasonable sum where 'the consideration for the service is not determined by the contract, left to be determined in a manner agreed

(b) the contract does not expressly fix a price or other consideration, and does not say how it is to be fixed, and
(c) anything that is to be treated under section 50 as included in the contract does not fix a price or other consideration either.

(2) In that case the contract is to be treated as including a term that the consumer must pay a reasonable price for the service, and no more.
(3) What is a reasonable price is a question of fact.

Here, therefore, where there is an express term fixing the price payable, the statutory term imposing a duty on the consumer to pay a reasonable sum will simply not exist. This approach is also sometimes taken to legal provisions which impose a duty on the trader rather than on the consumer. For example, section 28(2) and (3) of the CRA 2015 provides that:

(2) Unless the trader and the consumer have agreed otherwise, the contract is to be treated as including a term that the trader must deliver the goods to the consumer.
(3) Unless there is an agreed time or period, the contract is to be treated as including a term that the trader must deliver the goods—

(a) without undue delay, and
(b) in any event, not more than 30 days after the day on which the contract is entered into.[37]

This provision therefore sets default rules both as to the existence of an obligation to deliver and also as to the timing of delivery, but in both cases these rules apply only in the absence of contrary agreement (delivery itself) or differing agreement (its timing). These are, therefore, default rules in the sense that they will not arise if there is express agreement on the issue. Interestingly, however, they are in a sense *mandatory* default rules, as section 31(1)(j) of the CRA 2015 provides that 'a term of a contract to supply goods is not binding on the consumer to the extent that it would exclude or restrict the trader's liability arising under … section 28'. What this means is that if the parties do *not* agree that goods are *not* to be delivered (for example, they are instead to be collected at the trader's premises) or if they make no agreement as to the timing of delivery, the contract cannot exclude or restrict liability in the trader for breach of the statutory terms to deliver the goods within 30 days of the contract being made; but, as I have said, if the parties *do* agree on either of these matters, that agreement will, in principle, take effect on its terms. A similar approach is taken by the CRA 2015 to the provision of

by the contract or determined by the course of dealing between the parties'. Cf the position under the Sale of Goods Act 1979 s 8 which applies to all contracts for the sale of goods including those to consumers and imposes payment of a reasonable sum by the buyer in the absence of provision about the price in the contract. Notice also that there is no provision in the CRA 2015 governing payment by the consumer of a reasonable price in the case of digital content contracts given that both limbs of the dual definition of this category of contract in s 33 refer to price.

[37] CRA 2015 s 28 implemented the Consumer Rights Directive 2011 Art 18 and apparently would attract a special meaning of 'delivery' so as to refer to the transfer of physical possession or control of the goods: see 2011 Directive Art 18 and Recital 55 referring to 'delivery' for the purposes of Art 20 of the Directive. Cf the definition of 'delivery' in CRA 2015 s 59(1).

information by the trader to the consumer before entering the contract. For example, in the case of 'goods contracts', section 11(4) and (5) provide that:[38]

> (4) Any information that is provided by the trader about the goods and is information [relating to the main characteristics of the goods] is to be treated as included as a term of the contract.
>
> (5) A change to any of that information, made before entering into the contract or later, is not effective unless expressly agreed between the consumer and the trader.

Here, therefore, the CRA 2015 gives contractual force to any information of this nature provided by the trader, but, despite this, it allows changes to this information if they are *expressly* agreed between the consumer and the trader: their mere agreement (which could otherwise be implied) is not enough. But again, subject to this possibility of change to the information by agreement, any attempt by the trader to exclude or restrict its liability for breach of the statutory term relating to information provided by the trader will not bind the consumer.[39] This pattern reflects to a considerable extent a requirement in the Consumer Rights Directive 2011,[40] which also declares the 'imperative nature' of the Directive and provides that 'if the law applicable to the contract is the law of a Member State, consumers may not waive the rights conferred on them by the national measures transposing this Directive' and '[a]ny contractual terms which directly or indirectly waive or restrict the rights resulting from this Directive shall not be binding on the consumer'.[41] In this way, information provided by the trader to the consumer becomes a statutory term of the contract, but, despite this effect, that information may be changed with the express agreement of the parties; on the other hand, where the information (whether original or changed) is inaccurate, the trader is liable for breach of contract without the possibility of any exclusion or restriction by exemption clause.

B. Conditionally Non-mandatory Rules

Second, there are rules belonging to consumer contract law as I have defined it which are not mandatory in the sense of being completely immune to contrary or amending agreement, but nor are they 'default rules' in the sense of being rules which are fully capable of exclusion or derogation by the agreement of the parties. This is because (with two exceptions)[42] the CRA 2015 subjects *all the terms* of *all* consumer

[38] The CRA 2015 contains similar provisions as regards information provided by traders in relation to digital content contracts and services contracts: see (on the former) CRA 2015 s 36(3) and (4) (main characteristics, functionality and compatibility of the digital content) and for other information s 37(2) and (3); the control on the exclusion of liability is contained in s 47(1)(c) and (d); and for services see s 50 (the terms as to 'anything said or written') and s 57 (controls on the exclusion and restriction of liability).

[39] CRA 2015 s 31(1)(c); and for other information ss 12 and 31(1)(d).

[40] Consumer Rights Directive 2011 Art 6(1) and (5). For the details see *Chitty on Contracts* (n 25) paras 41-532–41-533, 41-585–41-586 and 41-609–41-612.

[41] Consumer Rights Directive 2011 Art 25.

[42] The exceptions are where the contract term reflects 'mandatory statutory or regulatory provisions' or provisions of international conventions to which the UK is a party (CRA 2015 s 73 and see below, s VI.A) and where the term falls within what is often called the 'core exclusion' set out in CRA 2015 s 64.

contracts[43] to a legislative requirement of fairness and provides that any term which fails this requirement does not bind the consumer.[44] As a result, a contract term which seeks to exclude or restrict the application of a non-mandatory rule of consumer contract law is only effective if it is fair: the rules are therefore only *conditionally* non-mandatory. I will give two examples.

First, and unlike the provisions governing goods contracts and digital content contracts noted earlier, the provisions in the CRA 2015 on services contracts distinguish between the *exclusion* and the *restriction* of liability arising for breach of the terms which it inserts into the contract. In this respect, section 57 provides that a term of a contract which seeks to *exclude* the trader's liability for breach of the contractual obligation to take reasonable care (section 49) or a contractual term relating to information provided (section 50) is simply not binding on the consumer, as are contractual *restrictions* on the trader's liability 'if [they] would prevent the consumer in an appropriate case from recovering the price paid or the value of any other consideration'.[45] However, this does not mean that limitation clauses which are set at or above the level of the contract price will necessarily bind the consumer, given that (as section 57(3) itself notes) they remain subject to the general controls on the fairness of contract terms contained in Part 2 of the Act (and in particular section 62) and limitation clauses are specifically mentioned by the 'indicative list' in Schedule 2 of the Act as examples of contract terms which *may* be unfair.[46] Overall, therefore, the provisions in sections 49 and 50 of the CRA 2015 are mandatory as regards the exclusion of liability but are otherwise *conditionally* non-mandatory, that is to say, they are non-mandatory as long as the contractual provision which derogates from them is fair.

My second example is much broader in scope. When the Consumer Protection from Unfair Trading Regulations were made in 2008, their purpose was to prohibit unfair commercial practices business to consumer (as defined generally and particularly), a prohibition buttressed by criminal offences and public enforcement measures; but the Regulations had no direct impact on the relative rights, duties or liabilities of the parties to any consumer contract related to such an unfair practice.[47] This position changed on the amendment of the 2008 Regulations by the UK government so as to create three 'rights to redress' (a right to unwind the contract, a right to a discount and a right to damages) in respect of two of the particular prohibited commercial practices, misleading actions and aggressive commercial practices.[48]

[43] CRA Act 2015 s 62(1) and (4) and for an explanation of this position see *Chitty on Contracts* (n 25) paras 41-266–41-275 (all types of consumer contract); paras 41-278 et seq (all contract terms, explaining the exceptions to this general position).

[44] CRA 2015 s 62(1) and (4).

[45] CRA 2015 s 57(3). This rule also applies to liabilities arising from breach of the statutory terms in ss 51 and 51 (reasonable price and reasonable time).

[46] CRA 2015 s 63(1) and Sch 2, Pt 1, para 2.

[47] This followed the then scope of the Unfair Commercial Practices Directive 2005 which the 2008 Regulations implemented, as Art 3(2) of the Directive provided that it was 'without prejudice to contract law and, in particular, to the rules on the validity, formation or effect of a contract'.

[48] Principally, 2008 Regulations Pt 4A as inserted by the Consumer Protection (Amendment) Regulations 2014 (SI 2014/870). The Digital Markets, Competition and Consumers Act 2024 Pt 4 Ch 1 provides for the repeal and replacement of the 2008 Regulations partly by its own provisions and partly by secondary legislation made under powers set out in the Act.

However, the 2008 Regulations, even as amended, make no provision as to their status, whether mandatory or non-mandatory[49] and this leaves the exclusion or restriction of the consumer's rights to redress to the general test of fairness in section 62 of the CRA 2015.[50]

Finally, at this stage, I should note that this pattern applies equally to rules governing the relationship of parties to a consumer contract which do not belong to consumer contract law in the narrower sense I earlier defined, but belong instead to the wider law which happens to apply in the circumstances. As earlier noted, this is the case of much of the common law governing contracts generally and in principle of the law of torts.[51] In the consumer context, this law provides default rules in the sense I earlier adopted, but any exclusion or amendment of them by way of contract term (or, indeed, non-contractual notice) is subject to the requirement of fairness. In the consumer context, therefore, in principle default rules governing their legal relationship are only conditionally non-mandatory.

VI. The Relevance of Default Rules to the Scope and Application of the Law of Unfair Contract Terms

However, default rules are also relevant to the law governing unfair contract terms in three further ways: as regards the scope of these controls, the assessment of fairness, and the results of unfairness.

A. The Exclusion of Terms which Reflect 'Mandatory Statutory or Regulatory Provisions' from Control of their Fairness or Transparency

The general scheme of controls on the fairness and transparency of the terms of consumer contracts set out in Part 2 of the CRA 2015 does not apply 'to a term of a contract … to the extent that it reflects – (a) mandatory statutory or regulatory provisions, or (b) the provisions or principles of an international convention to which the United Kingdom is

[49] The 2005 Directive does not state explicitly that its required prohibitions are mandatory, even after it was amended by Directive (EU) 2019/2161 Art 3(5) (inserting new Art 11(a) into the 2005 Directive) so as to require Member States to ensure that '[c]onsumers harmed by unfair commercial practices, shall have access to proportionate and effective remedies, including compensation for damage suffered by the consumer and, where relevant, a price reduction or the termination of the contract', it being added that 'Member States may determine the conditions for the application and effects of those remedies'.

[50] *Chitty on Contracts* (n 25) para 41-240.

[51] At common law, liability in the tort of negligence may be excluded or restricted by agreement or notice, but since 1977 there have been qualifications on this position as regards 'business liability': Unfair Contract Terms Act 1977 s 2. The equivalent provisions in the consumer context are CRA 2015 s 65 (special rule for liability for death or personal injuries) and s 62 (all exclusions or restrictions of liability other than those falling under s 65).

a party'.[52] This exclusion followed closely Art 1(2) of the EU Directive on Unfair Terms in Consumer Contracts 1993,[53] Recitals 13 and 14 of which explain that:

> Whereas the statutory or regulatory provisions of the Member States which directly or indirectly determine the terms of consumer contracts are presumed not to contain unfair terms; whereas, therefore, it does not appear to be necessary to subject the terms which reflect mandatory statutory or regulatory provisions …; whereas in that respect the wording 'mandatory statutory or regulatory provisions' in Article 1(2) also covers rules which, according to the law, shall apply between the contracting parties provided that no other arrangements have been established.

A first point to notice here is that 'mandatory' (in Article 1(2) of the 1993 Directive and therefore also section 73 of the CRA 2015) does not mean what it usually means – but instead refers *both* to mandatory rules in the usual sense and to what we earlier identified as non-mandatory or default rules. The justification for this exclusion is the idea that any contract terms which are 'directly or indirectly determined' by legislation are 'presumed not to contain unfair terms' as, according to the Court of Justice, 'it may legitimately be supposed that the national legislature struck a balance between all the rights and obligations of the parties to certain contracts'.[54] The Court of Justice has held that the exclusion should be interpreted strictly and should, therefore, not apply to the terms of a contract which are required by law for another, related type of contract.[55]

In the context of English law, the wording of the exception (and possibly also the reason just given) suggests that it does not apply to contract terms which reflect common law rules which apply to the contract, but it can be argued that the references to 'legislative or regulatory provisions' reflects the general approach to regulation in most Member States other than those of the Common law tradition, and the reason for the exception (as regards the law's striking a balance between the interests of the parties) applies equally to common law rules.[56] The question may not matter much in practice as a court is very unlikely to hold that a contract term which reflects the position otherwise applicable at common law is unfair under the test in section 62 of the 2015 Act.

B. Default Rules and the Assessment of the Fairness of Contract Terms

The test of unfairness of contract terms in section 62(4) of the CRA 2015 (which followed closely the test in the 1993 Directive except that it applies whether or not the term is 'individually negotiated'[57]) is a complex one, made up of a number of elements:

> A term is unfair if, contrary to the requirement of good faith, it causes a significant imbalance in the parties' rights and obligations under the contract to the detriment of the consumer.

[52] CRA 2015 s 73.
[53] Art 1(2).
[54] CJEU, C-92/11 *RWE Vertrieb AG v Verbraucherzentrale Nordrhein-Westfalen eV* EU:C:2013:180, para 29.
[55] ibid, where the CJEU distinguished between contract terms required for 'standard tariff contracts' to supply electricity where the supplier was under a legal obligation to conclude contracts with consumers, and 'special contracts', where they were not.
[56] See *Chitty on Contracts* (n 25) para 41-287.
[57] 1993 Directive Art 3.

In this respect, in *Aziz*, the Court of Justice observed that:

> in order to ascertain whether a term causes a 'significant imbalance' in the parties' rights and obligations arising under the contract, to the detriment of the consumer, it must in particular be considered what rules of national law would apply in the absence of an agreement by the parties in that regard. Such a comparative analysis will enable the national court to evaluate whether and, as the case may be, to what extent, the contract places the consumer in a legal situation less favourable than that provided for by the national law in force. To that end, an assessment should also be carried out of the legal situation of that consumer having regard to the means at his disposal, under national legislation, to prevent continued use of unfair terms.[58]

It will be seen, therefore, that the position on the issue governed by a contract term under 'rules of national law would apply in the absence of an agreement by the parties' (referring here to non-mandatory rules as the issue of the fairness of a term would not arise in relation to mandatory rules) is relevant 'in particular' to the assessment of the issue of significant imbalance. In this respect, the Court of Justice followed the Opinion of Advocate General Kokott, who had observed that:

> It is not possible to assess whether a term causes a significant imbalance in the parties' rights and obligations arising under the contract, to the detriment of the consumer, without a comparison with the legal situation under national law in the event that the parties themselves have not made any contractual provision. Only where the contractual term treats the consumer less favourably than the statutory provisions might the term actually cause an unfair shift in the rights and obligations arising under the contract, to the detriment of the consumer.[59]

She accepted, however, that not all terms which treat the consumer less favourably than statutory provisions will lead to a 'significant imbalance … contrary to good faith' and, in her view, '[c]onsequently, the principle of contractual freedom is observed and it is recognised that in many cases parties have a legitimate interest in organising their contractual relations in a manner which derogates from the statutory provisions'.[60] While this approach makes complete sense as a useful starting-point for assessing 'significant imbalance', it strikes me as one which reflects the Civil law tradition which gives prominence to the regulation of particular types of contract by legislation. This should perhaps not be surprising given that AG Kokott has an educational background in German law and that the German legislation which controls the reasonableness of standard contract terms (and which is not limited to consumer contracts) has long expressly related the assessment of their reasonableness to the question whether they derogate from default rules. Thus § 307 of the German Civil Code (BGB) states that '[p]rovisions in standard business terms are ineffective if, contrary to the requirement of good faith, they unreasonably disadvantage the other party to the contract with the user' and later provides that in the case of 'provisions in standard business terms on the basis

[58] CJEU, C-415/11 *Aziz v Caixa d'Estalvis de Catalunya, Tarragona i Manresa* EU:C:2013:164, para 68.

[59] CJEU, Opinion of AG Kokott of 8 November 2012, C-415/11 *Aziz v Caixa d'Estalvis de Catalunya, Tarragona i Manresa*, ECLI:EU:C:2012:700, para 71.

[60] ibid, para 73.

of which arrangements derogating from legal provisions, or arrangements supplementing those legal provisions, are agreed':[61]

> In case of doubt, an unreasonable disadvantage is to be assumed to exist if a provision
> 1. is not compatible with essential principles of the statutory provision from which it deviates, or
> 2. limits essential rights or duties inherent in the nature of the contract to such an extent that attainment of the purpose of the contract is jeopardised.[62]

It will be seen that the fact that a contract term deviates or derogates from an otherwise applicable legislative provision forms an important starting-point – and sometimes even a presumption – for the assessment of its 'reasonableness'. The provision had formed part of the German legislation of 1976 (again on standard business terms rather than just the standard terms of consumer contracts[63]) which in 2002 was 'slotted, en bloc' into the BGB.[64] And the legislation of 1976 itself had cast in legislative form a body of rules developed by the Federal Court of Justice to control the fairness of standard business terms developed under the aegis of § 242 BGB's general clause on good faith.[65] Despite this background in the Civil law tradition, the approach of the Court of Justice in *Aziz* was fully accepted and applied by the majority of the UK Supreme Court in its decision in *ParkingEye* which saw it as the 'leading case on the topic' of the test of fairness in the 1993 Directive decided by the Court of Justice.[66] However, even if this approach were 'domesticated' for English law by describing it in terms of deviation from 'the position which would have applied under national law apart from the challenged term', in the particular context of *ParkingEye* the underlying law otherwise applicable was not legislative and, at least according to Lord Mance JSC, not helpful in assessing the fairness of the term.[67]

C. Can a Default Rule Apply Instead of an Unfair Contract Term?

Finally, default rules may *exceptionally* play a role in the regulation of the legal relations of parties to a consumer contract where an express term has been held unfair and

[61] § 307(3) BGB.

[62] § 307(2) BGB (official English translation of German Federal Ministry of Justice provided by the Langenscheidt Translation Service, 'regularly updated by Neil Mussett and most recently by Samson Übersetzungen GmbH, Dr Carmen v Schöning' and available at www.gesetze-im-internet.de/englisch_bgb/).

[63] § 9 *Gesetz zur Regelung des Rechts der Allgemeinen Geschäftsbedingungen (AGB-Gesetz)* 1976 (translated by G Dannemann in Markesinis, *The German Law of Obligations*, vol I, *The Law of Contracts and Restitution: A Comparative Introduction* (Oxford, Clarendon Press, 1997) by BS Markesinis, W Lorenz and G Dannemann, Appendix II, 908).

[64] R Zimmermann, *The New German Law of Obligations, Historical and Comparative Perspectives* (Oxford, OUP, 2005) 188.

[65] ibid, 175.

[66] *ParkingEye v Beavis* [2015] UKSC 67, [2015] 3 WLR 1373 at [105] (Lord Neuberger of Abbotsbury, Lord Sumption and Lord Carnwath) (with whom Lord Hodge (at [289]) and Lord Clarke of Stone-cum-Ebony (at [291]) agreed on these points); [204]; Lord Toulson agreed on the importance of the *Aziz* decision (at [306]–[307]), but dissented on its significance on the facts of *ParkingEye Ltd*.

[67] According to Lord Mance, the CJEU's approach to the assessment of fairness in *Aziz* should be seen as providing relevant but not conclusive considerations. In his view, in *ParkingEye* itself the underlying legal position was that, but for the parking agreement, the consumer would not have had a right to park and would

therefore not binding on the consumer. In this respect, Article 6(1) of the EU Directive on Unfair Contract Terms declares merely that an unfair contract term shall:

> as provided for under their national law, not be binding on the consumer and that the contract shall continue to bind the parties upon those terms if it is capable of continuing in existence without the unfair terms.[68]

Interpreting this provision, the (retained/assimilated[69]) case law of the Court of Justice of the EU holds that *in principle* a court must *not* apply a legal rule which would otherwise apply (that is, a default rule) instead of the contract term.[70] For example, if the general law normally imposes a legal rate of interest for late payment of a debt by a consumer where no rate has been set by the contract, and a express contract term which seeks to imposes a higher rate is held unfair, the trader/lender is not entitled to recover *any* interest for late payment, neither under the unfair contract nor under the default rule.[71] According to the Court of Justice, Article 6(1) 'cannot be interpreted as allowing the national court … to reduce the amount of the penalty imposed on the consumer instead of excluding entirely the application of the clause';[72] such a power of revision would 'contribute to the elimination of the deterrent effect exercised on traders by the pure and simple non-application of such unfair contract terms as regards consumers', to the extent to which traders would be tempted to use them knowing that, if they were later invalidated, they could still look to the court to protect the interest with which the term was concerned.[73] In this way, an attempted contractual derogation from a default rule by a trader in the contract can lead to the *disapplication* of the default rule to the detriment of the trader. If taken to its logical conclusion, this general rule could have some very surprising effects. For example, if a penalty clause (in the sense of a clause imposing the payment of a sum of money on breach of contract) were held unfair and not binding on the consumer, the consumer would *not* be liable under the general law of damages for breach of contract; and if a contract term which created a right of termination by the

therefore be liable in damages for trespass for which it would, almost certainly, not have been worth the owner of the car park's while to pursue him; it would not have achieved any of that owner's aims, and could not therefore in the context be 'an appropriate comparator when assessing the legitimacy or fairness of the scheme put in place' by the owner and the managers of the car park (the latter of which was the trader party to the consumer contract: [2015] UKSC 67 at [208]. However, there is a certain wider resonance in English law with the approach of the CJEU in *Aziz* in what is sometimes called the '*Gilbert-Ash* principle', that is, that 'the court in construing the contract starts from the assumption that in the absence of clear words the parties did not intend the contract to derogate from [the] normal rights and obligations' established by the common law or statute: see *Triple Point Technology Inc v PTT Public Co Ltd* [2021] UKSC 29, [2021] 3 WLR 521 at [107] and [111] per Lord Leggatt JSC.

[68] 1993 Directive Art 6(1).

[69] The European Union (Withdrawal) Act 2018 as enacted (and as amended in 2020) referred to 'retained EU law' and 'retained EU case law' but this terminology changed on the coming into effect of the Retained EU Law (Revocation and Reform) Act 2023 s 5(1) and (2) (in force on 29 June 2023 under s 22(1)(a)) which provide that, at the end of 2023, 'retained EU law' is to be known as 'assimilated law' and 'retained EU case law' as 'assimilated EU case law'.

[70] CJEU, C-26/13 *Kásler v OTP Jelzálogbank Zrt* EU:C:2014:282, paras 82–84, and for further discussion of the complex case-law of the CJEU in this area (before and after IP completion day) see *Chitty on Contracts* (n 25) paras 41-434–41-440.

[71] CJEU, C-602/13 *Banco Bilbao Vizcaya Argentaria SA v Quintano Ujeta* EU:C:2015:397 (available only in French). The quotations in the text are translations from the French by the author.

[72] *Bilbao Vizcaya Argentaria SA* (n 71) para 34.

[73] *Bilbao Vizcaya Argentaria SA* (n 71) para 36.

trader on breach of contract by the consumer were held unfair and not binding on the consumer, the trader would not have a right to terminate the contract under the general law at least as regards the breach relevant to the express right of termination. However, given that these consequences are not explicitly spelt out by the retained/assimilated EU case law and given their practical implications, it may well be that an English court would either not see them as forming part of that case law or (if itself of the requisite appellate level) would choose to depart from it.[74]

However, the (retained/assimilated) EU case law recognises both a qualification and a true exception to this position. The qualification arises as a result of the fact that Article 6(1) of the 1993 Directive and section 62(4) of the CRA 2015 provide that the non-bindingness of an unfair terms leaves the rest of the contract binding as long as this is possible. So, for example, where a term in a contract of consumer credit fixing default interest has been held unfair and so not binding on the consumer, a national court may impose interest under *another* (fair) term of the contract which imposes 'ordinary interest'.[75] This therefore involves the application of another contract term rather than a default rule. Second, the (retained/assimilated) EU case law accepts a true exception to the general rule as a national court is not precluded 'in accordance with the principles of the law of contract, from deleting an unfair term and substituting for it a supplementary provision of national law' where this would enable 'real balance between the rights and obligations of the parties to be restored' and where otherwise the invalidity of the unfair term would require the court to annul the contract in its entirety with disadvantageous consequences to the consumer.[76] For example, where a contract term which sets the price or remuneration is held not 'transparent' *and* unfair[77] and national contract law would otherwise consider that the contract could not survive, the Court of Justice would allow a national court to apply a 'supplementary provision' to rescue the contract – and therefore the consumer. For example, where a term setting a variable interest rate in a contract of consumer credit is found unfair, a national court could replace that term by referring to a legislative index of interest rates applicable in the absence of agreement, as the annulment of the whole contract would be likely to lead to the immediate repayment of the capital by the consumer.[78] Even here, though, the consumer may object to being protected by the upholding of the contract in this way.[79]

In all this, though, it is clear that this case law is contingent on there *being* a relevant 'supplementary provision' of national law which could govern the issue dealt with

[74] At the time of writing, the powers of UK courts to depart from retained/assimilated EU case law are contained in the European Union (Withdrawal) Act 2018 s 6 and the European Union (Withdrawal) Act 2018 (Relevant Court) (Retained EU Case Law) Regulations 2020 (SI 2020/1525), but the Retained EU Law (Revocation and Reform) Act 2023 s 6 provided for the amendment of s 6 of the 2018 Act and, if brought into force, would change, in particular, the criteria to be used by the Supreme Court and certain appellate courts in deciding whether to depart from EU case law.

[75] CJEU, C-96/16 and C-94/17 *Banco Santander v Demba, Cortés v Banco de Sabadell SA* EU:C:2018:643, paras 73–79.

[76] *Kásler v OTP Jelzálogbank Zrt Kásler* (n 69) paras 82–84 and see also C-482/13, C-484/13, C-485/12 and C-487/13 *Unicaja Banco, SA v Hidalgo Rueda* EU:C:2015:21, para 33; C-70/17 and C-179/17 *Abanca Corporación Bancaria SA v Salamanca Santos, Bankia SA v Rodríquez Ramírez* EU:C:2019:250, paras 56–64.

[77] The condition of lack of transparency has to be satisfied in order for a price term to be assessed for its fairness under the 1993 Directive Art 4(2); in UK law, see CRA 2015 s 64 (which imposes an apparently further condition of prominence of the term).

[78] CJEU, C-125/18 *Gómez del Moral Guasch v Bankia SA* EU:C:2020:138, paras 60–67.

[79] CJEU, C-260/18 *Dziubak v Raiffeisen Bank International AG* EU:C:2019:819, paras 50 and 55.

by a term found unfair. For example, in English law, statutory provisions insert terms into contracts for the provision of goods or services by a trader to a consumer to pay a reasonable sum, but only where the price is *not* fixed by the contract, directly or indirectly.[80] Where a price clause is unfair and not binding on the consumer, can it be said as a matter of purely English law that the contract does not fix the price so as to allow the operation of the statutory terms? If so, and given that consumers may rely on a contract term even if it *is* unfair and so not binding on them[81] and that they may refuse to allow the court to rescue their contract in this way, in this situation the consumer would in effect have a choice between paying the contract price, paying a reasonable price or allowing the contract itself more generally no longer to apply.

VII. Conclusion

Given the dominance of mandatory rules in consumer contract law, it was, perhaps, inevitable that any discussion of the nature and role of default rules in consumer contract law should become a discussion of the relationship between mandatory and non-mandatory rules governing consumer contracts – and in this chapter I have not avoided this fate. However, in concluding my discussion of this relationship it can be seen that the distinction itself is by no means a simple dichotomy.[82] It is true that many rules dedicated to the legal relations of the parties to consumer contracts (whether expressed as terms 'treated as included in the contract', rights in the consumer or duties in the trader) are mandatory in the core sense that they themselves and/or liability for their infringement/breach cannot be excluded or restricted by agreement. However, the consumer context illustrates vividly that these legal rules may be buttressed by further levels of mandatoriness: in terms of the relations between the parties themselves, the law may also protect the consumer's rights from avoidance by choice of law (in practice by the trader), but even more the law does not leave the consumer's protection to private enforcement, as the courts themselves (in their duty to raise the issue of the consumer's rights in the proceedings of their own initiative) and designated public bodies have important powers designed to ensure the consumer's protection whether by court order or criminal prosecution.[83]

However, it is also clear that the dominance of mandatory rules in this area does not mean that default rules play no role in the consumer context. First, we have seen that sometimes consumer contract law recognises what I have called 'mandatory default rules'.[84] This oxymoron is intended to describe the situation where the law provides a

[80] In the case of sale of goods, the conditions are that the price was not fixed by the contract, left to be fixed in a manner agreed by the contract, or determined by the course of dealing between the parties: Sale of Goods Act 1979 s 8 (which applies to all contracts for the sale of goods including 'consumer contracts' falling under CRA 2015 Pt 1). In the case of contracts for the provision of a service by a trader to a consumer, the (cumulative) conditions are that '(a) the consumer has not paid a price or other consideration for the service, (b) the contract does not expressly fix a price or other consideration, and does not say how it is to be fixed, and (c) anything that is to be treated under section 50 as included in the contract does not fix a price or other consideration either': CRA 2015 s 51.

[81] CRA 2015 s 62(3).

[82] Cf Rudden's reference to a 'spectrum' rather than a split, above n 35.

[83] Above, s IV.

[84] Above, s V.A.

rule (setting a right or duty in the consumer in relation to an issue) but only where the parties have not themselves agreed on the issue in question: to this extent, the rule is a default rule. However, if the parties have *not* made an agreement on the issue with the result that the rule applies, the parties (and in practice the trader) cannot exclude or restrict liability arising from its infringement by an express contract term: to this extent, the rule is mandatory. Moreover, as we have seen, sometimes the law allows the legal position of the parties to be changed but only by their *express* agreement. This is true of the provision of information by a trader to a consumer in relation to a services contract, where in principle the information gains contractual force by way of a 'term treated as included' in the contract; but the parties can agree expressly to *change* the information and thereby in effect change the content of the term. Again, though, once the information (and the content of the term) is set, any liability arising from breach of the term cannot be excluded.[85]

Second, given that (with exceptions) the express terms of consumer contracts are effective only if they are fair, rules which are *not* in principle mandatory (in that in principle they are capable of exclusion or amendment by the contract and would therefore usually be seen as 'default rules') are equally binding on the consumer only if they are fair: the rules are therefore *conditionally* non-mandatory.[86] Moreover, sometimes the same legislative provision of consumer contract law may be mandatory *to an extent*, but may otherwise be conditionally non-mandatory (as in the case of the restriction of certain liabilities arising under services contracts).[87] Moreover, rules belonging to wider bodies of law (whether of contract or tort) which would apply to the legal relations of the parties to a consumer contract in the absence of contrary or different agreement are also conditionally mandatory in this sense.

Third, default rules are relevant to the general legal controls on the fairness of the terms of consumer contracts in three further ways. Where an express term reflects a rule (whether mandatory or non-mandatory) which would anyway apply to the particular contract between the parties, that term does not fall within the scope of the requirements of fairness or transparency.[88] Second, the relative rights and duties of the parties to consumer contracts under any applicable default rules (whether or not belonging to dedicated consumer contract law) should form the starting-point for a court's assessment of the fairness of any express term which seeks to exclude or amend those rights or duties.[89] Finally, where a term of a consumer contract has been found unfair and not binding on the consumer, a court may apply the default rules which would apply to the issue governed by that term, but only where the contract itself would not otherwise survive without this substitution and this preservation of the contract is in the interests of the consumer in the circumstances.[90]

[85] Above, s V.A. The position as regards the restriction of liability is more complex: above, s V.B.

[86] See above, s V.B.

[87] See above, s V.B in relation to the treatment of the exclusion or restriction of some of the statutory terms in consumer services contracts.

[88] Above, s VI.A.

[89] Above, s VI.B.

[90] Above, s VI.C.

9

The Nature and Function of Default Rules in Commercial Law

LOUISE GULLIFER

I. Introduction

The focus of this chapter is on default rules in commercial law. It argues that such rules are very prevalent in commercial law, where party autonomy is an important principle, but that the sources of the default rules vary, and the content of such rules depends on the source from which the rules come. As well as rules which can be modified or excluded by the parties to commercial transactions, international models developed in this area often include rules which can be excluded or modified by adopting States. In each case, the benefits of certainty and coordination, both very important in the commercial context, can render the rules stickier than an efficiency analysis alone would predict.

Since, in the area of commercial law, the dominant rhetoric is that of party autonomy, it is not surprising that many rules are default rules rather than mandatory rules.[1] However, one could ask, perhaps, why there are default rules at all if the parties are entirely, or nearly entirely, free to decide on their legal relationship, and so could define the legal rights and obligations between them from scratch.[2] That is one of the main questions explored in this chapter,[3] together with an examination of the relationship between source and content mentioned above.

In this chapter, the term 'commercial law' is broad, covering transactions involving not only the provision of goods and services, but also relating to finance (broadly defined), and the shifting of risk, such as insurance and derivative transactions. The focus will be on private law rather than regulation, that is, rules focused on a party's relationship with the state which are typically mandatory rules.

[1] See J Morgan, *Contract Law Minimalism* (Cambridge, CUP, 2013) 87 in relation to contract law.

[2] A Schwartz and R Scott, 'Contract Theory and the Limits of Contract Law' (2003) 113 *Yale LJ* 541 argue that default rules and default standards are not what commercial parties want; rather, they want contracts to be interpreted on a textual basis in order to give effect to the parties (efficient) bargaining. This robust defence of freedom of contract is at odds with the more traditional law and economics theory which favours default rules as reducing transaction costs (see s III below).

[3] See, especially, ss III and IV.

Given that this chapter focuses on commercial law, it is assumed that contracting parties are in a position to bargain, and that bargaining power is reasonably equal.[4] This does not mean that there are no mandatory private law rules, that is, those which cannot be excluded or modified by contrary agreement. Such rules exist, for example, to maintain minimum standards, to provide coordination and to protect third parties.[5] However, in the commercial law field, mandatory rules are kept to a minimum.

Default rules, however, are usually seen as rules which apply in the absence of contrary agreement (opt-out rules). In the commercial sphere, where relationships between market actors are, in most cases, governed by contracts between them, it is natural to focus on rules which apply either as terms of contracts or which apply in the absence of contrary contractual agreement. While this type of default rule is critically important in this area, harmonised rules in the international sphere can also take the form of default rules which apply unless opted out of by States when adopting a particular harmonising instrument.

As pointed out by Lord Leggatt in *Barton v Morris*,[6] one could see the body of contract law as providing a framework of default rules which apply unless the parties opt out of them. In one sense, in the commercial sphere, most private law (such as contract law, property law and even some tort law) and much regulation falls into this category: the rules (whatever their source) only apply if a person chooses to do a particular type of transaction, but if that person does choose to do the transaction governed by a particular applicable law, the rules apply unless the parties agree otherwise.

However, in this chapter, 'default rule' is a more granular concept, that is, a specific rule (or standard)[7] which applies as a result of legislation, case law or contract in the absence of contrary agreement, rather than referring to the entire body of private law. In this context, at least, there are various types of default rules. First, there are those which apply according to their terms in the absence of contrary agreement, such as section 20 of the Sale of Goods Act 1979 (SGA), which provides that, 'unless otherwise agreed', risk passes at the same time as property under a sales contract.[8] Even without express provision for contracting out, this is often permitted by the general law or a generalised provision, sometimes subject to some restriction.[9] Second, some default rules are drafted in such a way that some of their content has to be provided or modified by the parties to fit the specific transaction.[10] This tends to be the case in the model

[4] This does not mean that it is entirely equal, or that one party does not have another type of advantage over the other, such as an informational advantage or experience as a repeat player, see s IV below.

[5] See s IV below.

[6] *Barton v Morris* [2023] UKSC 3 at [126]. See also S Whittaker, ch 8 in this volume, 137–8.

[7] For the distinction between rules and standards, much discussed in US jurisprudence, see D Kennedy, 'Form and Substance in Private Law Adjudication' (1976) 89 *Harvard L Rev* 1685; P Schlag, 'Rules and Standards' (1985) 33 *UCLA L Rev* 379; and I Ehrlich and R Posner, 'An Economic Analysis of Legal Rulemaking' (1974) 3 *Journal of Legal Studies* 257.

[8] Another example of a default rule of this type, though couched in different terms, is s 18 of the SGA, which 'unless a different intention appears' provides rules for ascertaining the intention of the parties as to when property is to pass under a sale contract. S 17 of the SGA (which is a mandatory not a default rule) provides that the intention of the parties determines the time at which property passes under a sale contract.

[9] See the examples given in s II below.

[10] A legislative example is Art 11 of the Cape Town Convention 2001, which provides that the debtor and creditor may agree as to events which constitute default or otherwise give rise to the remedies provided by the Convention, although the rule also provides that in the absence of agreement 'default' means a default which substantially deprives the creditor of what it is entitled to expect under the agreement.

contracts provided by standard setting bodies,[11] such as the ISDA Master Agreement, where specific terms (for example, 'Credit Support Provider') in the agreement are given the meaning set out by the parties in the Schedule to the Master Agreement, and, for example, details of representations made (referred to in the Master Agreement) are given in the Schedule. This technique enables the standard agreement to apply to all transactions, but for it to be adapted to each particular transaction, for the reasons of coordination discussed below.[12]

After this Introduction, the second section of this chapter describes the sources of default rules in commercial law; the third and fourth sections address the question of why the rules in commercial law are default rules, as opposed to mandatory rules; the fifth addresses what the content of these rules should be and the sixth examines the way in which such rules are made. The seventh section concludes.

II. Sources of Default Rules in Commercial Law

A. Domestic Legislation

The first, and obvious, source of default rules, in common with all other areas of the law, is domestic legislation. The examples given in this section are from the law of England and Wales, but the same would be true of all states around the world. Statutory default rules in general contract law[13] (such as those under the Contracts (Rights of Third Parties) Act 1999) are of considerable importance in the commercial and financial law fields. Much of commercial law in the nineteenth century was codified in a number of statutes, such as the Bills of Exchange Act 1882, the Marine Insurance Act 1906 and the SGA[14] (plus related statutes, such as the Supply of Goods and Services Act 1982), which contain many default rules of which some examples will be used in this chapter.

Lord Leggatt, in *Barton v Morris*,[15] summarises the different techniques used in the SGA[16] to impose rules on contracting parties: express rules of law,[17] duties or rights of the seller or buyer[18] and implied terms of the contract of sale.[19] He concludes that nothing turns on these different formulations and, generally speaking, that is the case. In all three categories in these and other legislation, some rules are mandatory but many are default rules in one of the three senses set out above.[20]

[11] See s II.C below.

[12] See s II. Note, also, that some default rules in the ISDA Master agreement are of the first type, such as the cross-default provisions in clause 5(a)(vi), in respect to which parties can opt in or opt out of the Schedule.

[13] See J Cartwright, chapter 7 in this volume.

[14] Originally the Sale of Goods Act 1893.

[15] *Barton v Morris* (n 6) at [132].

[16] Similar techniques are used in many other commercial law statutes. For examples, the Marine Insurance Act 1906 provides for statutorily implied terms (ss 36, 39, 41, and 42) as does the Insurance Act 2015 (s 13A).

[17] Lord Leggatt cites ss 4–7, but could also have included many others, such as ss 9–10, ss 16–17, s 20, s 20A, the rules of transfer of title in ss 21–25 and ss 47, 35 (acceptance).

[18] Lord Leggatt cites ss 8 and 27, but could have also included others, such as ss 28–46, and ss 49–53 (remedies).

[19] Lord Leggatt cites ss 12, 14, and 15: it is not clear why s 13 was not included in this list.

[20] The statutorily implied terms can generally be contractually excluded or modified, often subject to restrictions, for example, the requirement of reasonableness imposed by the Unfair Contract Terms Act 1977 ss 6

B. International Conventions

Another important source of default rules in commercial law is international conventions, which become national law when ratified and implemented, but which are (largely) uniform between States. Prominent examples are the UNCITRAL[21] Convention on the International Sale of Goods 1980 (CISG) and the UNIDROIT[22] Cape Town Convention 2001 (CTC). The extent to which the rules in these international instruments are able to be modified or excluded by parties varies. Perhaps not surprisingly, the CISG, which deals purely with contractual rights and duties, permits derogation from, or modification of, any of its provisions[23] as well as permitting parties to opt out of it application altogether,[24] while the CTC, which largely deals with property rights, permits only more limited derogation and modification.[25] In another sense, the rules in commercial law treaties can be seen as default rules to the extent that the treaty permits implementing States to opt in or out of particular rules by a system of declarations.[26]

C. Models from Standard-Setting Bodies

Apart from international conventions, international inter-governmental bodies, such as UNIDROIT and UNCITRAL, also produce softer law, such as model laws and principles,[27] which are designed to guide and assist States in reforming their law, as well as acting as a means of harmonisation. These instruments are default rules on two levels. First, as the precise text is not binding, States can deviate from the model when enacting them.[28] Second, within the instrument itself, as with the treaties discussed above, there are likely to be provisions enabling parties to deviate from the rules on the basis of party autonomy.[29]

and 7, and the requirement of 'no worse position' in the case of deliberate or reckless breaches in Insurance Act 2015 s 16A. For an example of an unrestricted ability to exclude implied terms, see Marine Insurance Act 1906 s 87 (Unfair Contract Terms Act 1977 ss 2 and 3 do not apply to contracts of insurance, see Sch 1 s 1).

[21] United Nations Commission on International Trade Law.

[22] International Institute for Unification of Private Law.

[23] CISG Art 6. There is one small exception, relating to making or modifying a sale of goods contract in a form other than in writing, in respect of which a Contracting State can make a declaration that the articles permitting non-written contracts or modifications do not apply when any party has its place of business in that State (see Arts 12 and 96).

[24] CISG Art 6.

[25] CTC Art 15, in relation to Chapter III of the Convention, and see also express provision for contrary agreement in Arts 11(1), 13(1), 29(5), 31(1) and (4), 38(2) and 42. The same is true in relation to the Protocols to the CTC, see, for example, Art IV(3) of the Aircraft Protocol. A similar pattern can be observed in the UNIDROIT Geneva Securities Convention 2009 (GSC), which deals largely with proprietary rights, but which permits contractual deviation in rules which solely or largely affect only the parties to the contract.

[26] See CTC Art 56 and GSC Art 45. See also J Ungerer, chapter 13 in this volume, 246 et seq.

[27] Examples include (from UNICTRAL) the Model law on Cross-Border Insolvency 1997, the Model Law on Secured Transactions 2016, and the Model Law on Transferable Electronic Records 2017 and (from UNIDROIT) the Principles of International Commercial Contracts (latest version 2016), the Model Law on Leasing (2008) and the Principle on the Private Law of Digital Assets (2023).

[28] Some instruments include provisions which States can opt out of, or opt in, or choose from a 'menu' of options, eg UNCITRAL Model Law on Secured Transactions Art 38.

[29] See, for example, UNICITRAL Model Law on Secured Transaction Art 3(1).

In addition to such instruments, national and international trade bodies produce model rules and agreements for use in particular spheres. Examples are the Uniform Customs and Practice for Documentary Credits (eg UCP 600), produced by the International Chamber of Commerce (ICC), Incoterms (standardised rules for different types of international trade contracts, also produced by the ICC), the ISDA Master Agreement, produced by the International Swaps and Derivatives Association (ISDA), and the Loan Market Association (LMA) documentation, such as the Term and Revolving Facility Agreements.[30] Standardised documents such as these play a very significant role indeed in the financial markets, and it has been argued that they are as, or perhaps more, effective in producing harmonised rules in their particular areas than formal international instruments.[31] The debate as to whether such standardised rules form a new legal order[32] will continue to rage,[33] but for present purposes it is enough to see them as a set of rules which national courts, and arbitral tribunals, will enforce as (part or all of) the terms of a contract.[34]

There are at least three ways in which the terms in these model rules and agreements can be seen as default rules. First, there is no legal obligation on parties to use them when entering into a particular transaction: they could make up their own contract. There is, however, extreme market pressure to use them, and a party could find itself excluded from the market if it refused to use the standard agreement.[35] Second, as mentioned above, these models incorporate express possibilities for modification by the parties to suit their own transaction: these tend to be commercial modifications rather than legal modifications, for example, the parties are able to choose the particular content of a term or definition on the basis of the commercial agreement made between them,[36] or the model offers choices for a party between different commercial approaches. Third, it is always possible for a party to negotiate a change to a particular rule or term even if this not expressly envisaged in the standard agreement.[37]

Sometimes incorporating the model rules or agreements is in itself a method of contracting out of statutory default rules, as the former can be more nuanced and individualised. For example, the LMA standard forms for facility agreements contain better and more flexible constraints on dividend payments than the statutory provisions in section 830 of the Companies Act 2006, which are mandatory but can be gold-plated.

[30] There are many other standard agreements drawn up by even more narrowly focused bodies, for example, on an international level, the Grain and Feed Trade Association (GAFTA), which provides contracts of sale may of which are designed to coordinate with the Incoterms contracts (see www.gafta.com/All-Contracts) and, on a national level, the UK Warehousing Association conditions of contract (see www.ukwa.org.uk/membership/conditions-of-contract/).

[31] J Dalhuisen, 'The Operation of the International Commercial and Financial Legal Order: The Lex Mercatoria and its Application – Moving from the Theories of Legal Positivism and Formalism to the Practicalities of Legal Pluralism and Dynamism' (2008) 19 *European Business Law Review* 985, 1023–24.

[32] Sometimes called a new 'Lex Mercatoria'.

[33] See G Cuniberti, 'The Merchant who would not be King' in H Muir Watt and D Fernandez Arroyo (eds), *Private International Law and Global Governance* (Oxford, OUP, 2014) 141, 143.

[34] See, for example, Cuniberti (n 33) 144–46: A Riles, 'The Anti-Network: Private Global Governance, Legal Knowledge, and the Legitimacy of the State' (2008) 56 *American Journal of Comparative Law* 605, 612.

[35] See text to nn 81–83.

[36] An example would be the choice of the 'threshold amount' in Part 1(c) of the Schedule to the ISDA Master Agreement.

[37] There are often factual constraints on whether such negotiation is possible. See text to nn 81–86 and nn 133–139.

D. Case Law

It is also possible for a default rule to be established by case law. In commercial law, many of these case law rules have their genesis in custom and practice, and so will normally apply in the absence of contrary agreement. One, of many, examples is the rule that a common law possessory lien arises in certain specified circumstances but that express contractual agreement can prevent it from arising at all, or can modify its terms.[38] Another example is the rule that, in a FOB contract in the context of international trade, risk passes on shipment[39] unless the parties otherwise agree.[40] However, the extent to which courts in England and Wales are prepared to develop default rules in this area is constrained by the rules on the implication of contract terms. A term can be implied as a result of commercial custom and usage if it is notorious, certain and reasonable, but only if there is evidence that it is invariably used and treated as binding in a particular market.[41] Such a term will not be implied if it is inconsistent with the express terms of the contract. The result of this combination of contract law rules is that, to the extent that an implication of a term by one court based on commercial custom and usage is likely to be followed by other courts, the term becomes a default rule in that particular market.

In the absence of a trade custom, courts can imply terms in fact into an individual contract if certain very stringent conditions are satisfied, but this type of implication is not relevant here as such terms do not function as default rules in other situations.[42] However, courts can also imply a term in law on the basis that there is 'a general rule that in all contracts of a certain type – sale of goods, master and servant, landlord and tenant and so on – some provision is to be implied unless the parties have expressly excluded it'.[43] In other words, the courts can create a default rule. There is a lack of clarity in relation to the test to be applied for the implication of a term into a contract of a certain type.[44] The term must be 'a necessary incident to the type of contract in question'[45] but determining what is necessary in this context can involve considerations of policy.[46] Most, if not all, of the recent cases in which terms have been implied in law

[38] *Davis v Bowsher* (1794) 5 Term Rep 488; *Rolls Razor v Cox* [1967] 1 QB 552 (CA).

[39] This rule is established in a long line of cases, eg *Inglis v Stock* (1885) 10 App Cas 263. It is now part of the FOB (free on board) contract standardised by the Incoterms produced by the International Chamber of Commerce (see s 2(c)). See further n 87.

[40] *The Parchim* [1918] AC 157, 168.

[41] H Beale (gen ed), *Chitty on Contracts*, vol I, 35th edn (London, Sweet & Maxwell, 2023) para 17-036; *Black Sea Commodities Ltd v Lemarc Agromond Pte Ltd* [2021] EWHC 287 (Comm) at [29]–[30]. For a historical account of how English courts implied custom and practice into commercial contracts, see R Cranston, *Making Commercial Law Through Practice, 1830–1970* (Cambridge, CUP, 2021) 48–52.

[42] See *Barton v Morris* (n 6) at [135].

[43] *Liverpool City Council v Irwin* [1977] AC 239, 257–58.

[44] See, for example, the discussion in E Peden, 'Policy Concerns Behind Implication of Terms in Law' (2001) 117 *LQR* 459; A Phang, 'The Challenge of Principled Gap-filling: A Study of Implied Terms in Comparative Context' (2014) 4 *Journal of Business Law* 263, 295–311.

[45] *Geys v Société Générale, London Branch* [2013] 1 AC 523 at [55]; *Scally v Southern Health and Social Services Board* [1992] 1 AC 294, 307; *Liverpool City Council v Irwin* [1977] AC 239, 255.

[46] See *Crossley v Faithful & Gould Holdings Ltd* [2004] EWCA Civ 293 at [36], cited with approval in the Supreme Court in *Haywood v Newcastle upon Tyne Hospitals NHS Foundation Trust* [2018] UKSC 22 at [32], and see also Peden (n 44).

by the courts in this way have not been in the commercial context; it seems unlikely that the courts in England and Wales will imply terms into commercial contracts using this route,[47] given the possibility of implying a term as a result of trade custom, the fact that most terms implied in law are standards and not rules,[48] the fact that trade models[49] are usually comprehensive (and sometimes build on statutorily implied terms) and the fact that commercial parties are usually in a position to negotiate their own terms.

E. Questions Arising

Taking this rather wide view of the sources of default rules which applies in the field of commercial law, various questions arise. The first, already mentioned, is why there are default rules at all, given the ability of commercial parties to reach their own bargain. The second is why, if there are rules, they are not mandatory rules, and, why, if rules are mandatory, they are not default rules. The third is how the content of default rules in this area is, and should be, determined, and the fourth is the effect on these rules of the source and method by which they are created.

III. Why are there Default Rules at All?

The various arguments explaining the existence of default rules in commercial law centre around three main ideas. The first is that of reduction of transaction costs, which is said to promote market efficiency.[50] A set of default rules obviates the need for parties to negotiate their deal from scratch, and also the need for parties to consider what terms they need for a 'complete' contract:[51] the template is set out before them and they can decide whether they wish to change any of it. Moreover, a more complete contract (that is, one with fewer 'gaps') is less likely to lead to disputes or require litigation in order to determine how the gaps should be filled. Transaction costs are said to be reduced most effectively if the default rules mimic what most parties would agree, thereby reducing the need for negotiated modifications (majoritarianism), and thus reducing transaction

[47] One exception is where a type of commercial contract is very similar to that in which certain terms are implied by statute. This was the case for contracts for hire of goods and for goods and services in the period between the enactment of the 1893 SGA and the enactment of the Supply of Goods and Services Act 1982, see Peden (n 44) 471 citing *Stewart v Reavell's Garage* [1952] 2 QB 545; *G&H Myers & Co v Brent Cross Services Co* [1934] 1 KB 46, and is suggested by the Supreme Court (at [31]) to be the case in relation to a 'sui generis' contract of the type identified in *PST Energy 7 Shipping LLC v OW Bunker Malta Limited* [2016] UKSC 23, see text to n 63.

[48] See below text to nn 91–94.

[49] Such as those referred to in s II.C above.

[50] The basic idea came from the work of Ronald Coase, which is seen as the foundation of the law and economics movement. Coase argued that in the absence of transaction costs, parties would bargain for the most efficient contracts (see RH Coase, 'The Problem of Social Cost' (1960) 3 *Journal of Law and Economics* 1). In order to reach this position, transaction costs needed to be eliminated or at least minimised. See also R Korobkin, 'Status Quo Bias and Contract Default Rules' (1997–98) 83 *Cornell L Rev* 608, 613.

[51] Schwartz and Scott (n 2) 595–96; Korobkin (n 50); M Grochowski, 'The Majoritarian Concept of Default Rules: Towards a Shift in Paradigm' (2020) *Studies in Private Law* 63.

costs.[52] Moreover, time and effort can be focused on the specific areas in which the parties do need to negotiate.

Cost saving also has another aspect, and that is the reduction of errors by using a term or relying on a rule that has been used many times before, and which has therefore stood the test of time.[53] Moreover, the parties can rely on the expertise of those who have drafted the rule or the model term, rather than have to develop expertise themselves or expend costs in negotiating the drafting of the rule or term.[54]

Much of the debate on cost saving has appeared to be focused on an idea of a single default rule. Perhaps understandably, most examples discussed are of single rules (such as the damages rule in *Hadley v Baxendale*[55]) but the discourse seems, more widely, to be directed at the idea of rules or standards as individual norms.[56] However, in commercial law at least, much of the cost-saving benefit of default rules comes when they are put together into a coherent structure, either by legislation (national or international) or in a model law or model agreement. Parties (or States) can then use the resulting structure as a template, on the internal coherence of which they can rely. This reliance is in itself a cost-saver: the work to formulate a set of rules applying to, for example, the purchase of goods on board a ship, has already been done (in that case, originally by trade custom and the courts, and laterally by the formulation of the Incoterms model by the ICC). Parties can then decide how far, if at all, they wish to stray from the model: this will be a balancing act between reflecting commercial considerations but not losing the benefits of the legal coherence of the model.[57]

The second main idea is that of certainty. Legal certainty has long been a central tenet of English commercial and financial law.[58] Certainty will reduce costs, both ex ante and ex post, by reducing disputes and making disputes easier to resolve. Ex ante certainty can also be seen as a benefit as it enables more accurate pricing of the risks involved in the transaction (and any allied risk protection such as insurance or derivative

[52] There is a very wide literature on this subject, mainly, but not exclusively, from the US. See, for example, I Ayres and R Gertner, 'Filling Gaps in Incomplete Contracts: An Economic Theory of Default Rules' (1989) 99 *Yale LJ* 87; D Charny, 'Hypothetical Bargains: The Normative Structure of Contract Interpretation' (1991) 89 *Michigan L Rev* 1815, 1841–44; Korobkin (n 50) 611. For a concise judicial statement of the majoritarian position, see *Barton v Morris* (n 6) at [128] per Lord Leggatt. For further discussion, see s V below.

[53] M Kahan and M Klausner, 'Standardization and Innovation in Corporate Contracting (or "Economics of Boilerplate")' (1997) 83 *Virginia L Rev* 713, 720.

[54] D Wielsch, 'Global Law's Toolbox: Private Regulation by Standards' (2012) 60 *American Journal of Comparative Law* 1075, 1083; S Choi and M Gulati, 'Contract as Statute' (2006) 104 *Michigan L Rev* 1129, 1132.

[55] *Hadley v Baxendale* (1854) 9 Exch 341.

[56] See, for example, the excellent discussion on learning benefits in Kahan and Klausner (n 53) 719–25.

[57] An example of the dangers of deviation from the standard default rules is the situation in *Leigh & Sillivan Ltd v Aliakmon Shipping Co Ltd* [1986] AC 785. The contract started off as a standard C and F (carriage and freight) contract, in which risk passed as from shipment to the buyer, but the contract was then varied so that the buyer obtained the bill of lading only as agent of the seller, and so had neither a proprietary nor possessory title to the goods. It became, in effect, a sale from the warehouse at the destination port, but before that point risk had passed to the buyer. Under the legislation in force at the time, this meant that the buyer had no right in contract or tort to sue the carrier for damage to the goods during the voyage. Later legislation (the Carriage of Goods by Sea Act 1992) has probably changed this position (see *White v Jones* [1995] 2 AC 207, 265).

[58] For example, see *The Scaptrade* [1983] QB 529, 540 per Robert Goff LJ: 'if any particular event occurs which may affect the parties' respective rights under a commercial contract, they should know where they stand … and to act accordingly'.

contracts). Default rules in legislation, case law or market standard contracts, contribute to legal certainty in several ways. First, as long as the words in the rule are interpreted consistently,[59] market participants can rely upon a particular interpretation or meaning as settled, since the wording of the rule will not change (in the absence of contrary agreement).[60] Second, as mentioned above, since the rule applies to frequent and numerous transactions, potential errors will become apparent and can be corrected,[61] thus improving the 'quality' of the default rule(s).

The SGA is an example of codified default rules which provides a mixture of cost saving (the template of the rules themselves) and flexibility (the ability to contract out of the rules). Sales law is so widely codified, both at national and transnational level, that it seems odd to contemplate a counter-factual situation where it is not codified, and, therefore, where the cost saving and ex ante certainty benefits discussed above may not apply. However, the spectre of non-codified law applying to reasonably common transactions was raised after the case of *PST Energy 7 Shipping LLC v OW Bunker Malta Limited*,[62] in which what purported to be a sale of bunker oil on retention of title terms was characterised as a 'sui generis' contract rather than one governed by the SGA, on the grounds that, since the bunker oil was likely to be burnt before property was to pass, it was not a 'contract by which the seller transfers or agrees to transfer property in goods to the buyer for a money consideration' as set out in the definition of a contract for the sale of goods in section 2 of the SGA. In consequence, many contracts on retention of title terms are likely not to fall within the SGA. The uncertainty resulting from this (as it was not clear when the default rules in the Act would apply by analogy, and, if not, whether there was any basis for other default rules to apply) were pointed out by a number of commentators.[63]

The third main idea is that of coordination and harmonisation. This argument has several aspects. First, and perhaps most obviously, it is easier for there to be strings, network or back-to-back contracts if at least most of the terms of the contracts, or the rules applicable to them, are the same. Since commercial contracts are rarely entered

[59] This does not just refer to interpretation by the courts, but also by arbitrators and mediators, and by market participants themselves, leading to custom and practice. For a discussion of consistency, in the context of market standard terms, see L Gullifer, Interpretation of Market Standard Form Contracts (2021) 3 *Journal of Business Law* 227, 240.

[60] See, in the context of market standard terms, *Federal Commerce and Navigation Co Ltd v Tradax Export SA* [1978] AC 1, 8 per Lord Diplock, and *Pioneer Shipping Ltd v BTP Tioxide Ltd (The Nema)* [1982] AC 724, 730 per Lord Diplock: 'It is only if parties to commercial contracts can rely upon a uniform construction being given to standard terms that they can prudently incorporate them in their contracts without the need for detailed negotiation or discussion.'

[61] See, in the context of standard form contracts, J Braithwaite, 'Standard Form Contracts as Transnational Law: Evidence from the Derivatives Market' (2012) 75 *MLR* 779, 799–803; cf C Goetz and R Scott, 'The Limits of Expanded Choice: an Analysis of the Interactions Between Express and Implied Contract Terms' (1985) 73 *California L Rev* 261, who point out that sometimes the frequent use of a standard term means that its shortcomings are not even noticed because of its familiarity.

[62] *PST Energy 7 Shipping LLC v OW Bunker Malta Limited* (n 47).

[63] Second Supplement to the 9th edition of M Bridge (ed), *Benjamin on Sale of Goods* (London, Sweet & Maxwell, 2016) para 4-001; L Gullifer, '"Sales" on Retention of Title Terms: Is the English Law Analysis Broken?' (2017) 133 *LQR* 244, 258; K Low and K Loi, 'Bunkers in Wonderland: A Tale of How the Growth of Romalpa Clauses Shrank the English Law of Sales?' [2018] *Journal of Business Law* 229, 248; D Saidov, 'Sales Law post-Res Cogitans' [2019] *Journal of Business Law* 1, 4–5; R Goode, *Fundamental Concepts of Commercial Law* (Oxford, OUP, 2018) ch 14 at 238–42.

into in isolation, and networks of contracts[64] are widespread, coordination is an important virtue, and results in risk reduction. Second, coordination and harmonisation are particularly important in relation to transnational default rules applying to cross-border transactions, where parties may be unfamiliar with the law of each other's countries, and transaction costs would be raised by having to achieve that familiarity. Third, it has been argued that improved coordination can lead to 'network benefits' in that the reduction of risk means that market participants are encouraged to enter into more contracts, which improves liquidity and efficiency.[65]

The certainty and coordination arguments work best when the option to delete or modify (which exists because of the default nature of the rule) is in fact not exercised by market participants. We might, therefore, ask why the rules should not be mandatory, which would maximise at least the benefits of certainty and coordination and, to the extent that contracting out is itself costly, would probably maximise the reduction in transaction costs as well.

IV. Why are the Rules not Mandatory?

One answer to this question is that, in the commercial sphere, freedom of contract is fundamental as a matter of principle, and applies unless there is a good reason to restrict it.[66] As a matter of doctrinal law, freedom of contract can be justified on the basis of certainty, both ex ante (that the parties can be sure that what they have agreed will be enforced) and ex post (that disputes can be resolved quickly and efficiently on the basis of the parties' agreement). Seen through a law and economics lens, the answer to the question is that the parties are best able to judge what is economically efficient, and so should be given the option to change the rules to achieve that end. These answers can lead to an argument that commercial law should be minimalist, and should consist merely of rules about enforcement[67] and (few) default rules.[68]

Having said this, in most areas of commercial law there are some mandatory rules. In private law,[69] these rules are usually mandatory in the sense mentioned above,[70] namely that, if the parties (or one party) wish(es) to achieve a particular legal conclusion, they must do x. In English law, for example, there are not only basic requirements for

[64] This phrase is used here to include strings of contracts, back-to-back contracts and any other situation where contracts between different parties are closely related to each other, rather than the more specific concept of 'network contracts' that forms the basis of some academic discourse in relation to the privity rule, see JN Adams and R Brownsword, 'Privity and the Concept of a Network Contract' (1990) 10 *Legal Studies* 12.

[65] See, in the context of the widespread use of the ISDA Master agreement, A Gelpern and M Gulati, 'CDS Zombies' (2012) 13 *European Business Organisation Law Review* 347, 358, 385.

[66] This statement is treated as so fundamental that it is rarely articulated. For statements in the context of English law, see E McKendrick (ed), *Goode and McKendrick on Commercial Law* 6th edn (London, LexisNexis, 2020) para 4.02, and see also Morgan (n 1) 89. In an international context, see UNIDROIT, Principles of Commercial Contracts 2016, Art 1.1 and Comment 1.

[67] Schwartz and Scott (n 2) 546: '[E]nforcement, when needed, is by far the most important thing the state does.'

[68] See Morgan (n 1) and Schwartz and Scott (n 2).

[69] Regulatory rules are usually mandatory.

[70] s I.

making an enforceable contract, but also more fine-grained mandatory rules requiring formalities in the creation of particular types of contracts, such as writing in a contract of guarantee.[71] Another example of a mandatory rule is that very many legal systems require a security interest to be registered in order to be enforceable against third parties and on the insolvency of the grantor of the security interest.[72] Mandatory rules such as these, it is suggested, serve a number of purposes.[73] The first, and most important, is to protect third parties. This is the reason why many rules in relation to property rights are mandatory, such as registration requirements, numerus clausus restrictions and rules enabling a person acquiring something to take it free from previous conflicting property rights.[74] A second is to protect one or both of the parties to the transaction against exploitation and fraud.[75] A third is to impose minimum standards for particular types of contracts.[76]

The distinction between mandatory and default rules has been considerably blurred by the idea of 'stickiness' of default rules. This idea developed as a riposte to the view that parties would always contract out of default rules if it was economically efficient for them to do so, when economic efficiency was measured by the efficiency of the resulting agreement balanced against the transaction costs of contracting out. It has been observed that many contracting parties do not contract out of default rules even when the resulting agreement would be more efficient (at least in relation to the particular transaction), and that this is for a variety of reasons. Some of these situations can be explained by matters which form part of a wider economic efficiency calculation: for example, where the transaction costs of negotiation are high because one party would have to reveal confidential information to the other in order to negotiate,[77] or where proposing a negotiation sends an adverse signal to the other party, such as a willingness to disrupt an existing relationship, excess litigiousness or a bargaining weakness of which the other party could take advantage.[78] Another reason, in the context of commercial codes or models, is that deviation from the established set of default rules could upset the careful balance of rules and cause unforeseen consequences.

[71] Statute of Frauds 1677 s 4.

[72] In English law, see Companies Act 2006 Pt 25.

[73] The traditional economic view is that mandatory rules are required either to prevent externalities or market failure, see Schwartz and Scott (n 2) 610–11.

[74] Priority rules more generally can be contracted out of, but such priority agreements only bind those who are party to them. However, a priority agreement between two mortgagees is binding on the debtor even if the debtor is not a party to the agreement, see *Cheah Theam Swee v Equiticorp Finance Group Ltd* [1992] 1 AC 472.

[75] Writing requirements often come into this category, as writing provide evidence of the transaction and the date on which it occurred. Some rules are more specific such as the common law rule that liability for fraud cannot be excluded, see *HIH Casualty and General Insurance Ltd v Chase Manhattan Bank* [2003] UKHL 6 at [16].

[76] For example, SGA s 12 imposes an implied term on the seller of goods that he has the right to sell the goods: this term cannot be excluded (although it can be expressly qualified in the contract by a provision that the seller only agrees to transfer such title as he has (s 12(3)).

[77] Ayres and Gertner (n 52).

[78] O Ben-Shahar and J Pottow, 'On the Stickiness of Default Rules' (2006) 33 *Florida State Univ L Rev* 651, 657–58, referring to L Bernstein, 'Social Norms and Default Rules Analysis' (1993) 3 *Southern California Interdisciplinary LJ* 59, 70–71; KE Spier, 'Incomplete Contracts and Signalling' (1992) 23 *RAND Journal of Economics* 432.

However, other situations are less easily explained in this way. For example, human beings have a cognitive bias for the status quo, and therefore the fact that the rule is a default rule is seen as a good reason for retaining it.[79] Moreover, the benefits of certainty and coordination identified above are only gained if there are few, if any, opt outs from the relevant default rule, and parties who realise this will be much less likely to contract out of or modify the default rules in order to obtain these benefits.[80] For example, in some markets a standard term contract is 'commodified', that is, can be traded among market participants. A contract whose terms deviate from the standard is less likely to be tradeable.[81] Further, if market participants do not contract out of or modify a default rule on frequent occasions, this is likely to mean that others will be less likely to want to be seen as outliers, and will also not contract out.[82] Moreover, if a term or set of terms is used frequently by market participants, an assumption will arise that it or they are efficient (because everyone uses it or them), even if this is not always the case.[83] Finally, even in commercial situations, asymmetries such as inequality of bargaining power or informational asymmetry (in the sense that one party, perhaps a repeat player, may be better informed about the advantages and disadvantages of certain default rules) may mean that negotiation does not take place.[84] A default rule that is rarely subject to negotiation becomes 'quasi-mandatory' despite the possibility of contrary agreement.[85]

V. What should be the Content of a Default Rule or Set of Rules?

One might take the view that, since parties can bargain round a default rule, its content is (broadly speaking) irrelevant, but that what does matter is that it is certain and clear, so that parties know out of what they are contracting. However, because contracting out of the rule will usually entail transaction costs, a majoritarian approach is usually favoured, that is, for the rule to mirror what most parties would choose.[86] Contracting out is therefore minimised, and transaction costs are lowered.

Which approach is preferable may well depend on the context, and on how easy (and cheap) contracting out of the rule is. One example from English commercial law is the rule that risk passes with property in section 20 of the SGA. This is a rule which is very frequently subject to contrary agreement, for example, in a standard form contract such as a CIF or FOB international sales contract,[87] or where a sale contract includes a

[79] Korobkin (n 50).

[80] Ben-Shahar and Pottow (n 78), referring to Kahan and Klausner (n 53). See text to nn 114–115 below.

[81] Choi and Gulati (n 54) 1141; Wielsch (n 54) 1086.

[82] Ben-Shahar and Pottow (n 78) 667.

[83] Choi and Gulati (n 54) 1153–54.

[84] See, for example, C Bradley, 'Private International Law-making for the Financial Markets' (2005) 29 *Fordham International LJ* 127, 167–69.

[85] See Korobkin (n 50) 665. For a sociological description of how the ISDA Master Agreement was viewed by those who were using it for swaps contracts, namely as a 'document' which they had to fill in the blanks without question, see Riles (n 34) 608–10.

[86] See literature cited in n 52.

[87] In a CIF contract, risk passes as from shipment (see *The Julia* [1949] AC 293, 309) unless the parties agree otherwise (see *Houlder Brothers & Co Ltd v Commissioner of Public Works* [1908] AC 276 and *M Golodetz &*

retention of title clause so that property does not pass on delivery, but on payment.[88] In the latter type of contract, a provision that risk passes on delivery notwithstanding the later passing of property has become a boilerplate clause.[89] The potential transaction costs for contracting out of the default statutory rule have been lowered to virtually zero by the standardisation of contracting out.

A pure majoritarian approach raises the issue of how the content of the rules themselves is to be determined. A theme running through this and the next section of this chapter is that, in the commercial law sphere at least, the source of the rules is an important factor in this process. Thus, in relation to statutory and judge-made rules, strong arguments have been made for a minimalist approach. Schwartz and Scott (from a US viewpoint) argue that such default rules should be conditioned on as few states of the world as possible (because to do otherwise would be too expensive to be efficient), should be simple (because of the limits of 'institutional competence') and should be efficient for a wide variety of contracting parties.[90] The difficulty of meeting this last criterion, given the huge number of potential differences between contracting parties,[91] leads these writers to conclude that there should be very few default rules, as opposed to standards. However, they conclude that standards are also not appropriate as parties, who want more certainty, contract away from them, thus raising transaction costs.[92] Given these difficulties, Schwartz and Scott argue that, in commercial law, a majoritarian approach is actually achieved by minimal default rules and standards, since that is 'what most commercial parties want' and will avoid wasted transaction costs, both at the law-making level and the contract making level. Instead, the state should focus its attention in private law on resolving disputes, on the basis of textual interpretation.[93]

A similar argument is made by Ayres in relation to default rules. He argues that since default rules that apply in all or most states of the world will be contracted out of by many parties, a better alternative is 'tailored' default rules. These are rules that incorporate general standards[94] that can be adapted to fit the actual circumstances of the parties' transactions, and may be appropriate because parties will not expend costs in contracting out of or modifying the rule ex ante, even though, in the relatively rare event that there is a dispute, ex post costs will be incurred in a court or other tribunal having

Co Inc v Czarnikow-Rionda Co Inc [1980] 1 WLR 495, although contracting out of this provision can raise the question as to whether the contract is a CIF contract), and in a FOB contract it passes when the goods pass the ship's rail (again, this can be subject to contrary agreement) (see cases cited in nn 39 and 40).

[88] In this situation, the contract will almost inevitably provide that risk passes on delivery, see, for example, *Clough Mill Ltd v Martin* [1985] 1 WLR 111, 114.

[89] See, for example, the Encyclopedia of Forms and Precedents (LexisNexis) Volume 34 (Sale of Goods) forms 115–119.

[90] Schwartz and Scott (n 2).

[91] The majoritarian approach logically entails trying to find out what actual commercial parties, with a very wide degree of heterogeneity, would want, which seems a near impossible endeavour. For some thoughts on how this could be achieved by proxy, see Grochowski (n 51), and the discussion in s VI below.

[92] Schwartz and Scott (n 2) also argue that the efficiency of such contracting is further limited by moral hazard and information asymmetry (at 601–08).

[93] See the conclusion of Schwartz and Scott (n 2) 618–91. For a similar argument applied to English law, see Morgan (n 1).

[94] See above n 8.

to apply the standard to the particular situation.[95] However, in the commercial field, the ex ante uncertainty that such tailored rules or standards bring is often unacceptable.

Some commercial law default rules do fall into this category in that they incorporate a standard of (commercial) reasonableness or other similar concepts, often amplified by explanatory factors that can be taken into account to determine the reasonableness.[96] However, in many situations, particularly in standard form agreements or harmonisation instruments which apply to a particular market sector or particular activity, the benefits of certainty and coordination militate in favour of 'untailored' rules, which provide ex ante certainty. The more specific the model, the more likely such rules are to exist as they will be very granular in nature.[97] The costs of contracting out by individual parties identified by Schwartz and Scott are overcome by the collectivisation of the process of contracting out carried out by the trade body or standard setter.

In a (limited) riposte to majoritarianism, Ayres and Gertner suggest that, in some cases, the most efficient content of a default rule is a 'penalty default' rule, which represents what most parties do not want. They argue that parties are therefore incentivised to bargain round the rule, thus revealing previously hidden information to each other and making their contract more efficient.[98] If the penalty default rule is unpopular enough, it can also be useful in overcoming the problem of 'stickiness' of default rules.[99] While penalty defaults may work in some instances in the field of commercial law,[100] there at least two reasons why they are less often found. First, market specific models often include duties to disclose as the default rule, since what is needed to be disclosed is reasonably predictable. Second, at the general level there may well be less stickiness, since a more specific and granular model can be chosen which, as mentioned above, reduces the transaction costs of contracting out.

In the example given earlier, is section 20 of the SGA, a 'penalty default' rule? Probably not: not only was it not designed as such[101] but it is hard to see what

[95] I Ayres, 'Making a Difference: The Contractual Contributions of Easterbrook and Fischel' (1992) 59 *Univ of Chicago L Rev* 1391; I Ayres, 'Preliminary Thoughts on Optimal Tailoring of Contractual Rules' (1993) 3 *Southern California Interdisciplinary LJ* 1.

[96] One example is the implied term that the goods will be of a satisfactory quality in SGA s 14(2). SGA ss 14(2A) and (2B) set out factors which are relevant in determining whether goods are of a satisfactory quality. Note also the standard of good faith or (distinctively) commercial reasonableness which applies to many international instruments, eg Art 4 UNICITRAL Model Law on Secured Transactions 2016, or (in a limited way) Art 8(3) CTC.

[97] One example is the ISDA Master Agreement, which includes an absolute obligation to pay or deliver what is specified in the relevant Confirmation, a list of 'events of default' which are very specific and specific provisions on how close-out netting is to operate. Another is the duty of strict compliance in the UCP, which, even after the slight relaxation in UCP 600, is still very specific in its contours (the relaxation now builds in tolerances but within, for example, a defined percentage of permitted discrepancy in the quantity of goods (Art 30(b)).

[98] Ayres and Gertner (n 52). See also C Riley, 'Designing Default Rules in Contract Law' (2000) 20 *OJLS* 367, 384, Morgan (n 1) 92; Korobkin (n 50) 673–76.

[99] See text to nn 77–78. See also Korobkin (n 50) 673–76, and Ben-Shahar and Pottow (n 78) 669.

[100] For example, one could see SGA s 12 in this light: it implies a term that the seller has the right to sell the goods, which cannot be excluded unless s 12(3) applies. S 12(3) applies when it appears from the contract or is inferred from the circumstances that the seller only intends to pass such title as he or a third person has, in which case the seller's obligations are to disclose any charges or encumbrances known to the seller (s 12(4)). This rule, taken as a whole, therefore incentivises the seller to disclose important information to the buyer.

[101] As a matter of history it reflected what appeared to be the general view of the Roman law position ('res perit domino suo', ie the thing perishes for the owner) (see *Martineau v Kitching* (1872) LR 7 QB 436, 454).

efficiency gain results from contracting out of it, whether by increased revealing of information or by some other means. Instead, it is an example of a rule which, even if it once conformed largely to market practice, has become a 'bad' rule, in that it no longer meets market expectations. However, given the commercial context in which it operates,[102] the fact that it is a default rule, and that contracting out of it is neither is costly nor reduces legal certainty,[103] has meant that little harm is caused by its continuing existence.

Majoritarianism can be challenged on the basis that 'stickiness' results in default rules not being contracted out of even where the resulting contract is inefficient. Arguably, then, the content of default rules should also reflect other approaches, such as an increase in certainty and coordination, the benefits of which have been outlined above.[104]

Certainty can be achieved by clearly formulated rules, by rules which do not include vague or difficult to apply concepts,[105] and by rules which reflect well understood concepts or market practices. Certainty is best achieved by rules that are nearer the mandatory end of the default rule spectrum,[106] although as long as parties are able to contract out of the rule clearly enough, and the courts interpret such contracting out according to its terms,[107] ex ante certainty can be achieved.

The influence of coordination on the content of default rules in the commercial sphere cannot be overestimated. Coordination is best achieved with as little contracting out as possible. The default nature of sets of rules which heavily promote coordination is largely, in practice, limited to certain specific provisions which include gaps to be filled in or restricted menus of possible rules.[108] For example, the ISDA Master Agreement includes such 'gaps' in its schedules, which parties must (or in some cases, can) fill in. In theory, two transacting parties could contract out of other terms of the ISDA Master Agreement but the loss of coordination benefits would be so severe that this is rarely done.[109]

Coordination between different contracts in a network can be achieved reasonably easily by the use of model contracts from trade bodies. This can give rise to the network

This, however, was a misunderstanding, in that the Roman law linked the passing of risk to the perfection of the sale contract by agreement of the object of sale and the price rather than the passing of property, see Inst.3.23.3. In situations where the property was intended to pass with delivery, the passing of property was an appropriate time for risk to pass.

[102] A different, and more majoritarian, rule applies to consumers, see Consumer Rights Act 2015 s 29. This rule is not a default rule in that a term purporting to limit or exclude the trader's liability under it is invalid, see Consumer Rights Act 2015 s 31 (presumably it could be varied in the consumer's favour by agreement).

[103] See section III above.

[104] See text to nn 64–65.

[105] See text to nn 60–61.

[106] See text to nn 79–85.

[107] See n 59.

[108] An example of a menu is s 6(e)(i) of the 1992 ISDA Master Agreement, giving four alternative formulae for calculating early close-out payments on an early termination. For a discussion of menus, see I Ayres, 'Menus Matter' (2006) 73 *Univ of Chicago L Rev* 3.

[109] For an account of the ISDA Master Agreement as a mixture of default and mandatory rules (on the grounds that contracting out of such terms is not realistic for market participants), see M Borowicz, 'Contracts as Regulation: The ISDA Master Agreement' (2021) 16 *Capital Markets LJ* 72, esp 82–83. See also Braithwaite (n 61) 784, who points out that (in 2010) 90 per cent of all OTC derivative transactions were documented using the ISDA Master Agreement, and see also *Lomas v JFB Firth Rixson* [2010] EWHC 3372(Ch) at [5].

benefits mentioned earlier,[110] but only if there is no or minimal contracting out of the model, at least on the points of convergence required for the network to operate.

Second, a more general coordination can be achieved by aligning default rules to custom and practice. This is a practice of ancient origin, and, although the concept of custom and practice (and the benefit of aligning rules) can be challenged,[111] it has at least three advantages. First, market participants can be assumed to be familiar with the relevant customs and practices, so that the default rules have a majoritarian quality, and parties are less likely to contract out. Second, the customs and practices have grown up (and have been refined) over a number of years, and so are likely to be suited to the relevant market. Third, the content and meaning of custom and practice is likely to be reasonably consistent, and so default rules based on these are likely to give rise to both network benefits and certainty.

A third influence of coordination comes when considering international commercial transactions. The transaction cost saving from harmonised rules has already been mentioned. Because of this, harmonised rules are also likely to result in an increase in cross-border trade and finance. International instruments are default rules in at least two ways: they may well include choices for an implementing State to make,[112] and also many of the rules themselves are likely to be default rules. In relation to the first of these, there is a balance to be struck when formulating default rules. It may be necessary to include opt-outs, potential modifications or even opt-ins for implementing States to obtain agreement on the overall instrument, which agreement is necessary for the (economic) benefits of the instrument to be obtained.[113]

So far, this section has argued that there are a number of factors which determine, and should determine, what the content of default rules is in the commercial law sphere. As this discussion has shown, there are various levels of default rules in commercial law. The first, and most general, level are the legislative and judge-made rules which are either 'untailored' (and thus are often contractually excluded or modified) or 'tailored' in that they resemble standards. While a majoritarian approach can justify, and therefore underlie, the existence and content of these rules, it does not usually result in low levels of negotiation (except where stickiness results in an inefficient outcome) because of the heterogeneity of the parties to which they apply.

However, this is not necessarily a problem in commercial law. More specific rules drawn up by trade bodies in model agreements[114] and rules which can be incorporated into agreements[115] themselves modify the general default rules so that they can apply more specifically to particular commercial situations: these rules are untailored, but

[110] See text to n 65.

[111] See the discussion in Riley (n 98) 374–77, and the work of L Bernstein, including L Bernstein, 'The Questionable Empirical Basis of Article 2's Incorporation Strategy: A Preliminary Study' (1999) 66 *Univ of Chicago L Rev* 719.

[112] See text to nn 24–26.

[113] For example, in relation to CTC, see A Didenko, *The Cape Town Convention: A Documentary History* (Oxford, Hart, 2021) 143–51.

[114] Such as the ISDA Master Agreement, the Loan Market Association documentation, the GAFTA model agreements, and the UKWA model agreements (see text to n 38).

[115] Such as the Incoterms and the Uniform Customs and Practice for Documentary Credits produced by the ICC.

more majoritarian as they reflect specific situations, and trade practices within those situations. Although they are default rules, they are less likely to be subject to individual negotiation since they genuinely reflect what the parties are likely to want. Stickiness, here, is often logical and efficient, since it results in the benefits of certainty and coordination being realised.

The example mentioned earlier (section 20 of the SGA) illustrates this phenomenon. The general rule is, in many situations, modified by the more specific rules provided by a trade body (based on case law)[116] and by market practice as exemplified in commercially provided precedents.[117] Since these granular rules are also default rules, even more granularity can take place at the level of the parties to the actual transaction, but only to the extent necessary to achieve the parties' aims. Thus, in many circumstances, we can see that the market not only achieves a reduction in transaction costs by limiting modification or exclusion to where the parties' transaction is truly individual, but also enables the other benefits identified above (certainty and coordination) to be achieved.

Given the cross-border nature of much commercial activity, we can, to some extent, see a similar pattern in relation to transnational default rules. Those promulgated by international organisations are default rules vis-à-vis States,[118] thus permitting States to adopt and implement a more tailored version for their own national law, which, because it reflects better a majoritarian approach, and because parties at national level want certainty and coordination benefits, is likely to be stickier. The same, arguably, applies to transnational rules from trade bodies, many of which can be (and are) tailored to national law and requirements.[119]

VI. The Process of Formulating Default Rules or Sets of Rules in the Commercial Sphere

Having discussed how the content of the rules should be determined as a matter of theory, we now turn to who makes those determinations in the commercial law sphere and how this is done. Not only does the identity of the rule-maker affect the level of granularity of the rules, and therefore the factors taken into account when the rules are made, it also affects the actual method of rule-making. Certain bodies are better than others in answering questions which are relevant to determining the content of default rules, particularly in the application of majoritarianism.

Some of the literature does differentiate as to who is making the rules in terms of whether it is a legislative or judicial body. For example, Riley argues that the legislature is better placed than the courts to take efficiency criteria into account when formulating rules.[120] He argues convincingly that, while a judge cannot decide upon efficiency as a sole criterion, nor can she determine the correct majoritarian approach empirically, a

[116] Incoterms versions of CIF and FOB contracts.
[117] See n 89.
[118] See text to nn 21–26.
[119] See Riles (n 34) 613–14 in relation to the ISDA Master Agreement.
[120] Riley (n 98) 388–89.

suitable proxy is usually what he calls 'conventionalist norms', that is, the principles and standards 'immanent within the contractor's own community'.[121] The use by judges, in the commercial sphere, of trade custom and practice is an example of reliance on conventionalist norms, as is reliance on precedent or previously existing principle.[122]

While Riley differentiates between the approach based on efficiency criteria and that based on conventionalist norms, on the grounds that the latter will not necessarily give rise to terms which produce the most efficient outcomes, he acknowledges that the difference between the resulting terms will not always be very significant.[123] This is for a number of reasons, including that it is not always easy or even possible to determine whether a conventionalist norm is more or less efficient than one determined by efficiency criteria, and the fact that legislation often enacts judicially determined default rules, rather than being formulated as a result of a free-standing efficiency determination. While the latter reason is certainly true of codification exercises such as the SGA,[124] this is not necessarily true of much modern legislation, which is largely enacted to change rather than preserve the status quo,[125] and which usually only takes place after an economic impact assessment weighing up the costs and benefits of the legislation. This type of economic assessment will usually consider majoritarian considerations, that is, how likely it is that parties will negotiate around default rules, as well as whether the default rule itself is substantively efficient.[126]

While it is true that the judiciary cannot successfully carry out an efficiency calculation when they determine default rules, arguably, by following conventionalist norms such as trade custom and practice, and previously determined cases (both of which usually align with what a majority of commercial contracting parties want), they are following a majoritarian approach, tempered by considerations of certainty and coordination. Moreover, in England and Wales, judges are specialists: in the commercial court and the chancery division they are drawn from practitioners who have practised for many years in the areas of commercial and financial law, and who, as judges, decide cases in those areas all the time. For these reasons, judges, at least in English law where gap-filling is strictly limited by the criteria for the implication of terms into contracts,[127] are arguably good determiners of the content of default rules in the commercial sphere, when they do fill gaps.[128]

[121] ibid, 368.

[122] An example of the last of these is the formulation of the rule that risk passes with property in the nineteenth century, based on a view of the principle in Roman law (even though this turned out to be a flawed view), see n 101.

[123] Riley (n 98) 389–90.

[124] The original codification was in 1893.

[125] An example of recent legislation designed to preserve the status quo in all but one respect is the Electronic Trade Documents Act 2023, which provides that electronic documents which are the functional equivalent of paper trade documents can be possessed, thus enabling all the existing law in relation to such documents to apply to the electronic versions. The rule in s 3 of the Act which provides that such an electronic document can be possessed and has the same legal effect as a paper one is a default rule, in that parties can provide, by agreement, that it does not apply to a particular document (see s 5(1)).

[126] See, for example, the impact assessment for the (then) Electronic Trade Documents Bill (at www.gov.uk/government/publications/electronic-trade-documents-bill-impact-assessment/impact-assessment-of-the-electronic-trade-documents-bill) which considers the 'adoption rate' as part of the cost/benefit calculation.

[127] See s II.D above.

[128] For a more critical view of the ability of judges to determine default rules, at least using majoritarian criteria, see Grochowski (n 51) 69–70.

In considering the techniques used by legislatures to determine what default rule would best fit the majoritarian approach, Grochowski contrasts a direct approach, based on evidence of market contracts, to a comparative approach, that is, examining default rules in other states.[129] He considers neither approach particularly satisfactory. Both suffer from lack of comprehensive data[130] and rely on much speculation: how does the legislature know that most contracting parties will want to continue with the preferences of the past, or that the parties in one state will have the same preferences as parties in another state? These issues, while an inevitable part of any law-making process, can to some extent be overcome in the commercial sphere by the input of bodies representing market players in, for example, a consultation exercise. Such bodies can provide collectivised information which would be difficult to obtain from individual market players, and which does not raise the problem of confidentiality which would otherwise arise. Moreover, if trade bodies support a particular default rule, that alone is likely to incentivise market participants not to negotiate around it, as by adopting the rule they will obtain the benefits of certainty and coordination identified above.

As discussed above, rule-making in the commercial law sphere has become increasingly the province of trade bodies and international institutions. Are these better or worse able to determine the content of default rules? Taking international institutions first, the method of formulating default rules is not very different from that used by legislatures. The text of instruments is determined by committees of experts and delegates from many jurisdictions, usually with wide consultation with interested parties.[131] Of course, as mentioned above,[132] the 'default' nature of the rules here arises on two levels: States can, in many instances, opt out of or modify the rules in the international instrument and the instrument itself may permit parties to negotiate the rules. At the first level, the rule-making procedure of international institutions is often well designed to facilitate the process of determining the content of the rules. If many jurisdictions are represented, the majoritarian position can be determined quasi-empirically, that is, what most jurisdictions want, but the minority position can also be determined, so that a decision can be made as to whether a menu of choices or an opt-out or opt-in is optimal. In terms of the second level, in commercial law instruments there is likely to be input from trade bodies, often together with international financial organisations who, indirectly, represent the interests of lenders and financiers.[133] Consultation exercises, similar those run as part of the national legislative process, can cast the net even wider in the search for evidence for a majoritarian solution.

The formulation of default rules by trade bodies should, in theory, result in the most accurate application of the majoritarian approach, since such bodies can represent and 'aggregate' market preferences.[134] Coupled with the specificity of the rules promulgated

[129] ibid, 69.

[130] He suggests that this problem can, to some extent, be overcome by the use of AI and big data, but recognises that this brings its own problems, see ibid, 71–72.

[131] See www.unidroit.org/about-unidroit/overview/ and https://uncitral.un.org/en/about/methods.

[132] See s II.B.

[133] There is a danger, of course, that such input from trade bodies can favour one type of party over another: this danger, whether at national or international legislative level is hard to eliminate entirely.

[134] See Grochowski (n 51) 70–71.

by such bodies,[135] which also contributes to the suitability of the rules for most commercial parties in the particular market in question, one could argue that trade bodies are likely to be the most effective determiners of default rules in the commercial sphere.

There are, however, some potential drawbacks to the formulation of default rules by trade bodies. First, the benefits of certainty and coordination in the use of such rules are so strong (or perceived to be so strong) market participants rarely negotiate either individual rules or the use of the standard form contract. For this, and for other reasons set out above,[136] the default rules are very 'sticky'. Second, the stickiness of the rules could be seen as less than optimal if the formulation of a rule or set of rules did not, in fact, include aggregation of the views of all interest groups within the market. Concerns have been raised that some sets of such rules favour one type of party over another because of the influence that the former type of party has in the formulation process, and that type of party has a negotiation advantage over the other, particularly where the rules are sticky.[137] The stickiness of the rules has led some commentators to argue that they are 'quasi-statute'[138] and for one to call for a 'rule of recognition' which includes representation of all interests in the drafting process.[139] However, in the absence of an interaction with a court (at which point the lack of full representation can be taken into account in the manner in which the court interprets the standard terms),[140] such a 'rule' could only be effective if included in some form of regulation designed to enhance competition within standard default terms. Such a move, however, would jeopardise the coordination benefits referred to earlier.

VII. Conclusion

Default, as opposed to mandatory, rules are common in commercial law, given the importance attached to party autonomy, and the reduction in concerns about inequality of bargaining power.[141] The efficiency caused by the lowering of transaction costs through a majoritarian approach to the content of such rules is valuable to commercial parties. However, such rules can become 'sticky' for many reasons, including, in particular, the additional benefits of certainty and coordination that flow from the use of sets of default rules in this sphere. The degree of specificity of default rules will depend, in many cases, on their source. This applies particularly to more granular rules, which are often modifications of general default rules and which are adapted, by the courts, trade custom or trade bodies, for use in particular situations. While such rules can be further modified to fit individual situations, the resulting pattern provides a suitable balance between the transaction cost savings of majoritarianism and the benefits of certainty and coordination, particularly when these rules are harmonised across jurisdictions.

[135] See text to nn 114–15.
[136] See text to nn 79–85.
[137] See, for example, the discussion of the LMA standard terms in Bradley (n 84) 166–68; Ben-Shahar and Pottow (n 78) 670. See also Riles (n 34), discussing the ISDA Master Agreement.
[138] Choi and Gulati (n 54).
[139] Wielsch (n 54).
[140] See Gullifer (n 59).
[141] That is not to say that this concern is entirely eliminated, see n 4.

10

Default Norms in Labour Law: From Private Right to Public Law

ALAN BOGG

I. Introduction: The Problem of Default Norms in Labour Law

Even if the Latin terminology seems unfamiliar, the substantive matter of the distinction between *ius cogens* and *ius dispositivum* is fundamental to the historical development of British labour law. As we shall see, while there is some variation in the definition of these categories, *ius dispositivum* describes norms that may be varied by the will of the parties. By contrast, *ius cogens* describes mandatory or imperative norms that are imposed on the parties by operation of law and may not be varied by private agreement.

Broadly speaking, the historical development of British labour law may be understood as the journey from *ius dispositivum* to *ius cogens*. The legal 'cornerstone' of the structure of British labour law is still the employment contract.[1] Historically, the contract of employment was firmly in the realm of *ius dispositivum*. Its norms were amenable to variation by the parties. In part, this reflected the dominance of freedom of contract in English contract law. The unusual feature was the wide scope of 'the parties', which also included norms negotiated by employers and trade unions and that were incorporated into individual employment contracts from time to time. When statutory rights were introduced, such as wages regulation, unfair dismissal or trade union discrimination protections, these were generally defined in the legislation as *ius cogens*. This flowed from the basic justification for labour law itself.[2] Employment contracts were marked by an inequality of bargaining power. 'Contracting out' of statutory rights undercut the very reason for imposing those rights on the employment contract in the first place. Individual waivers in labour law always had dubious legitimacy given these background conditions of structural inequality. The widespread erosion of fundamental rights by

[1] O Kahn-Freund, 'Legal Framework' in A Flanders and HA Clegg (eds), *The System of Industrial Relations in Great Britain* (Oxford, Basil Blackwell, 1954) 42, 45.

[2] There is now a rich literature on waivers in employment law: see G Davidov, 'Non-waivability in Labour Law' (2020) 40 *OJLS* 482; and V Bogoeski, 'Nonwaivability of Labour Rights, Individual Waivers and the Emancipatory Function of Labour Law' (2023) 56 *Industrial LJ* 179.

'contracting out' could also undermine important public goods such as a decent labour market, or a culture of respect and equality in the workplace. In this way, *ius cogens* was inscribed into the very soul of labour law itself.

Like any broad brush portrait, this picture needs some adjustment to capture its subject with more precision. Some statutory norms are amenable to variation through individual agreement.[3] There are important debates around regulatory design, identifying procedural and substantive rules that can permit individual waivers while limiting the scope for abuse and coercion by the more powerful party.[4] And the vital regulatory role of collective agreements has always given *ius dispositivum* a stronger relevance to labour law than the statute book and mandatory individual rights might at first suggest. As will be discussed further below, the role of collective agreements in many labour law systems highlights the relativity of 'imperative-ness'. Where there are conflicting norms derived from multiple sources, this raises the issue of how to rank those norms. It is a well-established legal principle of 'favourability' in many European systems that accords primacy to the norm most favourable to the weaker party.[5]

This chapter will not engage with these important debates. Instead, it will consider a more basic issue which lurks in the foundation of British labour law itself. Generally speaking, imperative statutory norms supervene on an employment contract rooted in the agreement of the parties. This interface between statute and common law is absolutely fundamental.[6] Like tectonic plates, *ius dispositivum* and *ius cogens* are always in contact with each other, always in motion. From time to time, the seismic activity erupts into the English jurisprudence with spectacular legal effects.

In the next section (section II), I begin with three classic reflections on the distinction between default and imperative norms. As befits a workshop held at Brasenose College, Oxford, in which this chapter originated, these pieces all have a Brasenose connection. While there are some differences of emphasis and approach between them, they converge on an important proposition. This is the primacy of a notion of public policy or *ordre public* over *ius dispositivum*. Broadly speaking, where legal norms have a 'public law' quality, they tend to be less amenable to individual waiver.

In the third section (section III below), I examine two regulatory problems of modern labour law. They are problems because they arise principally out of the tectonic friction between statute and common law, between *ius cogens* and *ius dispositivum*. These are the problem of contractual employment status and the problem of terms implied in law. Drawing upon the notion of *ordre public* developed in the second section, I suggest some ways in which the law could limit *ius dispositivum* within appropriate boundaries. This is followed by a short conclusion and some reflections on rational and coherent legal development in light of the arguments in this chapter.

[3] The most widely discussed instance is the individual opt-out from the 48-hour maximum weekly working hours' limit in the Working Time Regulations 1998, Reg 5. For broader discussion of its practical operation, see C Barnard, S Deakin and R Hobbs, 'Opting Out of the 48-Hour Week: Employer Necessity or Individual Choice? An Empirical Study of the Operation of Article 18(1)(b) of the Working Time Directive in the UK' (2003) 32 *Industrial LJ* 223.

[4] A Bogg, 'The Regulation of Working Time in Europe' in A Bogg, C Costello and ACL Davies (eds), *Research Handbook on EU Labour Law* (Cheltenham, Edward Elgar, 2016) ch 12.

[5] M Freedland and N Kountouris, *The Legal Construction of Personal Work Relations* (Oxford, OUP, 2011) 186–87.

[6] A Bogg, 'Common Law and Statute in the Law of Employment' (2016) 69 *Current Legal Problems* 67.

II. Imperative Norms and Default Norms in Labour Law: A Brasenose Meditation

It is fitting to begin our reflections on the role of default norms in labour law with three papers authored by scholars with a Brasenose College connection: Professor Otto Kahn-Freund, Professor Bernard Rudden and Professor Mark Freedland. Kahn-Freund and Rudden were both holders of the prestigious Chair in Comparative Law at the University of Oxford, which is still associated with Brasenose College. Freedland arrived at Brasenose as a graduate student from University College London in 1966, before his election to a Junior Research Fellowship at St John's College in 1967. All three scholars were doyens of general comparative law, and across their distinguished careers Kahn-Freund and Freedland were also leading scholars of comparative labour law. It is surely no coincidence that the dimension of comparative law links these three foundational papers on default norms. The conceptual distinction between *ius cogens* (imperative norms) and *ius dispositivum* (waivable norms) was most highly developed in the Civilian legal tradition. The default norm is *ius dispositivum*. It is unsurprising, therefore, that it should be the legal comparatists grappling with the translation of systematic Civilian legal categories into a suitable Common law idiom.

A. Kahn-Freund on Status and Contract

The earliest of these three papers was Kahn-Freund's justly celebrated article, 'A Note on Status and Contract in Labour Law'. It was published shortly after his election to the Chair of Comparative Law in 1964, and it was focused on imperative and default norms in labour law.[7] At first glance, the relevance of the article to default norms is not obvious. In it, Kahn-Freund examined the ambiguities and difficulties in applying Maine's famous distinction between 'status' and 'contract'[8] to the modern development of societies and legal cultures. According to Kahn-Freund, the definition of 'status' in Maine's original sense described a situation where 'the sum total of the powers and disabilities, the rights and obligations, which society confers or imposes upon individuals' is operative regardless of their volition.[9] By contrast, 'contract' described the situation where the parties' rights and obligations arose out of the parties' own volition, and were reflected in their agreement. Broadly speaking, European societies had witnessed the eclipse of 'status' relations and the rise of 'contract'. This no doubt reflected the broader development of a liberal legal and constitutional culture. According to Kahn-Freund, the formal juridical category of 'status' was very narrow in scope. It was restricted to special statuses such as 'lunacy' or 'aliens' or 'citizens' where the ascription of legal incidents was entirely non-volitional. The puzzle for Kahn-Freund was the tendency of modern writers to describe a counter-movement from 'contract' back to 'status', particularly within the context of the welfare state and protective employment legislation. As he put it, in

[7] O Kahn-Freund, 'A Note on Status and Contract in Labour Law' (1967) 30 *Modern Law Review* 635.
[8] HS Maine, *Ancient Law* (London, John Murray, 1861) ch 5, esp 170 ('from status to contract').
[9] Kahn-Freund (n 7) 636.

these contexts, 'the law operates upon an existing contractual relation, but it moulds this relation through mandatory norms which cannot be contracted out of to the detriment of the weaker party (employee, passenger, consumer in general)'.[10] There was a tendency to treat this as a regression to 'status', a characterisation that was deliberately bound up with negative connotations.

Kahn-Freund rejected this status-based characterisation of mandatory norms in employment contracts. Employment contracts were volitional at their inception and termination. The fact that the content of these contractual agreements was shaped by statutory imperative norms to protect the economically weaker party did not justify their characterisation as status relations. Kahn-Freund traced this confusion of status and contract to a conceptual gap in the legal categories of the English Common law:

> The distinction between *jus cogens* and *jus dispositivum*, between 'imperative' and 'optional' norms of the law of contract, is familiar to every practising lawyer in any Continental legal system. It fits naturally into the thinking of lawyers brought up and working in a world of legal thought in which the systematic regulation of the law of contract through general norms applicable to all contracts and special norms applicable to defined types has for almost two centuries been a commonplace.[11]

This conceptual gap led some English lawyers to treat imperative norms in protective statutes as a status-based extra-contractual imposition on the employment contract. Such imperative norms were not integrated into the contract itself, because contractual norms were treated by the courts as *ius dispositivum* and rooted in the intention of the parties. According to Kahn-Freund, the clarification of these distinctive conceptual categories would assist in the task of rational codification.[12] It would also facilitate a deeper integration of imperative norms into the structure of the employment contract itself, thereby also providing a justification for the law's shaping of the normative content of those contracts.

How can we make sense of this conceptual gap in English contract law? In retrospect, there were four main factors explaining it. The first factor was the relatively under-developed body of doctrinally focused taxonomy and systematisation in the English universities compared with their European counterparts.[13] By contrast, 'dogmatic' legal science was well-established in the Law Faculties of the ancient universities of Europe. The second factor was the relative absence of a body of legal thought in English law based on 'systematic regulation of the law of contract through general norms applicable to all contracts and special norms applicable to defined types'.[14] The legal 'atrophy' of the employment contract, resulting from the primacy of dispute resolution through collective bargaining procedure, meant that a body of special norms for employment contracts had not developed.[15] This hobbled the emergence of a rich taxonomy of categories, concepts and legal distinctions. It also impeded the development of an autonomous body of special common law rules regulating personal employment contracts. The third

[10] ibid 640.
[11] ibid 641.
[12] ibid 644.
[13] G Samuel, 'Can Doctrinal Legal Scholarship Be Defended?' (2022) 4 *Amicus Curiae* 43.
[14] Kahn-Freund (n 7) 644.
[15] O Kahn-Freund, 'Blackstone's Neglected Child: The Contract of Employment' (1977) 93 *LQR* 508, 524.

factor was the general dominance of an 'oil' and 'water' approach to statute and common law in English legal thought.[16] The imperative norm was the domain of the legislator and statute law. The default or optional norm was the domain of the courts and the common law, which gave primacy to freedom of contract. This strong separation of statute and common law, which no doubt reflected broader constitutional ideas around separation of powers and parliamentary sovereignty, reinforced the exclusion of *ius cogens* from the law of contract.

The final factor was the relatively late development of many of the terms 'implied in law' in the employment contract, such as the implied term of mutual trust and confidence. Unlike express terms or terms implied in fact, such terms are not derived from the parties' intentions. They represent normative propositions, necessary legal incidents of a category of contracts, which reflect a judicial assessment of sound public policy such as promoting efficient cooperation or restricting party exploitation.[17] Terms implied in law represented the most powerful way in which the content and performance of the employment contract could be moulded by law other than through legislative intervention. This legal technique provided a more supple regulatory role than Kahn-Freund's rather blunt view that the common law of public policy 'in a few extreme cases, may destroy a contract, but which cannot mould it'.[18] Terms implied in law occupied an ambiguous place along the *ius cogens*/*ius dispositivum* axis. On the one hand, they are not derived from the parties' intentions but are grounded in independent normative arguments. On the other hand, contractual orthodoxy suggests they are highly vulnerable to exclusion by express agreement.

B. Rudden on *Ius Cogens* and *Ius Dispositivum*

Professor Rudden's article, 'Ius Cogens, Ius Dispositivum',[19] was specifically concerned with the conceptual distinction in the title. It was a fine piece of scholarship, steeped in legal learning and considering a wide range of material from Roman law, English legal history and modern Civilian legal systems. Rudden's background in comparative law enabled him to provide an acute perspective on the nature of the distinction. In terms of its substantive legal focus, the article focused particularly on problems drawn from the law of contracts, wills and property. This was because the conceptual distinction was of general relevance across a wide range of doctrinal areas. Interestingly, the article did not consider the application of these categories in labour law. It did however address the area of leaseholds and the protection of security of tenure in some detail, and the permissible role of contractual waiver. The parallels between the leasehold tenancy relation and the employment relation are striking, engaging similar regulatory challenges of protecting the security of the weaker party in a power relationship.[20] Where there are

[16] See J Beatson, 'The Role of Statute in the Development of Common Law Doctrine' (2001) 117 *LQR* 247.

[17] H Collins, 'Implied Terms in the Contract of Employment' in M Freedland, A Bogg and others (eds), *The Contract of Employment* (Oxford, OUP, 2016) ch 22 at 471 et seq.

[18] Kahn-Freund (n 7) 641.

[19] B Rudden, 'Ius Cogens, Ius Dispositivum' (1980) 11 *Cambrian L Rev* 87.

[20] See, for example, ACL Davies' comparative consideration of 'shams' in tenancies and employment in ACL Davies, 'Sensible Thinking About Sham Transactions: *Protectacoat Firthglow Ltd v Szilagyi* [2009] EWCA Civ 98; [2009] IRLR 365' (2009) 38 *Industrial LJ* 318.

standing concerns about the validity of consent, or a strong public interest in the effective enforcement of imperative norms, the scope for *ius dispositivum* might be legitimately curtailed. This had direct relevance to *ius dispositivum* in the law of employment.

Like Kahn-Freund before him, Rudden's analysis linked the distinction between *ius cogens* and *ius dispositivum* to the constitutional division between legislated norms and other types of norm: 'The issue I wish to consider is that of conflict between norms of the legislator or the general law and those made by citizens, sometimes by unilateral juridical act but usually by contract.'[21] Rudden also defined the categories in terms of the scope for norms to be waived or set aside by the will of the parties: 'I shall adopt the convenient jargon of *ius cogens* to mean norms which cannot be set aside by the will of the citizen, and *ius dispositivum* to mean those which can.'[22] Again, this was similar to Kahn-Freund's account of the distinction, which was framed around the role of the intention of the parties.

Beyond these definitional preliminaries, the true originality of Rudden's account was based in his elucidation of three maxims that provided the legal context to the distinction. These maxims could sometimes pull in different directions. One effect of this underlying normative complexity was that the division between *ius cogens* and *ius dispositivum* was better understood as a 'spectrum' rather than a simple categorical distinction.[23] It reflected the balance between maxims which was ultimately contingent on the balance of political forces. According to Rudden, these three underling maxims, derived from the works of Roman and English jurists, were: (i) public law cannot be altered by the agreement of private citizens; (ii) a benefit is not forced on the unwilling; (iii) agreement conquers law.[24] Freedland suggests that the third maxim may be understood as an overarching general principle.[25] The primary tension in legal systems is between the first and second maxims. The adjustment between them varies over time, across legal systems, and is relative to the specific issue being regulated. The private law default in the law of contract is the second maxim. Nevertheless, there is no simple relation of lexical priority of the second over the first, establishing a neat hierarchy of norms. The balance between them is far messier and less mechanistic than that. It depends upon shifting evaluative judgements of *ordre public*. There has never been a naturalised province of imperative norms.

The first maxim is most obviously concerned to vindicate imperative norms as *ius cogens*, whereas the other two maxims support a role for *ius dispositivum*. Given its importance as a foundation for imperative norms, what is the meaning of 'public' in this first maxim? It could describe the formal source of a legal norm, for example its basis in a statutory enactment. Alternatively, it could describe the basic legal taxonomy of a norm, such that it is properly described as a norm of public law rather than private law. This 'form' approach is overbroad. For example, it is demonstrably false that

[21] Rudden (n 19) 87. Note that Rudden adds 'or the general law' to 'norms of the legislator', which appears to suggest that some imperative norms may be based in the common law itself.

[22] ibid 87.

[23] ibid.

[24] ibid 88–91.

[25] M Freedland, 'Ius Cogens, Ius Dispositivum, and the Law of Personal Work Contracts' in P Birks and A Pretto (eds), *Themes in Comparative Law: In Honour of Bernard Rudden* (Oxford, OUP, 2002) 165, 168.

a statutory norm can never be altered by private agreement. In labour law specifically, there may be very good reasons why collective agreements should be permitted to vary statutory norms tailored to particular businesses or sectors. The taxonomical characterisation of a norm as one of public law is not straightforward either: many legal norms may be equally well situated within both private law and public law.[26] Rudden wisely rejects form-based approaches, of which source and taxonomy are examples. Instead, he favours a substantive test of 'public'. This substantive approach is based in a notion of public policy, captured in the Civilian idea that private agreement cannot derogate from legal norms concerned with *ordre public* and good morals.[27] As Rudden acknowledges, this category of imperative higher norm, understood in terms of *ordre public*, will vary in scope across different legal systems and different periods. It is also not easily translated into a common law formulation, where there is no exactly comparable doctrinal category. It would seem to capture those norms where there is a strong public interest in their universal application, perhaps because individual waiver threatens the dignity of the waiving party or where the erosion of the norm would undermine important public goods. While the flexibility of a substantive approach means that the maxim can accommodate a broad range of situations, this may also lead to a loss of predictive power. The clearest situation is where the statute itself prohibits contracting out of the statutory norm.[28] This is of fundamental importance in the law of employment, given the pivotal role of anti-contracting out provisions in the main employment statutes.[29]

If the first maxim supports the role of *ius cogens*, the second maxim both supports and demarcates the role of *ius dispositivum*. According to Rudden, it is an ancient principle that a beneficiary may renounce a benefit where it is conferred through a legal facility such as a gift, a will or under a trust.[30] This basic default in favour of waiving benefits represents an anti-paternalist approach to the legal subject. However, voluntary renunciation of benefits also has its legal limits. These legal limits represent the intersection of the first and second maxims, in that they turn upon the scope of public policy or *ordre public*. As Rudden explains, 'In the present context the difficulty stems from the fact that the best way to promote a public policy may be to confer rights on private citizens; and that policy may be thwarted if those rights can be discarded.'[31] He uses an example from the law of tenancies to demonstrate this limiting role of public policy. In relation to security of tenure for tenant farmers, non-waivable security of tenure was not only a 'protection of the weak against the strong', but supported the public interest in the stewardship and husbandry of the land.[32] We have already noted the significant affinities between security of tenure and security of employment. Many imperative norms in employment law are also concerned with the 'protection of the weak against the strong'. The constraints on waivability of statutory employment rights

[26] The classic account in this vein is D Oliver, *Common Values and the Public-Private Divide* (Cambridge, CUP, 1999).

[27] Rudden (n 19) 89 refers to a provision of the nineteenth-century *Code Napoléon* (ie the French Civil Code) as an example of this substantive approach.

[28] Rudden (n 19) 89.

[29] See eg Employment Rights Act 1996, s 203(1).

[30] Rudden (n 19) 90.

[31] ibid.

[32] ibid.

are also justified by important public goods. For example, mandatory rest and leave periods limit the health and safety risks posed by exhausted workers to co-workers and service users. More generally, a mandatory 'floor of rights' supports the public goods of a decent labour market and a stable protective framework for employment contracting. These public policy arguments are concerned with the integrity of the legal institutions within which employment contracting takes place, rather than the fairness of discrete individual waivers.

As already noted, Rudden examines the operation of *ius cogens* and *ius dispositivum* across the general areas of private law rather than in employment law. The most relevant of these general areas to employment law is contract law. Rudden's introduction to his analysis of general contract law draws a fundamental distinction between 'the operative fact of the parties' *agreement* and the legal consequences of *contract* ascribed thereto'.[33] How is this relevant to the *ius cogens*/*ius dispositivum* distinction? The ascription of legal consequences of 'contract' to an agreement seems to reflect the domain of *ius cogens*. For agreements to have contractual effect, this presupposes a general framework of norms within which those agreements must be embedded. The general doctrines concerned with enforceability, the construction and interpretation of terms and the remedial consequences of breach, all presuppose an overarching structural framework of legal rules. There is only so far that *ius dispositivum* can go. At some point, the framework must depend upon imperative norms and a stable structure for contracting, otherwise that basic structural framework will be undermined. In terms of the maxims, we might say that the structural preconditions of contract law represent a public good or *ordre public*. Since we all benefit from this structural integrity, and depend upon its stability for making our own contractual bargains, it cannot be a matter of private waiver and *ius dispositivum*.

This is reflected in his discussion of some specific doctrinal areas of general contract law, but ones which are also relevant to the modern law of the employment contract. The first is described as 'choosing the category'. The issue is crystallised with great perspicuity by Rudden: 'Given that the parties intend their agreement to have legal consequences, the question arises as to whether they can select those consequences by reference to some known category; whether, in short, their will, or some higher norm, classifies the deal.'[34] According to Rudden, the classification function in legal systems should be understood as *ius cogens* rather than *ius dispositivum*, an approach that originated in the courts of equity but in due course came to dominate the common law approach.[35] In other words, the legal characterisation of a contract, and the legal incidents of that characterisation, were critical elements in the structural framework for contracting. While the conceptual distinction is clear enough, this could be difficult to apply in practice. This is because the contract is based on the parties' own agreement, and the content of the agreement is the material upon which the legal characterisation is based. This meant that there were opportunities for stronger contracting parties to steer the characterisation through the imposition of terms in written documents. This fraught interaction between 'contract' and 'agreement' has formed the basis to the legal doctrine of sham

[33] ibid 92.
[34] ibid 93.
[35] ibid.

terms and arrangements.[36] While Rudden's discussion was focused on the law of mortgages and demise, it also had evident importance to the law of employment. The legal characterisation of personal work contracts is foundational to the entire law of employment, given that inderogable statutory protections (and certain terms implied in law) were allocated only to specific types of personal work contract. If the determination of the type of personal work contract was for the parties themselves, as a form of *ius dispositivum*, the entire basis of statutory imperative norms was constructed on foundations of sand. As we shall see, Rudden's rich insights on legal classification as *ius cogens* was taken up by Professor Freedland and developed specifically within the context of employment contracts.

The second doctrinal area in contract law was 'setting aside some of the norms'. Rudden's treatment of this issue again takes this notion of the background legal framework as its focus. In developing this argument, he engaged with Lord Diplock's speech in *Photo Production Ltd v Securicor Transport Ltd*.[37] In this case, Lord Diplock affirmed the centrality of *ius dispositivum* in the law of contract, which flowed from the default norm of freedom of contract. He also emphasised the limits of this default norm in terms of the structural legal preconditions of a law of contract. So, while the primary obligations of a contract may be modified by express agreement, the basic constitutive features for the agreement to be capable of qualifying as a contract could not be waived. This is because such a waiver would negate the very legal characteristics necessary for it to function as a contract at all. Similarly, the contractual exclusion of all remedies for breach would subvert the basic structural framework necessary for contracting practices to be reliably enforced. In terms of the first and second maxims, such exclusions would undermine *ordre public*.[38] Using examples from French law and Roman law, Rudden suggests that *ordre public* may go further than defending the basic structure of contract law. For example, a contractual waiver that concerned the 'integrity of the human body' or liability for deceit might undermine the human dignity of a contracting party or undermine norms of fair dealing upon which a system of contract law depends.[39] Interestingly, while the surest way to restrict contracting out is through *statutory* prohibition, Rudden's discussion certainly leaves open the possibility that public limits on *ius dispositivum* may sometimes be internal to the general Civil or Common law. In Common law systems, this could be derived from contractual techniques under the general umbrella of 'public policy'.

C. Freedland on *Ius Cogens*, *Ius Dispositivum* and the Law of Personal Work Contracts

The final piece in our Brasenose troika is a chapter by Professor Mark Freedland, published in a *festschrift* for Professor Rudden following his retirement from the Chair

[36] On which, see A Bogg, 'Sham Self-Employment in the Supreme Court' (2012) 41 *Industrial LJ* 328.

[37] *Photo Production Ltd v Securicor Transport Ltd* [1980] AC 827, esp 848–49.

[38] At the other end of the spectrum, *ordre public* may also explain why many legal systems are reluctant to enforce penalty clauses in contracts: see Rudden (n 19) 95.

[39] ibid. Rudden doesn't frame his examples in these dignitarian terms, but in my view it provides an attractive rationalisation of the law's reluctance to treat such waivers as valid.

in Comparative Law.[40] By this time, Freedland was Professor of Employment Law at the University of Oxford and Fellow at St John's College. The chapter is an extended reflection on Rudden's *Cambrian Law Review* piece from 1980, developing those themes within the specific context of the law of personal work contracts. As one would expect from the scholar, this chapter was neither hagiographic nor derivative of Rudden's earlier arguments. Indeed, the specificity of Freedland's focus on employment law provided a perceptive and original perspective on the *ius cogens*/*ius dispositivum* distinction. This reflected the distinctive shape of *ordre public* within the context of employment law as an autonomous legal discipline.

The significance of locating this discussion within the context of employment law is evident in the opening reflections on the definition of terms. The comparative context is as important as it was for Kahn-Freund and Rudden, but this is now identified by Freedland as based principally in European Community law. Freedland proposed the discourse of 'inderogability' as the most appropriate theoretical framework for analysing the distinction in employment law. This concept of 'inderogability' was first deployed in English labour law by Lord Wedderburn, drawing upon his own formidable grasp of comparative and European labour law.[41] 'Inderogability' was concerned with the hierarchy of sources of norms, such as norms derived from collective agreements, statutory norms and the individual contract of employment. In many European countries, collective agreements performed a public regulatory role, and so were much more akin to social legislation than private contract. This public characterisation was very significant in light of Rudden's three maxims and the pivotal role of *ordre public*. These issues were particularly acute in relation to the implementation of European Directives in employment law. For example, the Working Time Directive[42] contained a mix of inderogable norms (the right to paid annual leave), derogable norms through individual variation (the right to a weekly working hours' limit of 48 hours) and a role for collective agreements (on daily and weekly rest periods).

British collective labour law had developed in a rather haphazard way, subject to a liberal voluntarist ideology of collective laissez-faire.[43] By contrast, European labour law had been informed by a much more systematic taxonomy of legal sources. Interestingly, Freedland departed from the tendency of both Kahn-Freund and Rudden to overlay the treatment of imperative norms with a constitutional gloss – both had been keen to convey that *ius cogens* was especially characteristic of the legislative domain. Instead, Freedland's definition was constitutionally agnostic: '[W]e should think of *ius cogens* as referring to legal norms which are not derogable by agreement between employers and workers, and of *ius dispositivum* as referring to legal norms which are derogable by agreement between employers and workers.'[44] This agnosticism was surely facilitated by the regulatory wildcard of the collective agreement, which simultaneously displayed

[40] Freedland (n 25).

[41] Lord Wedderburn, 'Inderogability, Collective Agreements, and Community Law' (1992) 21 *Industrial LJ* 245.

[42] Directive 2003/88/EC of the European Parliament and of the Council of 4 November 2003 concerning certain aspects of the organisation of working time [2003] OJ L299/9.

[43] For a critical account of this legal concept, see K Ewing, 'The State and Industrial Relations: "Collective Laissez-Faire" Revisited' (1998) 5 *Historical Studies in Industrial Relations* 1.

[44] Freedland (n 25) 166.

both private and public characteristics. It was negotiated by private parties in circumstances of freedom of (collective) contract, but it was also a source of regulatory norms akin to social legislation. Even at the level of basic definitions, then, the specific focus on employment law opened up new intellectual vistas. Freedland was also astute to connect the fate of the particular distinction to the global fate of freedom of contract. The value of *ius dispositivum* was rooted in an ideology of freedom of contract, individual (between the worker and her employer) and collective (between the trade union and the employer). During political periods when 'deregulation' was a dominant economic policy, the frontiers of *ius cogens* were liable to constrict. At a deeper level, since general private law operated as the default legal regime for personal employment contracts, the underlying tilt of the legal system was to favour *ius dispositivum* over *ius cogens*. Consequently, 'deregulatory' employment statutes were moving very much with the legal grain of the law of contract. The effect of this legal default was to treat imperative norms in the personal employment contract as standing in need of special justification, as exceptions to the legitimate contractual default of *ius dispositivum*.

Having formulated the general regulatory issue as one concerning 'inderogability', Freedland then examined some specific legal problems in the contemporary adjudication of the employment contract. As indicated by Rudden's three maxims, the critical matter in tracing the complex boundary between *ius cogens* and *ius dispositivum* was the scope of *ordre public*. There was no single naturalised boundary to this legal category. What was 'public' depended on political ideologies and legal culture. Let us focus on two of the specific legal issues identified by Freedland, significant already in 2002, but with a significance that would only magnify in importance in the decades that followed. The first issue was the legal characterisation of the employment contract, given its public function as an allocative basis for statutory employment rights. Fundamentally, there was a tension between 'contract as agreement' and the use of that 'agreement' to allocate imperative statutory rights. Contract was the domain of *ius dispositivum*; statute was the domain of *ius cogens*. The conundrum was whether statutory *ius cogens* could be constructed on a foundation that was contractual *ius dispositivum*. Freedland described this problem as 'derogation by classification'.[45] Most statutory employment rights were allocated to a general type of contract, such as a 'contract of employment'. Under 'derogation by classification', the parties might exclude imperative statutory rights by selecting a different contractual form through their private agreement. The extent to which the law should defer to the parties' agreement has been central to employment status litigation over the last 50 years.

The second issue was the extent to which fundamental rights, as specified in the European Convention on Human Rights, were waivable through contractual agreement. This brought the tension between private law and public law into sharp relief. Convention rights constituted 'public law' in the broad sense of that terminology, in that it represented a body of norms that were constitutional in nature. They also represented *ordre public*. Some of these norms, such as privacy or freedom of conscience, were of such importance that there was arguably a public interest in restricting their negation by powerful private actors. Matters could be even more complex where

[45] ibid 173.

implied terms – a private law technique – might provide the legal vehicle for protecting human rights in the employment relation.[46] Decent work, which includes systematic protection of fundamental human rights in the labour market, is a strong candidate for a public good. The derogation from fundamental human rights, by private contract, could undermine decent work as a public good even where the weaker party was content to 'sell' her right through an agreed waiver free of coercion or manipulation.

For Freedland, both of these were areas where *ius dispositivum* could be seriously disruptive of *ordre public*. The integrity of the public interest could only be assured if imperative norms were protected through strong legal intervention. Unsurprisingly, perhaps, this was aligned with Kahn-Freund's own normative position defended in 1967. Both scholars have been leading proponents of worker-protective labour law. The objective of labour law was to protect the weaker party – the worker – from the risk of contractual exploitation by the stronger party – the employer. This supported a strong normative preference for imperative norms. If 'freedom of contract' was the basic normative problem of the law of personal work contracts, the *ius dispositivum* technique was hardly likely to be an effective general legal solution.

III. Default Norms and Imperative Norms in Employment Contracts: Two Regulatory Challenges

This section will examine two of the most fundamental regulatory challenges in modern labour law, in light of these classic reflections on *ius cogens/ius dispositivum*. The first regulatory challenge is the classification of personal work contracts. Most protective statutory rights are defined in legislation as *ius cogens*. The allocation of the statutory right depends upon the underlying characterisation of the contract. Depending on the statutory right, only 'employees' or 'workers' qualify for the statutory protection. Can an imperative statutory norm be transformed into a default norm in virtue of a private agreement to opt to provide labour through a commercial contract for services? Recent jurisprudential developments in English law reveal a greater conceptual grasp of the *ius cogens/ius dispositivum* distinction than the case law critiqued by Freedland in 2002. However, the contractual foundation of imperative statutory rights reveals an instability that is unlikely to be eliminated so long as 'agreement' continues to provide the basis to mandatory employment laws.[47] The second regulatory challenge is the entrenchment of terms implied in law, specifically mutual trust and confidence, from waiver. Can contractual norms ever be *ius cogens* in English contract law, given the dominance of freedom of contract? I argue that there is a strong case for regarding mutual trust and confidence as *ius cogens*, and I suggest three ways in which that might be achieved using existing legal techniques. These techniques do not go nearly far enough. There is

[46] H Collins and V Mantouvalou, 'Human Rights and the Contract of Employment' in Freedland, Bogg and others (n 17) 188, 200–02, 205–08.

[47] For an early and perceptive criticism of the role of 'agreement' in employment status, see B Hepple, 'Restructuring Employment Rights' (1986) 15 *Industrial LJ* 69.

a compelling case for a more expansive doctrine of public policy, developed within the specific domain of personal employment contracts.

A. The Classification of Personal Work Contracts

Both Rudden and Freedland discuss the legal classification of types of contract within the context of the *ius cogens/ius dispositivum* distinction. Freedland's discussion is especially instructive because it examines the most fundamental issue of employment law, the characterisation of the personal employment contract. It does so in a startlingly original way, using the idea of 'derogation by classification'.[48] The employment contract is based on a private agreement negotiated against a background common law regime of freedom of contract. It also has public significance as an institutional platform for the allocation of statutory employment rights. Many such rights are enacted by the legislator as inderogable. How far is the legal characterisation exercise sensitive to the parties' freedom of contract in negotiating their agreement? On the one hand, too much latitude to the parties' agreement, and there are risks that it can be manipulated by the employer to exclude employment status when the weaker party is in substantive need of the employment protection. This statutory protection depends upon contractual employment status, hence an inderogable statutory right rests upon a common law foundation. This could undermine parliamentary intention by allowing the stronger party to exclude work relations envisaged by the legislature as needing the relevant statutory protection from the statute's personal scope. This transforms rights that have been legislated as *ius cogens* into rights that are in practical reality *ius dispositivum*. The development and expansion of the 'sham' doctrine is testament to the regulatory challenge of 'derogation by classification'.[49] On the other hand, too little latitude to the agreement, there is a risk that genuine exercises of contractual autonomy would be obstructed where there is no justification for doing so. The unjustified encroachment on contractual liberty should certainly be avoided. Liberty is an important personal value, and the systemic protection of (genuine) contractual freedom is an important public good. The unjustified restriction of contractual liberty will also lead to inefficiencies and rigidities in the functioning of the labour market. This boundary between mandatory public categorisation of the contract and private agreement reflects the interaction between Rudden's first two maxims, and the vital role of *ordre public* in delineating imperative and derogable norms.

In retrospect, Freedland's analysis of this issue in 2002 was undertaken just as the judicial approach to employment status was entering a crucial transition point in the late 2000s. This began with the expansion of the sham doctrine, which originated in the now famous Employment Appeal Tribunal (EAT) judgment in *Consistent Group Ltd v Kalwak and Others*.[50] Although it was overruled by the Court of Appeal,[51] Sir Patrick Elias' judgment in the EAT has had an enduring influence on the law of employment

[48] Freedland (n 25) 173–74.
[49] See, generally, Bogg (n 36).
[50] *Consistent Group Ltd v Kalwak* [2007] IRLR 560 ('*Kalwack* EAT').
[51] *Consistent Group Ltd v Kalwak* [2008] EWCA Civ 430, [2008] IRLR 505.

status. The Court of Appeal judgment is now all but forgotten. He penned what must now be one of the most famous and frequently cited paragraphs in the history of the EAT:

> The concern to which tribunals must be alive is that armies of lawyers will simply place substitution clauses, or clauses denying any obligation to accept or provide work in employment contracts, as a matter of form, even where such terms do not begin to reflect the real relationship.[52]

Eventually, this overruled EAT judgment was the gateway to the one of the most important landmark judgments in employment law by the United Kingdom Supreme Court, *Autoclenz Ltd v Belcher*.[53] It is worth reflecting on Freedland's discussion of 'derogation by classification' in its own historical context. It is especially interesting to reflect on how that discussion might be conducted today, in 2025.

Let us begin with Freedland's discussion. Many of the early employment status cases were concerned with unfair dismissal claims. As with most statutory employment rights, unfair dismissal was enacted as an inderogable right. As Freedland observed, this was codified in section 203(1) of the Employment Rights Act (ERA) 1996, which provided that any provision in an agreement is void 'in so far as it purports … to limit the operation of any provision of this Act'.[54] At this stage of legal development, the existence of section 203(1) was treated as providing definitive confirmation that the statutory right was *ius cogens*. Nearly 20 years after Freedland's chapter, the United Kingdom Supreme Court in *Uber BV and others v Aslam and others* would treat section 203(1) as *directly relevant* to the underlying categorisation of employment contracts.[55] This, however, is to get ahead of our story.

Freedland examined two early employment status cases. In *Massey v Crown Life Assurance Co*, an accountant had entered into a contract for services; following his dismissal, he claimed unfair dismissal which required him to assert that he worked as an employee under a contract of employment.[56] There was little sympathy for the claimant, whom Lord Denning clearly regarded as opportunistic. This was because the claimant was viewed as attempting to resile from a legal arrangement which had suited the claimant perfectly well in better times when he benefited from important tax advantages. It was explicitly couched as an issue of fairness by Lawton LJ, with the claimant speaking in two different voices so as to take the benefit of favourable tax advantages while avoiding the burden of loss of employment rights. Accordingly, he was to be treated as self-employed, reflecting the valid agreement that had been made in 1973. In terms of the *ius cogens*/*ius dispositivum* distinction, we could understand *Massey* as exemplifying Rudden's second maxim. It is a situation where the law should respect the free disavowal of a benefit, in this case the suite of protective rights allocated to a contract of employment. This was compelling if that disavowal occurred in circumstances where the claimant enjoyed the fiscal advantages of self-employment.

[52] *Kalwak* EAT (n 50) [57].
[53] *Autoclenz Ltd v Belcher* [2011] UKSC 41, [2011] 4 All ER 745 ('*Autoclenz*').
[54] Freedland (n 25) 173.
[55] *Uber BV v Aslam* [2021] UKSC 5, [2021] 4 All ER 209 ('*Uber*').
[56] *Massey v Crown Life Assurance Co* [1978] ICR 590.

In the subsequent case of *Young & Woods Ltd v West*, the Court of Appeal supported the employee characterisation.[57] Freedland noted the reservations of two of the judges, and the perceived unfairness of an employee wanting his cake (in the law of personal taxation) and eating it too (in employment law).[58] Sir David Cairns, by contrast, identified the public policy that favoured the effective enforcement of the employer's statutory duties, such as health and safety or fair treatment, and the risk of abuse where contracting out of those duties was effectively facilitated by a permissive regime of freedom of contract.[59]

Freedland was surely correct to suggest that 'public policy has a rather precarious grasp on the distinction between *ius cogens* and *ius dispositivum* in the field of employment law'.[60] The cases considered by Freedland appeared to indicate a very pronounced tilt in favour of *ius dispositivum* and freedom of contract for the parties. In fact, many of these early employment status cases were also in the orbit of a well-established public policy, in the guise of the illegality doctrine. In circumstance of illegality in the performance of a contract, public policy may prevent its enforcement by the parties.[61] Where the renegotiation of work contracts strayed into the fraudulent misrepresentation of the true legal relationship to the tax authorities, for example by presenting an employment arrangement as one of self-employment, public policy might bar its enforcement (including the statutory rights that depended on the contract). This public policy was alluded to by Lord Denning in *Massey*. In the later case of *Daymond v Enterprise South Devon*, Underhill J considered the illegality doctrine within the context of an individual opting to be paid through a company rather than through the payroll as an employee.[62] Since this arrangement deprived the Revenue of payments to which it was entitled, the contract was unenforceable because of the public policy of illegality.[63] In its effects, this public policy often operated harshly and punitively against workers, many of whom may had been lured into 'self-employment' because of economic necessity.[64] This public policy aspect to contract categorisation was finally restrained in *Enfield Technical Services Ltd v Payne* and *Grace v BF Components Ltd*, where the Court of Appeal restricted the operation of illegality to situations where the parties had been acting in bad faith by deliberately misrepresenting self-employment.[65] Since the boundary of genuine self-employment was often ambiguous, illegality was a draconian intervention unless there was clear culpability in setting up the contractual arrangements. In circumstances where there was a joint intention to misrepresent the true nature of the legal arrangement to a third party for gain, the treatment of the contract as a 'sham' would usually be a Pyrrhic

[57] *Young & Woods Ltd v West* [1980] IRLR 201.

[58] Freedland (n 25) 174.

[59] *Young & Woods Ltd v West* (n 57) 209.

[60] Freedland (n 25) 174.

[61] This general topic is covered in S Green and A Bogg (eds), *Illegality After Patel v Mirza* (Oxford, Hart Publishing, 2018).

[62] *Daymond v Enterprise South Devon* (2007) UKEAT/0005/07.

[63] See also *Salvesen v Simons* [1994] ICR 409.

[64] A Bogg, 'Illegality in Labour Law after Patel v Mirza: Retrenchment and Restraint' in Green and Bogg (n 61) 257, 258.

[65] *Enfield Technical Services Ltd v Payne; Grace v BF Components Ltd* [2008] EWCA Civ 393, [2008] ICR 1423.

victory for the claimant, because any legal claims would presumably be barred by the illegality doctrine anyway.[66]

The EAT judgment in *Kalwak* marked a significant turning point in the categorisation of employment contracts. The true significance of the *Kalwak* judgment was realised more fully in the landmark Supreme Court judgment in *Autoclenz Ltd v Belcher* in 2011.[67] In *Autoclenz*, the Supreme Court considered the correct approach to categorising employees and 'limb (b) workers' for national minimum wage and working time claims under the relevant legislation. The claimants had been presented with comprehensive written contracts which contained specific terms that negated employment status. Those written contracts were signed by the workers. These written terms included a substitution clause (reserving a wide contractual power for the putative worker to designate a substitute to provide work to the employer) and a 'no mutuality' clause (no reciprocal duties to provide ongoing work or to accept work). There was no suggestion that these contracts involved a *Snook* sham. The employer had presented the written contracts on a take-it-or-leave-it basis, seemingly with the object of avoiding statutory protections; the workers signed the contracts and appeared to be oblivious to the legal ramifications of those written terms.

Lord Clarke delivered the unanimous judgment of the Supreme Court. It emphasised the important differences between commercial contracts and employment contracts, which sometimes justified the development of different legal rules. These differences were based upon the structural inequality of bargaining power between employers and workers. This inequality meant that there was a greater risk that written employment contracts might not reflect the parties' true legal obligations. This was because the written documentation was usually drafted by the employer's lawyers with little scope for genuine bilateral negotiation of terms. There were also significant economic incentives for employers to deflect a finding of employment status, because they could then get the benefits of subordinated labour without the costs of statutory employment protections. Some legal rules might be regarded as the 'general part' of contract law applying to all contracts, such as consideration or intention to create legal relations. This divergence in legal rules was reflected in the legal treatment of signatures for example. In the law applicable to written commercial contracts, the signatures of the contracting parties would generally be conclusive evidence of the parties' agreement.[68] In employment law, by contrast, the task of categorisation needed to be sensitive to discrepancies between the written agreement and the 'true agreement'. As Lord Clarke put it:

> So the relative bargaining power of the parties must be taken into account in deciding whether the terms of any written agreement in truth represent what was agreed and the true agreement will often have to be gleaned from all the circumstances of the case, of which the written agreement is only a part. This may be described as a purposive approach to the problem.[69]

[66] On this narrow sham doctrine as a joint intention to deceive third parties as to the true legal nature of the arrangement, see *Snook v London and West Riding Investments Ltd* [1967] 2 QB 786.
[67] *Autoclenz* (n 53).
[68] On the 'signature rule', see *L'Estrange v Graucob Ltd* [1934] 2 KB 394.
[69] *Autoclenz* (n 53) [35].

Where there was no realistic expectation that a written term would be treated as valid by the parties, such as a worker exercising a substitution clause, it was open to tribunals to disregard that written clause. They might conclude that the 'true agreement' was instead based upon an obligation of personal performance.

Autoclenz has been treated as a 'landmark' case of historic significance.[70] It certainly shifted the relevant contractual paradigm by signalling a relatively autonomous body of common law principles constituting a law of the personal employment contract. In practical terms, it also liberalised the strict law on shams, and this liberalisation gave workers much greater scope to challenge sham terms in written documentation. Reflecting back on Freedland's innovative use of the *ius cogens*/*ius dispositivum* framework for contract categorisation, did *Autoclenz* give the courts a less precarious grasp of this distinction compared with the early judgments analysed by Freedland? The answer to this is less clear. While *Autoclenz* is rightly regarded as a progressive landmark, the statutory context of *ius cogens*, while not entirely absent, is not a prominent aspect in Lord Clarke's reasoning.

There are certainly some important allusions to statute in the judgment. For example, in explaining counsel's appropriate reliance on authorities from landlord and tenant and housing law, Lord Clarke said, 'Those cases were examples of the courts concluding that relevant contractual provisions were not effective to avoid a particular statutory result.'[71] These cases included *Bankway Properties Ltd v Pensfold-Dunsford*.[72] A rent increase clause was inserted into a tenancy agreement in order to trigger a compulsory statutory ground for possession: it was 'real' in the sense that the landlord intended to rely on it. In holding that the clause was an impermissible attempt to contract out of the protective legislation, Arden LJ based her analysis primarily on statutory construction, and the court's role to give effect to the intention of Parliament in applying the statutory scheme.[73] She contrasted her own approach with that of Pill LJ who preferred 'an analysis of the terms of the contract'.[74] Pill LJ held the rent clause was not part of the true agreement because it was repugnant to the overarching commercial purpose, which was to enter into a statutorily protected assured tenancy. Arden LJ rightly emphasised the intention of Parliament, *not* the intention of the contracting parties, in identifying the legal nub of the issue. It is significant that Lord Clarke in *Autoclenz* referred approvingly to Arden LJ's judgment in *Bankway* as exemplifying an approach that relevant contractual provisions were not effective to avoid mandatory statutory protections. He did not refer to Pill LJ's contractual approach to the problem of statutory avoidance. In addition, Lord Clarke described his own approach as 'purposive'.[75] It was not immediately clear as to which 'purpose' Lord Clarke was referring to in his 'purposive' approach. It could have been referring to the commercial purpose of the contract or the protective statutory purpose of the right being claimed. In the immediate aftermath of *Autoclenz*, some

[70] See J Adams-Prassl, '*Autoclenz v Belcher* (2011): Divining "The True Agreement Between the Parties"' in J Adams-Prassl, A Bogg, and ACL Davies (eds), *Landmark Cases in Labour Law* (Oxford, Hart Publishing, 2022) ch 13.
[71] *Autoclenz* (n 53) [24].
[72] *Bankway Properties Ltd v Pensfold-Dunsford* [2001] EWCA Civ 528, [2001] WLR 1369.
[73] ibid [49].
[74] ibid [66].
[75] *Autoclenz* (n 53) [35].

commentators considered the potential range of 'purpose', and defended a preference for the statutory reading of 'purposive'.[76] Yet all of this remained to be clarified by later cases. The appearance of statute, as a marker for *ius cogens*, was still somewhat Delphic in 2011.

By contrast, the 'contract' dimension was a far more dominant feature of the judgment. Ultimately, it was still the *agreement* that was determinative in the categorisation exercise. Following *Autoclenz*, the main difference was that courts could now consider a broader range of evidence to determine the content of the 'true' contractual agreement as a basis for its categorisation. The tribunal was not restricted to the signed written documentation, as with a commercial contract. Yet the contractual agreement was still at the centre of things, the 'cornerstone', if you like. In terms of its contribution to legal taxonomy, the enduring importance of *Autoclenz* was internal to the common law of contract. The judgment recognised an important division between within the common law as it applied to commercial contracts and employment contracts. It was now possible to discern a relatively autonomous body of rules and principles that constituted a common law of the personal employment contract.[77] From this internal common law perspective, however, freedom of contract was still the keystone of the English law of contract(s). Consequently, *Autoclenz* and the notion of 'true agreement' had the likely effect of entrenching a strong tilt in favour of *ius dispositivum*. This was not merely a quibble about taxonomical elegance. It was also fraught with the potential for regressive effects on imperative statutory norms. In some cases, like *Autoclenz* and *Bankway*, the balance between contractual and statutory emphases was unlikely to lead to a practical difference in outcome. But what of a situation where there was no obvious discrepancy between the written contracts and the working practices? *Autoclenz* was always an easy case because there was never a realistic expectation that the substitution clauses would be operative and valid. What of the situation where the employer included a written term inconsistent with employment status, regarded by it as entirely genuine, but included with the overriding object of avoiding the mandatory statutory regime? The contractual validity of the term may even be sought by the employer as a way of putting the 'derogation by classification' beyond doubt. The Supreme Court had to confront this very dilemma a decade later in another landmark case, *Uber BV and others v Aslam and others*.[78] It was only after *Uber* that the Supreme Court displayed a much firmer grasp on the *ius cogens*/*ius dispositivum* distinction.

The facts in *Uber* revealed the elusiveness and instability of the 'purposive' approach of *Autoclenz*. This case was concerned with whether Uber drivers were 'workers' for the purpose of the National Minimum Wage Act 1998 (NMWA) and the Working Time Regulations 1998 (WTR). The legislative definition of 'worker' embraces both individuals who are employees at common law and a wider statutory category, usually called 'limb (b) workers'. This statutory category is sometimes described as an 'intermediate' category. This is because it is wider than 'employee' in including some self-employed

[76] See Bogg (n 36) 341–44. In a note that preceded the Supreme Court judgment (and which was referred to by Lord Clarke at [28]), I argued in favour of a 'purposive' approach linked to the statutory context: A Bogg, 'Sham Self-Employment in the Court of Appeal' (2010) 126 *LQR* 166.

[77] Bogg (n 36) 344–45.

[78] *Uber* (n 55).

workers within its scope. This is typically the case in situations where the worker undertakes to provide any personal work for the other party to the contract other than as a business undertaking to a customer. It is possible to be a 'limb (b) worker' without being an 'employee'. There may be fiscal and other advantages to being 'self-employed' workers, but not employees, in benefiting from a favourable tax regime while still enjoying some (but not all) statutory protections. For example, statutory unfair dismissal protection is still restricted to employees. The intermediate 'limb (b) worker' sometimes represents a compromise zone where workers opt for a trade-off in terms of economic advantages (including contractual flexibility) versus legal entitlements.

Crucially, this intermediate category still depends upon there being a 'contract' based upon an agreement between the parties. The drivers signed up to extensive written terms with Uber BV, a Dutch company which owns the app, stating that the acceptance of a trip by drivers created a contract between the driver and the passenger, to which no Uber entity was a party. Separate written terms between the passenger, Uber BV and Uber London Ltd (ULL) asserted that ULL accepted bookings as disclosed agent for drivers. It was these two sets of written terms, purporting to constitute ULL and Uber BV as no more than intermediaries facilitating contracts between passengers and drivers, which counsel for Uber argued the courts below had been wrong to disregard. Interestingly, there appeared to be no direct written terms between ULL and the drivers. The Employment Tribunal had concluded that the true agreement was that drivers were providing services under a contract to ULL, and so they were working for Uber, rather than Uber providing its services to the drivers as a commercial agent.

In the Court of Appeal, Underhill LJ delivered a powerfully reasoned dissent where he argued that *Autoclenz* was not triggered on the facts of the case.[79] There was no overt discrepancy between the written contracts and the actual working practices. While this may have constituted a disadvantageous bargain for the drivers, the task of the tribunal was to construe the agreement as it was, not to rewrite the agreement to assist the weaker party. In the Supreme Court, Lord Leggatt upheld the tribunal's original decision on worker status. In so doing, he clarified the scope of the *Autoclenz* principle: 'Critical to understanding the *Autoclenz* case, as I see it, is that the rights asserted by the claimants were not contractual rights but were created by legislation … In short, the primary question was one of statutory interpretation, not contractual interpretation.'[80] This entailed a purposive approach, in which the question is whether the worker protective legislation, construed *purposively*, was intended to apply to the relevant relationship, viewed *realistically*.[81] The relevant purpose was the worker-protective purpose of the statutory rights being claimed. Where the employment relationship displayed features of exploitation-vulnerability, such as economic dependence or subordination/control, this favoured applying the statutory definition of worker in an inclusive way.[82]

[79] *Uber BV v Aslam* [2018] EWCA Civ 2748, [2019] 3 All ER 489.

[80] *Uber* (n 55) [69].

[81] For an argument defending a purposive and realistic approach, based on statutory construction, see A Bogg and M Ford, 'Between Statute and Contract: Who is a Worker?' (2019) 135 *LQR* 347.

[82] It does *not* follow from this that the application of employment status definitions should be strained to exclude 'high status' professional workers such as lawyers or doctors, who would otherwise satisfy the relevant criteria. Factors indicating exploitation-vulnerability, such as economic dependence or direct/indirect

It followed from this that elevating the importance of the contractual documentation in the employment status enquiry risked subverting the protective statutory purpose:

> The efficacy of such protection would be seriously undermined if the putative employer could by the way in which the relationship is characterized in the written documents determine, even prima facie, whether or not the other party is to be classified as a worker.[83]

Lord Leggatt also linked this to the statutory restrictions on 'contracting out' of statutory employment rights which is a common feature of employment statutes conferring inderogable rights.

The relevant provision under the Employment Rights Act 1996, section 203(1), provides that:

> Any provision in an agreement (whether a contract of employment or not) is void in so far as it purports –
>
> (a) to exclude or limit the operation of any provision of this Act, or
>
> (b) to preclude a person from bringing any proceedings under this Act before an employment tribunal.

According to Lord Leggatt, this provision had a broad scope in rendering void provisions setting out 'agreed' legal classifications or even agreed 'facts' about their relationship which prevented workers claiming their statutory rights.[84] This approach acknowledged the imaginative range of ways in which drafting could be used as a subtle form of 'contracting out', particularly where 'armies of lawyers' were alive to the futility of more obvious forms of contractual evasion. Although there was no specific reference to section 203(1) in *Autoclenz*, Lord Leggatt indicated that it provided further legal support for the reasoning and outcome in that case.[85]

The explicit connection to section 203(1) is the decisive move in *Uber*'s statutory interpretation approach. Where inderogable statutory rights depend upon a contractual foundation, section 203(1) now tilts the law back in favour of statutory *ius cogens* rather than contractual *ius dispositvum*. Is *Uber* simply a rationalisation of *Autoclenz*, or is it an extension of it? Lord Leggatt's judgment certainly reads as a clarification of *Autoclenz* and its animating principles, which removed the genuine ambiguity reflected in the divergence in the Court of Appeal in *Uber*. In certain respects, however, *Uber* does seem like a genuine extension. The overriding emphasis in *Autoclenz* was on identifying the 'true agreement'. This is still very much located in the contractual land of *ius dispositivum*. Yet in *Uber*, the apparent absence of any direct contract between ULL and the drivers was passed over lightly by Lord Leggatt in treating ULL as the employer of the drivers. In *Autoclenz*, Lord Clarke suggested it was uncontroversial that

> If a contractual right, as for example a right to substitute, exists, it does not matter that it is not used. It does not follow from the fact that a term is not enforced that such a term is not part of the agreement.[86]

control, should only operate in borderline cases and in an inclusive way. In most cases, the relevant legal criteria can simply be applied in accordance with their ordinary meaning.

[83] *Uber* (n 55) [76].

[84] ibid [80].

[85] ibid [86] with reference to *Autoclenz* (n 53).

[86] *Autoclenz* (n 53) [19].

The emphasis on the 'realistic' application of statutory norms in *Uber* may now mean that evidence of non-exercise could be more relevant to negating the written term: it is not evidentially inert. Finally, the *Uber* approach may be engaged even where a term does form part of the 'true agreement' where it is deliberately inserted with the 'object' of avoiding statutory protections. This scenario would demonstrate clear blue water between *Autoclenz* and *Uber*, although the point has not yet arisen for consideration.

After *Uber*, we can certainly say that the courts have a less precarious grip on the *ius cogens/ius dispositivum* distinction than when Freedland considered it in 2002. To an ineradicable extent, however, there will always be some instability as a result of the importance of *agreement* to contractual employment status. Although this is somewhat speculative, I think this instability may be exacerbated by the presence of intermediate categories which imply a mode of selective contractual choice for workers themselves. Current proposals to adopt a 'single employment status' may reduce that instability. In the recent case of *Ter-Berg v Simply Smile Manor House Ltd*, for example, the EAT considered the status of *Autoclenz* after *Uber*.[87] This decision may be viewed as a reassertion of the primacy of contract (even if not the primacy of the *written* contract). The case considered the correct treatment of written documentation by the tribunal in determining employment status. After *Uber*, should the written terms in an agreement now be treated as having attenuated significance? Should they be disregarded, even? Or did they remain central to the characterisation exercise? The EAT offered a conservative reading of *Uber*. According to Auerbach J, *Uber* ought to be understood and applied as a clarification of *Autoclenz* rather than a displacement of it. Contract was still a central element of employment status, and the written terms could not simply be disregarded. Where there was doubt that the written agreement reflected the true agreement, it was legitimate for the tribunal to consider the wider context to the relationship (including the reality of working practices). But this approach was still decidedly contractual in focusing on the true agreement.

Of course, the statutory context meant that some relevant rules of commercial contract law, such as the signature rule or the parol evidence rule, needed to be modified for employment contracts. This much was clear from *Autoclenz* itself. It did not follow from that contract was irrelevant to the employment status enquiry, nor that the written terms could simply be overlooked in a roving examination of the whole context. It may even be legitimate in appropriate cases for a tribunal to have regard to the designated label in a written agreement.[88] Significantly, Auerbach J stated that the *Autoclenz/Uber* approach did

> not mean that it is no longer possible for parties genuinely and in an informed way to agree that they want to form a working relationship which is neither one of employee nor of worker, once consequence of which will be that various statutory employment protection rights will not apply to the individual who will be doing the work. Nor does it mean that a written agreement might not in a given case truly reflect everything that the parties have in fact agreed.[89]

[87] *Ter-Berg v Simply Smile Manor House Ltd* [2023] EAT 2.
[88] ibid [66].
[89] ibid [45].

The continuing presence of contract (and party agreement) probably means that the influence of *ius dispositivum* is liable to instability. It will likely continue to fluctuate in importance, sensitive to the facts in particular cases, the prevailing judicial culture, its view of freedom of contract and the proper approach to interpretation of statutes, and so forth. In the end, the full entrenchment of *ius cogens* probably necessitates detaching statutory rights from underlying contractual categories entirely.

B. The Implied Term of Mutual Trust and Confidence

One of the central issues in the law of the employment contract is whether the implied term of mutual trust and confidence is excludable by the parties through express agreement. As a mandatory term implied in law, and hence a necessary legal incident of all employment contracts, should it be regarded as *ius cogens* or *ius dispositivum*? The resolution of this conundrum depends upon the scope of Rudden's first maxim, that public law (or *ordre public*) cannot be altered by the agreement of private citizens. Given the tenacity of freedom of contract within the English law of contract, it is difficult to identify common law techniques to fortify implied terms against exclusion. In constitutional terms, this 'public law' dimension of *ius cogens* is still strongly determined by proximity to an inderogable statutory employment right. It is still an orthodox and fundamental proposition of English law that implied terms (even if not the background structural rules facilitating contractual agreements) must give way to express terms. As we have seen, *Autoclenz* indicated that some common law rules applying to general commercial contracts could be modified or even dispensed with for employment contracts. This is because employment contracts are marked by a structural inequality between employers and workers. In *Autoclenz*, for example, the 'signature rule' and the 'parol evidence rule' were displaced. As yet, this *Autoclenz* gateway into a distinct law of personal employment contracts has not yet been crossed within the context of derogation of implied terms. In the leading authority on mutual trust and confidence, the House of Lords decision in *Malik v BCCI*, Lord Steyn observed that '[s]uch implied terms operate as default rules. The parties are free to exclude or modify them'.[90] This still represents the orthodox position on derogation and the implied term in English law.

As we shall see, many specific applications of the implied term of mutual trust and confidence instantiate public law values to restrain abuses of power.[91] In basic normative terms, Lord Leggatt's articulation of the regulatory predicament in *Uber* is identical to the regulatory predicament here. The 'efficacy of such protection would be seriously undermined if the putative employer could by the way in which the relationship is characterized in the written documents determine' whether that protection applied at all.[92]

[90] *Malik and Mahmud v Bank of Credit and Commerce International (BCCI) SA* [1998] AC 20, 45 ('*Malik*').

[91] On the public law roots of mutual trust and confidence, see D Brodie, 'Beyond Exchange: The New Contract of Employment' (1998) 27 *Industrial LJ* 79. For a public law taxonomy for the case law on mutual trust and confidence, see A Bogg, '*Bournemouth University HEC v Buckland*: Re-establishing Orthodoxy at the Expense of Coherence?' (2010) 39 *Industrial LJ* 408. This taxonomy rationalises the case law into (i) avoiding dignitary injuries, (ii) ensuring rationality in exercise of contractual powers and (iii) promoting the rule of law (including the doctrine of legitimate expectations).

[92] *Uber* (n 55) [76]. Cf text to n 83 above.

By allowing the stronger party to exclude those common law norms targeted specifically at preventing abuse of power in an unequal relationship, public institutions are effectively creating the conditions for exploitation.[93] Contracting out subverts the very justification for the common law protective norm.

The implied term of mutual trust and confidence is now widely recognised as an integral element of the common law of employment contracts. It has been described by one of our leading appellate employment law judges of recent times as 'certainly amongst the most important developments in the law of the employment contract in the last 50 years'.[94] The context for its initial emergence was the statutory law on constructive dismissal in the unfair dismissal legislation.[95] As with the developing law on employment status, then, the complex interactions between statute and common law have been central to the evolution of the implied term. The statutory concept of constructive dismissal was defined as termination of the contract by the employee 'in circumstances in which he is entitled to terminate it by reason of the employer's conduct'.[96] This needed a coherent and stable judicial elaboration of the employee's 'entitlement to terminate'. Eventually, the courts adopted a contractual test of repudiatory breach for the entitlement.[97] This triggered 'a process of formulation of implied terms, which were in effect back-formations, in the sense that they were terms the breach of which would amount to expulsive or repudiatory conduct sufficient to constitute constructive dismissal by the employer'.[98] The elaboration of these behavioural standards, which often involved dignitary injuries against the employee, came to be rationalised at common law through the implied term. In practical terms, it involved bad contract-repudiating behaviour by employers and managers, such that the prospect of continued employment was intolerable for the employee. The encounter with statute was critical to the genesis and development of the term, especially in these early cases addressing behavioural standards.

The leading appellate case on the implied term is still the House of Lords decision in *Malik v BCCI*.[99] This was a pure common law claim rather than arising as a subsidiary aspect of a statutory claim. This decision confirmed the existence of the implied term, although it was already deeply embedded in the law of constructive dismissal. In *Malik*, the House of Lords concluded that the implied term could be engaged where the employer (in this case a collapsed bank) was operating a corrupt and dishonest business. The employees sought stigma damages, alleging that the taint of association with the bank's disreputable behaviour had damaged their future employability. Lord Nicholls referred approvingly to the development of the implied term as a fact of modern employment law. It reflected the fact that '[e]mployment, and job prospects, are matters

[93] On the role of public institutions in creating or maintaining 'structural injustice', see V Mantouvalou, *Structural Injustice and Workers' Rights* (Oxford, OUP, 2023).

[94] P Elias, 'Changes and Challenges to the Contract of Employment' (2018) 38 *OJLS* 869, 887.

[95] See A Bogg and M Freedland, 'The Wrongful Termination of the Contract of Employment' in Freedland, Bogg and others (n 17) 537, 545–47.

[96] Originally the Trade Union and Labour Relations Act 1974, sch 1, para 5(2)(c), now Employment Rights Act 1996, s 95(1)(c).

[97] *Western Excavating (ECC) Ltd v Sharp* [1978] QB 761 (CA).

[98] M Freedland, *The Personal Employment Contract* (Oxford, OUP, 2003) 155.

[99] *Malik* (n 90).

of vital concern to most people … An employment contract creates a close personal relationship, where there is often a disparity of power between the parties. Frequently the employee is vulnerable'.[100] This contributed to the shift in judicial perspective on the unequal nature of the employment contract, and the role of mutual trust and confidence in controlling abuse of power. Indeed, *Malik* may be regarded as facilitating the later recognition of a distinctive common law approach to employment contracts in *Autoclenz*.

If anything, the public law dimension of implied terms in employment contracts has intensified since *Malik*. In *Braganza v BP Shipping Ltd and Others*, the Supreme Court drew explicitly on doctrinal analogies with public law doctrines in scrutinising the exercise of a contractual discretionary power in the context of employment.[101] *Braganza* was concerned with the judicial review of a factual determination (under a relevant clause in the contract) by the employer that the employee, when he disappeared while employed on an oil tanker, had in fact committed suicide. The effect of this determination was to deprive his widow of death benefits under the contract of employment. The question for the Court was whether the decision-maker was entitled to form its opinion, that the employee committed suicide, on the basis of the evidence before it. A majority of the Supreme Court concluded that it was not so entitled because it had failed to take into account a relevant consideration – the inherent improbability of suicide – which could only be displaced by cogent evidence. There was no such cogent evidence on the facts in this case.

In the *Braganza* case, mutual trust and confidence was not centrally in issue, the question being whether the employer had acted 'reasonably' in a contractual sense in withholding death in service benefits from the widow. The majority judgments considered a broad range of authorities on judicial review of contractual discretions, including commercial contracts. Nevertheless, both Lady Hale and Lord Hodge made specific reference to mutual trust and confidence in their judgments. This should not surprise us, given its established significance as an overarching duty and constraint on abuse of discretionary powers in employment contracts. For Lady Hale, the specific contractual context in *Braganza* was important:

> [T]he party who is charged with making decisions which affect the rights of both parties to the contract has a clear conflict of interest. That conflict is heightened where there is a significant imbalance of power between the contracting parties as there often will be in an employment contract. The courts have therefore sought to ensure that such contractual powers are not abused. They have done so by implying a term as to the manner in which such powers may be exercised, a term which may vary according to the terms of the contract and the context in which the decision-making power is given.[102]

Lady Hale concluded that both limbs of the *Wednesbury* test from English administrative law applied.[103] This first limb, which is process-based, meant that the decision-maker needed to take into account relevant considerations and disregard

[100] ibid 37.
[101] *Braganza v BP Shipping Ltd* [2015] UKSC 17, [2015] WLR 1661 ('*Braganza*').
[102] ibid [18].
[103] *Associated Provincial Picture Houses Ltd v Wednesbury Corp* [1948] 1 KB 223.

irrelevant considerations in the decision-making process. The second limb, which is outcome-based, meant that the decision could be impugned where it was so outrageous that no reasonable decision-maker could have reached it. In *Braganza*, it was the process-based limb, and the failure to take into account a relevant consideration, that compromised the exercise of discretion. While this was presented as a general proposition applying in a broad range of contracts, its specific formulation in employment contracts was through mutual trust and confidence:

> Any decision-making function entrusted to the employer has to be exercised in accordance with the implied obligation of trust and confidence. This must be borne in mind in considering how the contractual decision-maker should approach the question of whether a person has committed suicide.[104]

Lord Hodge approached the matter in a similar way to Lady Hale. His judgment had particularly strong echoes of *Autoclenz* in emphasising that discretions in employment contracts might warrant more intensive scrutiny than ordinary commercial contracts because those contracts were personal and relational.[105] He also framed it as a matter of trust and confidence in the employment sphere, with the content of this implied term shaped by public law norms.[106]

Where a legal norm exists to protect a weaker party from abuse by a stronger party, as in *Braganza* itself, *ius dispositivum* effectively permits the stronger party to contract out of its public law restraints. This creates the conditions for exploitation and abuse of power. This may be part of the reason underlying Rudden's first maxim, that public law cannot be altered by the agreement of private citizens. It may also explain the hostility of some leading academic commentators to treating mutual trust and confidence as a derogable norm. We will first consider this united front against *ius dispositivum* in the work of Professors Douglas Brodie and Hugh Collins. Then, the chapter closes by reflecting on the utility of existing legal techniques for underpinning mutual trust and confidence as an inderogable norm.

Brodie's most recent consideration of the scope for contracting out of mutual trust and confidence are set out in his consideration of *Malik* as a landmark case.[107] Brodie notes the relative absence of case law directly on the express exclusion of mutual trust and confidence, which no doubt reflects the fact that very few employers are likely to insert an express exclusion of mutual trust and confidence into a written contract. The relevant case law has instead addressed the thorny issue of overlap between express terms and implied terms regulating similar subject-matter, such as procedural rights in disciplinary investigations.[108] The orthodox contractual position is that in a situation of overlap, the express term should have primacy over the implied term. But what of the hypothetical situation where an employment contract purported to reserve an absolute

[104] *Braganza* (n 101) [32].
[105] ibid [54]–[55].
[106] ibid [53]–[54].
[107] D Brodie, '*Malik v BCCI*: The Impact of Good Faith' in Adams-Prassl, Bogg and Davies (n 70) 245, 261–64.
[108] See eg *Burn v Alder Hey* [2021] EWHC 1674 (QB), where the court held that the implied term could not be used to extend procedural entitlements that had been specified with precision in an express term. Discussed by Brodie (n 107) 262.

entitlement to an employer to suspend an employee where there were allegations of sexual abuse, immunising that power from review even when exercised capriciously?[109] Brodie regards such an exclusion as intolerable. He suggests that the exclusion of fundamental procedural protections at the core of mutual trust and confidence should be void on the grounds of common law public policy. This development of public policy would depend upon the continuing development of the *Autoclenz* bifurcation between commercial contracts and employment contracts. This is because the courts are more favourably disposed to respecting freedom of contract where commercial parties negotiate an absolute entitlement to determine certain matters under their contract.[110] It is also interesting to note that the proposed restrictions on contractual exclusion are based on public policy. This has strong affinities with Rudden's first maxim on the priority of 'public law' over private agreement, as a basis for restricting *ius dispositivum*. The notion of an inderogable core of fundamental procedural guarantees within mutual trust and confidence is an attractive development of the *Autoclenz* principle. It would nevertheless be a bold step for a court to take given the existing state of jurisprudence, and it would be something more than an incremental step in common law development.

Hugh Collins has offered a nuanced exploration of the desirability of restrictions on contracting out of implied terms, while also acknowledging the doctrinal challenges given freedom of contract and the orthodox primacy of express terms.[111] Collins notes that some implied terms might go to the fundamental character of the employment contract, so that exclusion may lead to a different classification.[112] This raises the possibility of using the *Autoclenz* sham doctrine to challenge the exclusion in circumstances where it was designed to exclude employment status.[113] More broadly, Collins proposed an interesting middle way between *ius cogens* and *ius dispositivum*. For Collins, it ought to be possible to derogate from or modify specific particularised instances of mutual trust and confidence, while prohibiting complete derogation from the general abstract duty. This distinction between the general overarching duty and specific sub-duties is attractive. Interestingly, Lord Steyn in *Malik* described the implied term of mutual trust and confidence as developing out of the general duty of cooperation in contract law.[114] It is difficult to conceive of a functioning institution of contract law that is predicated upon *non*-cooperation, at least within the general category of relational contract. This duty of cooperation is therefore fundamental to the basic institution of relational contract. We might even regard it as part of the basic structure of contract law itself, rather than a feature of specific contracts. The restriction of wholesale exclusion of an element of the structure that makes contracting possible in the first place is exactly the kind of thing that should be encompassed by *ordre public* and imperative norms. Otherwise, agreement could destroy the very conditions that make it possible to contract in the first place.

[109] Brodie developed this hypothetical based around the facts in *Gogay v Hertfordshire CC* [2000] IRLR 703 (CA).

[110] Brodie (n 107) 262.

[111] Collins (n 17) 471, 483–90.

[112] ibid 484.

[113] ibid.

[114] *Malik* (n 90) 45.

In focusing on public policy or *ordre public*, these academic approaches are certainly engaged in the right sort of enquiry. I will suggest three arguments developing this idea that public policy may entrench the implied term as an imperative norm *ius cogens* and thereby limit contracting out. These arguments link to Rudden's first maxim. The first scenario draws upon common law public policy, and the illegality doctrine. The other two scenarios suggest ways in which the statutory restriction on contracting out in section 203(1) ERA 1996 might entrench mutual trust and confidence. This is because of the connections between the implied term and the enforcement of statutory employment rights, building on the critical role of section 203(1) in *Uber*.

Starting with common law public policy, *Malik* was concerned with the employer's dishonest and corrupt conduct of its business. On the assumed facts, the House of Lords concluded that this was a breach of mutual trust and confidence. Dishonesty and corruption represent very serious forms of wrongdoing in the marketplace. They are particularly insidious because their perpetration is usually concealed and clandestine. Corruption by its nature has a corrosive effect on the structures and practices of contractual exchange. It rots them from the inside. The stability of a social practice like contracting depends upon reliable expectations of trust and honest dealing. This is imperative in large organisations and professions, such as banking and legal services, that play an integral role in the operation of the market. These wrongs are often treated as public wrongs. It is perhaps for this reason that they have been treated as within the scope of the illegality doctrine. The illegality doctrine is a well-established public policy category. It prevents the enforcement of private law rights (including contractual rights) in circumstances where the claim is tainted by illegality.[115] The relevant turpitude in illegality extends beyond crimes to include 'quasi-criminal' acts that have a public character. This is set out in Lord Sumption's judgment in *Les Laboratoires Servier v Apotex Inc*:

> The ex turpi causa principle is concerned with claims founded on acts which are contrary to the public law of the state and engage the public interest. The paradigm case is … a criminal act. In addition, it is concerned with a limited category of acts which, while not necessarily criminal, can conveniently be described as 'quasi-criminal' because they engage the public interest in the same way … this additional category of non-criminal acts giving rise to the defence includes cases of dishonesty or corruption.[116]

This has obvious relevance to any attempts by an employer to limit or exclude mutual trust and confidence where this relates to 'quasi-criminal' behaviour, such as that in *Malik* itself. Where a *Malik*-type employer sought to rely upon a contractual exclusion of mutual trust and confidence, the exclusion would be contrary to the public interest. The underlying rationale of the public policy of illegality is the 'integrity of the legal system' and the importance of the law avoiding 'disharmony' and 'inconsistency'.[117] 'Quasi-criminal' acts, especially in the sphere of contract law, engage these normative concerns directly. Corruption and dishonesty are an attack on the foundations of the legal institution of contracting. Where the dishonest/corrupt wrongdoer attempts to

[115] *Patel v Mirza* [2016] UKSC 42, [2017] AC 467. See already the text to and following n 61 above.
[116] *Les Laboratoires Servier v Apotex Inc* [2014] UKSC 55, [2015] AC 430 at [25].
[117] *Patel v Mirza* (n 115) [100].

use the legal facility of contract to insulate itself from liability by excluding trust and confidence, permitting this would be a paradigm instance where the law is facilitating a self-defeating stipulation. It is a particularly strong manifestation of the maxim that public law cannot be altered by the agreement of private citizens. In this context, it is rooted in the common law of public policy rather than statute.

By contrast, the final two examples are focused on examining the scope (and limits) of section 203(1) ERA 1996. As we have seen, this statutory provision was central to Lord Leggatt's reasoning in *Uber*. According to Lord Leggatt, the statutory prohibition of any provision that purports 'to exclude or limit the operation of any provision of this Act' extends to the situation where the term has

> as its object excluding or limiting the operation of the legislation. It is just as inimical to the aims of the legislation to allow its protection to be limited or excluded indirectly by the terms of a contract as it is to allow that to be done in direct terms.[118]

This extension to 'indirect' exclusions was designed to limit the circumvention of imperative statutory rights by the manipulation of the underlying contractual form.

The first scenario involves an attempt by the employer at the complete exclusion of mutual trust and confidence. The implied term may fairly be described as fundamental to the identity of the employment contract. In this respect, it is akin to the obligation of personal performance, the successful exclusion of which may lead to the contract being treated as one of independent self-employment. As Lord Leggatt emphasised, section 203(1) must guard against 'indirect' exclusion of statutory employment rights. Otherwise, the statutory prohibition would risk becoming a dead letter because most well-advised employers would be savvy enough to avoid obvious exclusions or limitations couched in 'direct' terms. There is little evidence in practice of the total contractual exclusion of the implied term. If a court did encounter this extreme scenario, the immediate question would be: why, on an objective consideration of the facts, would an employer seek to exclude an implied term that goes to the fundamental identity of the contract? The inference that the 'object' of this contractual exclusion was to 'exclude or limit' the operation of the legislation may be irresistible. It would appear to be just another variant of the *Autoclenz* problem, where contractual stratagems mutate like a virus in response to adjustments by the legal system. This would leave some space for discrete qualifications to the overarching term by express agreement, focused on specific elements, while precluding its comprehensive exclusion by employers.[119]

The second scenario is focused on the symbiosis between the implied term of mutual trust and confidence and the statutory law of constructive dismissal. As we have seen, the elaboration of mutual trust and confidence flowed from the judicial concern to elaborate a contractual test for when an employee was 'entitled' to terminate the employment contract by reason of the employer's conduct. This led to an intensive focus on elaborating employer behavioural standards through the medium of the implied term.[120] Where this 'behavioural standard' dimension of mutual trust and confidence

[118] *Uber* (n 55) [80].
[119] On this compromise position, permitting targeted modifications of the content of mutual trust and confidence while barring blanket exclusion, see Collins (n 17) 489.
[120] Bogg (n 91) 414–15.

is excluded through the contract, the effect would be to curtail the operation of the unfair dismissal legislation very significantly. This is because it limits the scope for a constructive dismissal claim in circumstances of intolerable behaviour by the employer. The prospect of an employer limiting its statutory liabilities for intolerable behaviour that undermines the dignity and self-respect of an employee is likely to be highly unattractive to a court. The court may well take the view that the exclusion of contractual liability for dignitarian injury is an attempt to limit the operation of the statutory right not to be unfairly dismissed by removing constructive dismissal from its scope. This exclusion would also engage section 203(1) ERA 1996 as another form of 'indirect' exclusion.

Given the 'hybridity' of protective employment rights,[121] with statutory entitlements often intersecting with common law contractual categories, *Uber* has given fresh impetus to section 203(1) ERA 1996 as a powerful tool for restricting the illegitimate expansion of *ius dispositivum*. Ultimately, the reach of this statutory provision depends upon the proximity of the contractual term to an inderogable statutory right. In 'pure' common law cases like *Braganza*, where no statutory entitlement is even remotely at issue, section 203(1) can be of no assistance. These cases will depend upon the incremental development of a distinct common law of personal employment contracts, as indicated in *Autoclenz*. This is most likely to arise in a specifically tailored category of public policy for employment contracts. The starting point for those reflections is surely to be found in the Brasenose College 'classics' on the *ius cogens/ius dispositivum* distinction.[122] In particular, where public law standards are imposed on the employment contract to protect the weaker party from abuse of power, the exclusion of those common law restraints by the stronger party should be regarded as contrary to public policy. This provides an exact common law parallel to Lord Leggatt's concerns in *Uber* about the stronger party designing the contract so as to exclude *statutory* employment rights. Public law norms ought to have primacy over private contractual agreement, regardless of whether their source is statute or common law. This position is compelling for employment contracts, which often involve a close personal relationship, inequality of bargaining power and conflicting interests, with all the attendant risks of abuse and exploitation that these features bring in their wake.

IV. Conclusion: Section 203(1) ERA 1996 as the Philosopher's Stone?

In certain respects, section 203(1) ERA 1996 has led a rather obscure and diffident life in the history of British labour law. There are some scattered appearances in the case law and academic literature. The primary function has been to ensure access to a public forum, the employment tribunal, by regulating the role of settlement and arbitration agreements. It also addressed direct methods of contracting out of statutory employment

[121] The 'hybridity' description was provided by Sedley LJ in in *Bournemouth University Higher Education Corp v Buckland* [2010] EWCA Civ 121, [2011] QB 323 at [19].

[122] See above, under s II.

rights, such as express waivers in employment contracts. This quiet life may have led us to underappreciate the rather momentous significance of this statutory provision. It has prevented the destruction of a public system of enforceable rights by foreclosing the routine use of private arbitration clauses to shield employers from public accountability in a court, as in the US system.[123] In so doing, it has contributed to the systemic effectiveness of statutory employment rights and the Rule of Law as a public good. By channelling cases such as *Autoclenz* and *Uber* into the public courts, legal doctrine can evolve and address novel challenges in the labour market. The names of the litigants then stand as public and enduring monuments to the legal propositions those cases establish. Millions of workers have benefited from the legal principles established by Mr Aslam and Mr Farrar in *Uber*. Under a system of private arbitration, there is little scope for legal doctrine to develop as a living thing that governs everyone through authoritative legal norms. In the US, the dominance of private arbitration exemplifies a notion of public justice as *ius dispositivum*. In the British system, by contrast, section 203(1) has underpinned a framework of public justice and access to a court as *ius cogens*. Its importance cannot be overestimated.

The significance of this may be seen by considering the recent Canadian case of *Uber v Heller*.[124] This involved a legal challenge to a mandatory arbitration clause in a contract between Uber and an UberEATS driver. The arbitration clause required disputes to be referred to arbitration in Amsterdam, which would be subject to the law of the Netherlands. The clause also required the payment of US $14,500 as an administrative cost. The appellant earned $20,800–$31,200 per year before taxes, and expenses were deducted. Nor did the fee include other costs likely to be incurred in an arbitration, such as travel to Amsterdam, accommodation, and legal representation. In the Supreme Court of Canada, there were two distinct approaches supporting the invalidation of the arbitration clause. The majority favoured an unconscionability approach that was focused on the discrete transaction, specifically the inequality of bargaining power and the improvident nature of that bargain. This may be understood as a modified *ius dispositvum* approach, ensuring that the individual waiver of access to a court represents a valid exercise of a normative power. By contrast, Justice Brown favoured a 'public good' approach based on access to justice, scrutinising whether the arbitration clause effectively excluded the claimant from a just consideration of his legal rights. This was an established public policy enquiry addressing the ouster of courts from the determination of legal rights.[125] This public policy approach is very much in the realm of *ordre public*, and it treats the enquiry as an aspect of public rather than private law.

The enduring significance of *Uber* may yet be in enlivening the dynamic potential of section 203(1). In identifying its role in tackling the 'indirect' exclusion or limitation of inderogable statutory rights, Lord Leggatt's judgment may lead to this neglected statutory provision having a more prominent role. Much will depend upon how far

[123] The extensive use of private arbitration has been prevalent and devastating to justice as a public good in US labour law: see M Finkin, 'Privatization of Wrongful Dismissal Protection in Comparative Perspective' (2008) 37 *Industrial LJ* 149.

[124] *Uber Technologies Inc v Heller*, 2020 SCC 16.

[125] For further discussion, see A Bogg, '"Labour Law is a Subset of Employment Law" Revisited' (2020) 43 *Dalhousie Law Rev* 479, 500–11.

'indirect' goes. We now know that it extends to the inclusion of terms in written documentation with the 'object' of avoiding statutory rights that are legislated as *ius cogens*. I have suggested that 'indirect' may go even further to encompass purported contracting out of fundamental implied terms, such as mutual trust and confidence. It is also important that the statute not be treated as a ceiling, stymieing common law development. In this spirit, I have also suggested some ways in which the common law of public policy might be developed to tackle the undermining of *ius cogens* by private agreement in employment contracts. Proposals to redefine employment status have been mooted recently by the Government. While the details are still unclear, there is little sign that the legislator will dispense with 'contract' and adopt an exclusively statutory definition of an 'employment relationship'. If 'contract' is retained as a foundation for employment law, the tensions and instabilities explored in this chapter will endure. Ensuring that *ius dispositivum* stays within defensible limits will then depend upon a relatively autonomous common law of the personal employment contract. I have argued that this must be rooted in a strong notion of *ordre public*, supported by statutory restrictions on 'contracting out' and common law public policy. Such an achievement would be a fitting legal tribute to our Brasenose troika and their evident concern for justice and coherence in the law.

11

The Nature and Function of Default Rules in Succession Law: A Comparative Analysis

GREGOR CHRISTANDL

I. Types of Default Rules in Succession Law

The fundamental distinction between default rules and mandatory rules is well-known in the field of contract law,[1] where it has a long-standing tradition as an essential part of freedom of contract across jurisdictions.[2] In the area of succession law, the dichotomy of mandatory and default rules has received considerably less attention.[3] While in the realm of contract law, default rules typically operate as gap-fillers in contractual arrangements, in the field of succession law we can find different types of default rules.

First of all, there are those which apply where a person dies totally or partially intestate. Their purpose is to provide a complete set of rules for the transfer of wealth on death if and to the extent that the deceased failed to express his or her wishes in a will or other testamentary instrument. In line with their function, these rules can take the name of 'subsidiary' default rules; they apply in the (total or partial) absence of individual testamentary arrangements. Unlike under Roman law (*nemo pro parte testatus pro parte intestatus decedere potest*),[4] the rules on intestacy today[5] apply either to the whole

[1] On this distinction in contract law, see the contribution by J Cartwright, ch 7 in this volume.

[2] See Art 1:102 [Freedom of Contract] of the Principles of European Contract Law (PECL), on which E Hosemann in N Jansen and R Zimmermann (eds), *Commentaries on European Contract Law* (Oxford, Oxford University Press, 2018) 30. In the US, the dichotomy of mandatory and default rules has gained particular importance within the literature of law and economics, where default rules are perceived as a tool for increasing efficiency by reducing transaction costs: I Ayres, 'Valuing Modern Contract Scholarship' (2003) 112 *Yale LJ* 881, 885–92.

[3] For an in-depth discussion in the US, see AJ Hirsch, 'Default Rules in Inheritance Law: A Problem in Search of Its Context' (2004) 73 *Fordham L Rev* 1031; LF Tritt, 'Technical Correction or Tectonic Shift: Competing Default Rule Theories Under the New Uniform Probate Code' (2010) 61 *Alabama L Rev* 273.

[4] Digest 50.17.7 (Pomponius). On this rule, see F Schulz, *Classical Roman Law* (Oxford, OUP, 1951) 254. For a recent discussion in the light of its rejection under modern law, see W Borysiak, 'Roman Principle Nemo pro parte testatus pro parte intestatus decedere potest and the reasons of its modern rejection' in Z Benincasa and J Urbanik (eds), *Mater Familias: Scritti romanistici per Maria Zabłocka* (Łódz, Łódzkie Towarzystwo Naukowe, 2016) 63–82.

[5] But note that the law of Catalonia and of San Marino still stick to the Roman rule.

estate or only to part of it, depending on whether the deceased has disposed of all or only a part of the estate. By providing a complete regime of how the estate is going to be distributed among the members of the family of the deceased, intestacy rules turn out to be rather 'sticky'.[6] This is confirmed by a traditionally low incidence of will-making in many continental European jurisdictions. As a result, rules on intestacy are typically the most common, 'standard' succession regime, while testate succession is statistically the exception and dominates only in few European jurisdictions.[7]

Legal systems which allow for so-called 'negative wills' even grant the deceased the power to modify the rules on intestacy by excluding certain persons from the list of those who receive under such intestacy.[8] Except for this form of 'disinheritance' by will, the deceased cannot otherwise interfere with or modify the rules on intestacy, but is limited to simply excluding the applicability of the subsidiary regime. Hence, one can say that testate succession and intestate succession constitute two separate branches of succession law which stand on an equal level side by side, but with a different material scope of application:[9] the rules on intestacy apply only where the deceased dies totally or partially intestate, while the rules on testate succession apply when the deceased has left a valid will.

The rules on testate succession operate either as mandatory (eg rules on formalities) or as default rules (eg rules on the prior death of a beneficiary under the will). Default rules within the law on wills serve as 'suppletory' default rules since they govern mainly unexpected contingencies that testators leave unaddressed when drafting a will. As such, they apply either mechanically as rules of law to fill gaps, or they apply as discretionary default standards by granting courts the power to admit evidence of probable intent overriding the default standard.[10]

There is a third layer of rules in continental European succession laws which serves the purpose of family protection.[11] To a large extent these rules are mandatory, in the sense that they limit the private autonomy of the deceased in favour of family solidarity and thus apply regardless of contrary dispositions *inter vivos* or *mortis causa* by the testator. However, even in this layer of succession law, there is some margin for private autonomy. So, for example, in many legal systems, the deceased may deprive a person of his or her compulsory portion where the potential beneficiary is guilty of serious misconduct against the deceased or his family members.[12] Yet, this does not transform

[6] The inertia effect of default rules renders them 'sticky' in the terminology of I Ayres and R Gertner, 'Majoritarian vs. Minoritarian Defaults' (1999) 51 *Stanford L Rev* 1591, 1598.

[7] For an overview of available data on people who die without a will in different jurisdictions, see K Reid, M de Waal and R Zimmermann, 'Intestate Succession in Historical and Comparative Perspective' in K Reid, M de Waal and R Zimmermann (eds), *Comparative Succession Law (vol II): Intestate Succession* (Oxford, OUP, 2015) 442, 444–45.

[8] See eg § 1938 BGB for German law.

[9] E Ehrlich, *Das zwingende und nichtzwingende Recht im Bürgerlichen Gesetzbuch für das Deutsche Reich* (Jena, Gustav Fischer, 1899) 223.

[10] For criticism of this kind of default standards in succession law, see Hirsch (n 3) 1065 et seq.

[11] See R Zimmermann, 'Mandatory Family Protection in the Civilian Tradition' in K Reid, M de Waal and R Zimmermann (eds), *Comparative Succession Law (vol III) Mandatory Family Protection* (Oxford, Oxford University Press, 2020) 649.

[12] See eg the provisions in Austria (§§ 769–775 ABGB), Germany (§§ 2333–2335 BGB), Poland (Art 1008–1011 Polish Civil Code), Hungary (§§ 7:77–7:79 Hungarian Civil Code). By contrast, deprivation of the compulsory portion is unknown, for instance, in French and Italian law.

the rules in this area into defaults rules, since the law only exceptionally allows the deceased to disapply the mandatory rules without changing their content. By contrast, under Spanish law, the testator may redistribute the compulsory portion between those entitled and decide who among them is to receive the second half of the two thirds of the estate (*mejora*).[13] Exceptionally, in such a case, the mandatory family protection regime is partly constructed as a default, since the deceased may freely choose to disapply the default distribution rule (two thirds in equal shares) and change its content by redistributing one third in a different way.

The fundamental question that arises with regard to the different types of default rules in the realm of succession law concerns the policy considerations which shape their content. The first part of this chapter will focus on the rules governing intestacy in various jurisdictions and will deal with the question of which policy considerations have come into play when defining their specific content (section II). The second part will then focus on a number of default rules in the law concerning wills where these operate as suppletory rules or default standards, in order to determine whether there is any common ground on which they are founded (section III). This chapter will not specifically deal with the area of mandatory family protection, since this is an area where the law typically operates with mandatory rules and only exceptionally allows the deceased some limited margin of private autonomy in order perhaps to disapply, but not to change, the content of the mandatory rules.

I will argue that even though default rules in succession law all aim to effectuate the presumed intention of the average testator, they pursue a variety of different policy goals, which can however all be accommodated under the normative concept of presumed intention. Hence, a common and uniform policy goal for all default rules in succession law, namely that of reflecting testators' actual or presumed intentions, as suggested in the US literature on this issue,[14] is neither practicable nor desirable, considering the different purposes succession law default rules need to serve.

II. Rules on Intestacy

As has been pointed out, the rules on intestacy can be defined as default rules because they apply as a subsidiary regime where the deceased has failed to leave a valid will regarding the entire estate. When faced with the question of the rationale on which this default regime is based, the idea of the 'presumed will' or 'presumed intention' of the deceased is typically invoked.[15]

[13] Art 823 Spanish *Código civil*; see Zimmermann (n 11) 667; S Cámara Lapuente, 'Forced Heirship in Spain' in K Reid, M de Waal and R Zimmermann (eds), *Comparative Succession Law (vol III): Mandatory Family Protection* (Oxford, OUP, 2020) 139, 152.

[14] See Tritt (n 3) 278: '[S]uccession law should return to its roots and refocus solely on fulfilling the decedent's intent'.

[15] Reid, de Waal and Zimmermann (n 7) 446–48.

A. The 'Presumed Intention' of the Deceased

The idea of intestacy rules as an expression of the presumed intention of the deceased has its roots in the writings of Natural Law jurists like Grotius,[16] Pufendorf[17] and Stryk.[18] According to Grotius, the rules on intestacy are based on a conjecture of the will of the deceased ('a tacit will derived from inference as to wishes'[19]) so that the estate should go to the person to whom the deceased most likely would have wished it to belong. If, however, doubts remain about the actual will, then the presumption always applies that the deceased would have wanted what is most fair and honourable. Therefore, those to whom something is owed have priority as beneficiaries, and among these, those to whom something is *legally* owed enjoy priority over those to whom something is *morally* owed. This means that the first right of succession belongs to the children, because parents are believed to have wished to provide for them 'as parts of their own body and most abundantly', so that they receive all the property once their parents die.[20] Among other relatives, if there are no clear indications of intent, the deceased is believed to have wished what the law or custom prescribed.[21]

While at first glance it may appear as though Grotius is putting special emphasis on the presumed intent of the deceased himself, when taking a closer look it actually becomes evident that intestate succession, even according to Grotius, is not about individual wishes, but primarily about what is morally or legally due by the deceased. This idea of 'presumed intention', in the sense of what the deceased is expected to wish in line with his moral or legal duties, is even more evident in the writings of Pufendorf, who points out that in the area of intestate succession the intention of the deceased is considered not as it was, but as it *ought to have been* according to his legal or moral duties.[22]

The idea of 'presumed will' or 'presumed intention' was also adopted by the drafters of the two oldest codifications still in force on the Continent, namely the French Code civil of 1804 and the Austrian General Civil Code of 1811 (Allgemeines Bürgerliches Gesetzbuch, abbreviated ABGB). According to the drafters of the French Code, the rules on intestacy need to reflect the wishes which the deceased would have expressed if he had made a will in the last moments of his life.[23] Yet, here again, the drafters do not refer to the specific wishes of the individual testator, but to wishes that take into account all natural and legitimate affections a person owes to others. Accordingly, the drafters emphasise that 'if one goes deep into one's heart, one will find there the

[16] H Grotius, *De jure belli ac pacis* (Amsterdam, Janssonio-Waesbergios, 1680) lib II, cap VII, § 3. For an English translation, see SC Neff, *Hugo Grotius on the Law of War and Peace* (Cambridge, CUP, 2012) 145–48.

[17] S von Pufendorf, *De iure naturae et gentium* (Francofurt ad Moenum, 1694) lib IV, cap XI, § 1.

[18] S Stryk, *Tractatus de successione ab intestato* (Francofurtum ad Viadrum, 1697) diss I, cap 1, § 1.

[19] Grotius (n 16) lib II, cap VII, § 10 n 2: 'Successio autem ab intestato, de qua agimus, nil aliud est quam tacitum testamentum ex voluntatis conjectura.'

[20] Grotius (n 16) lib II, cap VII, § 5 n 2.

[21] Grotius (n 16) lib II, cap VII, § 11 n 2.

[22] Pufendorf (n 17) lib IV, cap XI, § 2: 'in hac materia voluntas defuncti respicitur non tam qualis fuerit, quam qualis esse debuerit.'

[23] PA Fenet, *Recueil complet des travaux préparatoires du Code civil*, vol 12 (Paris, 1836) 137: 'Elle doit donc prononcer comme eût prononcé le défunt lui-même, au dernier instant de sa vie, s'il eût pu, ou s'il eût voulu s'expliquer.'

order of successors engraved in inerasable characters'.[24] As a result, the children and their descendants are the first successors, irrespective of the fact that in a given case a father may not have loved his children as he should. With regard to so-called collateral relatives, the principle to be followed is that of proximity: closer collaterals exclude the rest. According to the French drafters, this order so naturally flows from a truth grounded in feelings that 'cursed be those who need further reasoning or discussion'.[25]

According to the drafters of the Austrian Civil Code, the idea of presumed intention was to be understood as the presumed affection that the deceased felt towards his or her relatives, so that according to this idea, the envisaged successors under the rules on intestacy had to be those whom the deceased presumably loved most. The question who this was ought to be answered according to the principle of *conserva te ipsum* which considers the individual person as a member of a closer and of a wider family. Hence, if a person dies, the members of the closer family will succeed and exclude the members of the wider family.[26]

In many later continental codifications, the idea of presumed intention was mentioned as one of the basic principles guiding the legislature in defining who should be the deceased's successors under the rules on intestacy.[27] However, by way of contrast, in Germany the idea of presumed intention was explicitly rejected by von Schmitt, the redactor who produced the first draft of the rules on intestate succession, as well as by the first commission consulting on the draft, since it was said to be one of a number of theories considered to be of doubtful value for defining the content of intestacy rules.[28] Yet, perhaps not surprisingly, the rejection of this idea does not seem to have had any relevant impact on the design and content of the intestacy rules in German law.

Across the Channel, the idea was promoted by Stair in Scotland; he echoed Grotius' idea of intestate succession as the law representing a presumed will of the deceased.[29] In England, the idea of presumed intention as the rationale of rules on intestacy is often attributed to a remark by Lord Cairns on the Statutes of Distributions of 1670 and 1675 in the nineteenth-century case of *Cooper v Cooper*, where he said that the intestacy rules should be regarded as 'nothing more than a will made by the Legislature for

[24] Fenet (n 23) 137: 'Que chacun descende dans son propre cœur, il y trouvera gravé en caractères ineffaçables le véritable ordre de succéder.'

[25] Fenet (n 23) 138.

[26] This idea goes back to Johann Bernhard Horten, the drafter of the Austrian rules on intestate succession, who was influenced by the Natural Law writer Joachim Georg Darjes. See G Christandl in A Fenyves, F Kerschner and A Vonkilch (eds), *Großkommentar zum ABGB (Klang Kommentar)* 3rd edn (Wien, Verlag Österreich, 2021) §§ 647–755 at 445–50.

[27] For Italy, see eg A Braun, 'Intestate Succession in Italy' in Reid, de Waal and Zimmermann, *Comparative Succession Law*, vol 2 (n 7) 67, 68–71.

[28] G von Schmitt, *Begründung des Entwurfes eines Rechtes der Erbfolge für das Deutsche Reich und des Entwurfes eines Einführungsgesetzes* (Berlin, Reichsdruckerei, 1879) 574; B Mugdan (ed), *Die gesammten Materialien zum Bürgerlichen Gesetzbuch für das Deutsche Reich*, vol 5 (Berlin, R v Decker's Verlag, 1899) 189. On this aspect, see R Zimmermann, 'Intestate Succession in Germany' in Reid, de Waal and Zimmermann, *Comparative Succession Law*, vol 2 (n 7) 181, 189–90.

[29] D Stair, *The Institution of the Law of Scotland* (Edinburgh, Andrew Andersen, 1693) Lib 3 Tit 4 § 2 and 3. On this see K Reid, 'Intestate Succession in Scotland' in Reid, de Waal and Zimmermann, *Comparative Succession Law*, vol 2 (n 7) 370, 382.

the intestate'.[30] This view was harshly criticised by Maitland, who thought that 'the law makes a will for intestates that no sane testator would make for himself';[31] Maitland was here referring to the law of descent, according to which land was, at the time, transferred to the eldest son without provision for the widow and younger children. By contrast, the modern rules on intestacy enacted by the Administration of Estates Act 1925 were explicitly based on the presumed intention of the deceased. As a consequence, a survey of wills was conducted to find out what the wishes of testators were, in order to allow the Parliament to make a will for the intestate.[32] A similar survey was also compiled in preparation for the 1952 Act,[33] although it might well be questioned to which extent wills drafting practice can be in any way conclusive evidence when it comes to determining what someone dying intestate would typically want.[34] In its 1989 report, the Law Commission of England and Wales emphasised presumed intention as the foundation of the rules on intestacy, and in more recent times several opinion surveys were commissioned, both by the Law Commission of England and Wales and the Law Commission of Scotland, in order to learn about the wishes of people dying intestate.[35]

That said, the idea of presumed intention as an empirical concept, as it seems to have been espoused by the English and Scottish Law Commissions in the past, is flawed for a variety of reasons, most of all because there is no way it can be assessed. And to the extent that the idea is built on the notion of an average testator, it has to be acknowledged that such an average testator does not exist.[36] The English Law Commission has thus emphasised that neither a will study[37] nor a public attitude survey alone offers a sufficient basis for reforming the law of intestate succession.[38]

It seems obvious, therefore, that 'presumed intention' can only be understood as a normative concept. For this reason, the theory of presumed intent and the theory of duty,[39] which is often presented as an alternative to the theory of presumed intent,

[30] *Cooper v Cooper* (1874) LR 7 HL 53, 66.

[31] FW Maitland, 'The Law of Real Property' in HAL Fisher (ed), *The Collected Papers of Frederic William Maitland*, vol I (Cambridge, CUP, 1911) 162, 172.

[32] B Sloan, *Borkowski's Law of Succession* 4th edn (Oxford, OUP, 2020) 21.

[33] Report of the Committee on the Law of Intestate Succession, Cmd 8310 (1951) para 18.

[34] See Reid, de Waal and Zimmermann (n 7) 447, who point out that wills are typically made by those who are better off and thus cannot be regarded as representative for the whole population. On the drawbacks of reliance on wills drafting practice, see also Law Commission, *Intestacy and Family Provision Claims on Death* (Law Com CP No 191, 2009) paras 1.40–1.411.

[35] Law Commission, *Intestacy and Family Provision Claims on Death* (Law Com No 331, 2011) benefited from the Nuffield survey published by the National Centre for Social Research, *Inheritance and the Family: Attitudes to Will-Making and Intestacy* (2010); Scottish Law Commission, *Report on Succession* (Scot Law Com No 215, 2009) para 1.4.

[36] F Burns, 'Surviving Spouses, Surviving Children and the Reform of Total Intestacy Law in England and Scotland: Past, Present and Future' (2013) 33 *Legal Studies* 85, 96; CH Sherrin and RC Bonehill, *The Law and Practice of Intestate Succession* 3rd edn (London, Sweet & Maxwell, 2004) paras 1.031–1.032.

[37] See Law Commission, *Intestacy and Family Provision Claims on Death* (Law Com CP No 191, 2009) paras 1.38–1.41.

[38] See Law Commission, *Intestacy and Family Provision Claims on Death* (Law Com CP No 191, 2009) para 1.41; on the value of public attitude surveys, see however, ibid, paras 1.42–1.45; Law Commission, *Intestacy and Family Provision Claims on Death* (Law Com No 331, 2011) para 1.24.

[39] For a discussion of this theory, see RJ Scalise, 'Honor Thy Father and Mother? How Intestacy Law Goes Too Far in Protecting Parents' (2006) 37 *Seton Hall L Rev* 171, 174–76, who admits that the theories have historically led to the same results.

largely coincide. Indeed, both refer to the presumed intention of the deceased not to how it actually *was* in an empirical sense, but to how it *ought to be* in a normative sense.

This normative concept of a presumed intention does not mean, however, that the legislature may arbitrarily define the rules on intestacy. The concept of presumed intention itself implies that a legislature will typically aim to model intestacy rules on the expectations of an average testator.[40] In this sense, intestacy rules must be at their core the legislature's best guess at the expectations of the majority of the population.[41] For this reason, one may say that, to a large extent, intestacy rules need to be 'majoritarian' default rules.[42] While in the realm of contract law, majoritarian default rules supply the missing terms of the contract by referring to the hypothetical bargain the parties would have struck had they addressed the issue themselves,[43] in the realm of intestacy law default rules need to meet the expectations of an average person who has not left a will. That children and, to a certain extent also a spouse, are included in the first class of beneficiaries certainly meets the expectations of the average person, and thus such a regime predictably reduces transaction costs[44] by sparing those who are content with the intestacy regime the expense of drafting a will, thereby reducing the overall number of cases where wills are made.[45]

With regard to how exactly the estate is to be distributed, however, the question becomes much trickier, so that other considerations need to step in to complete the picture. The same is true where a deceased dies without children or a spouse and the question arises who amongst the surviving relatives should receive the estate.[46] Since guessing the expectations of the average testator in cases where a person does not leave any close relatives seems impossible, a legislature could try to incentivise will-making by adopting intestacy rules which are purposefully *against* the wishes or the probable intention of the average testator. An intestacy rule to the effect that the State takes all if there are no children and no surviving spouse may incentivise will-making in an area where the expectations of an average testator cannot reasonably be predicted.[47] Yet, framing intestacy law in terms of such penalty defaults would most probably lead to undesired results, and it would certainly discriminate against those (in particular less wealthy) groups who are generally less likely to make wills.[48] Hence it is not surprising that legislatures across jurisdictions have refrained from instrumentalising intestacy rules as penalty defaults.[49]

[40] Reid, de Waal and Zimmermann (n 7) 446.

[41] Law Commission, *Intestacy and Family Provision Claims on Death* (Law Com No 331, 2011) para 1.24: 'The intestacy rules provide solutions that are designed to be generally acceptable, and to work in most families.'

[42] On this conceptual basis of default rules, see the contributions by B Häcker, ch 1 in this volume at 17–18 (but cf also 19), and by A Hellgardt, ch 2 in this volume at 33.

[43] Hirsch (n 348) 1039–42.

[44] Hirsch (n 3) 1038.

[45] This idea already existed in Prussia: see Schmitt (n 28) 144; TE Atkinson, 'Succession Among Collaterals' (1935) 20 *Iowa L Rev* 185, 187–88.

[46] On the question of whether a surviving spouse should exclude surviving parents, see Scalise (n 39) 176 et seq.

[47] Atkinson (n 45) 197.

[48] For this and other reasons against penalty defaults in intestacy rules: Hirsch (n 3) 1060.

[49] On the concept of penalty defaults, see Ayres and Gertner (n 6) 1606–10.

B. Fundamental Values: Equality and Fairness

Apart from simply trying to express the expectations of the average testator, intestacy rules also enshrine and promote fundamental values of a society. In the last decades, non-discrimination and fairness have gained ground as guiding principles of modern intestacy law across Western legal systems. It is, as will be shown, the above-mentioned normative force of the concept of presumed intention which allows these fundamental values to be implemented in the law on intestacy.

The radical reform of English intestacy law adopted with the Administration of Estates Act of 1925 abolished the precedence of male descendants of the same degree over females, and primogeniture with regard to realty.[50] Gender and age thus completely disappeared as relevant criteria from English intestacy law when the Act came into force in January 1926. In Austria, the first uniform law on intestacy for both movables and immovables was adopted in 1786,[51] and it was later integrated into the Austrian Civil Code of 1811. One of its main goals was to introduce a uniform set of rules for all classes and to remove the so-called *Mannesvorteil* (male privilege).[52] Similarly, the German draft of the rules on intestate succession was based on the principle of 'equality of heirs'.[53] Privileges on account of gender, age, religion, and so on, which had previously existed in regional or local laws, were abolished altogether. In France, the French Revolution swept away all kinds of privileges and discriminations which had existed under the *ancien droit*.[54] Thus, it paved the way for the Code civil, which in turn is grounded on the key principle of equality[55] even though it reintroduced some reactionary distinctions and discriminations.[56]

While it was relatively easy to jettison the most blatant examples of inequality and discrimination of the past based on gender and age, the case of succession rights for extramarital children was a much tougher nut to crack. Indeed, for centuries children born out of wedlock (so-called 'illegitimate children') had been the victims of both social and legal discrimination. The legal discrimination had its roots in Roman law, where extramarital children were neither agnatic nor cognatic relatives of their father, so that they were not entitled to any intestate succession rights after his death, while they could, on the other hand, become heirs to their mother and her relatives so long as she had not been *in manus* of her husband or father prior to her death.[57] Hence, in many jurisdictions for a very long time, extramarital children had a claim under

[50] With regard to personalty, no preference was given to male over female descendants, and there was no primogeniture even before the reform of 1925: see R Kerridge, 'Intestate Succession in England and Wales' in Reid, de Waal and Zimmermann, *Comparative Succession Law*, vol 2 (n 7) 323, 327–28.

[51] So-called *Josephinsches Erbfolgepatent* of 11 May 1786, JGS (*Justizgesetzsammlung*) 548. On this, see C Wendehorst, 'Intestate Succession in Austria' in Reid, de Waal and Zimmermann, *Comparative Succession Law*, vol 2 (n 7) 159, 163–64.

[52] See Christandl (n 26) 430–31.

[53] Schmitt (n 28) 555; Mugdan (n 28) 190.

[54] Décret du 15 mars 1790, tit 1, art 11; Décret du 8 avril 1791, art 1. On the multiple distinctions and privileges under the *ancient droit*, see LP Lévy and A Castaldo, *Histoire du droit civil* (Paris, Dalloz, 2002) 1100–56.

[55] Fenet (n 23) 144.

[56] Lévy and Castaldo (n 54) 1164–69.

[57] Digest 38.17.12 (Ulpian).

intestacy rules only as regards their mother, but not as regards their biological father. Once it had become permissible for paternity to be established with regard to extramarital children, the question of equal treatment became acute. Nonetheless, it was only during the second half of the twentieth and at the beginning of the twenty-first century that legislatures started to abolish or at least reduce the discrimination of extramarital children.[58] In Germany, for example, the reform of 1969 improving the position of extramarital children was prompted by a decision of the Federal Constitutional Court, which had urged the legislature to implement Article 6 paragraph 5 of the German Constitution (Grundgesetz or 'Basic Law') requiring equal treatment of extramarital children. The reform of 1969, however, did not fully achieve equal treatment, but – amongst other limitations – introduced only a monetary claim instead of a share in the estate. This discriminatory regime was finally abolished in 1997 when it was formally recognised that there can and should be only one rule for both marital and extramarital children.[59] Similarly, in Austria it took several attempts by the legislature and two decisions by the European Court of Human Rights to achieve equal treatment of extramarital children in 2004.[60] In France, any discrimination against extramarital children had already been abolished after the Revolution, but the reactionary forces during the codification process reintroduced a separate regime for them.[61] A first step towards improving the claims of extramarital children was taken in 1972.[62] Yet true equal treatment was not achieved until 2001,[63] following a decision of the European Court of Human Rights in 2000.[64] In Italy, the first improvement for extramarital children was introduced in 1975 with the reform of family law, while all remaining disparities of treatment of extramarital children under succession law were abolished only in 2014.[65] In England and Wales, it was section 18 of the Family Law Reform Act 1987 which brought about equal treatment for extramarital children under intestacy law.[66]

The example of extramarital children shows that the implementation of the principle of equal treatment and fairness in the rules on intestacy in European jurisdictions was extremely slow-moving and difficult and that, until very recently, equality in this regard

[58] For a comparative overview, see Reid, de Waal and Zimmermann (n 7) 481–84.

[59] Gesetz zur erbrechtlichen Gleichstellung nichtehelicher Kinder of 16 December 1997. Urged by the European Court of Human Rights, its application was later extended to children born before 1 July 1949 (Zweites Gesetz zur erbrechtlichen Gleichstellung nichtehelicher Kinder of 12 April 2011). For details, see Zimmermann (n 28) 197–202.

[60] Bundesgesetz über die Neuordnung der Rechtsstellung des unehelichen Kindes of 30 October 1970; Bundesgesetz über die Gleichstellung des unehelichen Kindes im Erbrecht und die Sicherung der Ehewohnung für den überlebenden Ehegatten of 13 December 1989; Familien- und Erbrechtsänderungsgesetz of 27 May 2004. For details, see Christandl (n 26) 436–41, 489–91.

[61] Fenet (n 23) 149–50.

[62] Loi n 72-3 du 3 janvier 1972 sur la filiation. See F Terré, Y Lequette and S Gaudemet, *Droit civil – Les Successions – Les liberalités* 4th edn (Paris, Dalloz, 2014) 96–99; C Pérès, 'Intestate Succession in France' in Reid, de Waal and Zimmermann, *Comparative Succession Law*, vol 2 (n 7) 33, 44.

[63] Loi n 2001-1135 du 3 décembre 2001 relative aux droits du conjoint survivant et des enfants adultérins et modernisant diverses dispositions de droit successoral. Apart from succession law, the distinction between marital and extramarital children was abolished by the Ordonnance n° 2005-759 du 4 juillet 2005 portant réforme de la filiation.

[64] ECtHR, *Mazurek v France*, 1 February 2000, no 34406/97.

[65] Braun (n 27) 76–77.

[66] Kerridge (n 50) 347.

had not yet been achieved. Cultural and religious reasons may have played a role, but the human rights perspective eventually won the day. It is the European Court of Human Rights that expressed the view that the right of succession as between children and parents, and between grandchildren and grandparents, is so closely related to family life that it is protected within the scope of Article 8 European Convention on Human Rights (ECHR).[67] In this respect, human rights have shaped modern intestacy rules.[68] As a result, the public policy objection can be invoked according to Article 35 of the EU Succession Regulation[69] in order to rule out the application of foreign law which discriminates on the basis of, for instance, sex, race, religion or against extramarital children.[70]

From this perspective, default rules in succession law also serve an expressive and transformative function,[71] namely insofar as they reject unfairness and discrimination in the devolution of wealth on death and thereby help at least indirectly to encourage the development of will-making preferences that reflect these values.[72]

However, one may ask why lawmakers do not impose these values generally by adopting mandatory rules that implement these basic values for everyone rather than only for those who die intestate. In other words, are mere default rules really the appropriate instrument for implementing these values? The answer is straightforward. The legislature's aim when drafting the rules on intestacy is not to abolish freedom of testation by introducing a mandatory regime, but to establish a default regime that reflects the societal judgement of how wealth ought to be distributed on death, and which thus fully respects, as required for any other law, the fundamental values of the legal system, such as human rights and the principles of equality and fairness. While the testator can discriminate and be unfair in his will, the legislature (and therefore the intestacy rules) cannot.

C. Other Policy Considerations

The normative dimension of the concept of presumed intention allows for a broad variety of policy considerations to be implemented in the rules governing intestacy. Among the many different policy considerations behind intestacy rules (which cannot all be recounted here), what needs to be mentioned is that certain provisions, especially those favouring spouses, fulfil the function of providing economic and social stability.

[67] ECtHR, *Marckx v Belgium*, 13 June 1979, no 6833/74 paras 51–52.

[68] On the human rights implications both of the current law and reforms of intestacy law, see Law Commission, *Intestacy and Family Provision Claims on Death* (Law Com CP No 191, 2009).

[69] Regulation (EU) No 650/2012 of the European Parliament and of the Council of 4 July 2012 on jurisdiction, applicable law, recognition and enforcement of decisions and acceptance and enforcement of authentic instruments in matters of succession and on the creation of a European Certificate of Succession [2012] OJ L201/107.

[70] G Contaldi and C Grieco, 'Art 35' in AL Calvo Caravaca, A Davì and HP Mansel (eds), *The EU Succession Regulation – A Commentary* (Cambridge, CUP, 2016) Art 35 para 20.

[71] For a critical view, see Hirsch (n 3) 1053–58.

[72] See ML Fellows, M Kirkpatrick Johnson and others, 'Committed Partners and Inheritance: An Empirical study' (1998) 16 *Law and Inequality Journal* 1, 8; EG Spitko, 'The Expressive Function of Succession Law and the Merits of Noon-Marital Inclusion' (1999) 41 *Arizona L Rev* 1063, 1065.

This holds true especially for those rules which assign to the surviving spouse a substantial part of the estate, as under English law, where the spouse's entitlement to the deceased's personal chattels and to the statutory legacy typically exhaust the estate;[73] under Scots law,[74] where the spouse's prior rights are so extensive that they will often exhaust the estate; or where the spouse takes all and the children only receive the remainder at the surviving spouse's death, as in Dutch law.[75] But it holds true also for those rules that assign to the surviving spouse a substantial share in the estate and, irrespective of a will, the lifelong right to live in the family home, as in France, Italy or Austria.[76]

Again, one may object that these goals can only be achieved if these rules are adopted as mandatory provisions. Indeed, in Austria or Italy, the rules that grant the surviving spouse a right to live in the family home until his or her death are mandatory provisions, so that the deceased cannot change them by his or her will. Yet, even where these rules favouring economic and social stability for the surviving spouse are not mandatory, they fulfil an important function in expressing how, according to a societal judgement, the spouse should be treated – even though testators remain completely free to dispose of their assets differently if for whatever reason they wish to do so. Nevertheless, the practical relevance of such a default rule should not be underestimated, considering that according to the 'iron rule of inertia'[77] default rules are typically 'sticky', so that the number of people who make a will to avoid the application of default rules will always be smaller than the number of people who just go with the default rules.[78]

D. Certainty, Predictability and Clarity

Intestate rules also fulfil the function of providing certainty, predictability and clarity about who is to receive a person's assets in the absence of a will. For this reason, lawmakers typically refrain[79] from any form of discretionary rules which delegate to a court the task of reconstructing intent *post mortem* in order to determine the distribution of the estate on a case-by-case basis.[80] Exceptionally, under English law, section 18 (1)(i) of the Mental Capacity Act 2005 allows the Court of Protection to make so called 'statutory wills' for living persons who lack testamentary capacity.[81] The Court's decision is based on the best interests[82] of the person who lacks testamentary capacity.

[73] Kerridge (n 50) 345.
[74] Reid (n 29) 392.
[75] W D Kolkman, 'Intestate Succession in the Netherlands' in Reid, de Waal and Zimmermann, *Comparative Succession Law*, vol 2 (n 7) 224, 242.
[76] Pérès (n 62) 46–48; Braun (n 27) 83–86; Wendehorst (n 51) 168–69.
[77] Ayres and Gertner (n 6) 1598.
[78] See ibid.
[79] For some examples to the contrary in US American law, see Hirsch (n 3) 1065.
[80] Sherrin and Bonehill (n 36) 19.
[81] On statutory wills, their practical relevance, and problems caused by them in law and practice, see Law Commission, *Making a Will* (Law Com CP No 231, 2017) paras 3.1–3.41.
[82] The subject's 'best interests' have been interpreted in the case law to mean that the statutory will should be made in a way which aims for the testator to be remembered as having 'done the right thing': *Re P* [2009] EWHC 163 (Ch), [2010] Ch 33; *Re M* [2009] EWHC 2525 (Fam), [2011] 1 WLR 344; *Re D (Statutory Will)*

For the same reason of certainty and clarity, intestacy law primarily focuses on formalised status rather than on de facto relationships when defining how the estate is to be distributed among the deceased's closest family members. Nonetheless, cohabitants in particular have gained ground as beneficiaries under intestacy rules and will, in the light of increasing numbers of unmarried couples in many European countries,[83] be granted an even more important role in the future.[84] Providing economic and social stability not only to spouses, but also to basically equivalent cohabitants is a growing concern that a lawmaker cannot ignore when modernising the rules on intestacy in the light of the principle of equal treatment and non-discrimination.

III. Rules on Wills

A. Default Rules as Gap-Fillers

It has been mentioned above that in the law on wills default rules are gap-fillers. They step in where the deceased, albeit making a will, has failed to provide for certain unexpected events. Hence, if a testator wants to leave everything to the spouse in the will, he or she might not think of the possibility that, at the time of death, the marriage may already have ended in divorce or be caught up in divorce proceedings. Similarly, a testator may not think of the possibility that. after making a will, he becomes father to a child, or to a further child, or that the child he thought was his turns out to be someone else's child. Also, where the person designated in the will has predeceased the testator, the question arises who should instead receive the benefit.

For all such contingencies, the legislature may provide specific default rules in order to prevent an outcome that conflicts with what the deceased most probably would have wished had he considered this case. Hence, the question to be answered is what the deceased would have wished had he been aware of these unforeseen events. It is thus the presumed intention of testators which guides the legislature in shaping certain default rules, so as to prevent unexpected results. A result is 'unexpected' in this sense if it fails to meet the expectations of an average testator. Again, we see that it is not the *individual* testator whose presumed intention is reconstrued, but the rules are based on the majoritarian default modelled on the presumed intention of an *average* testator and adapted to the basic values of fairness and non-discrimination to which the lawmaker is bound. So, even if it were true that an average testator does not want to include extramarital children among his or her beneficiaries, a rule to this effect would be as unacceptable as a rule that grants a right of representation only to male and not to female issue.

[2010] EWHC 2159 (Ch), [2012] Ch 57; *Re Meek* [2014] EWCOP 1, [2014] COPLR 535; *Re Jones* [2014] EWCOP 59; *Bagguley v E* [2020] Fam 267, 274.

[83] According to the Office for National Statistics, *People's Living Arrangements in England and Wales: Census 2021* (9 February 2023), the number of cohabiting couples (not in a marriage or civil partnership) has increased across all age groups from 20.6 per cent in 2011 to 24.3 per cent in 2021. The same trend can be seen in many other European countries: E Szandor and E Clerici (Eurofound), *Household Composition and Well-Being* (Luxembourg, Publications Office of the European Union, 2019) 15–20.

[84] For a comparative overview, see Reid, de Waal and Zimmermann (n 7) 504–8; G Christandl, 'Succession Rights for Cohabitants' (2020) 24 *Edinburgh Law Review* 138, 138–43.

But what if, according to the circumstances of the case, the default rule appears to be evidently contrary to the probable intent of the individual testator? Take the example of a person who has continuously declared that he or she wishes the divorced spouse to remain the beneficiary in the will, while according to the default rule all provisions in favour of a spouse lapse with divorce.[85] The question here is whether in the law on wills default standards should also be admitted in order to allow the beneficiaries to bring evidence of the deceased's probable intent which *differs* from the intent of the average testator reflected in the default standard. As we have seen, such standards are typically rejected in the area of intestacy, where they run against the policy goal of certainty and clarity.[86]

In the remainder of this chapter, three such unforeseen contingencies for which a legislature may provide will be examined, namely the case of the beneficiary predeceasing the testator (subsection B), the case of the deceased's marriage to the beneficiary being dissolved or annulled at the time of death (subsection C) and the case where the subject-matter of the disposition has ceased to exist as part of the testator's property on death (subsection D).

B. Predeceased Beneficiary

According to the doctrine of lapse under English law, a gift by will lapses if the beneficiary dies before the testator does.[87] Hence, in the absence of a provision to the effect that the beneficiary will be replaced by another beneficiary, the will fails. Yet there are two exceptions to this doctrine of lapse. If the beneficiary is a child or remoter descendant and the beneficiary predeceases the testator, the devise or bequest takes effect as a devise or bequest to the issue of the predeceased beneficiary living at the time of the testator's death, unless a contrary intention appears by the will (section 33(1) Wills Act 1837). The second exception is derived from case law and applies where the disposition is based on a moral obligation recognised by the testator in his will which continues to exist notwithstanding the beneficiary's prior death. In these cases, the intended gift is presumed to pass to the estate of the predeceased beneficiary.[88] This exception was applied, for example, where the testator intended to discharge a debt barred by the Statute of Limitations by making a corresponding gift to the beneficiary.[89]

In France, by contrast, the so-called doctrine of representation does not apply to testamentary dispositions, so that the descendants of the predeceased beneficiary cannot take instead of the predeceased (Article 1039 Code civil). This rule is commonly explained on the grounds that a testamentary disposition is always considered to be made in favour of a specific person.[90] Hence, the testator may also provide differently

[85] For such a rule, see § 725 of the Austrian Civil Code (ABGB).
[86] See the text accompanying n 79 above.
[87] R Kerridge, *Parry and Kerridge: The Law of Succession* 13th edn (London, Sweet & Maxwell, 2016) paras 14-11 et seq.
[88] *Stephen v King* [1904] 2 Ch 30, 33.
[89] *Williamson v Naylor* (1838) 3 Y & C 208.
[90] Terré, Lequette and Gaudemet (n 62) 418–19.

and either tacitly or explicitly express a wish regarding who should receive in case the beneficiary predeceases him or her. By contrast, under Italian law, the doctrine of representation operates for both testate and intestate succession if the predeceased beneficiary is a descendant or a sibling of the deceased (Article 467 paragraph 2 Codice civile). Under Austrian law, only the descendants of a predeceased child of the testator will take under the will, while the gift does not pass on to the descendants of other predeceased beneficiaries who are not the child of the testator (§ 605 ABGB).

The same rule applies under German law: the descendants of the predeceased beneficiary will take only if the predeceased beneficiary named in the will was a child of the testator (§ 2069 BGB). This rule cannot be extended by analogy to the descendants of other predeceased beneficiaries.[91] However, under German law, the court may, on the basis of a suppletory or hypothetical interpretation of the will (*ergänzende/hypothetische Testamentsauslegung*), extend the testamentary disposition to persons related to the predeceased beneficiary even in the absence of any hint to that effect in the will itself.[92] Courts may extend a disposition in a will not only to the descendants of the predeceased beneficiary,[93] but also to ascendants, the beneficiary's spouse or even to the second spouse instead of the predeceased children of the first marriage.[94] The extension of the disposition to these persons may be inferred from all the circumstances of the case allowing the court to determine the hypothetical will of the deceased. On the basis of these circumstances, the court determines what the testator would have wanted if, at the time of making the will, she or he had known of the changed circumstances.[95]

From a comparative perspective, thus, the general default rule (except for France) seems to be that if a child or other descendant is the beneficiary in a will and predeceases the testator, the descendants of the predeceased beneficiary will take in his or her stead. This is in line with the rule of representation in the area of intestacy. Only in Italy, this rule is further extended to descendants of predeceased siblings as primary beneficiaries. Unlike in any other jurisdiction considered here, German courts may fill gaps of a will by suppletory interpretation, taking into account elements outside the will which help assess the hypothetical will of the specific testator where a beneficiary named in the will is not a descendant of the testator and predeceases him or her. The hypothetical will of the specific testator is thus relevant only where the predeceased beneficiary is not a child or descendant, but some other person with regard to whom the general default rule does not apply.

[91] D Leipold in FJ Säcker, R Rixecker and others (eds), *Münchener Kommentar zum BGB*, vol 11, 9th edn (Munich, CH Beck, 2022) § 2069 para 37.

[92] Leipold in *Münchener Kommentar* (n 91) § 2069 paras 38–42. This point is debated since many courts require a 'hint' in the will in order to proceed to its suppletory interpretation. Yet such a requirement is contradictory, since the suppletory construction only applies when there is a gap (and thus not even a hint) in the will. See OLG Köln (10.11.2008), ZEV 2009, 241. What is required, however, is that the will can be understood as reflecting an intent that is sufficiently certain with respect to determinable legal consequences (even if not expressly mentioned in the will), allowing the court to construe the hypothetical wishes of the deceased on this basis. See Leipold in *Münchener Kommentar* (n 91) § 2084 para 100.

[93] Leipold in *Münchener Kommentar* (n 91) § 2084 paras 113–16.

[94] ibid.

[95] ibid para 97.

C. Dissolved or Annulled Marriage

Where a testator makes a will and is later divorced or where the marriage annulled before she or he dies without having made a new will, the question arises whether or not a disposition in the will in favour of the (then former) spouse should lapse. With regard to this question, the law in England changed over time. According to section 18 of the Wills Act of 1837, divorce had no effect on a will, unless the testator had remarried. In 1982, the Wills Act was amended by the Administration of Justice Act. Under the new section 18A, the will lapses with divorce, except where a contrary intention appears by the will. In order to avoid the application of intestacy rules in this case, the provision was amended by the Law Reform (Succession) Act of 1995, which now states that for most purposes the former spouse is deemed to have died on the day when marriage was dissolved or annulled, unless a contrary intention appears by the will. As a consequence, the former spouse is for most purposes considered to be (fictitiously) predeceased with no rights under the will.

Under French and Italian law, in the absence of any specific provision on this issue, the rule is still that divorce has no effect on a will unless a contrary intention can be found,[96] but the will may be voidable for mistake. In Germany, by contrast, a testamentary provision lapses if the marriage was dissolved before the death of the testator. It also lapses where the testator, at the time of death, had filed for divorce or annulment and all requirements for divorce or annulment were fulfilled (§ 2077 BGB). This rule does not apply if it can be established that the testator would have wished the will to take effect irrespective of the divorce or annulment.[97] Similarly, under Austrian law, the will lapses if the marriage is dissolved or annulled after the will was made, unless a contrary intention appears by the will (§ 725 ABGB). The Austrian Supreme Court, however, applies this default rule strictly and does not allow extrinsic evidence of the actual intent of the deceased where such intent cannot be inferred from the will itself.[98]

A provision to the effect that a testamentary disposition lapses upon divorce or annulment of marriage seems to be in line with the presumed intention of a typical testator who normally does not wish the former spouse to receive anything under the will,[99] even if the testator has failed to revoke the will before his or her death. Hence, a legal rule cutting out the former spouse is a rule that applies in the absence of a clear intention of the testator and serves the function of avoiding consequences that are most likely unintended. The question remains whether such a default should operate as a rule or, better, as a discretionary standard allowing extrinsic evidence of probable contrary intent to override the legal default.

[96] For French law, see: Cass civ 1er (4.12.2013) pourvoi n° 12-27.421. The contrary intention may also be deduced from extrinsic elements (writings, local usages, the nature of the personal relationship between the testator and the beneficiary, the individual habits of the testator): see P Malaurie and C Brenner, *Droit des successions et des liberalités* 10th edn (Paris, LGDJ, 2022) 318.

[97] Leipold in *Münchener Kommentar* (n 91) § 2077 para 25.

[98] OGH (29.4.2019), Az 2 Ob 192/18a, Zeitschrift für Familien- und Erbrecht (EF-Z) 2019, 130.

[99] See eg Law Commission, *Family Law The Effect of Divorce on Wills* (Law Com No 217, 1993) para 3.1: 'There are a number of principles upon which the law might be based, although the underlying object must be to seek to do what the testator himself, or herself, might have wished.'

D. Ademption

A third default rule under the law governing wills concerns specific legacies or specific devises which fail by 'ademption' if their subject-matter has ceased to form part of the testator's assets at the time of his or her death. Hence, under English law, if according to the will, beneficiary A is to receive the testator's jewellery and the testator destroys, sells or gives it away before his or her death, the specific legacy of the jewellery remains without effect. It is debated whether this rule is a rule of law applying irrespective of the probable wishes which the deceased would have expressed had he provided on his own to amend his testamentary provisions. By contrast, if ademption were to be considered a default standard (rule of construction), it would apply only if a different intention of the deceased cannot be made out by the court.[100] Considering it to be a default standard helps to achieve appropriate outcomes, especially in cases where only the name or form of the intended bequest changes, but the substance (value) remains in the estate of the deceased (eg stock or shares under a different name).[101]

Under German law, this rule applies to specific legacies where, for whatever reason, the subject-matter of the legacy is not part of the testator's assets at his or her death (§ 2169 BGB). The rule is considered to be one of construction and is based on the idea that a typical testator does not wish to dispose of assets which are not part of his property at death.[102] However, if the testator's intention is to be understood in the sense that the asset shall go to the beneficiary even though it is not part of the estate at the time of death, the legacy remains effective and obliges the heir to procure the asset for the beneficiary (*Verschaffungsvermächtnis*).[103] Similarly, under Austrian law, a legacy concerning a specific asset is presumed to be revoked if the asset was sold or the testator gave it away before death, unless the contrary is proven (§ 724 ABGB). Under French law (Article 1038 Code civil), a legacy is similarly considered to be revoked if the testator sells or gives away the asset before he or she dies, again unless the contrary is proven.[104]

What can be seen here is that the rule on ademption is deeply rooted in all legal systems, and is usually implemented as a default standard allowing a court to override it on the basis of evidence indicating a contrary intention by the testator.

IV. Conclusion

The analysis above has shown that there are three types of default rules in succession law, here described as subsidiary default rules, suppletory default rules and default standards.

Intestacy rules serve as subsidiary default rules insofar as they apply when a person dies totally or partially intestate. Their function is thus to provide for a complete and

[100] See Kerridge (n 87) para 14-38.
[101] *Re Slater* [1907] 1 Ch 665; Kerridge (n 87) paras 14-39 et seq.
[102] Mugdan (n 28) 76.
[103] H Lange and K Kuchinke, *Erbrecht* 5th edn (Munich, CH Beck, 2001) 644.
[104] Terré, Lequette and Gaudemet (n 62) 413–15.

exhaustive succession regime that is at once simple, clear and predictable. This is why intestacy rules operate mechanically without taking into account the actual intent of the person who died intestate.

The rules on wills may operate – first – as suppletory default rules, in the sense that they fill the gaps left in a will without having regard to the actual intent of the deceased as it may be determined by extrinsic evidence. Typical examples are the rule on representation according to which a predeceased child in a will is replaced by his or her descendants, or the rule according to which a will in favour of a spouse lapses with divorce.

In many jurisdictions, the law on wills also contains – second – discretionary default standards. Default standards grant courts discretion to establish probable intent on a case-by-case basis. Hence, these standards apply only if the beneficiaries cannot prove the contrary intent, either by the will or by some other extrinsic evidence. Among the examples above, the ademption rule is understood as a default standard in most legal systems cited here, even though the point is debated in English law. The rules on representation and on divorced spouses mentioned above are read as standards in some jurisdictions and as rules in others, with no evidence of contrary intent being allowed in the latter.

Some authors have argued that default standards should generally be avoided in succession law, since they create litigation costs for the beneficiaries and fail to bring about an obvious advantage for testators, who are of course free to make a new will whenever they feel that the default rule no longer accommodates their wishes.[105] Even though certainty, predictability and efficiency clearly speak against default standards in succession law, the goal of achieving a just result for the specific testator ex post may convince a lawmaker to introduce default standards into the law governing wills.

From a comparative perspective it becomes clear that both the law on intestacy and the law on wills pursue one common goal, which is implementing the presumed intention of the average testator. However, presumed intention is not an empirical, but a normative concept that allows for a variety of different policy goals to be effectuated by succession law. The historical sources of the concept in succession law confirm this conclusion, since 'presumed intention' was always about what an average testator *ought to have* wanted rather than what an average testator *actually* wanted. As a consequence, default rules in succession law have long served numerous policy goals.

The fact that succession law rules are based on an amalgamation of different policy goals has been heavily criticised in the US.[106] According to this view, the 'once-central value' of the deceased's intent has been marginalised for an amorphous bunch of policy goals leading to an 'identity crisis' of the whole field of succession law, while the 'only goal of succession law default rules should be to effectuate testator's intent'.[107] This criticism, however, is ahistorical and unfounded. It is ahistorical because succession law has always served a variety of different policy goals which have been changing over time according to what eventually came to be considered just and fair. But it is also unfounded because the concept of presumed intention is normative, which means that

[105] Hirsch (n 3) 1065–66, 1079.
[106] Hirsch (n 3) 1036 et seq; Tritt (n 3) 274: 'identity crisis'.
[107] Tritt (n 3) 336.

a variety of different policy considerations have inevitably influenced succession law rules over time.

Hence, it is evident that the expectations of a typical testator can always only be one aspect to be taken into account when defining the default rules under intestacy and the law governing wills. In order to ascertain the expectations of an average person, it might be helpful to conduct quantitative and qualitative sociological research, but such studies can never be conclusive, since what becomes the law, after all, is the result of a policy-oriented process that needs to be in line with the basic principles of fairness and non-discrimination as well as with the other values underpinning the rules on intestacy.

It has thus become clear that default rules, both in the law on intestacy and the law on wills, serve a variety of different policy goals, which can nonetheless all be accommodated under the normative concept of presumed intention. Presumed intention thus serves as a vehicle for accommodating a variety of different policy goals by adjusting succession law default rules not only to changing expectations of the average testator, but also to changing fundamental values.

12

The (Changing) Role of Default Rules in Civil Procedure and Arbitration

GIESELA RÜHL

I. Introduction

This chapter is devoted to 'default rules in civil procedure'. And at first sight this is an unlikely topic. After all, civil procedure is traditionally regarded as the stronghold of rigorous procedures and mandatory rules – and not of party autonomy.[1] Party autonomy, however, is the very basis of default rules – because default rules only come into the picture when the parties are free to regulate their own affairs but abstain from doing so. Seen from this perspective, the topic of this chapter is a non-topic. However, a closer look reveals that the story is more complicated. In fact, it seems that there is more room for party autonomy in civil procedure than we tend to think and that, in fact, the room for party autonomy has recently been growing. The chapter will shed some light on this observation.

However, the chapter will not stop here but also look at the role of default rules in arbitration. This is because party autonomy is commonly regarded as the cornerstone of arbitration in the sense that parties are free to agree on arbitration and to design the rules of procedure.[2] With a view to party autonomy the law of arbitration is, thus, usually regarded as the complete opposite of civil procedure. However, here again the story is more complicated. In fact, as in civil procedure, there are recent developments that show that the role of party autonomy is changing. In particular, there are court

[1] See, for example, O Bülow, 'Dispositives Civilprozessrecht und die verbindliche Kraft der Rechtsordnung' (1881) 64 *Archiv für die civilistische Praxis* 1; K Hellwig, 'Prozeßhandlung und Rechtsgeschäft' in Juristische Fakultät der Friedrich-Wilhelms-Universität Berlin (ed), *Festgabe für Otto Gierke* (Breslau, Marcus, 1910) 41, 88 et seq. See for a detailed and nuanced overview G Wagner, *Prozeßverträge. Privatautonomie im Verfahrensrecht* (Tübingen, Mohr Siebeck, 1998) 49 et seq (with further references).

[2] See only N Blackaby, C Partasides and A Redfern, *Redfern and Hunter on International Arbitration* (Oxford, OUP, 2023) paras 2.01, 6.07; G Born, *International Commercial Arbitration* (Alphen aan den Rijn, Kluwer Law International, 2021) 229–30, 2295; J Lew, L Mistelis and S Kröll, *Comparative Commercial Arbitration* (The Hague/London/New York, Kluwer Law International, 2003) 4, para 1-11 as well as F Ferrari and F Rosenfeld, 'Limitations to Party Autonomy in International Arbitration' in S Kröll, AK Bjorklund and F Ferrari (eds), *Cambridge Compendium of International commercial and Investment Arbitration* (Cambridge, CUP, 2023) 47–48 (with further references).

judgments, including from the European Court of Justice and the European Court of Human Rights, that limit both parties' freedom to agree on arbitration and their freedom to design the applicable rules of procedure.

The chapter will offer some thoughts on these two trends, that is, the increasing role of party autonomy in civil procedure and the decreasing role of party autonomy in arbitration. It will show that the two fields of law – which are coming from opposing ends of the party autonomy spectrum – are currently in the process of converging.[3] The chapter will, hence, add to the debate about the increasing 'arbitralization of litigation'[4] on the one hand and the increasing 'judicialization of arbitration'[5] on the other. Before going into the details, however, two caveats are in order.

First, the chapter will discuss the role of default rules in civil procedure and arbitration with a reference to the role of party autonomy. However, this is not to say that the role (or reach) of default rules is defined by the role (or reach) of party autonomy.[6] In fact, while there is significant overlap, the realm of party autonomy is broader than the realm of default rules. Specifically, party autonomy does not only cover cases in which there is a rule that regulates a certain state of affair and (explicitly or implicitly) allows parties to agree to proceed otherwise (so-called norm disposition). It also covers situations in which the law simply allows the parties to agree to proceed in a certain way (so-called rights disposition).[7] If, for example, the law allows the claimant to withdraw his claim before the oral hearing (as does § 269 of the German Code of Civil Procedure) and the claimant agrees with the defendant that he will actually do so, party autonomy is at work. However, the agreement will not lead to the derogation of any otherwise applicable legal rule. It follows that the existence and exercise of party autonomy does not necessarily require the existence of a default rule.[8]

Second, the chapter will discuss the role of default and mandatory rules with regards to civil procedure and arbitration as such – and not with regards to the substantive laws that courts or arbitration tribunals are bound to apply. This means that the chapter will

[3] See for a similar observation P Bookman, 'The Adjudication Business' (2022) 45 *Yale Journal of International Law* 227, 275–76; P Bookman, 'Arbitral Courts' (2021) 61 *Virginia Journal of International Law* 161, 169 et seq; A King, 'Global Civil Procedure' (2021) 62 *Harvard Journal of International Law* 223.

[4] See for this term and this trend G Antonopoulou, 'The "Arbitralization" of Courts: The Role of International Commercial Arbitration in the Establishment and the Procedural Design of International Commercial Courts' [2023] *Journal of Dispute Settlement* 1; Bookman, 'The Adjudication Business' (n 3) 276 et seq; Bookman, 'Arbitral Courts' (n 3) 179 et seq. See generally on the "privatization of procedure" RG Bone, 'Party Rulemaking: Making Procedural Rules through Party Choice' (2012) 90 *Texas L Rev* 1329; D Hoffman, 'Whither Bespoke Procedure?' 2014 *Univ of Illinois L Rev* 389; E Effron, 'Ousted' (2018) 98 *Boston Univ L Rev* 127; D Kapeliuk and A Klement, 'Changing the Litigation Game: An Ex Ante Perspective on Contractualized Procedures' (2013) 91 *Texas L Rev* 1475; J Resnik, 'Procedure as Contract' (2005) 80 *Notre Dame L Rev* 593.

[5] See, for example, C Brower, 'W(h)ither International Commercial Arbitration?' (2008) 27 *Arbitration International* 181; R Gerbay, 'Is the End Nigh Again? An Empirical Assessment of the "Judicialization" of International Arbitration' (2014) 25 *American Review of International Arbitration* 223; T Stipanowich, 'Arbitration: The New "Litigation"' 2010 *Univ of Illinois L Rev* 1; A Stone Sweet and F Grisel, *The Evolution of International Arbitration: Judicialization, Governance, Legitimacy* (Oxford, OUP, 2017) 84 et seq; L Trakman and H Montgomery, 'The "Judicialization" of International Commercial Arbitration: Pitfall or Virtue?' (2017) 30 *Leiden Journal of International Law* 405.

[6] Wagner (n 1) 53.

[7] See for this distinction Wagner (n 1) 52 et seq.

[8] Wagner (n 1) 53.

not delve into the question of whether and to what extent courts and arbitration tribunals have to apply (overriding) mandatory rules to the substance of a dispute.[9]

II. Default Rules and Party Autonomy in the Law of Civil Procedure

As mentioned at the beginning of this chapter, the law of civil procedure is traditionally regarded as the stronghold of mandatory rules. It is usually conceived as part of public law[10] and as such beyond the reach of the parties.[11] Referring to the Roman principles of 'ius publicum privatorum pactis mutari non potest'[12] and 'privatorum conventio juri publico non derogat'[13] it is generally held that parties have no or little say in the design and the conduct of state court proceedings.[14] A closer look, however, reveals that this view is misleading at best.[15] In fact, there is room for party autonomy on (at least) three different levels.

A. Choosing whether to Litigate: Arbitration Clauses

The first level relates to the question of *whether* to litigate a dispute at all. In fact, parties are usually free to decide whether they want to take their case to state courts – or whether they want to submit disputes to arbitration instead. The very existence of arbitration – and the world-wide acceptance of arbitration as an alternative dispute resolution mechanism – thus suggests that the entire law of civil procedure for litigation in state courts is, in fact, a set of default rules that only comes into play if the parties decide not to go to arbitration. This holds true even though there are certain requirements that need to be met to opt out of the state's civil justice system. In particular, the dispute needs to be arbitrable[16] and the arbitration agreement needs to be binding and valid under the applicable law.[17] Also, states reserve the right to review arbitral awards for compliance with public policy concerns before they are recognised and enforced.[18] However, all this does not change the fact that civil justice systems around the world, as a matter of principle, allow parties to (completely) opt out of the public court system.

[9] See for a detailed discussion G Bermann, 'Mandatory Rules of Law in International Arbitration' in F Ferrari and S Kröll (eds), *Conflict of Laws in International Arbitration* (Berlin/New York, Otto Schmidt/De Gruyter European Law Pub, 2010) 325 et seq.

[10] Wagner (n 1) 14–15 (with further references). See for a comprehensive comparative account A Nylund and A Cabral, 'General Report: Contractualisation of Civil Litigation' in A Nylund and A Cabral (eds), *Contractualisation of Civil Litigation* (Cambridge, Intersentia, 2023) 3 et seq.

[11] See for a detailed discussion Wagner (n 1) 48 et seq.

[12] D. 2.14.38 (Papin. 2 quaest.).

[13] D. 50.17.45.1 (Ulp. 30 ad ed.). See also D. 26.7.5.7 (Ulp. 35 ad ed.).

[14] See for a comprehensive and nuanced account Wagner (n 1) 57 et seq.

[15] Wagner (n 1) 57 et seq. See also with a view to US law HN Aragaki, 'Arbitration: Creature of Contract, Pillar of Procedure' (2016) 8 *Yearbook on Arbitration and Mediation* 2 et seq, 8–9, 10–11; Bone (n 4) 1329 et seq. See for a comprehensive comparative account Nylund and Cabral (n 10) 3 et seq.

[16] See below s III.A.i.

[17] See below s III.A.i.

[18] See below s III.A.ii.

B. Choosing where to Litigate: International Choice of Court Clauses

The second level, on which there is room for party autonomy in civil procedure, relates to the question of *where* to litigate. Even if parties decide to go to court rather than to arbitration, they may usually choose the place of litigation. Especially with regards to international transactions, parties may choose the courts of the country where they wish to litigate their dispute. According to Article 25 of the Brussels Ia Regulation[19] and according to Article 3 of the 2005 Hague Choice of Court Convention,[20] for example, parties may enter into a choice of court agreement which, if found to be valid (and exclusive), will lead the chosen court to accept jurisdiction while other courts, if seized, will (have to) decline to hear the case.[21] It follows that parties to an international transaction are essentially free to choose the law of civil procedure by choosing the forum. And this is also what parties do in practice. In fact, they very often choose to litigate before English courts, notably the London Commercial Court,[22] and, hence, make a choice in favour of the English law of civil procedure.

However, it should be noted that the parties' right to choose the competent court and, hence, the law of civil procedure is limited in that parties may only choose the law of civil procedure as such, that is, as a 'package'. In contrast, they cannot combine procedural rules from different countries. In that respect, a choice of court agreement is remarkedly different from a choice of law agreement which can usually relate to the entire relationship or only to parts of it. Take, for example, a choice of contract law. According to Article 3(1) of the Rome I Regulation,[23] which applies to disputes before EU Member State courts and in its retained form to disputes before British courts, the parties may choose the applicable law for the entire contract or for parts of the contract. They may, hence, submit one part of the contract to one law and another part to some other law. In civil procedure, in contrast, parties may not submit parts of the procedure to one law and another part to some other law. They may only choose the law of civil procedure as such by choosing the forum. Nonetheless, choice of court clauses offer parties some choice with regards to the rules of procedure showing, again, that the law of civil procedure may be conceived, in essence, as a set of default rules.

[19] Regulation (EU) No 1215/2012 of the European Parliament and of the Council of 12 December 2012 on jurisdiction and the recognition and enforcement of judgments in civil and commercial matters (recast) [2012] OJ L351/1.

[20] Hague Convention of 30 June 2005 on Choice of Court Agreements, available at www.hcch.net/en/instruments/conventions/full-text/?cid=98.

[21] See Art 31(3) of the Brussel Ia Regulation and Arts 5 and 6 of the Hague Choice of Court Convention.

[22] According to numerous studies, English courts and especially the London Commercial Court are the courts most frequently chosen by parties to settle disputes. See, for example, S Vogenauer and C Hodges, *Civil Justice Systems in Europe: Implications for Choice of Law and Choice of Forum – A Business Survey* (2008) 25 et seq, available at www.fondation-droitcontinental.org/fr/wp-content/uploads/2013/12/oxford_civil_justice_survey_-_summary_of_results_final.pdf. See for a detailed analysis of the available empirical data G Rühl, *Building Competence in Commercial Law in the Members States, Study for the European Parliament's Committee on Legal Affairs* (2018) 29 et seq available at www.europarl.europa.eu/thinktank/en/document/IPOL_STU(2018)604980.

[23] Regulation (EC) No 593/2008 of the European Parliament and of the Council of 17 June 2008 on the law applicable to contractual obligations (Rome I) [2008] OJ L177/6.

C. Choosing how to Litigate: Conduct of the Proceedings

The third level, on which there is room for party autonomy, finally, relates to the question of *how* to litigate, that is, the conduct of civil proceedings as such. It comes into the picture if the law of civil procedure of a particular country applies because the parties have chosen to litigate in that country. Insofar, the traditional view is that this is where party autonomy ends and the realm of mandatory rules begins. However, while many rules of civil procedure are, indeed, mandatory in nature, there are also a number of default rules.

i. Traditional Room for Party Autonomy: Examples from Germany and England

To begin with, there are a number of rules in civil procedure that have traditionally – and explicitly – been conceived as default rules. I shall demonstrate this by way of two examples.

The first example is to be found in German law and relates to the provisions on (subject-matter) competence of civil courts.[24] According to § 23(1) No 1 and § 71 of the German Court Constitution Act (Gerichtsverfassungsgesetz – GVG),[25] disputes with a value of up to € 5,000.00 will be heard by the local courts (Amtsgerichte), while disputes with a value above € 5,000.00 will be dealt with by the district courts (Landgerichte).[26] In addition, §§ 12, 17 of the German Code of Civil Procedure (Zivilprozessordnung – ZPO)[27] provide that a claim must usually be brought before the local or district court where the defendant has his or her domicile (Wohnsitz). However, German law – like other legal systems – allows parties to agree that other courts may hear a particular case (§§ 38, 40 of the German Code of Civil Procedure). Parties may, therefore, decide that their dispute will be heard by the district court rather than by the local court. And they may decide that the courts at the claimant's domicile instead of at the defendant's domicile are competent to hear the case. These rules on court competence to be found in the German are, hence, default rules.

That being said, it should be noted that the parties' right to determine the competent court is not without limits. In fact, there are instances where the parties may not agree on the court competence, meaning that the legally defined competence is mandatory. According to § 40(2) No 1 of the German Code of Civil Procedure, for example, a choice of court is inadmissible with regards to non-pecuniary claims which fall into the jurisdiction of the local courts by virtue of § 23 No 2 of the German Court Constitution Act. And by virtue of § 40(2) No 2 of the German Code of Civil Procedure, parties may not

[24] For more examples with regards to German law see Hellwig (n 1) 79 et seq; Wagner (n 1) 11 and 48 (referring to § 108(1) sentence 2, § 224(1) sentence 1, § 404(4), § 816(1), (2) and § 825(1) sentence 2 ZPO).

[25] An English language translation of the German Court Constitution Act (current as of 2023) is available at www.gesetze-im-internet.de/englisch_gvg/englisch_gvg.html.

[26] Exceptions from this rule are to be found in § 23 No 2 GVG.

[27] An English language translation of the German Code of Civil Procedure (current as of 2013) is available at www.gesetze-im-internet.de/englisch_zpo/englisch_zpo.html.

choose where to litigate if a court has exclusive jurisdiction. The latter is the case, for example, with regards to claims *in rem* relating to immovable property.[28]

The second example originates in English law and concerns the determination of the applicable substantive law. Here, famously, English courts will only apply foreign law to the substance of a dispute insofar as the parties plead and prove foreign law.[29] If the responsible party fails to do so, that is, if foreign law is either not pleaded or not sufficiently proved, English courts will simply apply English law.[30] It follows that the English law of civil procedure allows parties to plead and prove foreign law but does not require them to do so. Rather, it contains a – very pragmatic – default rule that leads to the application of English law.[31]

In the light of the above it is fair to conclude that the concept of default rules – contrary to common belief – is well-known in the law of civil procedure. However, two caveats should be made. First, there is no agreement across jurisdictions about which provisions may or may not be conceived as default rules. Take, for example, the determination of the applicable law. While English courts apply the above-mentioned default rule and apply English law if the parties do not plead and prove the content of foreign law,[32] courts in Civil law countries, notably Germany, always resort to the rules of choice of law to determine the applicable substantive law.[33] In Civil law countries there is, hence, no default rule that automatically leads to the application of the *lex fori* if the parties do not plead and prove foreign law.

Second, while there is agreement across countries that rules in civil procedure may explicitly be default rules, it is unclear whether the default nature of a rule may also be

[28] See § 24 ZPO.

[29] See only *Roberts v Soldiers, Sailors, Airmen and Families Association* [2020] EWHC 994 (QB), para 187; *FS Cairo (Nile Plaza) LLC v Lady Brownlie* [2021] UKSC 45, [2022] AC 995, paras 100 et seq as well as A Critchley, *The Application of Foreign Law in the British and German Courts* (Oxford/London/New York, Hart Publishing 2022) 3–4; A Dickinson, 'United Kingdom' in J Basedow, G Rühl, F Ferrari and P de Miguel Asensio (eds), *Encyclopedia of Private International Law*, vol 3 (Cheltenham/Northampton, Edward Elgar, 2017) 2612, 2615-16; C Esplugues and G Palao, 'Foreign Law, Application and Ascertainment' in J Basedow, G Rühl, F Ferrari and P de Miguel Asensio (eds), *Encyclopedia of Private International Law*, vol 1 (Cheltenham/Northampton, Edward Elgar, 2017) 769, 771; R Fentiman, *Foreign Law in English Courts* (Oxford, OUP, 1998) 3–4; T Hartley, 'Pleading and Proof of Foreign Law: The Major European Systems Compared' (1996) 45 *ICLQ* 45 (1996) 271, 273, 282 et seq; C Trautmann, 'Ausländisches Recht vor deutschen und englischen Gerichten' [2006] *Zeitschrift für Europäisches Privatrecht* 283, 290.

[30] See only *MCC Proceeds Inc v Bishopsgate Investment Trust plc* [1999] CLC 417 para 10; *PT Pan Indonesia Bank Limited TBK v Marconi Communications International Limited* [2005] EWCA Civ 422, para 70; *Sharp v Ministry of Defence* [2007] EWHC 224 (QB), paras 11–12; *FS Cairo (Nile Plaza) LLC v Lady Brownlie* [2021] UKSC 45, [2022] AC 995, paras 100 et seq; Critchley (n 29) 4; Dickinson (n 29) 2616; Esplugues and Palao (n 29) 771; Fentiman (n 29) 4; Hartley (n 29) 273, 282–83; Trautmann (n 29) 302–03.

[31] *Shaker v Al-Bedrawi* [2002] EWCA Civ 1452, para 65; R Fentiman, 'Laws, Foreign Laws, and Facts' (2006) 59 *Current Legal Problems* 391, 421 et seq; Hartley (n 29) 285. See, however, the discussion in *FS Cairo (Nile Plaza) LLC v Lady Brownlie* [2021] UKSC 45, [2022] AC 995, paras 113 et seq in which Lord Leggatt distinguishes between cases in which application of foreign law is not pleaded and those in which it is pleaded, but not sufficiently proven. According to Lord Leggat, English law applies in the first case because there is a default rule that English law applies whereas English law applies in the second case because there is a presumption that, in the absence of evidence to the contrary, foreign law is presumed to be the same as English law.

[32] See for possible exceptions Critchley (n 29) 104 et seq; Fentiman (n 29) 4; Trautmann (n 29) 291 et seq.

[33] Critchley (n 29) 95–96; Fentiman (n 29) 269; J von Hein, 'Germany' in J Basedow, G Rühl, F Ferrari and P de Miguel Asensio (eds), *Encyclopedia of Private International Law*, vol 3 (Cheltenham/Northampton, Edward Elgar, 2017) 2101, 2104; Hartley (n 29) 273, 275; Trautmann (n 29) 287–88.

the result of interpretation.[34] In fact, while some authors believe that there is no room for such implicit default rules, others are more open. Specifically, it has recently been argued that rules of civil procedure should always be conceived as default rules unless they serve to protect public interests or private (weaker or third) parties.[35] A comprehensive analysis of this – very country-specific – discussion, however, is beyond the scope of this chapter.

ii. Recent Trends: The Case of International Commercial Courts

In addition to the traditional default rules, that is, default rules that have long been recognised by laws of civil procedure, there are also default rules that are of more recent origin. In fact, there are reasons to believe that the number of default rules and, hence, the room for party autonomy has been growing in recent years.[36] A case in point are international commercial courts which have been established over the past two decades in the Gulf region (Abu Dhabi,[37] Dubai,[38] Qatar),[39] in Asia (China,[40] Kazakhstan,[41] Singapore)[42] and in Europe (Netherlands,[43] France,[44] Germany[45]). Despite their name these courts are national courts (or court chambers) which are designed to deal with international commercial cases.[46] And even though they differ in detail, it is fair to say that they all have one feature in common: they all attempt to offer attractive dispute resolution through procedural innovations.[47] In particular, they all attempt to attract international litigants by borrowing heavily from international commercial arbitration, notably by giving more room to party autonomy.[48] I will demonstrate this by way of three examples.

a. English as Court Language

The first example relates to the court language, notably the use of English as a court language. Insofar, the traditional position of all countries is that the language

[34] See for a detailed presentation of the various views Wagner (n 1) 48 et seq.
[35] Wagner (n 1) 64 et seq, 77 et seq.
[36] See for a more detailed and much broader comparative analysis Nylund and Cabral (n 10).
[37] Abu Dhabi Global Market Courts (ADGM Courts): www.adgm.com/adgm-courts.
[38] Dubai International Financial Centre Courts (DIFC Courts): www.difccourts.ae.
[39] Qatar International Court and Dispute Resolution Center (QICDRC): www.qicdrc.gov.qa.
[40] China International Commercial Court (CICC): https://cicc.court.gov.cn/html/1/219/index.html.
[41] Astana International Financial Centre Court (AIFC Courts): https://court.aifc.kz/en.
[42] Singapore International Commercial Court (SICC): www.sicc.gov.sg.
[43] Netherlands Commercial Court: www.rechtspraak.nl/English/NCC/Pages/default.aspx.
[44] International Commercial Chamber at the Paris Court of Appeal (ICCP-CA): www.cours-appel.justice.fr/paris/presentation-generale-ccip-ca-iccp-ca.
[45] Various chambers at various regional courts (Landgerichte). See for a detailed presentation T Riehm and Q Thomas, 'Germany' in M Yip and G Rühl (eds), *New International Commercial Courts. A Comparative Perspective* (Cambridge, Intersentia, 2024) 293, 302 et seq.
[46] See for a detailed account M Yip and G Rühl, 'General Report: New International Commercial Courts' in M Yip and G Rühl (eds), *New International Commercial Courts. A Comparative Perspective* (Cambridge, Intersentia, 2024) 4 et seq.
[47] Yip and Rühl (n 46) 9 et seq.
[48] Yip and Rühl (n 46) 38 et seq. See also Antonopoulou (n 4) 7 et seq; Bookman, 'Arbitral Courts' (n 3) 180–81.

to be used in courts is the language that is officially spoken in the country in which the court is located.[49] In Germany, for example, the Court Constitution Act (Gerichtsverfassungsgesetz – GVG) establishes that the language of the courts is German meaning that court proceedings have to be conducted in German.[50] However, with regards to international commercial courts more and more countries are willing to depart from that rule.[51] In fact, with the exception of China where proceedings before the Chinese International Commercial Courts must be conducted in 'languages commonly used in China',[52] allowing English language proceedings seems to be an important – if not the most important – point on the agenda of all countries that have recently established international commercial courts.[53]

Take, for example, the international commercial courts established in Abu Dhabi, Dubai, Qatar, Kazakhstan and the Netherlands.[54] They offer fully fledged English language proceedings from beginning to end – if the parties agree on English as the language of the proceedings. The parties may, hence, file their briefs and all their statements in English, the oral hearings will be held in English and witnesses will be examined in English. In addition, the courts will communicate with the parties in English and write all orders, decisions and the final judgment in English. The traditional rule that court proceedings have to be conducted in the local language is, thus, effectively converted into a default rule for the purposes of proceedings before these international commercial courts.

That being said, it should be noted that other international commercial courts adopt a more cautious approach to the use of English as a court language. Examples relate to France and Germany.[55] In both of these countries, international commercial courts are only allowed to conduct the oral hearing in the English language and to receive documents in English, whereas submissions, court orders or judgments must be drafted in German and French, respectively. The use of English as a court language is accordingly limited. However, it should be noted that the German legislator has recently adopted a law[56] that will affect the legal situation in Germany. The law allows the German federal states (Bundesländer) to establish so-called commercial chambers at selected district courts (Landgerichte) that will,

[49] Note that in countries where more than one language is spoken or where a different language is spoken by a minority, parties usually have a choice which language to use in courts. According to § 184 sentence 2 of the German Court Constitution Act (Gerichtsverfassungsgesetz – GVG), for example, Sorbs may speak Sorbian before the courts in the home districts of the Sorbian population, ie in some parts of Saxony and Brandenburg. In a similar vein, parties may choose to either speak English or Welsh in Welsh courts.

[50] § 184 sentence 2 GVG.

[51] Bookman, 'Arbitral Courts' (n 3) 182.

[52] Civil Procedure Law (2021 Amendment) art 11. See further Z Huo and F Guo, 'China' in M Yip and G Rühl (eds), *New International Commercial Courts. A Comparative Perspective* (Cambridge, Intersentia, 2024) 175, 194 et seq.

[53] Yip and Rühl (n 46) 36 et seq.

[54] ibid.

[55] Yip and Rühl (n 46) 37 et seq. See for details regarding France and Germany Cerqueira, 'France' in M Yip and G Rühl (eds), *New International Commercial Courts. A Comparative Perspective* (Cambridge, Intersentia, 2024) 247, 264 et seq; Riehm and Thomas (n 45) 309 et seq.

[56] Gesetz zur Stärkung des Justizstandortes Deutschland durch Einführung von Commercial Courts und der Gerichtssprache Englisch in der Zivilgerichtsbarkeit (Justizstandort-Stärkungsgesetz), 7 October 2024, Bundesgesetzblatt (BGBl.) 2024, I, No. 302.

if the parties so wish, conduct (certain)[57] civil proceedings completely in English.[58] The law further provides that appeals against decisions of these commercial chambers will be heard (completely) in English at second instance in the higher regional courts (Oberlandesgerichte)[59] and possibly also at third instance in the Federal Court of Justice (Bundesgerichtshof).[60] As in Abu Dhabi, Dubai, Qatar, Kazakhstan and the Netherlands, the legal provision that requires court proceedings to be conducted (completely) in the local language will, therefore, most likely be turned into a mere default rule very soon.

b. Taking of Evidence

The second example that shows that the role of party autonomy and, hence, the number of default rules is growing before international commercial courts, relates to the taking of evidence. In fact, while ordinary courts are bound to apply the local rules of evidence, some international commercial courts allow parties to decide that other rules should be applicable.[61]

A prime example is the Singapore International Commercial Court (SICC): it may apply rules of evidence found under any foreign law or otherwise if the parties so agree.[62] Parties are, thus, given the power to (i) disapply by agreement the normally applicable national rules of evidence to be found in the law of Singapore and (ii) to apply some other rules of evidence instead. These other rules may either be taken from a foreign country or, interestingly, from other sources, notably non-state, soft law instruments. According to the SICC User Guides, the parties may, for example, agree on the application of the IBA Rules on the Taking of Evidence in International Arbitration.[63] It follows that before the Singapore International Commercial Court the local Singapore rules on evidence are downgraded to mere default rules that only apply if the parties do not agree otherwise.[64]

[57] Note, that according to the new law only 1) disputes between professionals (Unternehmer), 2) disputes arising out of or in connection with the acquisition of a company or shares in a company, and 3) disputes between a company and members of the management or the board qualify for English language proceedings. See for details §§ 184a (1), 119b(1) GVG as amended by the Justizstandort-Stärkungsgesetz (n 56).

[58] See § 184a (1) No 1 GVG as amended by the Justizstandort-Stärkungsgesetz (n 56).

[59] ibid.

[60] The Federal Court of Justice, however, may decline to hear cases in English and continue the proceedings in German. See § 184b (1) No 1 GVG as amended by the Justizstandort-Stärkungsgesetz (n 56).

[61] Antonopoulou (n 4) 8–9; Bookman, 'Arbitral Courts' (n 3) 180–81.

[62] Section 18K Supreme Court of Judicature Act; SICC Rules, Order 13, Rule 15(1) and (2). See also J Ho Lau, 'Singapore' in M Yip and G Rühl, *New International Commercial Courts: A Comparative Perspective* (Cambridge, Intersentia, 2024) 411, 426; Z Huo and M Yip, 'Comparing the International Commercial Courts of China with the Singapore International Commercial Court' (2019) 68 *ICLQ* 903, 934; J Landbrecht, 'The Singapore International Commercial Court (SICC) – an Alternative to International Arbitration?' (2016) 34 *ASA Bulletin* 112, 120; L The, 'The Singapore International Commercial Court' (2017) 11 *Dispute Resolution International* 143, 146; M Yip, 'The Singapore International Commercial Court: The Future of Litigation?' (2019) 12 *Erasmus L Rev* 82, 88–89.

[63] SICC Court User Guides, Note 4 – Disapplication of Singapore Evidence Law, para 25, available at www.sicc.gov.sg/docs/default-source/legislation-rules-pd/20211221-sicc-user-guides-wef-1-apr.pdf.

[64] With regards to the SICC it is worth noting that it allows parties to prove foreign law by mere party submission (cf Section 18L Supreme Court of Judicature Act, SICC Rules, Order 16, Rule 8). The mandatory common law rule that the content of foreign law must be proven through expert evidence is, thus, equally

The situation is similar in the Netherlands with regards to the national Dutch rules of evidence in proceedings before the Netherlands International Commercial Court (NICC). According to Article 153 of the Dutch Code of Civil Procedure and Article 8.3 of the Rules applicable to the NICC,[65] parties may, within certain limits, enter into an agreement to depart from the otherwise applicable Dutch rules of evidence.[66] And even though these provisions – in contrast to the provisions to be found in Singapore – do not detail which rules of evidence the parties may choose to apply instead, it becomes clear that the normal Dutch rules of evidence can by displaced by party agreement turning them, like in Singapore, into mere default rules.

c. Privacy and Confidentiality

A final example that highlights the growing importance of party autonomy before international commercial courts relates to privacy and confidentiality of court proceedings.[67] While publicity is one of the hallmark features of court proceedings requiring courts to conduct their proceedings publicly,[68] some international commercial courts allow parties to agree that proceedings should be conducted (completely or partly) in private.[69]

A case in point is, again, the Singapore International Commercial Court. It allows any party to apply for three different types of confidentiality orders: (i) an order that the case be heard in private, (ii) an order that no person may reveal or publish any information or document relating to the case or (iii) an order that the court file be sealed.[70] And while it is ultimately for the SICC to decide whether to issue the order or not, the parties' wishes play an important role in the decision-making process. In fact, according to the applicable rules, the SICC has to take into account any agreement that the parties have reached with regards to the confidentiality of the proceedings.[71] The traditional rules on the publicity of court hearings – and court proceedings as such – are, thus, largely placed into the hands of the parties.[72]

The situation will be similar in Germany, under the earlier mentioned, recently adopted law. It allows courts, upon application of one party, to classify relevant information as confidential if they constitute a trade secret within the meaning of § 2 No 1 of the Act on the Protection of Trade Secrets (Gesetz zum Schutz von Geschäftsgeheimnissen – GeschGehG).[73] If the court decides to grant the application, §§ 16 to 20 of the Act on

turned into a mere default rule. See also Z Huo and M Yip (n 62) 933; Landbrecht (n 62) 120; The (n 62) 146; Yip (n 62) 89.

[65] Rules of Procedure for the International Commercial Chambers of the Amsterdam District Court (NCC District Court) and the Amsterdam Court of Appeal (NCC Court of Appeal), available at www.rechtspraak.nl/SiteCollectionDocuments/NCC-Rules2-rules.pdf.

[66] See for details E Bauw, 'Commercial Litigation in Europe in Transformation: The Case of the Netherlands Commercial Court' (2019) *Erasmus L Rev* 15, 18 et seq.

[67] Antonopoulou (n 4) 14–15.

[68] See, for example, Article 6(1) of the European Convention on Human Rights: 'In the determination of his civil rights and obligations …, everyone is entitled to a fair and public hearing'.

[69] Antonopoulou (n 4) 14–15; Bookman, 'Arbitral Courts' (n 3) 181.

[70] SICC Rules, Order 16, Rule 9(1). See also Huo and Yip (n 62) 934; Landbrecht (n 62) 120; The (n 62) 146; Yip (n 62) 90–91.

[71] SICC Rules, Order 16, Rule 9(2).

[72] See for a critical account Antonopoulou (n 4) 20–21.

[73] See § 273a ZPO as amended by the Justizstandort-Stärkungsgesetz (n 56).

the Protection of Trade Secrets will apply meaning that all information classified as a trade secret must be treated confidentially during and after the proceedings (§ 16(2) and § 18 of the Act on the Protection of Trade Secrets). In addition, the court may restrict access to the information at the request of a party and exclude the public from the oral hearing (§ 19 of the Act on the Protection of Trade Secrets). Like in Singapore, court proceedings can, thus, be conducted largely in private if the parties so wish. However, the new German provision will be both more and less far-reaching than its Singapore counterpart. It will be more far-reaching in that the provisions on privacy and confidentiality are not limited to international commercial courts but may be applied by all civil courts. It is less far-reaching in that only information that qualifies as a trade secret will be protected. In contrast, the proceedings as such cannot be kept from the public. In particular, the fact that there are proceedings pending cannot be kept private and confidential.

III. Default Rules and Party Autonomy and the Law of Arbitration

In light of the above it seems fair to say that the law of civil procedure is not as mandatory as we tend to think and that it leaves far more room for party autonomy than is commonly assumed. In fact, even though the law of civil procedure is part of public law and serves to protect public interests, there are more and more instances where parties are allowed to deviate from legal norms, thus, turning more and more provisions of civil procedure into default rules. Against this background, what is the situation in international arbitration?

As set out at the beginning, arbitration is fundamentally built on the principle of party autonomy.[74] This holds true for the commencement of arbitration proceedings which requires an agreement between the parties.[75] And it holds true for the conduct of the arbitration proceedings which is left to the parties.[76] However, and again as indicated at the beginning, the full story is more complicated.

A. Traditional Limits to Party Autonomy: Mandatory Rules and Public Policy

To begin with, there are a number of limitations that have traditionally been imposed on the parties. They relate to both the parties' freedom to submit a dispute to arbitration and their freedom to design the rules of procedure.[77]

[74] See references in n 2.

[75] See only Born (n 2) 229–30, 255; Lew, Mistelis and Kröll (n 2) 99, paras 6-1 et seq; Blackaby, Partasides and Redfern (n 2) para 2.01.

[76] See for a detailed discussion Born (n 2) 2295 et seq; Lew, Mistelis and Kröll (n 2) 521, paras 21-1 et seq; Blackaby, Partasides and Redfern (n 2) paras 6.07, 6.09 et seq.

[77] See for a recent comprehensive account Ferrari and Rosenfeld (n 2) 49 et seq.

i. Limits as to whether to Arbitrate

The parties' right to submit a dispute to arbitration is traditionally limited through the concept of 'arbitrability'. Embodied, for example, in Articles II(1) and V(2) lit a) of the New York Convention,[78] it refers to the question of whether a particular dispute may be decided through arbitration or not. And while different national laws take different approaches and limit arbitrability in different situations, two categories of (potential) non-arbitrability can be distinguished.[79] The first category relates to the parties and excludes (or limits) arbitrability when one party is a state, a public entity or a public body (subjective arbitrability or abitrability *ratione personae*). The second category relates to the subject matter of the dispute and excludes (or limits) arbitrability when the subject matter relates to public law or touches upon public interests (objective arbitrability or arbitrability *ratione materiae*). The details are complicated and disputed – including the question of which law should be applied to determine arbitrability.[80] But the bottom line is that the arbitrability of a dispute traditionally limits the parties' right to submit a dispute to arbitration.

In a similar vein, the parties' right to go to arbitration is limited through the requirement, for example, in Article II(3) of the New York Convention, that the arbitration agreement – just like any other contract – needs to be valid and binding.[81] Again, the details are complex and disputed. In particular, it is disputed which (substantive) law determines the validity of the arbitration agreement if the parties have not agreed on the applicable law.[82] But irrespective of which law applies – the relevant law always establishes requirements for a valid arbitration agreement and thereby limits the parties' freedom to submit a dispute to arbitration.

ii. Limits as to how to Conduct the Proceedings

Further limits traditionally apply to the parties' right to design the arbitration proceedings. Certainly, the applicable law usually grants parties great freedom to agree on the

[78] The New York Convention on the Recognition and Enforcement of Foreign Arbitral Awards (short: New Yok Convention) was adopted on 10 June 1958 and has been ratified by more than 170 states, including Germany and the United Kingdom. For details see the information available at www.newyorkconvention.org.

[79] See for a detailed discussion Blackaby, Partasides and Redfern (n 2) paras 2.125, 2.128 et seq; Born (n 2) 1028–29, 1033–34; F Ferrari and F Rosenfeld (n 2) 63 et seq; E Gaillard and G Bermann, *Guide on the Convention on the Recognition and Enforcement of Foreign Arbitral Awards* (New York, Brill/Nijhoff, 2017) 245 et seq; Lew, Mistelis and Kröll (n 2) 187–88, para 9-2, 199, paras 9-35 et seq; D Quinke, 'Article V' in R Wolff (ed), *New York Convention: Convention on the Recognition and Enforcement of Foreign Arbitral Awards of 10 June 1958. Commentary* (Munich/Baden-Baden/Oxford, CH Beck/Nomos/Hart, 2019) 380 et seq, para 418 et seq.

[80] See for the choice of law aspects B Hanotiau, 'The Law Applicable to Arbitrability' (2014) 26 *Singapore Academy of Law Journal* 874 et seq; Gaillard and Bermann (n 79) 56 et seq; Lew, Mistelis and Kröll (n 2) 188 et seq, paras 9-5 et seq; R Wolff, 'Article II' in R Wolff, *New York Convention: Convention on the Recognition and Enforcement of Foreign Arbitral Awards of 10 June 1958. Commentary* (Munich/Baden-Baden/Oxford, CH Beck/Nomos/Hart, 2019) 143 et seq, para 159 et seq.

[81] See for a detailed account comprehensive account Ferrari and Rosenfeld (n 2) 49 et seq.

[82] See for a detailed discussion Blackaby, Partasides and Redfern (n 2) paras 3.12 et seq; Born (n 2) 526 et seq; Lew, Mistelis and Kröll (n 2) 108, paras 6-25 et seq; S Wilske and TJ Fox, 'Article II' in R Wolff (ed), *New York Convention: Convention on the Recognition and Enforcement of Foreign Arbitral Awards of 10 June 1958. Commentary* (Munich/Baden-Baden/Oxford, CH Beck/Nomos/Hart, 2019) 164, paras 228 et seq.

procedure to be followed by the arbitral tribunal.[83] For example, parties are allowed to choose between ad hoc or institutional arbitration, to agree on the means of communication and the procedure for the taking of evidence, or to set time limits for the termination of the proceedings. However, the *lex arbitri* – usually the law of the place of arbitration[84] – limits as to what the parties may do.[85] According to Article 19(1) of the UNCITRAL Model Law on International Commercial Arbitration,[86] for example, the parties' freedom to agree on the conduct of the arbitration proceedings is 'subject to the provisions of this Law', which indicates that there are certain mandatory provisions that the parties may not derogate from by agreement. And according to section 4(1) of the English Arbitration Act, the mandatory provisions set out in Schedule 1 have effect notwithstanding any agreement by the parties.[87] It follows that there are certain provisions that the parties cannot derogate from. And while not all arbitration laws label mandatory provisions as clearly as the English Arbitration Act, national laws largely agree that fundamental principles of arbitration limit the parties' freedom to design the arbitration proceedings.[88] A frequently cited example is the principle of equal treatment, enshrined, among others, in Article 18 of the UNCITRAL Model Law on International Commercial Arbitration and section 33 of the English Arbitration Act. It requires the arbitral tribunal to give both parties full opportunity of presenting their case.

Limits to the parties' freedom to design the arbitration proceedings, however, do not only follow from the *lex arbitri*. They also come from the provisions on recognition and enforcement of arbitral awards such as Article V(2)(b) of the New York Convention. The provisions state that recognition and enforcement may be refused if recognition would be contrary to the public policy of the country in which recognition and enforcement is sought.[89] And while Article V(2) only applies after an award has been rendered, it may have an ex ante effect on the conduct of proceedings since any arbitration

[83] See, for example, Article 19(1) of the UNCITRAL Model Law on International Commercial Arbitration; Section 1(b) of the English Arbitration Act 1996.

[84] See only Born (n 2) 1650 et seq; Lew, Mistelis and Kröll (n 2) 525, para 21-14; Blackaby, Partasides and Redfern (n 2) paras 3.42 et seq.

[85] See for a detailed discussion Born (n 2) 1651, 1671 et seq, 2318 et seq; Lew, Mistelis and Kröll (n 2) 525, paras 21-14 et seq; Blackaby, Partasides and Redfern (n 2) paras 3.50 et seq.

[86] The UNCITRAL Model Law on International Commercial Arbitration is a model law drafted and adopted by the United National Commission on International Trade Law (UNCITRAL) on 21 June 1985 and substantially revised in 2006. The model law is not binding but has been adopted in 88 states, including Germany and the United Kingdom. For details see the information available at https://uncitral.un.org/en/texts/arbitration/modellaw/commercial_arbitration/status.

[87] See for a similar approach S 4 of the (American) Revised Uniform Arbitration Act (RUAA).

[88] Blackaby, Partasides and Redfern (n 2) paras 3.50–51, 3.57; Born (n 2) 1706 et seq, 2326–27; Lew, Mistelis and Kröll (n 2) 525, paras 21-14 et seq. See generally on the question of how to distinguish mandatory and default rules in arbitration CR Drahozal, 'Default Rule Theory and International Arbitration (with Comments an Expanded Review and Ex Parte Interim Relief)' (2005) 5 *Transnational Dispute Management* 2.

[89] See for a detailed discussion of what public policy means and how it is interpreted in different jurisdictions Blackaby, Partasides and Redfern (n 2) paras 11.63, 11.110 et seq; Born (n 2) 3760 et seq; Ferrari and Rosenfeld (n 2) 65 et seq; Gaillard and Bermann (n 79) 254 et seq; Lew, Mistelis and Kröll (n 2) 722, paras 26-114 et seq; R Wolff, 'Article V' in R Wolff (ed), *New York Convention: Convention on the Recognition and Enforcement of Foreign Arbitral Awards of 10 June 1958. Article-by-Article commentary* (Munich/Baden-Baden/Oxford, CH Beck/Nomos/Hart, 2019) 402 et seq, paras 480 et seq. See also International Bar Association (IBA), Report on the Public Policy Exception in the New York Convention, October 2015.

proceeding has as its aim to produce an enforceable award.[90] When designing arbitration proceedings, parties are, therefore, well advised to comply with the public policy requirements of the country in which an award will most likely be enforced. In particular, they are well advised to comply with the most basic and fundamental procedural rules of that country: these rules form the so-called procedural public policy and comprise, for example, the right to be heard, the right to equal opportunity to present one's case and the principle of independence and impartiality of arbitrators.[91]

B. Recent Trends: The Case of Investment and Sports Arbitration

The above considerations show that the law of arbitration establishes a number of limits to the parties' freedom to agree on arbitration and to design the proceedings. However, by and large it is fair to say that the traditional limits still leave a lot of room for party autonomy. In fact, they can best be described as mere minimum standards that arbitration agreements and proceedings must comply with. The same cannot be said with regards to more recently introduced limits. They touch upon both the reach of arbitration as a dispute settlement mechanism and the way arbitration proceedings are conducted – and potentially have an enormous impact on the role of arbitration in the European Union and beyond.

i. Investment Arbitration and the Achmea *Case*

The first limitation relates to the field of investment arbitration and was brought about by the – by now – infamous *Achmea* judgment of the Court of Justice of the European Union (CJEU) in 2018.[92] The case revolved around the Dutch health insurance company Achmea which had sold health insurances in Slovakia following the opening of the Slovakian health insurance market in 2004. In 2006, Slovakia decided to partly undo the opening of its market. In particular, it decided to prohibit the distribution

[90] Blackaby, Partasides and Redfern (n 2) paras 9.15 et seq; Born (n 2) 2909 et seq; Lew, Mistelis and Kröll (n 2) 30, para 2-49.

[91] Blackaby, Partasides and Redfern (n 2) paras 6.13 et seq, 10.04; Born (n 2) 2318 et seq, 2326 et seq; Gaillard and Bermann (n 79) 267 et seq; Lew, Mistelis and Kröll (n 2) paras 21-2, 21-16 et seq; Wolff (n 89) 434 et seq, paras 522 et seq, 437 et seq, paras 530 et seq, 439 et seq, paras 537 et seq. See also International Bar Association (n 89) 14 et seq.

[92] CJEU, C-284/16 *Slovak Republic v Achmea BV* ECLI:EU:C:2018:158. See for a detailed discussion of the case only M Andenas and C Contartese, 'EU Autonomy and Investor-State Dispute Settlement under Inter Se Agreements between EU Member States: Achmea' (2019) 56 *CMLR* 157; A Dimopoulos, 'Achmea: The principle of autonomy and its implications for intra and extra-EU BITs' *EJIL: Talk!*, 27 March 2018; S Gáspár-Szilágyi, 'It Is not Just About Investor-State Arbitration: A Look at Case C-284/16, Achmea BV' (2018) 3 *European Papers* 357; B Hess, 'A European Law Reading of Achmea' *Conflictoflaws.net*, 8 March 2018; N Lavranos, 'Black Tuesday: The End of Intra-EU BITs' *Arbitration Blog*, 7 March 2018; S Hindelang, 'The Limited Immediate Effects of CJEU's Achmea Judgment' *Verfassungsblog*, 9 March 2018; P Niemelä, 'Achmea – A Perspective from International (Investment) Law' *European Law Blog*, 15 March 2018; D Restrepo Amariles, A Ardelan Farhadi and A Van Waeyenberge, 'Reconciling International Investment Law and European Union Law in the Wake of Achmea' (2020) 69 *ICLQ* 907; H Schepel, 'From Conflicts-Rules to Field Preemption: Achmea and the Relationship Between EU Law and International Investment Law and Arbitration' *European Law Blog*, 23 March 2018.

of profits generated by health insurance activities. Achmea, therefore, sought relief from the Slovak Republic before an arbitration tribunal established in Germany in accordance with the terms of a Bilateral Investment Treaty concluded between the Netherlands and the Czech and Slovak Federative Republic, the predecessor of the Slovak Republic.[93] The claim was eventually successful and Achmea was awarded a large sum of money by the tribunal. However, Slovakia lodged an appeal against the award with the competent German courts which eventually referred the case to the CJEU asking whether investment arbitration in intra-EU cases was in line with European Union law, in particular Articles 18, 267 and 344 Treaty on the Functioning of the European Union (TFEU). And the Court held – much to the surprise of everybody – that it was not.[94]

The CJEU argued that investment arbitration tribunals might be called upon to apply and interpret EU law without being able to submit preliminary references to the CJEU.[95] Allowing investor-state arbitration to go forward under these circumstances could, therefore, not ensure the full effectiveness of EU law.[96] As a consequence, the Court found that EU Member States were *not* allowed to settle intra-EU investor-state disputes by means of arbitration.[97] The Court, thus, effectively put an end to investor-state arbitration within the EU – and, hence, to party autonomy in intra-EU investment disputes. This holds also true because the Court, extended *Achmea* in a later decision to ad hoc arbitration agreements, that is, to arbitration agreements concluded between a Member State and an investor on an individual basis and outside of a Bilateral Investment Treaty.[98]

ii. Sports Arbitration and the Pechstein *Case*

The second example that shows that party autonomy is losing ground in arbitration concerns the field of sports arbitration and revolves around the – by now equally infamous – *Pechstein* case.[99] At the heart of the matter was the (very successful) German speed skater Claudia Pechstein who had signed an arbitration agreement with the German Speed Skating Federation (Deutsche Eisschnelllaufgemeinschaft – DESG) and the International Skating Union (ISU) in favour of the CAS, the Court of Arbitration for

[93] Agreement on encouragement and reciprocal protection of investments between the Kingdom of the Netherlands and the Czech and Slovak Federative Republic, concluded in 1991 and entered into force on 1 January 1992.

[94] CJEU, *Achmea* (n 92) para 60.

[95] ibid, para 58.

[96] ibid para 56.

[97] ibid, para 60.

[98] CJEU, C-109/20 *Poland v PL Holdings* ECLI:EU:C:2021:875.

[99] See for an overview of the case history B Ehle and I Guaia, 'Bundesgerichtshof, Az. KZR 6/15, Pechstein v. International Skating Union (ISU), 7 June 2016' 2016 *Yearbook of International Sports Arbitration* 415; Kleen, 'Sport arbitration and competition law: Long-awaited verdict of the Bundesverfassungsgericht gives Pechstein new hope' *Kluwer Competition Law Blog*, 26 July 2022; R Morbach, 'The Pechstein Saga Continues: The German Federal Constitutional Court Grants Another Round on the Rink' *Kluwer Arbitration Blog*, 27 July 2022; P Nacimiento, S Schenk and A Covi, 'Landmark ruling of Germany's Constitutional Court: Arbitration Clause Violates Access to Justice' *Arbitration Notes*, 15 July 2022; G Wagner and O Samanci, 'Justizgrundrechte im Schiedsverfahren? – Pechstein und die Folgen für die Handelsschiedsgerichtsbarkeit' [2024] *Zeitschrift für Europäisches Privatrecht* 533, 536 et seq.

And it could be argued that at least some businesses have no choice but have to sign arbitration clauses in order to stay in business.[112]

Against this background, it remains to be seen whether the trend to curtail party autonomy in arbitration continues – or whether the trend away from default rules will remain confined to investment and sports arbitration. In addition, it remains to be seen whether further suggestions to limit party autonomy in arbitration will eventually gain ground. This seems particularly relevant with a view to suggestions to invalidate arbitration agreements or exclude the arbitrability of a dispute in light of the principle of effectiveness of EU law if it is not guaranteed that the arbitral tribunal will apply mandatory rules of EU law, such as competition law.[113] The CJEU itself has not ruled on the issue. However, it has held that a choice of law clause in favour of a Third State is ineffective if it leads to the inapplicability of (overriding) mandatory rules of EU law (in the case in question: the Commercial Agents Directive).[114] Building on this case law, the German Federal Court of Justice (Bundesgerichtshof) invalidated a choice of court clause in favour of a court in a Third State, arguing that submission of a dispute to a court located outside the EU would impair the obligation to give effect to the (overriding mandatory) provisions of the Commercial Agents Directive.[115] For the same reason, the Austrian Federal Court of Justice (Oberster Gerichtshof) invalidated an arbitration agreement.[116] Should this reasoning be applied more broadly, possibly to all disputes involving (overriding) mandatory EU law, the parties' rights to arbitrate rather than to litigate their dispute would be further limited.

IV. Conclusion and Outlook

Civil procedure and arbitration are conventionally perceived to be located at opposing ends of the party autonomy spectrum. They are considered to 'represent the public and private sides of the binding dispute resolution coin'.[117] However, recent developments have suggested that the role of party autonomy is increasing in civil procedure in the shape of default rules, while its role is decreasing in arbitration. The two fields of law are, therefore, in the process of convergence. This gives rise to (at least) two questions: why are civil procedure and arbitration converging? And are there any limits?

With regards to the first question, it seems fair to assume that the convergence is caused, at least in part, by a change of what we perceive to be the role of civil procedure and arbitration, respectively. In fact, while civil procedure was traditionally perceived as an instrument that increasingly serves public interests, it is now increasingly understood as an instrument that serves party interests. Just like arbitration, civil procedure

[112] See for a detailed discussion of this aspect Longrée (n 105) 1252-53; Wagner and Samanci (n 99) at 556 et seq.

[113] See with a view to competition law C Heinze, 'Antitrust Damages Claims and Arbitration Agreements' in F Ferrari (ed), *The Impact of EU Law on International Commercial Arbitration* (Huntington/New York, Juris, 2017) 383, 409 et seq. See for a more detailed discussion Kodek (n 108) 204 et seq.

[114] CJEU, C-391/98 *Ingmar* ECLI:EU:C:1999:519, para 26.

[115] BGH, 5 September 2012, VII ZR 25/12.

[116] OGH, 1 March 2017, 5 Ob 72/16y.

[117] Bookman, 'Arbitral Courts' (n 3) 169.

is therefore increasingly constructed as a service for private parties,[118] which in turn makes it more amenable to party agreements and, hence, to characterisation of the procedural rules as default rules. With regards to arbitration, in contrast, the development has been different. While it was originally seen as the paradigmatic instrument to serve party interests, it has recently been used in situations that involve public interests and/or weaker parties. The law of arbitration, therefore, has had to learn how to deal with these kinds of situations – and it has chosen to go down the classic way of introducing more mandatory rules.

More difficult to answer is the second question relating to the limits of the convergence of civil procedure and arbitration. Will the two mechanisms to settle private disputes eventually become indistinguishable from one another? Will convergence in the end lead to a merger of litigation and arbitration? For want of a crystal ball we cannot be sure. However, it seems that there are certain limits to the 'arbitralization' of court proceedings on the one hand, and the 'juditialization' of arbitration on the other. These limits derive from the fact that courts base their authority and legitimacy on public sources and sovereignty, whereas arbitral tribunals derive their authority and legitimacy from private sources and autonomy.[119] Courts have, therefore, both more powers and more responsibilities than arbitral tribunals. Most importantly, they may declare and develop law in the public interest.[120] Against this background, it seems more likely that differences between litigation and arbitration will persist in one form or the other. And this most likely means that default rules will (continue to) play a different, most likely more limited role in civil procedure than in arbitration.

[118] G Wagner, *Rechtsstandort Deutschland im Wettbewerb* (Munich, CH Beck, 2017) 216 et seq; R Susskind, *Online Courts and the Future of Justice* (Oxford, OUP, 2019) 95 et seq.

[119] Bookman, 'Arbitral Courts' (n 3) 170.

[120] ibid 202.

13

Private International Default Rules

JOHANNES UNGERER

I. Introduction

This chapter will discuss the role of default rules in situations where private parties interact across national borders. Whether it is an international contract that is to be concluded or an international tort that has been committed, the complexity of the situation is significantly greater than in the purely domestic context. In these international situations, default rules can, on the one hand, be seen as a fallback option and safety net for private parties who have not made their own arrangements as to the governing law or the litigation location. It has thus to be investigated whether and how default rules succeed in providing suitable solutions and which objectives are promoted by these solutions. On the other hand, it has to be examined whether and how private parties can indeed make their own deviating arrangements.

The discussion of what is here called 'private international default rules' will address two issues. It will deal with the issue of the applicable law, which will cover both international uniform law and choice of law, and with the issue of which court has international jurisdiction to adjudicate disputes.[1] Both issues will be discussed with reference to the two most important and interesting types of legal sources – international conventions and EU law – because they cover most of the ground of our modern private international law.[2] The discussion will focus on civil and commercial matters of international contracts and torts since default rules are most relevant and widespread in these areas, whereas in other areas of private law mandatory rules are prevalent, such as in international property law.

At the outset, it is helpful to clarify the understanding of the nature of private international law. The term is used as a synonym to the conflict of laws. Yet private international

[1] Questions concerning arbitration are addressed by G Rühl, ch 12 in this volume. Questions concerning the recognition and enforcement of judgments are not commonly governed by default rules and are therefore excluded here.

[2] With regard to the UK post-Brexit, limiting the discussion to EU law is not a problem in respect of choice of law since the Rome I and II Regulations have been retained, see below n 47. The change from the Brussels Ia Regulation to the national rules for determining the international jurisdiction of British courts will be briefly addressed below, nn 77–78.

law could be misconceived to be completely mandatory instead of providing default rules in certain areas, such as contract and tort. This could be true from the perspective of the courts, which must apply the rules of private international law in order to determine their international jurisdiction or the applicable law. In this sense, indeed, private international law is not private, nor very international, let alone non-mandatory. However, the chapter will mainly consider private international law from the perspective of private parties in cross-border situations. Taking this perspective, the discussion will address legal interactions of a private and international nature in which the parties rely on rules applicable by default in order to have the applicable law or international jurisdiction determined if the parties themselves have not (validly) made a choice of law or court within the discretion awarded to them.

II. Default Rules in International Uniform Private Law

Cross-border legal relations between private parties can, in certain situations, be governed by international uniform rules adopted by states in international conventions.[3] What is particularly interesting is the design which makes these conventions – instead of national law – applicable by default.[4]

A prime example of this default applicability is the 1980 United Nations Convention on Contracts for the International Sale of Goods (CISG).[5] It is widely known across the globe and highly relevant in cross-border business practice, which is why it has been chosen here for a detailed discussion. There are also other international conventions which are applicable by default, for instance the Convention on International Factoring and the Convention on International Financial Leasing, both of which were concluded in Ottawa in 1988, but neither of them has been ratified by more than ten states.

Since the present discussion will focus on the applicability by default of an entire international convention containing international uniform private law, it will not engage with specific default rules *within* an international convention. Such specific default rules do not differ significantly from default rules in national law, apart from the fact that they are drafted and adopted on the international level; yet this difference in origin does not warrant separate discussion concerning the private international default design in this chapter. An example of a specific rule not discussed further here is the default compensation limit in the 1956 Convention on the Contract for the International Carriage of Goods by Road,[6] which is transposed into national law, for instance by the Carriage of Goods by Road Act 1965 in the UK and in the Commercial

[3] Applying law of international origin to private legal interactions is an exception to the rule that the applicable law is a national private law which is identified with the help of the seized court's conflict of laws rules, an aspect that will be discussed further below, s III.

[4] The following discussion contains excerpts from the author's chapter 'Behavioural Economics of Internationally Unifying Private Law' in B Köhler, R Gulati and T John and (eds), *Elgar Companion to UNIDROIT* (Cheltenham, Edward Elgar Publishing, 2024).

[5] United Nations Convention on Contracts for the International Sale of Goods (Vienna, 11 April 1980), UN Treaty Series, vol 1489, p 3.

[6] Art 23(3) and 24 United Nations Convention on the Contract for the International Carriage of Goods by Road (Geneva, 19 May 1956), UN Treaty Series, vol 399, p 189. On this, see A Hellgardt, ch 2 in this volume.

Code in Germany.[7] Apart from its international origin, however, there is nothing special about this limitation by default, which means that it could equally have been adopted on national levels without any international inception.

A. The Default Design of the CISG

The CISG was prepared by the United Nations Commission on International Trade Law (UNCITRAL) as a successor to the not very successful 1964 Conventions relating to a Uniform Law on the Formation of Contracts for the International Sale of Goods (ULFC) and relating to a Uniform Law on the International Sale of Goods (ULIS), which had been drafted by the International Institute for the Unification of Private Law (UNIDROIT). The CISG has to date been ratified by close to 100 states and thereby covers national economies that make up two-thirds of global trade.[8] The Contracting States include both Civil law and Common law countries, for instance all EU Member States (apart from Ireland and Malta), the United States, Canada, and Australia. One of the most prominent states that has not ratified the CISG is the United Kingdom; instead, the UK, together only with the Gambia, is still a party to the ULFC/ULIS Conventions, which were denounced by all other states in order to be able to accede to the CISG.

The applicability of the CISG is determined in principle by its Article 1(1), which stipulates:

> This Convention applies to contracts of sale of goods between parties whose places of business are in different States: (a) when the States are Contracting States; or (b) when the rules of private international law lead to the application of the law of a Contracting State.

The scope of the CISG is limited, and also slightly extended, by further rules.[9] In other words, the CISG applies to most cross-border sales when either both seller and buyer are in CISG States (such as the US and Germany) or, if at least one of the parties is in a Non-Contracting State (such as the UK), when the law of a Contracting State (such as Germany) applies because of the seized court's conflict of laws rules pointing to that law. However, the private parties to the sales contract can deviate and exclude the CISG, which thus only applies by default and is not mandatory. This is evident from Article 6 which permits full deviation or partial modification by the parties.[10] The default design is not an innovation of the CISG; the ULFC/ULIS Conventions already contained comparable rules.[11]

The CISG default design makes it easy for the parties to deviate because it neither stipulates a high threshold for the validity of a deviating choice nor forces them to make choices. Yet it would not have been the only imaginable design, as can be demonstrated by contrasting it with two stricter models. Instead of a very flexible default

[7] §§ 431 and 449 German Commercial Code (Handelsgesetzbuch, abbreviated HGB).

[8] See https://uncitral.un.org/en/texts/salegoods/conventions/sale_of_goods/cisg/status.

[9] Arts 2–5 CISG.

[10] Partial modification is subject to Art 12, according to which Contracting States can make declarations that CISG contracts by parties in their territories must always be made in writing.

[11] Art 2(1) ULFC; Arts 1 and 3 ULIS.

design, the CISG could have implemented a 'penalty default rule' design, which intentionally disadvantages (penalises) one party to the contract, who is typically stronger than the other, and requires this party to provide information to the other party in order to initiate a deviation from the default to its advantage.[12] However, in the case of the CISG, neither of the business parties is typically stronger, and consumer contracts are excluded from its scope.[13] Simply making it harder to opt out of the default applicability of the CISG would not be helpful in this regard; if anything, it would only raise the threshold for both parties to modify the default regime. Equally, the CISG did not adopt an alternative solution in the style of a mandated choice design, where both parties are forced to actively make a choice about the applicability of the international uniform law. Mandated choice would reduce the freedom of private parties further and would require them to pick one or another option.[14] Mandating a choice for international sales contracts would not only go against the very idea and helpful nature of the default design, it would also be very difficult to enforce such an obligation on the parties to make the choice.

B. Deviation from the CISG Default

Looking more closely into the design adopted for the CISG, the international uniform rules apply to cross-border sales contracts within the scope of the CISG unless the parties have made alternative arrangements in order to deviate. This begs the question as to what deviation means on this international level and how it differs from deviation from national rules. The answer will be helpful for understanding the default design of this international uniform law instrument.

Private parties may modify specific CISG rules.[15] For example, private parties might wish to vary the CISG in order to include an Incoterm into their contract.[16] The validity of such deviation is judged only by the CISG itself.[17] This is comparable to private parties deviating from national law, albeit that on the international level private parties have much greater discretion than most national laws would award them when transacting domestically. But apart from that, this modification of the default regime is not uniquely different on the international level.

Private parties may however also deviate from the CISG entirely in two ways, which is unique with regard to international default rules. On the one hand, parties can simply include a term in their contract that they wish to exclude the CISG as a whole, without stipulating which rules shall apply in its stead. This is rare in practice, but a court deciding the dispute between the contractual parties would then have to determine the

[12] I Ayres and R Gertner, 'Filling Gaps in Incomplete Contracts: An Economic Theory of Default Rules' (1989) 99 *Yale LJ* 87, 95 et seq.

[13] Art 2(a) CISG.

[14] Mandated choice in private law is, for instance, discussed by A Karampatzos, *Private Law, Nudging and Behavioural Economic Analysis* (London/New York, Routledge, 2020) 77 et seq.

[15] Art 6, 2nd alternative, in conjunction with Art 12 CISG.

[16] P Hachem, 'Article 6' in I Schwenzer and U Schroeter (eds), *Commentary on the UN Convention on the International Sale of Goods (CISG)* 5th edn (Oxford, OUP, 2022) 118.

[17] Arts 14–24 and 29 CISG.

applicable national law by virtue of its conflict of laws rules objectively.[18] For instance, the default choice of law rules might stipulate that the law of the residence of the seller ought to apply to the contract; if the seller is resident in France, French law ought to govern the contract.

On the other hand, instead of including a term as to the mere exclusion of the CISG, the parties may choose a particular national jurisdiction to govern their international contract, for instance the law of England and Wales. The validity of such a choice of law clause will be discussed in greater detail below,[19] but in principle it depends on the requirements contained in the choice of law rules of the seized court. Apart from general issues with choice of law, this choice and, as a logical corollary, the exclusion of the CISG are largely unproblematic if the chosen law, for instance English law, is the national law of a state that is not a Contracting State of the CISG.[20] If, however, the chosen law is, for instance, the law of Germany, which – unlike the UK – is a Contracting State, the issue arises whether the CISG is not excluded but is rather applicable 'through the backdoor' as part of the chosen German law. This is indeed regularly affirmed.[21]

If the parties want to ensure that they solely choose German substantive national law and if they want to exclude the CISG completely, then it is recommendable that the choice of law clause is accompanied by a clause that additionally clarifies the CISG exclusion. Such combination is common business practice for jurisdictions which are Contracting States.[22] In any event, it must not be forgotten that the parties can of course also make further deviations from the governing national law; this is a question to be decided within the governing national law as to whether, and to what extent, parties may deviate from the default rules of that national law and entirely 'make up' their own contract rules.

C. Intended Benefits of the CISG Default

The CISG's default design can thus be seen to fulfil functions in principle similar to default rules on the national level, yet it goes beyond due to its setting on the international level. Indeed, on the international level, benefiting from the advantages of defaults is of even greater significance against the background of the increased complexity of cross-border legal interactions of private parties.

It has been recognised that international uniform private law, such as the CISG, increases legal certainty through balanced default rules, which are easily ascertainable as well as accessible in English and other major languages of international trade.[23]

[18] See below, s III.A.
[19] See below, s III.D.
[20] Hachem (n 16) 122–23.
[21] See, for instance, the judgment of the German Federal Court of Justice (*Bundesgerichtshof*) BGH (11.05.2010) NJW-RR 2010, 2017 at 2019; Austrian Supreme Court (*Oberster Gerichtshof*) OGH (12.02.2012) case 10 Ob 4/12d, IHR 2012, 193 at 195, para 1.2. However, for the opposite view without substantive reasoning, see OLG München (02.10.2013) IHR 2014, 68, at 69.
[22] Hachem (n 16) 125–26.
[23] See only MJJ Bonell, 'Introduction to the Convention' in CM Bianca and MJ Bonell (eds), *Commentary on the International Sales Law* (Milan, Giuffrè, 1987) 14–15; I Schwenzer, 'Introduction' in I Schwenzer (ed),

This suggests that, in contrast to national rules, the CISG and similar international instruments are less prone to promote and impose controversial political and economic values. Greater fairness and efficiency of international rules can indeed be expected from the drafting process involving international organisations, such as UNCITRAL and UNIDROIT, and their expert groups; moreover, states review the rules before making their respective decision about whether to accede to the international convention, and the decision to accede then affirms the quality of the rules of the international convention.

The CISG may also be seen as promoting rules particularly suited for international sales, which the parties would have agreed on had they crafted their own rules (hypothetical bargains).[24] Insofar as the CISG applies and is not excluded, it saves the parties and the courts from needing to establish the national law governing the cross-border contract, which would require employing the complex rules of the conflict of laws. These rules can differ from jurisdiction to jurisdiction and hence depend on which court adjudicates the dispute, thus bringing about the risks of forum shopping.

Therefore, even more so than national default rules, which let private parties reduce transaction costs domestically,[25] international uniform law can be understood as a means of minimising transnational transaction costs.[26] From the perspective of (neo)classical economics, this suggests that following the default rules of international uniform private law would be highly advantageous for private parties.

D. Factual Default Inversion

In practice, however, private parties oftentimes opt out of the CISG, regularly in conjunction with choosing a national law to govern their international contract. Whilst not fully representative, empirical surveys in recent decades have shed some light on this: in summary, they found that private parties were advised to exclude the CISG in roughly 40–70 per cent of the cases.[27] This means that the theoretical intention of

Schlechtriem & Schwenzer: Commentary on the UN Convention on the International Sale of Goods (CISG) 4th edn (Oxford, OUP, 2016) 6. This is called into question by G Cuniberti, 'Is the CISG Benefiting Anybody?' (2006) 39 *Vanderbilt Journal of Transnational Law* 1511, 1514 et seq.

[24] D Charny, 'Hypothetical Bargains: The Normative Structure of Contract Interpretation' (1990) 89 *Michigan L Rev* 1815, 1819 et seq, based on, for instance, Ayres and Gertner (n 12), and JL Coleman, DD Heckathorn and SM Maser, 'Bargaining Theory Approach to Default Provisions and Disclosure Rules in Contract Law' (1989) 12 *Harvard Journal of Law & Public Policy* 637.

[25] R Korobkin, 'Status Quo Bias and Contract Default Rules' (1997) 83 *Cornell L Rev* 608, 613 et seq; CA Riley, 'Designing Default Rules in Contract Law: Consent, Conventionalism, and Efficiency' [2000] *OJLS* 367, 382 et seq. Also see Ayres and Gertner (n 12).

[26] M Cenini and F Parisi, 'An Economic Analysis of the CISG' in A Janssen and O Meyer (eds), *CISG Methodology* (München, Sellier, 2009).

[27] See, for instance, JF Coyle, 'The Role of the CISG in U.S. Contract Practice: An Empirical Study' (2016) 38 *Univ of Pennsylvania Journal of International Law* 195, 206–07; J Meyer, 'Die praktische Bedeutung des UN-Kaufrechts in Deutschland' (2021) 85 *Rabels Zeitschrift für ausländisches und internationales Privatrecht* 357, 375–76, 384–86; UG Schroeter, 'Empirical Evidence of Courts' and Counsels' Approach to the CISG (with Some Remarks on Professional Liability)' in LA DiMatteo (ed), *International Sales Law* (Cambridge, CUP, 2014) 661; L Spagnolo, 'Green Eggs and Ham: The CISG, Path Dependence, and the Behavioural Economics of Lawyers' Choices of Law in International Sales Contracts' (2010) 6 *Journal of Private International Law* 417, 419–21.

making the international uniform law of the CISG applicable by default to international sale contracts has in fact been inverted frequently. Private parties have established behaviours which result in what may be called a 'factual default inversion'.[28]

Several factors can be considered to have led to this factual default inversion. Whilst both Common law and Civil law jurisdictions are among the CISG Contracting States, the CISG rules are somewhat closer to Civil law conceptions of contract law than to the Common law ones. For instance, in terms of contract formation, the CISG does not require consideration or any equivalent demonstration of reciprocity/seriousness; offer and acceptance suffice.[29] In terms of contractual remedies, the CISG adheres to the principle of *favor contractus*[30] and therefore provides for price reduction and damages, instead of terminating the contract prematurely, and it also provides for additional time (*Nachfrist*) in case of non-delivery of the goods.[31] These features differ significantly from the Common law tradition where, in principle, contracts require consideration and where specific performance is very much the exception and damages are the ordinary remedy.[32] Accordingly, it is understandable why private parties from Common law jurisdictions would be sceptical of and tend to exclude the CISG. They might prefer the economic clarity and harshness of the Common law remedies.

Equally, private parties from Civil law jurisdictions might generally be more amenable to the CISG rules but could be seen to still prefer their national rules instead of the international regime, which for instance only acknowledges the observance of good faith as an element for the interpretation of the CISG[33] but not for the parties' obligations and performance.[34] Hence, they too might choose to exclude the CISG.

E. The Behavioural Economics of Deviating

Appreciating the complexity of cross-border contracts and, in particular, of comparing international uniform law with national alternatives and identifying which is better, it appears very likely that the exclusion of international uniform law is not always and solely based on rational reasoning considered so far. Instead, private parties can be affected by psychological biases, that is, patterns of deviation from rational judgment,[35]

[28] Ungerer (n 4) 127. G Low, 'The (Ir)Relevance of Harmonization and Legal Diversity to European Contract Law: A Perspective from Psychology' (2010) 18 *ERPL* 285, 301 uses the phrase 'real default'.

[29] Art 14 et seq CISG.

[30] B Keller, 'Favor Contractus: Reading the CISG in Favor of the Contract' in CB Andersen and UG Schroeter (eds), *Sharing International Commercial Law Across National Boundaries: Festschrift for Albert H. Kritzer* (London, Wildy, 2008) 247.

[31] Art 25 et seq CISG. Cf L Spagnolo, *CISG Exclusion and Legal Efficiency* (Alphen aan den Rijn, Kluwer Law International, 2014) 48 et seq.

[32] The CISG tries to reduce some of the friction in its Art 28 but this essentially amounts to a public policy exception and does not solve the substantive issue.

[33] Art 7(1) CISG.

[34] P Hachem, 'Article 7' in I Schwenzer and U Schroeter (eds), *Commentary on the UN Convention on the International Sale of Goods (CISG)* 5th edn (Oxford, OUP, 2022) 143. See also Court of Appeal (*Gerechtshof*) Arnhem, judgment of 18 July 2006, case 2005/1005 AY5784, CISG-online.org number 1266.

[35] D Kahneman and A Tversky, 'Prospect Theory: An Analysis of Decision under Risk' (1979) 47 *Econometrica* 263; D Kahneman, P Slovic and A Tversky, *Judgment under Uncertainty: Heuristics and Biases* (Cambridge, CUP, 1982).

to determining the applicable law, also establish the court's international jurisdiction to adjudicate. For both issues, applicable law and adjudicatory jurisdiction, private international law relies heavily on default rules. In addition to illuminating the default rules themselves, it will be explored how private parties can deviate through agreeing on a choice of court and/or choice of law and which boundaries are set for this.[42]

Before delving into default rules in private international law, it should be clarified that, in Common law jurisdictions, there is typically yet another default rule when it comes to the application of foreign law. For instance, in an English court, there is a default rule that, in a cross-border case, English law applies if foreign law is not pleaded (and even if foreign law is pleaded, there is a presumption that its content is similar to English law unless a deviation of the foreign law is proved).[43] This is a default rule which forms part of the procedural law in English courts; it helps to resolve *non liquet* situations in a highly adversarial court system, but it is not part of private international law and therefore does not form part of the exercises of determining the court's jurisdiction or the applicable law. Neither is it a rule universally followed because courts in Civil law jurisdictions apply the governing foreign law *ex officio*, if necessary with the assistance of experts called upon by the court instead of the parties.[44] Thus, the Common law approach to pleading and proving foreign law is not a private international default rule to be discussed further here.[45]

A. Default Choice of Law Rules

In order to determine the applicable law for a cross-border contract or tort, courts of EU Member States follow the objective connecting factors in the Rome I and II Regulations if the parties have not agreed upon a (valid) choice of law.[46] Even post-Brexit, British courts still adhere to the retained versions of these Regulations;[47] the Retained EU Law (Revocation and Reform) Act 2023 does not affect them either, although the Act requires referring to them as 'assimilated law'.[48]

Like its predecessor, the 1980 Rome Convention, the Rome I Regulation stipulates for international contracts that the characteristic contractual obligation is the basis for

[42] The subsequent discussion contains excerpts from the author's article 'Nudging in Private International Law' (2022) 86 *Rabels Zeitschrift für ausländisches und internationales Privatrecht* 1.

[43] *FS Cairo (Nile Plaza) LLC v Lady Brownlie* [2021] UKSC 45, [2022] AC 995, at [96] et seq (per Lord Leggatt).

[44] See, for instance, for German courts, § 293 German Code of Civil Procedure (*Zivilprozessordnung*, abbreviated ZPO).

[45] But see Rühl, ch 12 in this volume on procedure.

[46] Regulation (EC) No 593/2008 of the European Parliament and of the Council of 17 June 2008 on the law applicable to contractual obligations (Rome I) [2008] OJ L177/6; Regulation (EC) No 864/2007 of the European Parliament and of the Council of 11 July 2007 on the law applicable to non-contractual obligations (Rome II), [2007] OJ L199/40.

[47] The Law Applicable to Contractual Obligations and Non-Contractual Obligations (Amendment etc.) (EU Exit) Regulations SI 2019/834, as amended by SI 2020/1574. See further A Dickinson, 'Realignment of the Planets – Brexit and European Private International Law' [2021] *Praxis des Internationalen Privat- und Verfahrensrechts* 213, 218–19.

[48] J Ungerer, 'No Sunset of Retained EU Conflict of Laws in the UK, but Increased Risk of Sunburn', 26 July 2023, https://conflictoflaws.net/2023/no-sunset-of-retained-eu-conflict-of-laws-in-the-uk-but-increased-risk-of-sunburn/.

the default rule.[49] This differs from earlier ideas of applying the law of the place where the contract is concluded (*lex loci contractus*)[50] or where the contract is to be fulfilled (*lex loci solutionis*).[51] Focusing on the characteristic obligation means applying the law at the place of the party who owes the non-monetary obligation.[52] The Regulation states this as the default rule,[53] and it also lists various contracts and clarifies which party performs the characteristic obligations. For instance, for an international contract for the sale of goods (insofar as this is not governed by the CISG), the law of the country where the seller is habitually resident applies according to the default rule.[54] In an example given above, if the seller is habitually resident in France, then French law governs the sale contract by default. Similarly, the law of the country where the service provider is habitually resident applies by default to a contract for the provision of services.[55] Exceptions to these general default rules are only made in the shape of specific default rules where they are necessary on account of the nature of the contract, for instance for contracts relating to rights in rem[56] or contracts concluded in a specially regulated procedure.[57]

For international torts, parallel to the usually applicable criminal law, the general default rule for the applicable law has been guided by the policy of *lex loci delicti*.[58] Whilst its interpretation has varied between referring to the place of conduct and to the place of injury,[59] these differences only matter in cases where the tortious conduct and its resulting injury occur in separate jurisdictions.[60] The Rome II Regulation's default rule places the emphasis on the place of the injury or direct damage,[61] and it thus stipulates that 'the law of the country in which the damage occurs' shall primarily apply by default.[62] This is further clarified by the addition that, for the default rule, it is irrelevant where 'the event giving rise to the damage occurred and [where] the indirect

[49] L Collins, 'Contractual Obligations – The EEC Preliminary Draft Convention on Private International Law' (1976) 25 *ICLQ* 35, 44 et seq; FK Juenger, 'The European Convention on the Law Applicable to Contractual Obligations: Some Critical Observations' (1981) 22 *Virginia Journal of International Law* 123, 132 et seq.

[50] O Lando, 'Contracts', *International Encyclopedia of Comparative Law*, vol III (1977) ch 24, sec I.

[51] FC von Savigny, *System des heutigen Römischen Rechts*, vol 8 (Berlin, Veit & Co, 1849) 207–08.

[52] M Giuliano and P Lagarde, 'Report on the Convention on the law applicable to contractual obligations' [1980] OJ C282/1, 20; P Torremans (ed), *Cheshire, North & Fawcett Private International Law* 15th edn (Oxford, OUP, 2017) 732; F Vischer, 'The Principle of the Typical Performance in International Contracts and the Draft Convention' in K Lipstein (ed), *Harmonisation of Private International Law by the E.E.C.* (London, Institute of Advanced Legal Studies, 1978) 25.

[53] Art 4(2) Rome I Regulation.

[54] Art 4(1)(a) Rome I Regulation.

[55] Art 4(1)(b) Rome I Regulation.

[56] Art 4(1)(c) and (d) Rome I Regulation.

[57] Art 4(1)(g) and (h) Rome I Regulation.

[58] E Rabel, *The Conflict of Laws*, vol 2, 2nd edn (Ann Arbor, University of Michigan Law School, 1960) 235.

[59] SC Symeonides, 'Rome II and Tort Conflicts: A Missed Opportunity' (2008) 56 *Am J Comp L* 173, 186 et seq.

[60] U Magnus, 'Article 4 Rome II' in U Magnus and P Mankowski (eds), *European Commentaries on Private International Law: Rome II Regulation*, vol 3 (Köln, Otto Schmidt, 2019) para 66.

[61] Recital 17 Rome II Regulation: 'the country in which the damage occurs should be the country where the injury was sustained or the property was damaged respectively'.

[62] Art 4(1) Rome II Regulation; see further, for instance, R Fentiman, 'The Significance of Close Connection' in J Ahern and W Binchy (eds), *The Rome II Regulation on the Law Applicable to Non-Contractual Obligations* (Leiden, Martinus Nijhoff, 2009) 86 et seq.

consequences of that event occur'.[63] Exceptions are again made in the form of specific default rules for specific tortious contexts, for instance cases of product liability,[64] and for other non-contractual obligations, such as unjust enrichment.[65] However, for some other torts, the objective connecting factors are mandatory rules instead of default rules because they cannot be deviated from, for instance in cases of unfair competition or infringement of intellectual property.[66]

B. The Closest Connection and Other Default Objectives for Choice of Law

Both Rome Regulations have in common that their default rules in the shape of objective connecting factors seek the legal seat of the cross-border legal relation in order to declare its law applicable.[67] In other words, the closest connection has been identified as the intention that underlies the default rules.[68] This is expressly confirmed by the fact that, under the Rome I Regulation for international contracts, ultimately 'the contract shall be governed by the law of the country with which it is most closely connected' if the characteristic contractual performance cannot be determined.[69]

On the other hand, both Regulations not only allow for deviation from their default rules by choice of the parties (albeit to varying extents),[70] they also contain what private international lawyers call 'escape clauses'.[71] These are still very much objective connecting factors, but they modify the default design in order to ensure that the law with the closest connection is indeed applied. The escape clauses of the Regulations determine that the law of another country shall be the applicable law if 'it is clear from all the circumstances of the case that the contract/tort is manifestly more closely connected with [that other] country'.[72]

The Rome II Regulation goes even further specifically for torts by stipulating in another escape clause, whose rationale can be traced back to a case that led to the 'American conflicts revolution',[73] that the default rule differs if the tortfeasor and victim had 'their habitual residence in the same country at the time when the damage occur[ed]'; then, the law of that country is to be applied by default.[74]

[63] Art 4(1) Rome II Regulation.
[64] Art 5 Rome II Regulation.
[65] Art 10 Rome II Regulation.
[66] Art 6 and 8 Rome II Regulation, see Art 6(4) and 8(3). Yet this mandatory nature is not uncontroversial; see, for instance, in respect of intellectual property: I Bach, 'Art. 14' in P Huber (ed), Rome II Regulation (Munich, Sellier 2011) para 3 and fn 4, with reference to S Leible, 'Rechtswahl im IPR der außervertraglichen Schuldverhältnisse nach der Rom II-Verordnung' [2008] *Recht der internationalen Wirtschaft* 257, 259.
[67] von Savigny (n 51) 108, 118.
[68] Vischer (n 52); S Symeonides, *The American Choice-of-Law Revolution: Past, Present and Future* (Leiden, Martinus Nijhoff, 2006) 33.
[69] Art 4(4) Rome I Regulation, which was the primary rule in Art 4(1) Rome Convention.
[70] Discussed in subsection D below.
[71] Recital 20 Rome I Regulation; Recital 18 Rome II Regulation.
[72] Art 4(3) Rome I and Rome II Regulations.
[73] *Babcock v Jackson* 191 NE 2d 279 (NY 1963); cf Symeonides (n 68) 38, 101 et seq.
[74] Art 4(2) Rome II Regulation.

C. Default Jurisdictional Rules and the Proximity Objective

Turning from the applicable law issue to the question of international jurisdiction of courts for adjudicating cross-border disputes over contracts and torts, this is governed in the EU by the Brussels Ia Regulation.[75] In the UK after Brexit, England and Wales (and Northern Ireland) have mostly reverted to the common law principles for determining the international jurisdiction of their courts,[76] apart from the Regulation's protective rules for consumers and employees which have been largely retained,[77] whereas Scotland still follows a statutory regime which is generally more closely modelled on the Regulation's predecessor, the 1968 Brussels Convention.[78]

The Regulation's heads of jurisdiction are applied by default in the absence of a (valid) choice of court agreement. Comparable to the design of the Rome I and Rome II Regulations, the Brussels Ia Regulation lists various types of disputes and specifies which courts have jurisdiction to adjudicate by default. For instance, for an international contractual dispute, 'the courts for the place of performance of the obligation in question' shall have international jurisdiction.[79] The Brussels Ia Regulation sets out a further default rule for defining the 'place of performance of the obligation in question', which stipulates that, unless otherwise agreed upon, this place shall be the place of (intended) delivery in case of the sale of goods.[80] In case of an international tort, 'the courts for the place where the harmful event occurred' have international jurisdiction.[81] Exceptions are again made by way of mandatory rules for disputes that shall be decided by certain courts with exclusive jurisdiction, for instance over rights in rem or entries in public registers.[82]

Although there are some natural differences in substance, the jurisdictional default rules seek to determine the closest connection of a dispute with a forum,[83] which is comparable to the aim of the default rules for determining the applicable law discussed above. The differences in substance are a result of the different functions that the default rules have to fulfil in establishing international jurisdiction and in determining the applicable law, respectively. The rules on international jurisdiction have to strike a fair balance between enabling access to courts on the one hand and avoiding exorbitant competence on the other hand. The jurisdictional rules have steered away from basing jurisdiction to adjudicate on considerations of territorial power and sovereign allegiance; instead, the modern defaults are based on the proximity of both the parties and their dispute to the forum.[84]

[75] Regulation (EU) No 1215/2012 of the European Parliament and of the Council of 12 December 2012 on jurisdiction and the recognition and enforcement of judgments in civil and commercial matters (Brussels Ia Regulation), OJ 2012 L 351/1.

[76] Dickinson (n 47) 215 et seq.

[77] Civil Jurisdiction and Judgments Act 1982 ss 15A–15E.

[78] Civil Jurisdiction and Judgments Act 1982 Pt III and Sch 8 and 9.

[79] Art 7(1)(a) Brussels Ia Regulation.

[80] Art 7(1)(b) first bullet point Brussels Ia Regulation.

[81] Art 7(2) Brussels Ia Regulation.

[82] Art 24 Brussels Ia Regulation.

[83] H-P Mansel, 'Connecting Factor' in J Basedow and others (eds), *Encyclopedia of Private International Law* (Cheltenham, Edward Elgar, 2017) 450.

[84] For an overview, see R Michaels, 'Jurisdiction, Foundations' in *Encyclopedia of Private International Law* (n 83) 1047 et seq. The CJEU has also emphasised proximity since the times of the 1968 Brussels Convention:

D. Deviation by Agreeing on a Choice of Law or Court

The default character of the objective connecting factors which are employed for determining international jurisdiction and the applicable law can only be fully understood if the subjective connecting factors are examined in turn. These permit private parties to make their own deviating arrangements. The freedom to make a choice of law or court was established in private international law in the nineteenth century as a result of the emerging philosophical, political and economic ideas of individualism and libertarianism.[85] Party autonomy is nowadays widely recognised for international contracts and, to a more limited extent, for international torts.[86]

According to the Rome I Regulation, party autonomy is indeed considered to be 'one of the cornerstones of the system of conflict-of-law rules in matters of contractual obligations',[87] and thus parties may fairly freely choose the applicable contract law at any time.[88] The validity of the choice is in principle assessed by the rules of the chosen law itself.[89] More recently, choice of law has also been permitted with respect to torts:[90] the Rome II Regulation lets the parties choose the governing law, but non-commercial parties may only make a choice after the damage has occurred.[91]

In terms of choice of court, this is nowadays so widely recognised that it is even considered to be customary international law.[92] The Brussels Ia Regulation stipulates that the parties can agree on jurisdiction of Member State courts to settle any disputes in connection with a particular legal relation, such as an international contract or tort; this agreement is enforced unless it fails to meet the requirements set by the Regulation and the substantive law of the chosen jurisdiction.[93] Beside the Brussels Ia Regulation, there is the 2005 Hague Convention on Choice of Court Agreements for exclusive jurisdiction agreements, which are made within the Convention's scope among commercial parties; this is particularly relevant for the choice of British courts after Brexit since the Brussels Ia Regulation no longer applies in the UK.

Case 133/81 *Roger Ivenel v Helmut Schwab*, ECLI:EU:C:1982:199, paras 11, 15; Case 34/82 *Martin Peters Bauunternehmung GmbH v Zuid Nederlandse Aannemers Vereniging*, ECLI:EU:C:1983:87, paras 11–12; C-220/88 *Dumez France SA and Tracoba SARL v Hessische Landesbank*, ECLI:EU:C:1990:8, para 17.

[85] A Mills, *Party Autonomy in Private International Law* (Cambridge, CUP, 2018) 29 et seq.

[86] See ibid 91 et seq, 313 et seq.

[87] Recital 11 Rome I Regulation.

[88] Art 3(1) and (2) Rome I Regulation.

[89] Arts 3(5) and 10(1) Rome I Regulation. Additional limitations are effectively imposed, for instance, by prohibiting deviation from mandatory rules of the country to which all elements of the case save the choice of foreign law are connected to (Art 3(3) Rome I Regulation, similarly for EU mandatory rules in Art 3(4) Rome I Regulation), by letting courts superimpose overriding mandatory rules of their own law (Art 9(2) Rome I Regulation) or of the *lex solutionis* under certain conditions (Art 9(3) Rome I Regulation), and by letting courts take account of even other laws (cf CJEU C-135/15 *Republik Griechenland v Nikiforidis* ECLI:EU:C:2016:774; critically discussed in M Lehmann and J Ungerer, 'Applying or Taking Account of Foreign Overriding Mandatory Provisions – Sophism Under the Rome I Regulation' (2017) XIX *Yearbook of Private International Law* 53).

[90] F Maultzsch, 'Party Autonomy in European Private International Law: Uniform Principle or Context-Dependent Instrument' (2016) 12 *Journal of Private International Law* 466, 470 et seq.

[91] Art 14(1) Rome II Regulation.

[92] AF Lowenfeld, *International Litigation and the Quest for Reasonableness* (Oxford, Clarendon Press, 1996) 200.

[93] Art 25 Brussels Ia Regulation. This freedom is limited, for instance, in Art 25(5) in respect of matters for which the Regulation stipulates that certain courts have exclusive jurisdiction under Art 24.

E. Shortcomings in Orthodox Explanations of Defaults and Deviation

From an orthodox point of view, the default design in private international law can be seen as seeking a balanced and fair decision on which law to apply and where to litigate by looking for the closest connection, whilst at the same time letting parties make their own choices. In terms of neoclassical economics, the defaults are explained by the hypothetical bargain model mentioned above; in the context of the conflict of laws, this model promotes the law or court which the parties would have autonomously chosen if they had made a choice.[94] It emphasises the importance of party autonomy and seeks to effectuate this freedom even where this can only be achieved hypothetically through default rules.

In turn, party autonomy in private international law has often been explained by analogy to private autonomy in substantive law, based on either a naturalist or positivist understanding of the law.[95] Such a 'proper law' doctrine seems plausible and pragmatically appealing. Furthermore, the neoclassical economic analysis of private international law has suggested that granting private parties autonomy promotes efficiency and wealth increase: it promotes the market-orientated freedom for individuals within a world of free competition of legal systems.[96] Where parties have not actually made a choice, following their hypothetical choice by way of default rules seems the second-best option then.

However, the main problem of the neoclassical model is its assumption of rationality, which cannot realistically accommodate human behaviour affected by bounded rationality, especially against the background of the complexity of cross-border legal interactions.[97] For instance, especially in international cases, parties might not be aware of the possibility, or might not be able, to deviate from what they have done previously. They might simply stick to what has been allocated to them in the first place due to the endowment effect and path-dependence (which were already discussed above for international uniform law).

In addition, individuals making decisions regarding a choice of law or court can be affected by over-optimism.[98] Individuals overestimate the prospects of positive

[94] EA O'Hara and LE Ribstein, 'From Politics to Efficiency in Choice of Law' (2000) 67 *Univ of Chicago L Rev* 1151, 1190–91; EA O'Hara and LE Ribstein, 'Rules and Institutions in Developing a Law Market: Views from the United States and Europe' (2007) 82 *Tulane L Rev* 2147, 2158; M Whincop and M Keyes, 'Economic Analysis of Conflict of Laws in Torts Cases: Discrete and Relational Torts' (1998) 22 *Melbourne Univ L Rev* 370, 390 et seq.

[95] O Kahn-Freund, *General Problems of Private International Law* (Leiden, Sijthoff, 1976) 195 et seq; for a more recent account, see, for instance, A Briggs, *Agreements on Jurisdiction and Choice of Law* (Oxford, OUP, 2008) para 2.30; M McParland, *The Rome I Regulation on the Law Applicable to Contractual Obligations* (Oxford, OUP, 2015) para 9.04.

[96] FJ Garcimartin Alferez, 'Regulatory Competition: A Private International Law Approach' (1999) 8 *European Journal of Law and Economics* 251, 258 et seq; EA O'Hara and LE Ribstein, *The Law Market* (Oxford, OUP, 2009) 65 et seq; MJ Whincop and M Keyes, *Policy and Pragmatism in the Conflict of Laws* (Aldershot, Ashgate, 2001) 38 et seq.

[97] See above, s II.E.

[98] On over-optimism: Arlen (n 39) 1773 et seq, 1781 et seq; Jolls, Sunstein and Thaler (n 39) 1524–25; Korobkin and Ulen (n 39) 1091 et seq.

outcomes and underestimate the prospects of negative ones.[99] So, if private parties get excited about choosing for themselves a potentially better law than the one applicable by default, then they might make the choice even if they cannot evaluate all advantages and disadvantages properly but feel that choosing themselves is better in any case.

Moreover, the framing effect can influence how choices are made or not made, because the behaviour of private parties might depend on how a setting is presented to and regarded by them.[100] If it is presented as desirable to make a particular choice in an international setting, such as of a presumably beneficial jurisdiction allegedly known for its low-cost efficiency, private parties might choose it even without being rationally convinced of it; conversely, parties might not actively consider insisting on a rationally beneficial choice simply because it is not made obvious or it is not presented as advantageous.

Whilst granting choice of law and court to private parties is valuable because it allows them to benefit from the assumed popularity, impartiality, and reliability of the chosen law or court,[101] party autonomy and a 'hypothetical bargain' are not always suitable explanations for the content of default rules and the rules on permissible deviation in private international law. In particular, the hypothetical bargain model either unrealistically assumes rationality or covertly infers supposedly rational decisions on individuals which they would however not have been able to make but which are made for them by the intervening lawmaker. Indeed, directly applied, the hypothetical bargain model would in any event be too imprecise to decide what the parties would hypothetically have agreed upon because many outcomes are imaginable but not verifiable.[102] Uncertainty and indeterminacy can already be demonstrated by reference to the scholarly disaccord over whether, for instance with regard to choice of law, parties would hypothetically agree on the law which provides a 'comparative regulatory advantage'[103] or on the law which results in the lowest overall costs.[104]

F. Reconceptualisation Based on Behavioural Economics

Following the more realistic understanding of behavioural economics, which appreciates the effects of bounded rationality, the 'libertarian paternalism'[105] incorporated

[99] E Zamir, 'Law and Behavioral Economics' in M Sellers and S Kirste (eds), *Encyclopedia of the Philosophy of Law and Social Philosophy* (Dordrecht, Springer Netherlands, 2018).

[100] On the framing effect: D Kahneman, 'Maps of Bounded Rationality: Psychology for Behavioral Economics' (2003) 93 *American Economic Review* 1449, 1458 et seq; Korobkin and Ulen (n 39) 1105; Sunstein (n 39) 123, 129.

[101] O'Hara and Ribstein, *Law Market* (n 96) esp 65 et seq; MJ Whincop and M Keyes, 'Towards an Economic Theory of Private International Law' (2000) 25 *Australian Journal of Legal Philosophy* 1, 21.

[102] G Rühl, *Statut und Effizienz: ökonomische Grundlagen des Internationalen Privatrechts* (Tübingen, Mohr Siebeck, 2011) 364 et seq.

[103] O'Hara and Ribstein, 'Politics to Efficiency' (n 94) 1190 et seq, 1216 et seq.

[104] R Michaels, 'Two Economists, Three Opinions? – Economic Models for Private International Law – Cross-Border Torts as Example' in J Basedow and T Kono (eds), *An Economic Analysis of Private International Law* (Tübingen, Mohr Siebeck, 2006) 153 et seq; H-B Schäfer and K Lantermann, 'Choice of Law from an Economic Perspective' in Basedow and Kono (ibid) 98–99.

[105] RH Thaler and CR Sunstein, 'Libertarian Paternalism' (2003) 93 *American Economic Review* 175.

in objective connecting factors applicable by default can be openly acknowledged.[106] Default rules steer private parties intentionally by virtue of the specific objective connecting factors outlined above and, as an underlying safety net, the residual defaults of the closest connection or escape clauses. In this sense, the steering achieved by default rules can be seen as a form of 'nudging'. Nudging is one of the tools which the lawmaker can employ to overcome the bounded rationality of private parties and to promote a beneficial outcome.[107]

The specific direction of nudges in the shape of objective connecting factors may be set in line with certain policy considerations, such as efficiency. Yet default rules are not mandatory, which means they are only liberally paternalistic because their result-orientation is generally intended to make private parties better off than if they had solely followed their own judgement. Importantly, the beneficial result towards which the parties are nudged does not have to be solely identified by efficiency considerations. When setting the default rules, the lawmaker can include a variety of considerations. These can, for example, be relevant for: the protection of third parties, the public at large, the efficient administration of justice, the protection of vulnerable groups of the population, international relations, or the environment. This is where the significant difference can be found in comparison to the neoclassical hypothetical bargain model, which is limited to aiming for efficiency for the parties themselves. In turn, defaults are not strictly paternalistic and mandatory because they do not limit rational people who want to minimise transactional costs further and who are in a socioeconomic position to opt out in order to make individual arrangements according to their rational insights.[108] Yet, at the same time, these defaults ensure that those other people whose actions are determined by bounded rationality and who usually stick to the status quo are not disadvantaged.[109] The crucial characteristic of libertarian paternalism in this context is that defaults are both choice-preserving and de-biasing without being coercive.[110]

Against this background, it is beneficial that the characteristic contractual obligation is selected for the default rule to determine the applicable law for cross-border contracts. It nudges the parties, who have not validly made an independent choice, towards the jurisdiction which most likely has the closest connection, and it ensures neutrality, predictability, and legal certainty, from which third parties might also benefit. Similarly, for international torts, making the law of the place where the damage occurred the default is justified due to the fact that the parties involved presumably had no previous intention to establish contact with one another, as they met most likely by 'accident' in the true sense of the word. The place of damage is the only objective link

[106] On the following, cf Ungerer (n 42) 13 et seq.

[107] RH Thaler and CR Sunstein, *Nudge: Improving Decisions about Health, Wealth, and Happiness* (Yale, Yale University Press, 2008); see also CR Sunstein, *Why Nudge? The Politics of Libertarian Paternalism* (Yale, Yale University Press, 2014).

[108] Cf MJ Whincop and ME Keyes, 'Statutes' Domains in Private International Law: An Economic Theory of the Limits of Mandatory Rules' (1998) 20 *Sydney L Rev* 435, 436 et seq differentiating mandatory and default rules; Whincop and Keyes, 'Economic Theory' (n 101) 17 et seq; Whincop and Keyes, *Policy and Pragmatism* (n 96) 35 et seq.

[109] See also Korobkin (n 25) 668 et seq.

[110] C Jolls and CR Sunstein, 'Debiasing through Law' (2006) 35 *Journal of Legal Studies* 199.

between them, so that they are suitably nudged towards the tort law of that place. In terms of international jurisdiction, the concept of proximity most importantly ensures fairness in determining the internationally competent courts. Moreover, nudging the litigating parties in this direction is also beneficial in practical terms, such as for taking evidence, and it might increase the chances that the law of the forum coincides with the applicable law, and that the judgment to be rendered will be recognisable and enforceable in another jurisdiction.

G. Overcoming the Stickiness of Default Rules

The only major concern with default rules is their potential 'stickiness'.[111] Due to the omission bias and endowment effect, private parties might avoid active choices and, in this way, default arrangements might have a strong direct distributive effect.[112] This can lead to problematic outcomes in situations where private parties who could have done better for themselves did not take action.[113] Moreover, due to socioeconomic constraints, the costs of opting out can be a burden for weaker parties.[114] Therefore, the design of default rules has to accommodate the need to provide sufficient opportunity for diverging from them, so that they do not end up being too restrictive.[115] To this end, clear and reasonable validity requirements for exercising party autonomy are vital.

The EU Regulations on private international law contain straightforward and transparent opportunities for deviating from the defaults: the Rome I and Rome II Regulations stipulate, respectively, that 'the choice shall be made expressly' or 'shall be expressed', and they allow alternatively that it is sufficient for the choice to be, respectively, 'clearly demonstrated' or 'demonstrated with reasonable certainty' by the terms of the contract or the circumstances of the case.[116] As already mentioned, the EU rules submit the issue of consensual agreement about the choice to the chosen governing law,[117] which is the foreseeable and probably most reasonable law to decide it; in addition, a safeguarding provision protects private parties from being surprised by having their alleged consent to the choice assessed by the allegedly chosen foreign law if it 'would not be reasonable to determine the effect of [their] conduct in accordance with [that] law'.[118] In sum, these validity requirements create a clear and not overly restrictive framework for a deviating choice of law.

Correspondingly, the Brussels Ia Regulation sets out in some detail the formal criteria for a choice of court agreement;[119] likewise, the 2005 Hague Convention contains

[111] R Bubb and RH Pildes, 'How Behavioral Economics Trims Its Sails and Why' (2013) 127 *Harvard L Rev* 1593, 1647 et seq; E Zamir and D Teichman, *Behavioral Law and Economics* (Oxford, OUP, 2018) 179–80.

[112] G Mitchell, 'Libertarian Paternalism Is an Oxymoron' (2005) 99 *Northwestern Univ L Rev* 1245, 1269 et seq; Zamir and Teichman (n 111) 181.

[113] BC Madrian, 'Applying Insights from Behavioral Economics to Policy Design' (2014) 6 *Annual Review of Economics* 663, 668 et seq; see also Bubb and Pildes (n 111) 1616 et seq.

[114] Zamir and Teichman (n 111) 181.

[115] See ibid 182.

[116] Art 3(1) Rome I Regulation; Art 14(1) Rome II Regulation.

[117] Art 3(5) and 10(1) Rome I Regulation.

[118] Art 10(2) Rome I Regulation.

[119] Art 25 Brussels Ia Regulation.

(slightly different) rules on this.[120] Although the Regulation's condition of there being a written agreement or evidence in writing seems strict at first,[121] there are plenty of possible alternatives which simplify breaking away from the defaults and accommodate the needs of international commerce: 'communication by electronic means which provides a durable record of the agreement shall be equivalent to "writing"',[122] and it also suffices to obey 'a form which accords with practices which the parties have established between themselves' or

> which accords with a usage of which the parties are or ought to have been aware and which in such trade or commerce is widely known to, and regularly observed by, parties to contracts of the type involved in the particular trade or commerce concerned.[123]

The additional requirement of the Brussels Ia Regulation that the substantive validity of the agreement is to be determined in accordance with the law of the chosen jurisdiction might not instantly seem transparent and might not be aligned with the governing law of the contract or tort in question; yet this rule is the most choice-preserving way of setting substantive standards which have to be fulfilled by the parties' choice, because these standards are essentially included in the choice and not objectively imposed by any rule of the Regulation itself.

H. Alternative Design Considerations

It is worthwhile to contrast the existing regime with how the design of the rules on deviating from the defaults could further counteract the default stickiness. Insofar as the design of the default rules itself is concerned, reducing stickiness could additionally benefit from, for instance, putting the cost of deviation onto the cheapest cost avoider, which usually is the stronger party. This could, as similarly discussed above in respect of the CISG, suggest introducing a penalty default rule design, which intentionally disadvantages the stronger party and requires it to provide information and to initiate the necessary steps for a valid deviation working to its advantage.

This would have the benefit of accommodating the need to counteract socioeconomic disadvantages of a weaker party in addition to psychological biases. However, this approach would create serious problems for the default design because it cannot easily be established who – generally – would be the stronger party and which information – generally – should be provided.[124] Only if it was ensured that the costs related to providing information and settling on a choice of law or court were not disproportionate to the potential benefit of making a deviating choice, the default stickiness could be further reduced; otherwise, the imbalance would simply swing the other way. Hence, a penalty default rule design does not seem recommendable.

[120] Art 3 of the 2005 Hague Convention.
[121] Art 25(1)(a) Brussels Ia Regulation.
[122] Art 25(2) Brussels Ia Regulation.
[123] Art 25(1)(b) and (c) Brussels Ia Regulation.
[124] See also Whincop and Keyes, 'Economic Theory' (n 101) 439–40, 448.

If, alternatively, a mandated choice system was to be introduced, private parties would be further limited in their freedom insofar as they would be asked directly which available option they prefer. They would be required to choose a law and jurisdiction for their cross-border legal relationship. In addition to the obvious practical challenges of implementing such a system and enforcing it, the mandated choice would limit individual freedom more than is necessary without creating a benefit for the individuals or the public. It would make cross-border relationships even more complex if it became mandatory to choose the law and court (instead of being able to rely on an otherwise objectively determined in the absence of a truly voluntary choice). Private parties might not even realise that they are interacting cross-border, which is not a problem if they can easily rely at any time on the safety net of defaults; yet under a mandated choice system, complications would arise if a mandatory choice was missed or turned out to be imperfect.

In consequence, neither a penalty default design nor a mandated choice system is recommendable for default rules in the conflict of laws. These alternative models might work well for certain areas and purposes on the national level, but they are ill-suited for helping private parties resolve the complexity of international interactions.

I. Design Modification for Consumer Protection: Semi-Compulsory Default Rules

The EU Regulations do however modify the default rules for special situations, in particular for the protection of consumers[125] (or, for instance, employees[126]); these modifications have proved to be so important that the UK has decided to keep them even post-Brexit.[127]

Examining consumer protection in private international law is worthwhile not only because of the high practical importance of the topic. It seems fair to say that consumers are most prone to be affected by the consequences of bounded rationality in cross-border cases, which can help explain why they receive the most refined normative protection in comparison with the ordinary default rules in the Regulations. More specifically, the modified default rules for consumer protection are a prime example of what might be called 'semi-compulsory default rules'. This is not an oxymoron; it rather highlights that the rules intend to ensure a beneficial outcome for consumers by preventing (potentially biased) choices to their detriment, though the rules do not restrict the freedom to agree on a beneficial choice. In comparison with the original suggestion of the European Commission to prohibit choice of law for consumer contracts,[128] the adopted EU semi-compulsory default regime does not one-sidedly discriminate against international business for the sake of counteracting the bounded

[125] Art 6 Rome I Regulation; Art 17 et seq Brussels Ia Regulation.

[126] Art 8 Rome I Regulation; Art 20 et seq Brussels Ia Regulation.

[127] In the shape of the retained ('assimilated') Rome Regulations and in the Civil Jurisdiction and Judgments Act 1982 ss 15A–15E.

[128] European Commission, Proposal for a Regulation of the European Parliament and the Council on the law applicable to contractual obligations (Rome I), COM(2005)650 final, Art 5(1).

rationality of consumers;[129] instead, it seeks to strike a balance between business autonomy and protective intervention.

Choice of law for consumer contracts is restricted in terms of substance in the Rome I Regulation.[130] The restrictions apply, roughly speaking, if a professional contracting party pursues its activities in the country of the consumer's habitual residence or has directed its activities to that country.[131] Then choice of law is, in principle, limited by the semi-compulsory regime insofar as the choice may not result in the consumer being deprived of the protection granted by mandatory provisions of the law which would apply by default.[132] This requires an issue-by-issue analysis of the individual case,[133] so that a combined regime is essentially applicable to the individual case.[134] Where the subjectively chosen law is less advantageous for the consumer concerning one particular issue, the governing law is not the chosen one but is rather objectively determined by the specific default rule for consumers, which means that the law of the country where the consumer is habitually resident is applicable.[135] However, where the validly chosen law favours the consumer, the choice takes priority over any default determination. What has to be noted is that this preferential treatment is limited because under the Rome I Regulation certain types of contracts are excluded from this sketched regime of consumer protection, for instance most contracts concerning rights in rem.[136] Outside the scope of the consumer semi-compulsory restrictions, the ordinary connecting factors determine the applicable law, namely a subjective specification of the chosen law or an objective reference by the default rule pointing to the law of the place of the party performing the characteristic obligation or, as the residual default rule, the law of the closest connection.[137]

Similarly, for international jurisdiction over consumer contracts, the Brussels Ia Regulation establishes semi-compulsory default rules in favour of the consumer provided that, in principle, the contract has been concluded by the consumer with a professional party who pursues activities in the Member State of the consumer's domicile or directs its activities to that Member State.[138] Then, the

> consumer may bring proceedings against the other party to a contract either in the courts of the Member State in which that party is domiciled or, regardless of the domicile of the other party, in the courts for the place where the consumer is domiciled.[139]

Conversely, however, proceedings against the consumer may only be brought 'in the courts of the Member State in which the consumer is domiciled'.[140] Deviation from

[129] See also Karampatzos (n 14) 60–61.
[130] Art 6(2) Rome I Regulation.
[131] Art 6(1)(a) and (b) Rome I Regulation.
[132] Art 6(2) Rome I Regulation; on this, see, for instance, R Plender and M Wilderspin, *The European Private International Law of Obligations* 5th edn (London, Sweet & Maxwell, 2019) paras 9–064 et seq.
[133] G Rühl, 'Consumer Protection in Choice of Law' (2011) 44 *Cornell International LJ* 569, 591.
[134] G Rühl, 'The Protection of Weaker Parties in the Private International Law of the European Union: A Portrait of Inconsistency and Conceptual Truancy' (2014) 10 *Journal of Private International Law* 335, 352.
[135] Art 6(1) Rome I Regulation.
[136] Art 6(4) Rome I Regulation.
[137] Art 6(3), 3 and 4 Rome I Regulation.
[138] Art 17(1)(c) Brussels Ia Regulation; the only exceptions in Art 17(1)(a) and (b) relate to special cases of payment by instalments.
[139] Art 18(1) Brussels Ia Regulation.
[140] Art 18(2) Brussels Ia Regulation.

either of these consumer jurisdiction default provisions by way of a choice of court agreement is, in principle, only valid if the choice is made 'after the dispute has arisen',[141] unless both the consumer and the other party choose the courts of the Member State in which they are both domiciled at the time[142] or the chosen courts are only extending the possible default jurisdictions.[143]

For torts and similar non-contractual obligations, whilst there are no protective jurisdictional provisions for consumers, the choice of law is comparably restricted in terms of time by the Rome II Regulation.[144] As already mentioned, where not all parties to a non-contractual obligation are pursuing commercial activities, so essentially where a consumer is involved, the governing law may only be chosen 'after the event giving rise to the damage occurred'. The wording of the Regulation does not refer to the term 'consumer', but the personal scope of the temporal restriction is functionally congruent with the consumer protection idea.[145]

IV. Conclusion

Private international default rules can be understood to help private parties resolve complex questions about the applicable law for a cross-border legal relationships and the international jurisdiction of courts to adjudicate disputes. These default rules ensure that the applicable law and litigation location are determined on the basis of predictable and balanced factors, which can accommodate policy considerations both related to and external to the parties. At the same time, the default rules help debias decision-making when giving private parties the necessary freedom to make their own arrangements with a safety net and certain limitations in place.

Such defaults can, on the one hand, occasionally be found in international conventions for the unification of private law. The CISG has been discussed as an example of such an international regime which applies by default to international sales contracts instead of national law. It offers legal certainty through balanced rules. Private parties can, and in practice oftentimes do, deviate from the international default rules by choosing a national law. However, where this amounts to a factual default inversion, it is questionable whether the deviation is a conscious and beneficial decision; it is more likely a consequence of bounded rationality and misconceptions about the learning costs associated with international uniform law.

Default rules come into play, on the other hand, where no international uniform law governs the cross-border legal obligations and the applicable law has to be determined instead by the choice of law rules of the seized court. Insofar as the parties have not (validly) chosen the applicable law themselves, default rules containing objective connecting factors are employed for determining the governing national law. The design of these default rules in the Rome I and Rome II Regulations submits the contract or

[141] Art 19(1) Brussels Ia Regulation.
[142] Art 19(3) Brussels Ia Regulation.
[143] Art 19(2) Brussels Ia Regulation.
[144] Art 14(1) Rome II Regulation.
[145] Rühl, 'Protection of Weaker Parties' (n 134) 340.

tort to the national law of the closest connection, which is balanced and predictable for all involved and affected. Likewise, for their international jurisdiction to adjudicate, courts rely on default rules when the parties have not agreed upon a choice of court. The Brussels Ia Regulation's heads of jurisdiction seek to ensure by default that the forum has the greatest proximity to the dispute. Additionally, the Regulations use a variety of residual default rules to accommodate specific constellations.

The default design of these EU Regulations, which have to some extent been retained in the UK, can overall be best explained with the help of behavioural economics, because this perspective appreciates how important it is for private parties to be nudged towards a beneficial jurisdiction given the complexity of international interactions and the effects of bounded rationality. Yet private parties can deviate from these defaults, for which clear rules are established in the Regulations whose specific requirements for choice of law or court ensure that the default rules are not overly sticky. The Regulations also modify the default rules as well as the choice restrictions for special instances where one side of the cross-border obligation requires greater protection, such as a consumer; this is achieved through semi-compulsory default rules which allow deviation for the benefit of the protected party but restrict choice to their detriment.

Private international default rules can thus be considered to be default rules *par excellence*, with both the typical benefits and problems. Yet they have to provide the answers for the unique legal issues of cross-border relationships, which makes these default rules and their objectives stand out and distinguishes them from any default rule at the purely domestic level.

INDEX

www.ingramcontent.com/pod-product-compliance
Ingram Content Group UK Ltd.
Pitfield, Milton Keynes, MK11 3LW, UK
UKHW020247290926
15470UKWH00002B/786

9 781509 973521